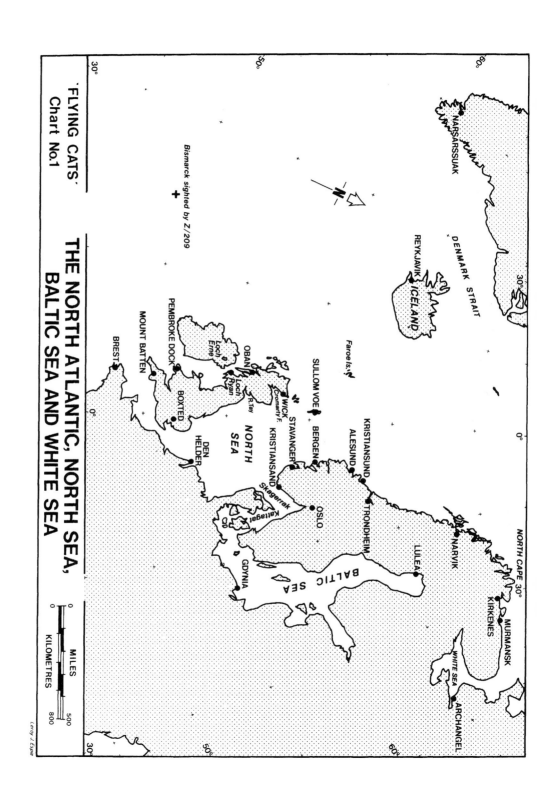

'FLYING CATS'
Chart No.1

THE NORTH ATLANTIC, NORTH SEA, BALTIC SEA AND WHITE SEA

Bismarck sighted by Z/209

NARSARSSUAK

DENMARK STRAIT

REYKJAVIK ICELAND

Faroe Is.

SULLOM VOE

OBAN
Loch Erne
Loch Ryan
R.Tay
Cromarty F.
WICK
STAVANGER
BERGEN
KRISTIANSUND
ALESUND
KRISTIANSAND
Skagerrak
Kattegat
OSLO
TRONDHEIM
LULEA
NARVIK
NORTH CAPE 30°
KIRKENES
MURMANSK
WHITE SEA
ARCHANGEL

PEMBROKE DOCK
MOUNT BATTEN
BREST
BOXTED
DEN HELDER
NORTH SEA
GDYNIA
BALTIC SEA

MILES
KILOMETRES
0   500   800

Leroy J. Espe

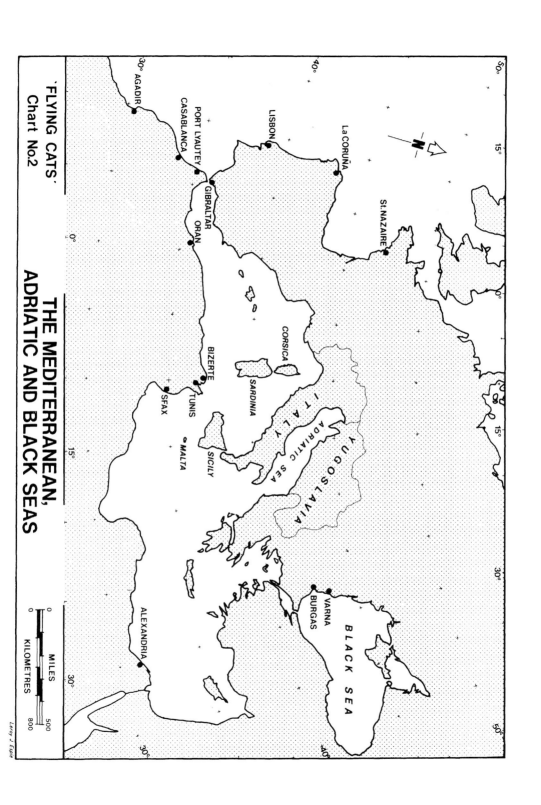

'FLYING CATS'
Chart No.2

THE MEDITERRANEAN,
ADRIATIC AND BLACK SEAS

N

AGADIR
CASABLANCA
PORT LYAUTEY
GIBRALTAR
ORAN
LISBON
La CORUÑA
St. NAZAIRE
BIZERTE
TUNIS
SFAX
MALTA
SICILY
SARDINIA
CORSICA
ITALY
ADRIATIC SEA
YUGOSLAVIA
ALEXANDRIA
BURGAS
VARNA
BLACK SEA

30°
40°
50°
15°
0°
15°
30°

MILES
0   500
KILOMETRES
0   800

Leroy J. Espie

FLYING CATALINAS

THE CONSOLIDATED PBY CATALINA IN WORLD WAR II

FLYING CATALINAS

THE CONSOLIDATED PBY CATALINA IN WORLD WAR II

by
Andrew Hendrie

Pen & Sword
AVIATION

First published in Great Britain in 1988 by
Airlife Publishing Ltd.

Reprinted in this format in 2012 by
PEN & SWORD AVIATION
An imprint of
Pen & Sword Books Ltd
47 Church Street
Barnsley
South Yorkshire
S70 2AS

Copyright © Andrew Hendrie 1988, 2012

ISBN 978 1 84884 780 4

A CIP catalogue record for this book is
available from the British Library

Printed and bound in England
By CPI Group (UK) Ltd, Croydon, CR0 4YY

Pen & Sword Books Ltd incorporates the Imprints of Pen & Sword Aviation,
Pen & Sword Family History, Pen & Sword Maritime, Pen & Sword Military,
Pen & Sword Discovery, Wharncliffe Local History, Wharncliffe True Crime,
Wharncliffe Transport, Pen & Sword Select, Pen & Sword Military Classics,
Leo Cooper, The Praetorian Press, Remember When,
Seaforth Publishing and Frontline Publishing

For a complete list of Pen & Sword titles please contact
PEN & SWORD BOOKS LIMITED
47 Church Street, Barnsley, South Yorkshire, S70 2AS, England
E-mail: enquiries@pen-and-sword.co.uk
Website: www.pen-and-sword.co.uk

Contents

For this edition, I would like to extend my thanks to the following individuals: Martin Mace, John Grehan and Sara Mitchell for their assistance in preparing the manuscript; David Legg of The Catalina Society. Following Andrew's death in 2004, his collection of Catalina photographs was presented to the society's archive. For more information on this organisation, visit: www.sunderlandtrust.org.uk

Evelyn Hendrie, Storrington, 2011.

Foreword

By Air Marshal Sir Richard Wakeford, KCB, LVO, OBE, AFC, RAF(Retired)

In the early summer of 1941 a small group of Royal Air Force trainee pilots arrived at The United States Naval Air Station, Pensacola, Florida. They were the first of many thousand aircrew to be trained in the United States under The Arnold Scheme during World War 2. As one of that group I was destined to fly Catalinas for the remaining war years.

All aircrew believe that the aircraft they fly is the best, but those of us privileged to fly 'The Cat' were perhaps more justified than most in believing this to be so. This aircraft served with distinction as an air-sea-rescue platform, anti-submarine bomber and torpedo carrier, convoy escort, mail freight and passenger transport and even as a glider tug during World War 2.

Flying Cats as the result of considerable research has drawn together in remarkable detail the history of a remarkable aircraft. In doing so the author has not only produced a very informative and interesting book but a valuable contribution to aviation history.

Introduction

Three reported sightings by Catalina crews in World War 2 have given the aircraft a unique place in history; Briggs and the battleship *Bismarck*, Birchall against the Japanese fleet off Ceylon, and Reid off Midway. A fourth, off Pearl Harbor, is sometimes forgotten. In selecting the Catalina as a subject, I was prompted by none of these sightings, but by the many successful attacks on enemy submarines made by Coastal Command-controlled Catalinas which rival even those by the lordly Liberator.

The part played by the Catalina in anti-submarine warfare will be seen as its major role in World War 2, and I have endeavoured to cover every recorded successful attack by Catalinas against German, Italian and Japanese submarines, despite some anomalies in official records. That the Catalina featured so strongly in an anti-submarine role may be attributed to its long range, a useful bomb load, and the fact that it was available. It had been designed as a maritime patrol plane and was free of prior claim by Bomber Command, unlike the Liberator which was to follow.

Its long range and useful bomb load enabled the Catalina to be employed by the RAAF in mine-laying extending to the coast of China. Although essentially a 'patrol plane' sponsored by the US Navy, it was used by that service in torpedo attacks, and in their quite exceptional shipping strikes in the South Pacific by their celebrated 'Black Cats'. After major battles such as Midway, the formerly aggressive aircraft were employed on mercy missions in the rescue of ditched aircrew.

Unlike the Sunderland flying boat, the Catalina could be literally 'dropped in' using any reasonable stretch of water. Its long range, plus this ability, enabled it to be used by both Norwegians over Norway, and the RAF in the Far East on 'special ops', ie, landing agents or picking them up from enemy-occupied territory. Requiring no expensive runways, the Catalina flying boat could follow both withdrawal movements and subsequent advances, as exemplified by US Navy PBYs in the Philippines campaigns.

Both the RNZAF and the American AAF used the Catalina on open sea rescue or 'Dumbo' missions, so often risking damage to both hull and floats. The RCAF gained their first wartime VC during the period when their 162 Squadron was operating Cansos with the RAF.

Other services to operate Catalinas in World War 2 were the Netherlands Naval Air Service, the Russian Fleet Air Arm and the Brazilian Air Force. The United States Coast Guard service flew their 'ice patrols'.

The Catalina followed the Hudson in the Atlantic Ferry using various routes over both the North and South Atlantic. Other Catalinas were ferried across the Pacific for both the RAAF and RNZAF.

The Catalina will be seen to have operated in all the major theatres of the Second World War and certainly flew over the 'seven seas'. Both the aircraft and the aircrews proved able to withstand the extremes of the White Sea, the Black Sea, the Bering Sea, the China or Coral Seas.

Since the Second World War, the Catalina has continued to fly with many services, including those of Indonesia, Brazil, Denmark and Sweden.

In this project I have endeavoured to contact representatives of every country or service known to have operated Catalinas. For wartime operations, I have tried to gain the help of as many ex-service personnel as possible, acting upon the assumption that aircrew with their log books are a most reliable source. Such has proved the case for perhaps the most celebrated Catalina sortie — 'Bismarck' Briggs as captain of *AH545*. He regretfully received his 'final posting' just a week before I heard from his 2nd pilot, Ensign (now Capt) Smith of the US Navy.

Personal accounts given by those directly concerned with operating aircraft frequently give details not found in official records; I have included a number of such personal reminiscences.

Andrew Hendrie
Storrington, January 1988.

Chapter 1
The Machine

Development of the Catalina flying boat

The first mention of the Catalina flying boat in the official US Naval Aviation history[1] is under the date 28 January 1928. On that day a contract was awarded to the Consolidated Aircraft Corporation for the XPY-1 flying boat, the 'first large monoplane. . . procured by the Navy'. It was designed to have installed either two or three engines. The abbreviation 'XPY' follows the US Navy's code with 'X' for 'experimental', 'P' for 'patrol plane' and 'Y' for 'Consolidated' — the manufacturer.

The $150,000 contract was for the development and construction of the prototype. On completion however, the contract for a batch of aircraft to be produced was awarded to the Glen Martin Company which, with no development costs, was able to under-bid Consolidated.

The Consolidated design team, led by Isaac Machlin Laddon, developed a civil version based on the XPY design. From what was to become a successful passenger-carrying aircraft, a military version was prepared and on 7 July 1931 Consolidated was awarded a contract for 23 flying boats which were designated 'P2Y-1'. Six of these aircraft on 7/8 September 1933, then with Patrol Squadron 5F and under the command of Lt-Cdr H. E. Halland, flew direct from Norfolk, Virginia, to Coco Solo in the Canal Zone, a record distance formation flight of 2,059 miles in 25 hr 19 min.

What may well be considered a true early type of Catalina was now to follow. This was the XP3Y-1 flying boat, for which Consolidated was awarded a contract on 28 October

The P2Y flying boat as used in training at Pensacola *circa* 1942.

1933 and, as the USN official history indicates, the Navy sponsored the 'development of the PBY Catalina series. . .'

The XP3Y-1 was to be fitted with Pratt and Whitney Twin Wasp XR-1830-58 engines of 825 hp each. When airborne, this aircraft proved to have clean lines with retractable floats at the wing tips, was free of struts to the tailplane, and the waist positions had not yet received 'blisters'.

On 14/15 October 1935, Lt-Cdr K. McGinnis commanded an XP3Y-1 patrol plane of the US Navy on a flight from Cristobal Harbor in the Canal Zone, to Alameda, California, establishing a new world record for that class of aircraft by covering 3,281.4 miles in 343/4 hours. In 1937, on 21/22 October, VP-3 of the USN flew Catalinas (PBY-1s) non-stop from San Diego to Coco Solo in 27hr 58min.

An amphibian version of the Catalina was first ordered by the US Navy from the

An advertisement of March 1944 by the Consolidated Vultee Aircraft Corporation of New Orleans for workers to build PBY Catalinas.

Consolidated Corporation on 7 April 1939. It was to become the prototype of the PBY-5A which is still flying in 1986 over various parts of the world.

One of the most obvious changes in the development of the Catalina is seen in modifications to the tailplane and fin assembly. Such variations began on the XP3Y-1 and were to continue up to the PBY-6A.

With the PBY-3 came the use of a Pratt and Whitney R1830-66 engine rated at 900hp and the type was distinguished from the PBY-2 by an air intake on top of the engine nacelles as required for a downdraught carburettor.

Of the Catalina variants, the PBY-4 was the first to be received by the Royal Air Force. The service in fact received only one — *P9630*[2]. The PBY-4s were fitted with engines rated at 1,050hp, the Pratt and Whitney R1830-72, and with a further change — the addition of spinners to the propeller hubs.

The Aeroplane[1] refers to the RAF's experimental Catalina, albeit as a 'PBY-5', flying from San Diego to Felixstowe via Newfoundland in July 1939 and taking 15 hours to cover the 2,450-mile Atlantic leg. The same account gives the engines as being 1,200 hp P&W Twin Wasps, R.1830-S1C3-G.

Delivery of a PBY-4 to the RAF

Consolidated's European agent in 1939 was J. H. Millar, FRAeS, who received an order from the Air Ministry in February for one PBY-4.

As Mr Millar now recalls: 'Consolidated took one from the US Navy's production line and, using Dick Archbold's private air crew — Russell Rogers, pilot; Lon Yancey, navigator and 2nd pilot; a radio operator and a flight engineer — the PBY-4 was flight delivered via Halifax, Nova Scotia to the Marine Aircraft Experimental Establishment, Felixstowe, England in June 1939.

'I arranged for the Press to witness the touchdown. Many refused to believe the PBY-4 had flown the Atlantic non-stop to Felixstowe because the engines were not covered with oil. In those days, British radial engines did not have effective rocker box seals and threw oil, so some pressmen thought the Pratt and Whitney engines should do the same.

'The RAF sent a launch to collect the crew after the boat had been put on a mooring, but were astonished when the crew disembarked wearing country clothes and hats and carrying golf clubs, etc.

'That night, Wing Commander Wigglesworth in charge at Felixstowe gave a dinner party in the Mess and a question was asked about the range of the radio in the flying boat. When the crew said they had been working San Diego as they were landing, there was a "hush", and I felt they were disbelieved.

'However, as the contract provided for the American crew to remain for two weeks and to familiarize the RAF, it was arranged that the RAF would be taken up for a flight the next day. On that flight, the American crew called up San Diego using the Bendix radio which was standard equipment on all PBY-4s, but the RAF had never seen anything like it — the range of the radio in the Short Sunderlands at that time was very short.

'After "familiarizing" the RAF at Felixstowe and checking out pilots to fly it, Russell Rogers and his crew returned to America by boat. RAF Felixstowe then went on leave, and those who had been indoctrinated and taught to fly the PBY-4 were dispersed. When the war broke out, the PBY-4 was still on a mooring at Felixstowe and it was the only long-range — 4,500 miles — aircraft England had . . . I had to scratch around and finally Larry Skey, a Canadian with PBY-4 experience, came from Canada and flew it to the Clyde for better safety.

'Air Marshal Sir Roderick Hill asked me to go to Harrogate to see him and told me they were going to order 40 or more. Eventually they took over the French contracts which I had negotiated. I had to go back to San Diego with drawings of brackets the Air Ministry wanted mounted on the leading edge of the wings. They were for ASV. I begged them to remove the "Top Secret" markings on the drawings — I felt that as they were very ordinary looking brackets it was a mistake to draw attention to them by marking the drawings "Top Secret", but the Air Ministry insisted.

'Much more important was the need to order the beaching gear to arrive ahead of the boats so there would be no delay in bringing the Catalinas ashore to have guns fitted, etc,

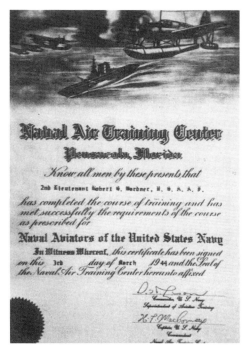

A Naval Aviator's Certificate as awarded by the US Navy, Pensacola to pilots who had completed their training successfully.

but the Ministry of Aircraft Production refused to do so . . .'

Development of the Catalina flying boat

Obvious visible differences between the PBY-4 and the PBY-5 which followed, were 'blisters' in the waist position replacing hatches, and modifications to the tail assembly. In the latter, the rudder was squared off and with a modified trimming tab.

The outbreak of war in September 1939 resulted in orders being placed immediately for the RAF and the US Navy. The RAF referred to the PBY-5s as 'Mark Is'. The name given to the aircraft by the RAF — 'Catalina' — was adopted by the US Navy in October 1941. Due to its neutrality patrol commitments, the US Navy placed an order on 20 December 1939 with Consolidated for 200

3

PBY-5s, the largest single order for American naval aircraft since World War 1.

Between March 1941 and January 1942, the RAF were to receive 92 of the Mark I Catalinas; a further seven PBY-5s were delivered to the RAF in early 1941, but due to differences in equipment, these were designated 'Mark IIs'. In 1942, 21 more PBY-5s were received by the RAF to be designated 'Mark IIAs'.

An amphibian version of the Catalina flying boat was first ordered by the US Navy on 7 April 1939, and for this a PBY-4 was converted using a retractable tricycle undercarriage. This increased the empty weight in relation to the PBY-5 by over 3,300lb and reduced the maximum speed by 6mph, rate of climb by 70ft/min, ceiling by 5,000ft and the range by 640 miles. Other disadvantages, due to the installation of landing gear, mentioned to me by Dennis Briggs were reduced living space and the collection of water in the wells which located the landing wheels.

In 1940, Boeing Canada was licensed to build PBYs in Vancouver and, in 1941, Canadian Vickers Ltd agreed to construct them in Cartierville, Quebec. The Canadian version of the Catalina came to be known as the 'Canso'. By 17 May 1945, Canadian Vickers Ltd had delivered 369 of these aircraft to the USAAF and the RCAF. Boeing on Sea Island, Vancouver produced 240 Catalinas which were designated PB2B-1s, but the first of Boeing's PBYs at Vancouver were 55 Canso-A amphibians.

In 1941, the American Naval Air Factory in Philadelphia was contracted to build 156 Catalinas. The design of these aircraft incorporated changes in the hull, wing and tail, with modifications to the wing-tip floats. The fuel capacity was increased and a power operated turret in the nose was equipped with a 0·5 calibre gun replacing the earlier 0·3. These flying boats were designated PBN 'Nomads'. Some of the design variants were to be repeated in the Boeing 2B2B-2 flying boats including tall tail and radome. The 2B2B-2 was one of the variants operated by the RAAF.

The final production variation to the Catalina line was the PBY-6A, of which there is now an example at the Aerospace Museum, RAF Cosford. Apart from the tricycle landing gear, perhaps the most obvious difference between this aircraft and those flown by the RAF is the tall tail fin, but there are also alterations in the hull design.

Catalinas operated by the USAAF and, later, by the USAF, were designated OA-10s ('A's or 'B's). A number of Catalinas were ferried to Russia, and the Russians were licensed to build their own machines — characteristically with strengthened hulls to withstand the Arctic conditions. Although I received some data from Moscow, such help did not include numbers of aircraft either used or constructed[4]. Capt Scarborough gives the total PBY/Catalina/Canso production as 3,272, which includes 1,418 amphibians.

The successors to the Consolidated Corporation — General Dynamics — state that the Convair workers built 2,393 of these aircraft, thus the difference in the totals is represented by the production from Canadian Vickers, Boeing Canada, and the US Navy factory in Philadelphia.

The price quoted for the Catalina in the early war years was $90,000, the same as that for a Lockheed Hudson, and at 1938 exchange rates, about £17,000 sterling.

Conversion of Catalinas by Saunders-Roe at Beaumaris

The Consolidated Model 28-5ME was the USN type PBY-5. In modifications for the British, alterations were made to the hull to cope with stowage of different equipment. In the wing, structural changes were made for the carriage of British bombs on British bomb carriers in lieu of the American-type carriers which were fitted to all RAF marks except Mark IB.

The first aircraft arrived on the Clyde in February 1941 and conversion work on Mark Is was undertaken both at Greenock and Beaumaris. Greenock at that time was better equipped with hangars, roadways and an electric winch for hauling up flying boats, all of which were lacking at Beaumaris. Consequently most of the aircraft were dealt with at Greenock.

One of the earliest alterations was the provision of new ASV aerials which were followed in a few months by an urgent request for long range ASV. The resulting installation proved satisfactory and became standard on

The first PBY-2 Bu.No.0454, patrol plane 12 of VP-11 USN; note air intake below engine nacelle.

Marks I and IB aircraft. Another early requirement was provision for a 1,500lb bomb rather than the previous maximum of 500lb. No structural change in the wing was necessary. Following the development of the Leigh light for anti-submarine night operations, suitable alterations were made for its installation on all marks intended for operational flying.

The first Mark I arrived at Beaumaris in June 1941 and became the aircraft on which most of the trial installations were made until February 1944, when it became unrepresentative of the Mark IVs then being received and was replaced by a new aircraft.

Catalina IBs began to arrive at Beaumaris on 15 July 1942 and were the first supplied under the lend-lease arrangements. Although these were basically the same as Mark Is, attempts had been made to meet subsequent requirements, notably with the fitting of long-range ASV. Some electrical aspects of the American installation gave trouble and an RAF party became attached to Beaumaris to deal with the SI problems.

Repeated hull bottom failures were being reported at Gibraltar in late 1942 due to the exceptional water conditions there, together with the overloading resulting from additional fuel tanks. Ultimately the problem was overcome by considerably strengthening the two stiffeners inboard of the chine between bulkheads 4 and 5, immediately forward of the main step. The modification was applied to all in-service and subsequent aircraft, covering all marks.

The limited Catalina armament was increased by fitting two guns instead of one in the bows. This followed the change of tactics by U-boats to remaining on the surface during attacks.

Saunders-Roe began fitting Leigh lights towards the end of the run of Mark IB aircraft when deliveries from America had ceased and Mark IVs were awaited. Earlier, the work had been undertaken by the RAF.

There was a special allotment of PBY-5s — seven Catalina Mark IIs — arranged personally by Mr Churchill. The first of these (AM264) went to MAEE Helensburgh in January 1941 for trials, and the subsequent conversion was undertaken by Scottish Aviation Ltd at Greenock. Three others were also converted by them. Of these other three, one was lost in transit (AM265) and two were converted at Beaumaris.

Some RCAF aircraft, Consolidated Model 28-5MCs, were diverted to the United Kingdom. These were Catalina IIAs which had a hull lay-out similar to Catalina Is, although the wings and thus the bomb installations were similar to Catalina IIs. The first arrived on 10 February 1942.

The initial batch of Mark IIIs arrived on 13 April 1942. They were PBY-5A amphibians and, due to the difference in operating procedure, they were moored out as flying boats rather than in the American way of using them as land-based aircraft. A number of defects arose, and subsequently the aircraft were

5

A PBY-2 of VP-2 USN. The insignia on the port bow is believed to be that of a Keystone Cop, representative of VP-2 in 1937.

converted to flying boats by removal of the chassis.

Catalina Mark IVs were being delivered from May 1943 until January 1945, but a variant of the Mark IV, the PB2B-1 manufactured by the Boeing Aircraft Corporation of Canada, became known as the Mark IVB, while the other Mark IVs became Mark IVAs.

In the Mark IVs the ASV had been replaced by radar with a new aerial system, and there was provision for American bombs and bomb racks only. Ultimately, alterations provided for a British bomb rack external to the wing. A Proportional Bank Adapter fitted to the Sperry auto-pilot proved unsatisfactory; existing installations were therefore put out of action and the Proportional Bank Adapter was not fitted to later aircraft.

Due to inferior workmanship resulting from diluted labour, some Mark IVs were received with leaking integral tanks, due also to different jointing material being used. Leaks were remedied by the injection of a neoprene compound using a high-pressure lubrication gun. Some auxiliary power units (APUs), were wrongly assembled in America with locking wire instead of split pins at the big ends. All APUs were then dismantled and checked.

By June 1944, seventy alterations were being carried out on each aircraft, including the fitting of Leigh lights.

In October 1944, aircraft were arriving with a new type of cabin heater. As it interfered with several British requirements, the heater was removed in favour of electrically heated flying clothing.

Normal operation of the Catalina flying boat

Capt Vic A. Hodgkinson, DFC, served with the RAAF from March 1942 until April 1946, flying on operations with No 20 Squadron, and as Chief Flying Instructor at Rathmines. After the war his experience was to include that of Comets and Boeing 707s, and he eventually completed a total of almost 20,000 hours' flying.

Many Catalina pilots and other aircrew refer to the reliability of the Pratt and Whitney twin Wasp engines, and Vic Hodgkinson echoes this view. He has also however, given a detailed account of a normal Catalina trip.

'In the air, marine aircraft handle the same as landplanes. It is only when in contact with the water that problems begin. Flying boats, amphibians and float planes had their own built-in waterborne characteristics and these required various techniques to keep the aircraft under control.

'The Catalina was no exception. Following is a brief description of a normal operation:

'On arrival at the aircraft by dinghy and boarding through the port blister, the rigger in the crew would detach the storm pennant from the buoy and prepare the aircraft on the short slip, ready for slipping the mooring. Other members of the crew would carry out their respective pre-flight checks, etc. Due to low battery capacity, the Auxiliary Power Unit was always run to provide electrical power for starting engines and to operate the radio until the engine generators could provide output. The APU was also fitted with a pump for refuelling or "bilging" the hull.

'When ready, the Captain would indicate to the Flight Engineer the sequence of engine starting. This would depend on the lay of the aircraft, surrounding obstructions, such as shipping, buoys, etc, and shallow water.

'The mooring was slipped once the first engine was running, otherwise the aircraft might rotate round the buoy. Engine revolutions below 1,000rpm were recommended until the oil temperature reached 40°C.

'Once clear of moorings and obstructions, engines were warmed up and tested on the way to the take-off point. This might be near the moorings or some distance away. If a long taxi downwind was required, the run up would be delayed until near the downwind take-off point.

A PBY-3 of VP-9 on Lake Washington in 1938; air intakes are fitted above the engine nacelles.

'Due to the close inboard position of the engines, the Catalina was not the easiest of aircraft to turn and taxi downwind in strong wind conditions, especially when this was accompanied by swell or rough water. This would result in reduced visibility due to spray and the sea coming over the windscreen. The natural tendency of the aircraft to weathercock into wind added to this problem. To turn the aircraft in these conditions, opposite aileron and same rudder were applied together with full power from the appropriate engine.

'Having turned the aircraft as far out of wind that way, the controls were reversed, power reduced on that engine and the other engine opened to full power. This was repeated until the aircraft came downwind. Anticipating this, the idling engine was opened up and power reduced slightly on the other and flying controls operated in the opposite sense to "into wind" settings, ie, to turn the aircraft, same aileron but opposite rudder.

'A fair amount of power was required to maintain the aircraft at a speed to control it downwind. In certain conditions the engines could be stopped and the aircraft sailed downwind, but it was a slow process and restricted to obstruction-free areas.

'One feature of the Catalina put to frequent use was its ability in light winds to revolve about its float, eg, should the aircraft be in a confined area or the take-off point was near the moorings, and it was required to warm up the engines, one engine was opened up to turn the aircraft. The drag of the inboard float and the relative flat section of the planing bottom of the hull ensured that the aircraft would continue turning in a circle.

'The engines were generally set at 1,200rpm to warm up.

'Having selected the take-off path (hopefully free of obstructions), with all checks completed, the aircraft was headed in a general direction. Control column hard back, ailerons set to raise the float dragging in the water, rudder to maintain direction, the engines were gradually opened with the object of reducing the amount of spray likely to cause damage to the propellers. Assuming that aircraft had not swung or porpoised and that one was on the step, the control column was eased to a position to allow the hull to plane on the step and gain speed. When aileron control had been gained, the floats were raised.

'This gave less drag and a little more lift, also in swell conditions it reduced damage to the floats and if taking off around the bends of rivers, allowed bank to be applied on the water to reduce slip.

'Once on the step, if the windscreen visibility was reduced by spray, rudder could be applied to skid it sideways and see ahead through the side window for a quick look, although the aircraft was fitted with windscreen wipers.

7

'There was no set speed for take-off. It depended on temperature, wind, state of the sea, weight, etc, and the skill of the pilot. The length of the run was also affected by these factors. Even so, take-offs could take up to three miles or more.

'After the aircraft had become unstuck from the water, it was levelled out to gain speed for the climb. The power was reduced to climb settings[5] (2,300rpm 35inHg 85kt) and climb commenced. Climb performance was never spectacular especially when fully laden in high temperatures. In these conditions it took up to two hours to attain 2-3,000ft. On reaching cruise altitude, power was reduced to cruise settings and once engine temperatures had reduced to a reasonable figure, the mixture was set to Auto Lean.

'A further leaning off of the mixture (giving greater range), was possible by moving the mixture lever towards the Idle Cut-off position. The engine temperatures had to be closely monitored to keep them within limits (120°C min — 205° max).

'On a normal landing approach, settings were Floats Down, Auto Rich and 2,300rpm. Approach speed 85-90 kt. Engine-assisted approaches (glassy surface, night landings and fully stalled landings), the speed was reduced to 75kt at around 200ft when the throttles were set to maintain a rate of descent of 200ft/min.

'Touch-down on a normal landing was in the take-off planing attitude. As the aircraft lost speed and came off the step, the control column was eased back to be then held hard back.

A fully stalled landing undertaken by a Catalina. This method was employed under exceptional conditions such as prevailed in special duty operations, but also in areas such as Gibraltar.

'On approaching the moorings, the rigger would extend the bollard and prepare the mooring lines, while two other crew members in the blisters made the drogues ready for streaming. On a signal from the pilot, the drogues would be streamed to take the way off the aircraft. The mooring line from the buoy was placed over the bollard and the engines shut down. Propellers were trimmed with one blade of each pointing downwards towards the hull. This was to give clear passage to marine craft passing under the mainplane and causing possible damage to the propeller.

'Landing in swell conditions required a different technique. With the aircraft set up for an engine-assisted approach, sufficient power was applied at about 50ft to hold the aircraft in a nose-up attitude at around 65kt. Floats were kept in the retracted position. When a reasonable landing spot appeared amongst the waves, the throttles were closed and the control column pulled hard back. The aircraft stalled and hit the water with a thump and generally only travelled a couple of lengths of the hull. One wing would drop into the water and the retracted float supported it.

'The flight engineer would crank the floats down by hand and there you were! The float operating motor was not used as it would have been overloaded. A stall landing under glassy calm conditions required the control column to be pushed fully forward on contact with the water to prevent the aircraft becoming airborne again in a stalled condition.

'For night take-offs and landings, flarepaths normally consisted of three flares (electric or kerosene), mounted on floats with anchors. Three marine craft showed white lights or — as at Cairns — the lights of moored aircraft were switched on. Flarepaths never stretched the full length of the take-off run, so one normally commenced the take-off run well downwind of the flarepath. Aircraft landing lights were never used for landing due to danger of the pilot relying on them to see the surface of the water. In glassy conditions the beam is not reflected from the surface and many an inexperienced pilot has come unstuck on that one. So it was a matter of experience to judge one's height on approach prior to touching down.

'Pilots were also trained on night landings without the aid of a flarepath. An area was

The cockpit of a PBY-6A. The auto-pilot may be seen bottom left.

selected ostensibly free from obstructions; the approach made as for night landing and the power set for a rate of descent of 200ft per minute at 65 to 70kt. This gave the correct attitude for touch-down.

'To me it was not a pleasant experience waiting for contact with the water. Like landing into a bottomless pit! On touch-down one would hear the water on the planing bottom and feel the drag on the hull with a tendency for the nose to dig in. The control column was eased back as the speed reduced and the throttles were closed.

'A restriction was placed on the number of persons permitted in the blister compartment in flight to four, because more than that would give a dangerous aft centre of gravity and cause the tailplane to stall. This was demonstrated to all pilots on training. Flying on one engine presented no problems when moderately loaded due to the engines being close to the centre of the hull.'

1. *United States Naval Aviation 1910-1970* US Govt office.
2. *Ibid.*
3. *The Aeroplane*, 8 May 1941, p151.
4. Figures given in the *Illustrated Encyclopaedia of Aircraft*, Vol 3, issue 28, p552, are 1,000-1,500 built in the USSR.
5. See appendix.

Chapter 2
US Navy Catalinas over the Atlantic and Caribbean

American neutrality patrols

Following the outbreak of war in Europe, President Roosevelt ordered neutrality patrols to be undertaken by the United States Navy. This was on 5 September 1939 and resulted in the Commander of the USN Atlantic Squadron establishing both surface and air reconnaissance of the approaches to the West Indies and the USA.

At a conference of the American republics held at Panama in late September-early October, Roosevelt's policy of maintaining a security zone, was endorsed by the 21 delegates on 2/3 October, the datum line being roughly longitude 60°W down to latitude 20°N, thence to a point 600 miles west of the Cape Verde Islands, and then south-west roughly parallel to the South American coast. Churchill welcomed this move, considering it to the Allies' advantage provided that the United States played an active role with its strong forces.

The US Navy had given immediate response to Roosevelt's directive and the first re-deployment of Catalina squadrons was on 11 September with VP-33 transferring from the Canal Zone (Coco Solo), to Guantanamo, Cuba, to operate over the Caribbean. By the 12th, eight surface units were covering offshore waters from Newfoundland down to French Guiana. On the 13th, Catalinas of VP-51 arrived at San Juan, Puerto Rico, from Norfolk, Virginia, their duties being to patrol the Lesser Antilles area.

Arising from these neutrality patrol requirements, a contract was issued to the Consolidated Aircraft Corporation on 20 December for 200 Catalinas. This was the largest single order for naval aircraft placed since the 1914-18 war.

Following the collapse of France, America became aware of the increasing danger to its security, and an agreement of mutual benefit was reached on 2 September 1940 between America and Britain for the supply of fifty ancient destroyers to Britain in exchange for bases in the West Indies and Bermuda. This agreement effectively extended the American frontier for the USN by several hundred miles.

When US Navy air operations began from Bermuda on 15 November 1940, VP-54 was the first to operate aircraft using as a base the tender USS *George F. Badger* (AVD-3), initially with three PBY-2s.

There was an obvious need to cover sea routes from ports such as Halifax, Nova Scotia, so a naval base was constructed at Argentia, Newfoundland, where the American flag was raised on 13 February 1941. The seaplane tender *Albermarle* (AV-5) arrived at Argentia on 15 May serving as a prelude to the deployment of VP-52 which, with PBY-5s, was the first USN squadron to patrol the North Atlantic convoy routes. Admiral A. L. Bristol flew there on the 20th in one of the PBYs, and the base was commissioned on 15 July. A month later, the base became famous for the meeting of Roosevelt with Churchill on HMS *Prince of Wales*.

On 10 December, VP-52 initiated antisubmarine air patrols for the US Navy over the South Atlantic by operating Catalinas from Natal where six of the PBY-5s were welcomed by the Brazilian Air Force. They used bases at Norfolk, Antigua, St Lucia, Trinidad, Panama and Bermuda with their patrols ranging from 600 to 1,200 miles. Although searching for U-boats, they were reporting the sinking of many Allied ships. From Panama, they patrolled the Galapagos Islands and the Gulf of Fonseca, Honduras. From Bermuda, convoy escorts were flown up to a radius of 600 miles.

52-P-8, a PBY-5 with landing gear at Quonset Point, Rhode Island in 1941.

From September 1941, the US Navy was effectively involved in the Battle of the Atlantic and, like the Royal Navy, resources were stretched. Their Caribbean patrol unit at San Juan, Puerto Rico, consisted of VP-31 Catalinas with a tender USS *Lapwing* (AVP-1), a converted minesweeper, and two destroyers.

When the first American convoy scheduled for the Middle East, WS-12X, left Halifax on 10 November 1941, it was covered by aircraft of VP-31 en route to Trinidad via the Mona Passage; the closure of the Mediterranean resulted in a re-routing to Cape Town where WS-12X arrived on 9 December after a 8,132-mile trip.

American Catalina air patrols

At the beginning of the war US Navy aircraft were organized in the form of seven patrol wings, each with four squadrons, and each squadron with 12 PBYs. By 31 December 1941 the numbers in each squadron varied between four and 22[1].

Lack of positive support by the Central American republics left the US Navy almost alone to respond to U-boats entering the American zone in June 1942 and air patrols by Patrol Wing 3 were required to cover the Panama and Caribbean areas from bases at Coco Solo and San Juan with only 24 Catalinas (PBY-3s and PBY-5s).

An abortive attack was made on *U-159* on 14 June but a Pacific convoy negotiated the Panama Canal safely on the 17th. By 2 July a number of Allied ships had been sunk by U-boats which themselves had suffered only one attack, and that from the air.

Equipment of US Navy PBYs had begun with ASV and IFF in July 1941 to VP-71, VP-72 and VP-73. In July 1942, radar-equipped Catalinas were operating from Coco Solo. In addition, other PBYs operated from Grand Cayman, and Port Royal Bay, Jamaica, while the small seaplane tender USS *Matagorda*, AVP-22, provided a base for flying boats at Puerto Castilla, Honduras.

The first kill in this area by the American forces was on 13 July. It followed a torpedo attack on the net tender *Mimosa* on the 11th. First on the scene was a Catalina which obtained a radar contact and attacked the U-boat with depth charges which were thought to have damaged the submarine. A second Catalina arrived in addition to AAF planes, but the final attack was by the destroyer

11

Lansdowne which released four 600lb depth charges. *U-153* was sunk in position 45°50′N 48°50′W.

The sinking of *U-94*

VP-92 of the US Navy was formed on 26 December 1941, and in that month was at Quonset Point with VP-91.

Jack Bruce[2] was a VP-92 pilot who joined the squadron in February 1942 as one of the 35-40 pilots with the unit. His aircraft was *92-P-7* No *7254*, one of the squadron's fifteen PBYs.

Bruce was airborne from NAS Alameda on 5 March in *7254* and flew via San Bernardino, El Paso, Pensacola and Miami to San Juan where he arrived on the 10th. While based at San Juan in Puerto Rico, VP-92 undertook patrols of the Caribbean from Trinidad to the beginning of the Old Bahama Channel north of Cuba. Although headquarters remained at San Juan, the squadron was in four sections with detachments operating from St Lucia and Guantanamo Bay. About 26 June, those at St Lucia moved on to Camaquey, Cuba. While there, personnel were billeted in hotels in the town and operated from the city's airport about five miles out in the country. Their main area of responsibility was to patrol the Old Bahama Channel. Other squadron planes patrolled the south side of Cuba covering the Windward Channel between Haiti and Cuba. The area covered by the Camaquey detachment included also the lower end of the Old Bahama Channel.

The San Juan element of VP-92 flew north of Puerto Rico and undertook sweeps of the Mona Channel between Mona Island and the Dominican Republic. Other patrols extended out as far as Antiqua while a few went southwards of the island towards the coast of South America.

It was during this period that VP-92 claimed one of its first anti-submarine successes. A Catalina commanded by Lt Gordon R. Fiss was airborne from Guantanamo and involved in the protection of convoy TAW-15. A U-boat had entered the convoy's escort screen when it was attacked by Fiss who released four 650lb depth charges together with a flare. The flare indicated the U-boat's position to an escort — HMCS *Oakville*.

Although the U-boat had sighted the Catalina just before the attack and had crash-dived, it was too late as the depth charges blew off his forward hydroplanes, brought him to the surface, and the vessel was unable to submerge again. HMCS *Oakville* rammed the U-boat causing further damage and the crew abandoned ship. Twenty-six survivors were rescued by *Oakville* before *U-94* sank in the Windward Passage on 28 August.

VP-92 also experienced losses while in the Caribbean area. Against orders one aircraft attempted a night landing in the Bahamas and was lost. While taking off from St Lucia Lt Hanset lost power and splashed into the surf. The aircraft was lost but there were no major injuries to the crew.

There was a happier side, as Jack Bruce recalls: 'Life in the town of Camaguey was a fairy tale to the crews who were stationed there. Most of the citizenry of this town had never been away from their homes and knew little of the outside world. We were treated with all the kindness and respect possible. Two of our pilots married local girls from Camaguey.'

VP-92 shared patrols with B-18s of the Army Air Force. Three Catalinas at Camaguey flew night patrols while the AAF B-18s flew mainly day missions. In the latter half of September 1942, VP-92 was alerted that a move was imminent. The detachment at Camaquey made its last flight on 24 September and then moved back to Guantanamo to await further orders. There was much uncertainty due to the prospect of self-sealing tanks being fitted to the Catalinas. The order for this modification was then countermanded because the fuel capacity would be reduced by such tanks, and a South Atlantic crossing was intended.

The main squadron and Guantanamo elements of VP-92 joined at Trinidad on 25 October. From Trinidad, the squadron moved down to Natal in Brazil, arriving on the 27th after stopping en route in Belém.

The next move was to Casablanca, ferrying via Ascension Island on 9 November, Freetown and Bathurst. The longest leg for PBY *7254* was Bathurst to Casablanca, a flight of 13hr 25min. One section of the squadron arrived at about the time of the French surrender, and a Catalina from VP-92 attacked a French submarine en route. Another crew, after the failure of an engine and the jettisoning of much equipment, realized that there were depth charges still on the wings but touched down successfully. Yet another missed the airport at Casablanca and landed in a field.

1942-44 VP-92 in North Africa

Jack Bruce in Catalina *7254* arrived in Casablanca on 14 November. Of the conditions he remembers: 'The squadron scrounged as best it could. We lived in the airplanes and in one of the hotels nearby. Squadron mess was a large 10ft x 10ft section of ¼ in steel plate which was mounted on large boulders inside a hangar. Cooking was done here. We ate from mountains of supplies dumped on the docks by the supply ships.'

Their patrol area extended from near the Canary Islands, north along the coast to near Gibraltar, and a detachment was maintained at Agadir. Sometime around June/July 1943 the squadron moved from Casablanca to Port Lyautey.

It was during this period that U-boats changed their tactics, when attacked by aircraft, by remaining on the surface and relying on AA fire for their defence. When one of VP-92's Catalinas encountered a U-boat off the Canary Islands and made a bombing run over the vessel, return fire from the U-boat killed one of the crew and severed the elevator controls of the aircraft. The pilot was able to return to Agadir by adjustment of trim controls and movement of crew members.

The casualties of the squadron included Catalinas *7251* and *7247*. At 05:08hr on 10 April PBY-5A*7251* crashed during take-off: two of the crew killed and others severely injured. It was suggested by some pilots that, in reaching forward under the yoke to the lower right of the instrument panel for the landing-gear handle, the yoke was pushed forward causing the aircraft to nose into the ground, then catching fire. This was at Port Lyautey. Also, there was *7247* which is believed to have crashed in the sea just off the coast about the middle of September with the loss of all the crew.

VP-92 personnel saw a note at 11:00 hours on 23 January which read: 'Army transport leaving Casablanca at approximately 13:00hr going to Safi and to Tedela, then flying over Casablanca harbour and then landing at Casablanca. This is an inspection tour and all rules and restrictions of aircraft flying in this sector will in all probability be disregarded.' They learned later that the aircraft, a DC-4, carried Churchill and President Roosevelt with some of their staffs.

VP-92 remained for a time during 1944 at Port Lyautey before later being deployed at Atkinson Field, Georgetown, British Guiana.

1. From data supplied by Capt W. Scarborough, USN (Ret).
2. Commander Jack Bruce, USN (Ret).

13

Chapter 3
Brazil

Brazilian-American liaison

In April 1941 President Roosevelt informed Churchill of a possible extension of the US security zone to Brazil and by June the US Navy Task Force No 3 was patrolling to Brazil, with bases made available at Recife and Bahia.

In October the Brazilian Navy began training for merchant vessels to sail in convoy. There was American liaison with Brazil and, following Pearl Harbor, six PBYs of VP-52 were welcomed at Natal on 11 December by the Brazilian Air Force. There was a merger of Brazilian Military and Naval Air Corps to form the BAF in 1941, and their Air Ministry initiated the establishment of a chain of air bases along the Brazilian coast. By early 1942, airfields were being constructed at Belém, Fortaleza, Recife, Natal and Bahia. On 28 January Brazil broke off diplomatic relations with the Axis powers, and in the following months there was a series of attacks by enemy submarines on Brazilian ships.

On 1 April VP-52 was relieved by a section of VP-83 commanded by Lt-Cdr Sperry Clark, the second section arriving on 13 June, equipped with PBY-5As.

Ten U-boats left French ports in July and were refuelled off the Brazilian coast by the 'milch cow' — U-460. There was concern at the time that, with co-operation from the Vichy French, the Germans could utilize bases on French colonies and harass communications, not only along the Brazilian coast-line, but also on the important South Atlantic routes to West Africa.

Following the sinking of seven Brazilian ships by U-boats, some with serious loss of life, Brazil declared war on Germany and Italy on 22 August. During the latter half of 1942, a number of US Navy squadrons equipped with Hudsons or Catalinas operated with the 4th Fleet and used bases at Belém, São Luis, Fortaleza, Natal and Recife.

The American 4th Fleet was responsible for the co-ordination of all operations in anti-submarine warfare in the South Atlantic, as the BAF was then not fully trained and organized.

Convoys along the Brazilian coast started in October 1942. Between Trinidad and Recife, the escorts were from the US Navy; from Recife to the south, Brazilian warships took over. Air cover along the length of the Brazilian coast was undertaken jointly by American and Brazilian aircraft.

1943: U-boats sunk off the Brazilian coast

The first attack by an aircraft of the Forca Aerea Brasileira on a U-boat occurred on 26 August 1943 with a V-11 'Vultee' operating from Porto Alegre off Santa Catarina.

The first kill in this area for the US Navy Catalinas was by VP-83 on 6 January 1943. PBY-5A, *83-P-2* commanded by Lt W. R. Ford had been on a three-day coverage of convoy JT-1 and on that day was airborne from Belém to return to base at Natal. He had been flying for almost six hours and was at 5,500ft when a gunner — B. Goodell — sighted a white streak on the horizon 25 miles away. Ford turned to port and increased speed from 83 to 184kt losing height meanwhile. When at a range of three to four miles he gave full revs and boost, increasing speed to 225kt. Four depth charges of 325lb each were released from 35ft altitude while the U-boat was still on the surface. Three of these exploded simultaneously within 5ft to port of the conning tower; the vessel rose out of the water breaking into two sections and releasing three large tanks and much debris.

Three survivors appeared and, after *83-P-2* circled, one was seen clinging to a pipe on one of the tanks. A rubber dinghy was dropped, followed by a second. One survivor reached the dinghy and attempted to help a second man, but there was a 25kt wind and the sea was rough. Contact was lost, although Ford remained in the area for 3½ hours before returning to base due to lack of fuel.

Following a belated sighting report due to a broken aerial, a surface vessel left Camocim to rescue survivors from the U-boat. No oil slick had been seen. At the time it was thought to have been an Italian submarine but it was subsquently identified as *U-164*, lost in position 01°58'S 39°23'W about eighty miles north of Fortaleza.

A report sent to the C-in-C of the US Atlantic Fleet in January 1943 indicated that VP-83 had by then reached a high standard in their anti-submarine operations.

One week after Lt Ford's success, Lt Lloyd Ludwig was airborne in *83-P-10* at 05:00 hours on 13 January from Fortaleza, his duty being to escort convoy TR-1. There was scattered cumulus cloud at 2,000ft with a 25kt wind from the east giving a rough sea, but visibility was twenty miles despite some haze.

Ludwig's PBY-5A was armed with depth charges of 625lb and 325lb set at 25ft depth — formidable DCs compared with those of 250lb used by RAF Coastal Command!

After they had been flying for about 1¾ hours, the co-pilot Lt M. G. Taylor sighted a white wake at twenty miles. The Catalina was then at 5,500 ft on a course of 300° at 110kt, and on the look-out for a convoy. At first the wake was thought to be that of a patrol boat but, when a submarine was identified, the Catalina dropped down, even though there was no effective cloud cover. The vessel was steaming with decks awash, but the conning tower was clearly visible.

From two miles out, Ludwig swooped on the submarine, although by then it had started to dive. Four depth charges were released by the navigator Ensign Holt from 40ft altitude; two of 625lb and two of 325lb, 200ft directly ahead of the submarine's conning tower. They struck the water 50ft ahead of the conning tower.

The Brazilian Catalina which attacked *U-199* on 31 July 1943. It was subsequently dubbed 'Arara' after a ship which had been sunk.

After about four minutes, a large oil slick appeared and a photograph which was taken showed it to be 175ft by 75ft wide. It was apparent that the submarine *(U-507* as it proved to be), was on a course following the convoy TR-1 on which it would, no doubt, have made an attack by dusk.

Only 'slight damage' was claimed by VP-83 for their Catalina, but in fact *U-507* was sunk in position 01°38'S 39°52'W. Ludwig remained in the area for 1¾ hours until he had to leave due to fuel shortage. He was relieved by Catalina *83-P-28* and USS *Jouett*, a destroyer of the American surface patrol force.

1943: Caribbean Convoy

U-156 is likely to be best remembered as the one which sank *Laconia* on 12 September 1942 while that ship was carrying 1,800 Italian PoWs, and then took four lifeboats in tow. In March 1943 however, it was very much the hunted vessel, this period coinciding with the sailing of convoy TG-4 en route from Trinidad to Guantanamo. On 2 March, *U-156* was subjected to attacks by two AAF bombers which were followed on the 3rd by USS *Nelson*, when the latter must have caused some damage to at least the U-boat's fuel tanks.

Catalina *53-P-1*, a PBY-5, was airborne at 06:15hr on the 8th detailed for an anti-submarine sweep to the north-east. Visibility was fifteen to eighteen miles with scattered cumulus cloud at 1,200-1,500ft and an 18-20kt wind from the east. At 13:10 hours the plane was being flown by the third pilot, J. M. Cleary, who sighted a fully surfaced submarine eight miles away and steaming at about 9kt. The plane commander, Lt J. E. Dryden, immediately took over the controls with the aircraft flying at 4,500ft and 115kt.

By making good use of cloud cover, Dryden was able to get within a quarter of a mile of the U-boat, then he broke cover at 1,500ft altitude and went into a dive at 150kt from 1,200ft.

All four Torpex-filled depth charges were released manually in a salvo from between 75 and 100ft altitude. J. F. Connely in the port blister saw two charges hit the water 10-15ft to starboard and just aft of the conning tower, followed by the vessel lifting and breaking into two sections which then sank centre first with

the bow and stern last to go under.

A heavy explosion caused debris, smoke and water to rise about 35ft into the air. A large oil slick developed and within it were eleven or more survivors; three were swimming, others clinging to wreckage. A dinghy was dropped to them from the Catalina, and five of the U-boat survivors managed to reach it and board the dinghy. A second dinghy was dropped and, although it did not inflate, it remained afloat. Emergency rations were also dropped, tied to two Mae Wests, and survivors rowed towards them. Photographs were taken and Dryden remained in the area for more than 1½ hours before returning to base.

An analysis of this attack by the USN attributes the success to VP-53's high degree of anti-submarine training, the altitude of the PBY above broken cloud, its white camouflage, and the maximum use which Dryden made of this camouflage during his approach. The report endorses the drop in salvo of depth charges by a well-trained crew.

Subsequent records confirm the sinking of *U-156* by VP-53 in position 12°38'N 54°39'W. According to Professor Morison's account[1], the US Navy searched for several days to rescue the U-boat's survivors but they were not recovered.

Italian submarines operating off Brazil

In the early part of 1943 five Italian submarines were detailed to operate off the coast of Brazil. They were *Cappellini*, *Barbarigo*, *Bagnolini*, *Torelli* and *Archimede*.

Cappellini sailed from La Pallice on 26 December 1942 and by 21 January was off the coast of Brazil in the area of Fortaleza. After reaching Martinique in February, the submarine was short of fuel and returned to Bordeaux on 4 March.

Barbarigo and *Bagnolini* followed from La Pallice in January and February respectively. All three were subjected to attacks by aircraft but they suffered no serious damage and *Barbarigo* returned to Le Verdon on 3 April followed by *Bagnolini* ten days later.

Torelli left Le Verdon on 21 February captained by Lt-Cmdr Antonia de Giacomo. On 11 March he received 25 tons of oil from *Barbarigo*. Later, when about 270 miles from Fernando de Noronha Island, *Torelli* was located by a reconnaissance aircraft. The submarine then had to endure a series of attacks from the air in which the radio was damaged and she suffered a considerable loss of oil. De Giacomo decided to return to port.

The final foray was by *Archimede*, commanded by Lt Guido Sacardo who sailed from Le Verdon on 26 February and was scheduled to operate off the Brazilian coast in the Pernambuco or Recife area. This involved following the coastline from about 23° South to 20° South. On reaching position 16°45′S 37°30′W, Lt Sacardo found himself short of fuel and contemplated returning to port, although there was the possibility of a rendezvous with a German supply submarine.

Now, from 10 April, the United States Navy had organised sweeps by aircraft operating from Natal to counter any Axis vessels which might break through the Allied blockade. For this operation, five aircraft were flown on a daily basis. One of the American Catalinas engaged on just such a sortie was commanded by Ens Robertson on 15 April. After about ten hours flying, he was 350 miles east of Natal when the Italian submarine *Archimede* was sighted.

According to an official Italian account², Robertson attacked *Archimede* releasing a 650lb depth charge at 17:00hr, and (*vide* Professor Morison³), made two strafing runs. This was to be followed by another aircraft flown by Lt jg G. Bradford Jr, who released four depth charges.

The submarine broke into two sections, with twenty of the crew thrown into the sea while others went down with the vessel. Three rubber dinghies had been released and some of the survivors managed to reach at least one of the dinghies which, however, was without food or water.

On 12 May, some Brazilian fishermen located one of the dinghies. There were three occupants, two dead and one barely alive. He was taken ashore and was handed over by the Brazilian authorities to the Americans to become a prisoner of war.

1943: The loss of *U-590* off Maraca Island

During the month of July, there was a concentration of U-boats off the Brazilian coast and Allied counter measures were stretched. Convoy TJ-1 from Trinidad with twenty merchant vessels was with six escorts which were largely patrol craft, and three of the merchant ships were lost on 8/9 July due to attacks by *U-510*.

On the 9th, VP-94 had five aircraft based at Belém⁴ and one of these was *94-P-1* commanded by Lt S. E. Auslander who was airborne at 08:44hr to provide escort for convoy TJ-1. En route to the convoy, just before noon, a swirl made by a submerging submarine was sighted.

At 12:30 a second Catalina, *94-P-10* with Lt Frank F. Hare as commander, was sweeping the area of the convoy when a surfaced U-boat was sighted sixty miles from the position in which Auslander had reported a swirl. It was Lt Hare's co-pilot who spotted the submarine 12 miles away in position 03°54′N 48°52′W. The Catalina was prepared to attack and, when at a distance of one mile, the U-boat opened fire with cannon; the PBY suffered shrapnel strikes through the port bow, killing Hare who was hit in the head, heart and body. The instrument panel was damaged and oil released from the automatic pilot caught fire.

The bombing run was continued with Lt J. P. Phelps the co-pilot taking command. Depth charges were released and two detonated 30ft from the U-boat's starboard quarter. Phelps left the scene with the U-boat still surfaced, but when *94-P-1* and another aircraft, *107-B-5*, investigated at 13:00hr there was no sign of the submarine.

At 14:24hr Auslander was flying at 3,700ft. There was about 5/10th cumulus cloud, but a submarine could still be seen surfacing three miles away in position 03°22′N 48°38′W. After passing through cloud, Auslander saw the U-boat still on course at 15kt. It dived and, when the Catalina was at 150ft with a speed of 200kt, depth charges were released spaced at 73ft and with a 25ft depth setting. Some use had been made of cloud cover and the U-boat crew must have been caught by surprise as, although there were three or four in the conning tower, there was no AA fire.

One depth charge exploded 20ft to port, a second 12ft between bow and conning tower, while two others were 30ft and 100ft ahead of the vessel. Three men were seen in the water

17

with two swimming in an oil slick which stretched 300yd. A dinghy was dropped to the survivors but drifted away from them. After an hour, the oil slick had spread over three-quarters of a mile. It was the demise of *U-590*, lost off Maraca Island, Brazil.

Catalina *94-P-4* sinks *U-662*

At 02:30 hours on 21 July Catalina *94-P-4* was airborne from Belém to undertake the escort of convoy TJ-2 and thus relieve *94-P-7*. By 05:30 hours Lt Richard H. Rowland, the commander of *94-P-4*, had reached the convoy area and just over thirty minutes later sighted a U-boat which was awash and steaming at 6-7kt, while the Catalina was cruising at 1,200ft and 95kt. The submarine was two to three miles away in position 03°56′N 48°46′W and Rowland rolled his aircraft to gain a better view while his 2nd pilot, Lt A. Anselmo, obtained a camera.

While the Catalina was on its approach there was some trouble with its bow gun, and AA fire from the U-boat made Rowland turn to port before going into a shallow-dive bombing run. Shrapnel from the AA fire damaged the base of the rudder fin and wounded the radio operator, Watson, in the leg and ankle; he was replaced by Garren.

Depth charges were released when the Catalina had reached 75ft altitude and was flying at about 145kt. One charge hung up, but two were seen to explode to port and aft of the conning tower, while a third detonated off the starboard bow of the submarine. Lt Anselmo saw the U-boat go down: it was later confirmed as being *U-662*. There were survivors, and according to Professor Morison's account[5], the German skipper (Müller), was picked up a week later with three of his crew by an American patrol craft — *PC-494*.

Attacks on U-boats by the Brazilian Air Force

Aircraft of the Brazilian Air Force had made two attacks on U-boats in April and May, one off Aracaju, the other off Maceió, but with no confirmed kill.

U-199 commanded by Kapitän-Leutnant Hans Werner Kraus had sailed from Germany on 13 May. It attacked an unescorted Liberty ship on 27 June about fifty miles off Rio de Janeiro and on 3 July shot down a PBM Mariner of the US Navy. On the 24th it sank a British merchant vessel, but on the 31st, *U-199* was attacked by another PBM flown by Lt W. F. Smith and suffered damage which precluded submerging again. This was at 07:18hr, sixty miles off Sugar Loaf and about the time that convoy JT-3 was due to sail from Rio de Janeiro en route to Trinidad.

Two Brazilian aircraft arrived at about the same time and were able to co-ordinate their attacks. One of the aircraft, a Hudson, made a bombing run, following with two strafing runs against the U-boat's fire. The second aircraft, a Catalina, now followed with two bombing attacks at 09:00 hours, releasing two depth charges on each run. The first two depth charges must have proved lethal as the German crew were ordered to abandon ship, and after the second run the vessel sank within seconds.

There were twelve survivors including the captain. The Catalina dropped dinghies and circled the area until the American tender *Barnegat* arrived.

On 28 August, during a ceremony held by the Brazilian Minister for Aeronautics, the Catalina which sank *U-199* in position 23°54′S 42°54′W off Rio de Janeiro was named *Arara*.

In October another attack was made by a Brazilian Catalina on an enemy submarine, but apparently without achieving a kill.

From April 1944 the US Navy began to withdraw its squadrons from the Brazilian coast. Churchill's charts[6] for U-boat sinkings in the Battle of the Atlantic show the Brazilian coastline ‛free of recorded losses from 19 September 1943 to 15 May 1944, apart from eight sinkings in the South Atlantic east of the Natal-Recife area, and six of these sinkings were well out from the coast.

Seven PBY-5 Catalinas had been incorporated into the Brazilian Air Force in 1943. They were flown to Belém, state of Para to undertake patrols for the 7th Air Base Corps.

In 1944, the Brazilian Air Force created three patrol groups. These were 1st Patrol Group, based at Belém; the 2nd Patrol Group located at Galeão, Rio; and the 3rd Patrol Group at Air Base Florianopolis, Sta Caterina. Three Catalinas remained at Belém, three at Galeão, and one Catalina at Florianopolis.

C-10A 6527, an ex-Brazilian Air Force (Forca Aerea Brasileira) PBY-5A which is now at the Aerospace Museum, Rio de Janeiro. During the anti-submarine campaign in 1943, the BAF was operating seven Catalinas from Bélem, but the total number received was 31 including seven PBY-5s.

By the end of 1944 the Brazilian Air Force was at full operational strength and considered able to maintain efficient patrols of its own coastline. The Brazilian Minister of Aeronautics obtained amphibian Catalinas for this purpose. They had a crew of four, a range of 3,100 miles and a cruising speed of about 124mph. These were PBY-5As and were designated 'PA-10s'.

1947-82 Brazilian Catalinas in the post-war period

In 1947 the Air Force discontinued the Patrol Groups and they were transformed into the 1st and 2nd Aviation Groups at Belém, where all the Catalinas were concentrated.

In the post-war period, the PBY-5As were incorporated into the Correio Aero Nacional (CAN). The amphibians' long range and adaptability made them particularly suitable for covering the Amazon region, since they were able to touch down at riverside communities without needing special landing facilities. The river people dubbed the Catalina 'The Angel of Space'. Air Force personnel devised a less reverent name, 'Pata Choca' (broody duck), and in the mid-1970s it was still in service carrying mail as well as medical and other supplies. Catalina flights in the Amazon region resulted in the formation of many new villages and the growth of a number of towns.

In 1950 the Brazilian Air Force changed the designation PA-10 to CA-10 (CA for cargo). Under this designation they operated until 1969 when the 1st and 2nd Aviation Groups were deactivated, but continued to function as the 'Primeiro Esquadrão de Transporte Aéreo' (First Air Transport Squadron, or 1st ETA).

All the Catalinas continued to fly with the 1st ETA until 1982, when they were replaced by Embraer 110s with the designation C-95.

A tribute to the Catalina by Brazil and headed 'Adeus' with text in Portuguese has been translated thus:

'Goodbye to the Catalina aircraft, which has been withdrawn from services in June 1982,

19

received a highly emotional farewell in several regions of our country after having rendered highly important services, not only to the Brazilian Air Force as a military aircraft, but also to the people of several states, and, especially to those of the Amazon region, transporting supplies for over forty years.

'In Florianopolis, Salvador, Natal and obviously, the Amazon region, this veteran and still efficient aircraft has been greeted with gratitude and sadness, as if it were not a mere flying machine, but a character, which in reality it was for the evolution of Brazil . . . '

1. SEM, Vol 1, p352.
2. In *I Sommergibili Negli Oceani*, 2nd edn, Rome, 1976, pp310-17.
3. SEM, Vol 1, p390.
4. Some aircraft of VP-94 were operating from Amapa.
5. SEM, Vol 10, p216.
6. WSC, Vol V, p14.
7. Data from *Correio Aero Nacional;* translation of 'Adeus', courtesy of the Brazilian Air Attache.

Chapter 4
RAF Coastal Command Operations

The first of the many

Of the 579 Catalinas and Cansos listed as being delivered to the Royal Air Force, the first was a PBY-4, serial No *P9630*, which was received in July 1939 and became a trials aircraft. In September 1939 it made a historic flight to Iceland[1] captained by Wg Cmdr Barnes, but before its demise in February of 1940, *P9630* was flown by a number of other RAF pilots including, notably, Dennis 'Bismarck' Briggs and the late Sir Geoffrey Bromet.

Sir Geoffrey had retired from the RAF in 1938 but was recalled on the outbreak of war and posted to Headquarters Coastal Command as SASO (Senior Air Staff Officer).

Catalina *P9630* was flown by Sqn Ldr Riley from Dumbarton to Rhu on 7 November, followed on the 12th by Flt Lt Isacke taking the aircraft to Invergordon. Two days later, Air Commodore Bromet with Dennis Briggs as 2nd pilot and a crew of four, took the Catalina from Invergordon to Sullom Voe.

Writing about this trip Air Commodore Bromet commented: 'The Pratt and Whitney engines are about 1,050hp each. Fuel 1,460 gallons and a range of some 4,000 miles at economical height. Speed 120 knots cruising. A good trip to the Shetlands cutting across land south of Wick to Thurso and west of Orkneys to Yell Sound — south to Sullom Voe. Fired at by a trawler near the boom defence and by a destroyer in the Voe. Thank you very much and we landed in a hurry.'

For 16 November, Briggs gives in his log: 'A/Com Bromet, S/Ldr Chaplin, 6 passengers; attempt to return to Invergordon — return owing to weather; 1hr.'

The PBY-4 was again flown by Air Commodore Bromet on 17 November and he records: '. . . good trip after Shetlands, sleet storms and visibility 40-50 miles from Orkneys onwards. A Hun arrived over the Shetlands at 10:45 taking photographs and *Coventry* and *Cardiff* pooped off at her. Night train to London.'

Briggs' log includes more trips in *P9630* including one on 23/24 November when it was captained by Wg Cdr Cahill on a night patrol in a search for the German pocket battleship *Deutschland* which had sailed for the Atlantic in August.

Dennis Briggs' last trip in *P9630* was on 10 February 1940, a flight from Rhu to Dumbarton. The Catalina was captained by Flt Lt Butler and in addition to Briggs, in the crew of six were Sqn Ldr Knyvett and Mr Drake. After a flight of 15 minutes the aircraft crashed on landing and sank.

According to an Air Ministry list, *P9630* had been allocated to three squadrons: 228, 240 and 210. Its all too brief operational role was in addition to serving as a trials aircraft.

The battleship *Bismarck*

Following the sinking or capture of 22 ships totalling 115,622 tons[2] by the battlecruisers *Scharnhorst* and *Gneisenau* in the first quarter of 1941, the Germans made plans for further operations in commerce raiding. These were to involve the two new battleships *Bismarck* and *Tirpitz* together with *Scharnhorst*, *Gneisenau* and the heavy cruiser *Prinz Eugen*.

Tirpitz was to prove unready until the following November and *Scharnhorst* and *Gneisenau* at Brest were subjected to a series of attacks by the RAF, such as on 6 April when F/O Campbell of 22 Squadron in a Beaufort torpedoed *Gneisenau*, putting the vessel out of action for a few months.

The Germans decided to use *Bismarck* in conjunction with *Prinz Eugen*. Even this limited force would have required Allied convoys to have a heavy escort, as no single battleship of the Royal Navy could have matched the modern, heavily armed *Bismarck*.

Under the code name 'Exercise Rhine', *Bismarck* and its consort *Prinz Eugen* sailed from Gdynia on 18 May for the Atlantic, their intended procedure being for *Bismarck* to engage escorts of convoys while the cruiser would dispose of as many merchant vessels as possible, leaving perhaps just one to pick up survivors.

En route through the Kattegat they were spotted by Swedish craft, but on the 20th were in Grimstad fjord and with three destroyers sailed into Kalvanes Bay. A Coastal Command PRU Spitfire flown by F/O M. Suckling photographed the battleship from 24,000ft on 21 May. The following day the German raiders sailed northward and, off Trondheim, the escorting destroyers departed. The absence of the battleship was reported by a Fleet Air Arm Maryland on reconnaissance which flew over Bergen at 200ft in 10/10th cloud.

By 23 May *Bismarck* and *Prinz Eugen* had entered the Denmark Strait. This route into the Atlantic was covered by the Royal Navy cruisers HMS *Norfolk* and HMS *Suffolk,* and that same evening *Suffolk* made contact at seven miles, whereupon the German vessels attempted to evade the cruisers by increasing speed to 30kt.

Subsequently, in an engagement between the new, but untried battleship HMS *Prince of Wales* and the battlecruiser HMS *Hood* against *Bismarck* and *Prinze Eugen,* HMS *Hood* blew up following hits to ammunition and a magazine; this within sixteen minutes of the first shot being fired. There were only three survivors.

Meanwhile, HMS *Prince of Wales* received hits on her bridge and below the waterline and withdrew. She had, however, caused significant damage to *Bismarck* with 14in shells, one having passed through *Bismarck* just above the waterline but below the bow wave, and about 2,000 tons of water were taken aboard. Another shell had damaged oil tanks which resulted not only in an oil slick, but also reduced the vessel's fuel supply. Admiral Lütjens in *Bismarck* now decided to abandon his Atlantic foray and head for St Nazaire.

The escape of *Prinz Eugen* was covered in the evening of the 24th by *Bismarck* turning back to make a short attack against the shadowing cruisers. She herself was attacked by aircraft flown off from HMS *Victorious* but suffered no damage. Then, just after 03:00 hours on the 25th, the shadowing cruisers lost contact with *Bismarck*.

Many Royal Navy units had been drawn away from other duties, including convoy escort, to intercept the enemy battleship. Coastal Command aireraft including Hudsons, Sunderlands and Catalinas were patrolling areas from the Faroes to Iceland, southwards and westwards from Iceland, and north-west and south-west from bases in Northern Ireland. There was a real prospect however, of the warships of the Royal Navy running short of fuel before *Bismarck* could be intercepted and gain cover by German aircraft.

The Air Officer Commanding-in-Chief, Coastal Command, Air Chief Marshal Sir Frederick W. Bowhill, laid on long-range sorties for Catalinas further south than was within the Admiralty's appreciation.

His initiative proved crucial.

Catalina *AH545* was now destined to become part of history. *AH545* of No 209 Squadron coded *WQ-Z* was airborne from Lough Erne in Northern Ireland at 03:45 hours on 26 May captained by Dennis A. Briggs, who had been detailed for a cross-over patrol. With him as crew members were P/O Otter, F/O Lowe, Sgts Edmonds, Burton, Leigh, Dunning and Stenning. By no means least was LAC Martin as wireless operator. From the USN was co-pilot Ens Leonard B. Smith, one of seventeen reported pilots from the US Navy operating with Coastal Command.

The rank of Pilot Officer belied Briggs' experience and ability, as by that time in his service he had completed about 1,500 hours' flying and was rated by his CO as an 'above average pilot-navigator'.

The weather conditions were reported as 7/10ths cumulus cloud at 1,500ft with visibility three miles at 800ft and eight miles at the surface, with a 30kt wind blowing from 300°. The sea was rough.

After flying south-west for six hours the Catalina reached its search area where the wind was reported as 40kt. At 10:30 hours they sighted the enemy battleship.

P9630, the RAF's PBY-4. It was flown by W/Cmdr Barnes on a recce of Iceland in September 1939 and by Dennis Briggs in a search for the pocket battleship *Deutschland* in November 1939.

Of this Capt Leonard B. Smith now writes: 'The weather was ideal for the mission, reasonably good visibility below 1,500ft altitude and plenty of nice clouds to hide in if one had encountered air opposition.

'After the original sighting, Briggs turned the controls over to me and went aft to prepare the contact report. The general idea was to take cover in the clouds and close the range somewhat in order to make positive identification. While in the clouds I misjudged the wind rather badly, and as the record shows, got much too close — right over the ship.'

The Catalina had broken cloud on the port beam of the battleship which immediately opened fire and the aircraft was holed in several places by shrapnel. Briggs' concern was that he'd be shot down before getting off a sighting report, and in a conversation with me he stressed his respect for his wireless operator, LAC Martin, who wished to gain promotion only by merit.

Bismarck's position was given in the coded co-ordinates 'KRGP 3215' (49°20'N 21°50'W), course 150°, speed 20kt. A survivor from *Bismarck*, Baron von Müllenheim-Rechberg', acknowledges the RAF's navigation to have given a more accurate position that that obtained by *Bismarck's* navigation by some 55

nautical miles — a position roughly 700 miles west of Brest.

The Catalina's radio transmission was received by Capt P.I. Vian, RN, commanding a destroyer flotilla, and also by the aircraft carrier HMS *Ark Royal*. Capt Vian, like Sir Frederick Bowhill, was prepared to act on his own initiative, and for Vian that meant torpedo attacks against *Bismarck*.

Despite damage to his aircraft, Briggs did not give up his objective of shadowing the battleship. He altered course and at 14:45 hours sighted another Catalina 'M' of 240 Squadron, which indicated the approximate bearing of the ship to Briggs. *M/240* had also picked up Briggs' original sighting report while patrolling north of *Z/209*. The two Catalinas formated on each other and signalled through cockpit windows. Briggs, who needed to touch down in daylight because of damage to the hull of his flying boat, set course for base at 15:10hr.

While Briggs was en route to base, aircraft from HMS *Ark Royal* were airborne, but with torpedoes. At 20:30hr on 26 May *Bismarck* gave an aircraft alarm. At 20:47hr the battleship was subjected to a torpedo attack by Swordfish of 810, 818 and 820 Squadrons. Fifteen aircraft released thirteen torpedoes, one of which struck the vulnerable stern,

23

flooding the steering gear room and jamming the twin rudders at 'left 12°'. The jamming of the rudders was to prove the decisive factor in an attack lasting 38 minutes.

Catalina *AH545* captained by P/O Dennis Briggs, whose sighting report brought the Royal Navy back in a position to attack, landed at 21:30hr. In the column of his log book headed 'Duty, including results and remarks' is written: 'Spotted and shadowed *Bismarck*, holed by A/A shrapnel'.

At 08:47hr on 27 May the battleships HMS *Rodney* and HMS *King George V* opened fire on *Bismarck;* it became a floating hulk. Joining the action were the cruisers *Norfolk* and *Dorsetshire*. The latter remained on the scene to fire torpedoes at *Bismarck*, although meantime scuttling charges had been placed against her condenser intakes.

Bismarck sank in position 48°10′N 16°12′W at 10:36hr[4].

From Captain Dennis Briggs, DFC and Bar, it is understood that LAC Martin gained his wish of being promoted to Corporal on *merit*. This was in addition to the award of a DFM.

Attack by Catalina *AH545* on *U-81*

Catalina *AH545* survived the AA fire from *Bismarck*, and in October was still with 209 Squadron but then operating from Pembroke Dock.

On 30 October it was detailed for an anti-submarine cross-over patrol, captained by F/O Ryan. The weather in the operational area was given as fine with ³⁄₁₀ths cloud at 2,500ft and with a north-easterly wind of 23kt.

Ryan was airborne at 08:00hr but was flying for almost seven hours before a first sighting was made: this was of a submarine heading due east on the surface at 15kt. Those in the vessel must have also spotted the aircraft as they fired green pyrotechnics and turned to port.

Ryan circled the submarine, during which time there was an exchange of fire. A shell from the U-boat exploded in the tail of the Catalina causing damage to the IFF and a dinghy air bottle.

A Lockheed Hudson[5] aircraft was now seen flying at 600ft altitude on a reciprocal course to the Catalina. Although by now the U-boat had commenced diving, the Hudson attacked with three anti-submarine bombs.

Ryan, in the Catalina, then followed with his attack in which he released three depth charges, a fourth having hung up. He circled the area for 15 minutes during which time an oil patch appeared with some air bubbles. As there were now some signs of trouble with the Catalina's engines, Ryan set course for base where he touched down after a sortie lasting 10hr 15 min.

Coastal Command credited both the Hudson and Catalina as having caused damage to the submarine, *U-81*, such that it returned to port. Just a fortnight later, however, it was *U-81* with *U-205* which torpedoed HMS *Ark Royal* when she was en route to Gibraltar[6].

The sinking of *U-253*

During September 1942, Sullom Voe in the Shetlands was the base for 210 Squadron, although their Catalinas were not confined to that area. Thus just one page of the operational record, for the 18th to the 23rd, indicates the use of Grasnaya in Russia, and Akureyri in Iceland, in addition to Sullom Voe. The use of such widely dispersed bases must have stemmed from the intention to give the maximum possible cover to convoys PQ18 and QP14.

The same single page reflects the overall attitude of the squadron with regard to its close attention to details: a 'press on' attitude, but not 'regardless'[7]. Dates, bases, serial numbers and letters of aircraft and the names of *all* crew members are recorded, in addition to the accounts of each sortie.

On 18 September Flt Lt D. E. Healy, captain of 'S' *FP113*, was airborne from Grasnaya to escort PQ18 which was on a course of 200° at 8kt. He exchanged visual signals with the convoy which he then had to leave because of deteriorating weather and the close proximity to land, and he had to await first light after making a landfall at Cape Kanin before flying to Lake Lakhta.

P/O J. G. Walker in 'P' *VA729* took off from Sullom Voe to escort convoy QP14. While with the convoy he was informed by the Senior Naval Officer (SNO), that the area was 'full of U-boats'. From the positions given, he must have flown north of Jan Mayen Island before returning to Akureyri.

From the times given, 'round the clock' coverage must have been provided for convoy

QP14, as following P/O Walker were F/O Martin on the 21st and Flt Sgt J. W. Semmens on the 22nd.

Semmens was airborne from Sullom Voe just before midnight on the 22nd in Catalina 'U' *FP115*. Just over six hours later, while on the track of the convoy, a surfaced U-boat was sighted three-quarters of a mile away on a north-westerly course, travelling at 6kt. Semmens attacked from a height of 50ft releasing six 250lb Torpex-filled depth charges.

The U-boat — *U-253* — was straddled, although completely submerged at the time of release. It rose again to the surface but on its side, sank again; then rose again on its side before rolling over. The stern came up almost vertically before the U-boat disappeared for the last time. This was in position 68°19N′ 13°50′W to the north and east of Iceland.

Attack on *U-465* by Catalina 'M', 210 Squadron

In April 1943, 210 Squadron was under the control of 19 Group, Coastal Command, and based at Pembroke Dock in South Wales. In the first half of April their Catalinas were flown on a series of patrols with the aircraft on each occasion being airborne at about 19:20 hours.

One of these patrols was on the 10th — Catalina *M/210* captained by Flt Lt Squire flying with a crew of ten. Throughout the flight, a constant radar watch was maintained. It was at 22:41 hours that night that a radar contact was reported at a distance of six miles. The radar blip disappeared at 3 ½ miles but, after Squire had turned a slow circle, contact was re-established at four miles. Shortly afterwards, a U-boat was sighted steaming on a westerly course at 15kt, but still four miles away and on the starboard bow.

In an attack by Squire made from about 60ft altitude, four depth charges were released. It was estimated that they had straddled the submarine. Although not stated in the squadron's operational record, it is likely that at that stage in the war the charges would have been of 250lb each and filled with Torpex rather than Amatol.

Subsequent records credit *M/210* with causing damage to *U-465* on 10 April 1943, in a patrol of sixteen hours' duration.

A Catalina believed to be undergoing modifications for the RAF at Beaumaris.

Anti-submarine operations by 190 Squadron

No 190 Squadron was re-formed in March 1943 at Sullom Voe and equipped with Catalinas. Duties undertaken by the unit were largely anti-submarine patrols in the northwest approaches.

A flight engineer who was with 190 Squadron during much of the time they operated Catalinas was John Robertson, whose first trip was an A/S patrol between the Faeroes and Iceland. This was in *FP113* with Sqn Ldr King on 22 May when, after 17 hours' flying they landed at Vaagar in the Faeroes, returning to Sullom Voe on the 24th.

On 15 September he was airborne from Reykjavik in *FP113* with F/O McKirdy. During the take-off, which was in severe weather conditions, the port float was ripped off. However, flying speed had been reached, and with little room left there was no option but to take off. They circled the area, and after much fuel had been dumped, attempted a touch-down. During the landing, an ASR launch ran alongside and under the wing, now devoid of its float. Gradually McKirdy allowed the wing to rest on the launch. Both crew and aircraft were thereby saved.

For their return flight to Sullom Voe on 18 September the duties included escorting a convoy which was en route to Murmansk. They touched down in the Shetlands after flying for over 24 hours.

To assist the Royal Navy in routing the convoys to Russia, the squadron detailed a Catalina to fly an ice patrol as far north as Bear Isle, returning via Ice Fjord and Jan Mayen Island. This was *FP324* captained by F/O Walker whose navigator, Flt Sgt Woodland, had the additional task of taking a series of photographs of the sea. Due to strong head winds, the trip was cut short, but 23½ hours were flown.

In the first half of 1943, this anti-submarine campaign was building towards a peak which was to be reached in May. On 23 March F/O Fish attacked a U-boat with six depth charges. It was later confirmed as being *U-339* which was damaged. F/O Walker in *FP183* sighted two U-boats on 21 April but was able to attack only one.

A second confirmed attack occurred on 17 May by Catalina *E/190* which was operating from Castle Archdale on Lough Erne. It was airborne at 11:32hr captained by Flt Lt Gosling who, after flying for almost eight hours, was then above 10/10th cloud. His radar operator obtained an SE contact at five miles on the starboard bow. Four minutes later when they were at 1,500ft a fully surfaced U-boat was sighted 1½ miles away.

In his first run, Gosling was unable to pull out from a steep turn in time to make a satisfactory release of depth charges. During a second run, the submarine was beginning to submerge with about a third of the hull between the conning tower and bow below surface. Four depth charges were released, one falling 12ft from the starboard side, another on the stern. All four exploded and the vessel's bow was lifted about 30ft out of the water. A few seconds later part of the U-boat came out of the water at a steep angle before sliding down again.

Gosling adopted waiting tactics and, on returning to the scene of the attack, he saw a large oil patch a mile long by 200yd wide. The convoy (TA42), was located at 22:21 hours, informed of the attack, and was then escorted for a further period.

The U-boat — *U-229* — had indeed been damaged by the Catalina's depth charges but survived to be sunk later in the year by HMS *Keppel*.

Catalina *FP280* was airborne from Sullom Voe at 10:50 hours on 10 October captained by F/O Vaughan, who had been detailed for an anti-submarine patrol. With him in the crew were 2nd pilot Flt Sgt Graham, the Canadian navigator F/O Merrick, Engineer Sgts Ludgate and Pepperday, W/AGs Sgts Gibbons, Carter and Bennett, and air gunner Sgt Tindall.

After completing the patrol which proved uneventful in the atrocious weather, they were diverted three times. On each occasion the weather closed in before the diversion was reached. By now they were seriously short of fuel and an attempt was made to return to base, but without success.

Vaughan had now no alternative to putting the Catalina down in open sea, west of the Shetlands. This was at 18:50hr on the 11th, after they had been flying for 22 hours. There was a heavy sea running and the radio transmitter was defective, although they were able to receive messages.

TJ-S JX269, the last of the RAF Mark IVAs in formation flying over Northern Ireland with another Catalina of 202 Sqn.

As the aircraft was by now overdue, surface search vessels were sent out but were unable to locate the Catalina. Signals transmitted by an emergency-type transmitter proved too weak to be received by base.

At some Coastal Command stations at that time there was provision for aircraft to carry homing pigeons: *FP280* was fortunately one of these. The Catalina's estimated position was given on a note fixed to the ring on a pigeon's leg, the bird released, and some time later the pigeon entered the loft near control. An RAF ASR launch was sent out, in addition to the lifeboat from Aith in the Shetlands.

The aircraft was abandoned at 02:10hr on the 12th, with Sgts Ludgate, Pepperday and Bennett being picked up by the lifeboat, while the remainder of the crew were taken in the ASR launch. The fate of the Catalina, according to the Air Ministry list, was that it was struck by the ASR launch and foundered on 12 October.

Subsequent press reports included a photograph of the pigeon which was to be named 'Saviour'. It had been bred by the Fleming brothers of Motherwell and presented to the RAF pigeon service.

On 1 January 1944, 190 Squadron was renumbered 210, and Catalina aircraft continued to be operated under that designation with great success.

Anti-submarine operations by 210 Squadron

Sqn Ldr F. J. French was captain of Catalina 'M' of 210 Squadron on 24 February. He was airborne just before midnight from Sullom Voe detailed for an A/S escort to a convoy, and eight hours later he was in position 69°52'N 08°33'E. Not having met the convoy, he commenced a rectangular search by radar. At 09:20hr he was flying at 1,500ft when a blip on the radar screen indicated a contact 24 miles away. French closed the range and within five minutes a U-boat, with decks awash, was sighted from four miles.

French attacked with depth charges at 50ft altitude, and during the bombing run was subjected to cannon and machine-gun fire which missed its target. After the attack, wreckage with eight or ten survivors from the U-boat were seen. It was the demise of *U-601*.

In May 1944, Dönitz was sending U-boats to Northern Norway for the purpose of operating against Allied Arctic convoys. This was despite the obvious disadvantages of there being only about three hours of darkness in such latitudes during which submarines might surface to charge their batteries.

On the 18th, F/O Bastable was one of two captains detailed for an A/S patrol. He was airborne from Sullom Voe in Catalina 'S' at 06:43hr and in less than three hours had reached his patrol area at position 63°15'N 01°47'E — roughly north-east of the Faeroes and due west of Trondheim. Visibility was five to eight miles, and he was flying at 200ft altitude when a submarine was sighted heading north-west at 12-15kt. Tracers were seen from the U-boat, which had immediately opened fire; Bastable took evasive action while two of his gunners responded, with hits being scored on the conning tower of the vessel from which a body was seen to fall in the water.

At 50ft Bastable released six Torpex depth charges, achieving a straddle midships of the vessel. Fortunately, the Catalina suffered only some damage to the tailplane. After the attack, the U-boat sank stern first at an angle of 30°; an oil patch appeared and a number of survivors were seen in the water. They were from *U-241*, which was lost in position 63°36'N 01°42'E.

Within a week, this squadron was able to claim another U-boat sunk. This time it was just south of the Arctic Circle in the Norwegian Sea.

Catalina 'V', captained by Capt F. W. L. Maxwell, was airborne from Sullom Voe just before midnight on 23 May. He flew at 900ft altitude and, after 7½ hours sighted a fully surfaced U-boat five miles away. It was heading south-west at 12kt. As Maxwell closed to attack, there was heavy but inaccurate flak from the vessel and he was able to release six Torpex depth charges. They all exploded, and one was very close to the U-boat. The vessel spun round on its stern almost full circle, then lay still before sinking by the stern. The U-boat then pivoted at the conning tower with the bows rising out of the water at a steep angle. It rose again for a minute as though all the tanks had been blown, with the conning tower and foredeck out of the water, before again sinking slowly. There was then no further trace of the submarine in position 65°08'N 04°53'E where *U-476* was lost on 24 May.

Royal Air Force squadron operational records from the period of the *Bismarck* sighting show, all too frequently perhaps, just half a line of detail, and with the names of many crew members omitted. During 1943 and 1944 however, a change is seen in some Coastal

Command records with the names and categories of aircrews being given, in addition to much more detail concerning the sorties.

A new aircrew category is listed against an entry in 210 Squadron's record for 28 June 1944 — 'Wop/Air', ie, aircrew whose duties were specifically those of a wireless operator. It was at about this time that a new flying badge was issued with the letter 'S' for 'signals' (and not for 'sprog' as might have been suggested!).

Three of the crew of Catalina 'Q' on 28 June are listed as 'Wop/Air', namely Sgt A. Smith, Sgt J. McLean and Flt Sgt W. Thirwell. Exceptionally also, are given in plain language the messages apparently received and transmitted by the 'Wops/Air' while in flight. They, together with others in the crew, were captained by F/O J. C. Campbell.

Catalina 'Q' was airborne at 09:45 hours and reached the patrol area just over an hour later. It was to be exactly nine hours after beginning the patrol that a radar contact was made 4½ miles ahead of the Catalina, when the aircraft was at 750ft altitude with very limited visibility. On closing to investigate, the crew sighted a surfaced U-boat steaming eastwards at 16kt.

Campbell attacked with depth charges from the U-boat's starboard quarter, and the charges appeared to straddle the vessel 30ft ahead of the conning tower. The U-boat had responded with AA fire and Campbell took evasive action before making a second attack with machine-gun fire. The U-boat maintained its speed as it subjected the Catalina to further AA fire. It was thought that a second U-boat was in the vicinity about 1½ miles away, but a search was difficult due to sea fog.

After obtaining a fix on the attack position — 62°30'N 01°07'E — a sea-marker was dropped with a two-hour delay setting and Campbell was ordered to remain until PLE (Prudent Limit of Endurance), being diverted to Alness if necessary. A Liberator now arrived on the scene; the Catalina returned to base, touching down in the early hours of the following morning.

The U-boat *U-396* was damaged as a result of the Catalina's attack. It was then sunk by Liberator 'V' of 86 Squadron in position 59°29'N 05°22'W on St George's Day, 1944.

On 17 July three fleet carriers of the Royal Navy were used to launch an attack by

Barracuda aircraft against *Tirpitz* in Altenfjord. In addition to *Tirpitz* there were five destroyers and 32 U-boats in Northern Norway. To cover the Navy's withdrawal, Coastal Command laid on air patrols deploying Nos 59, 120 and 210 Squadrons.

On that day, Catalina 'Y' of 210 Squadron was airborne from Sullom Voe at 13:45 hours captained by F/O J. A. Cruickshank. With him were F/O J. C. Dickson, navigator; Flt Sgt J. S. Garnett, 2nd pilot; Sgt F. Fidler, 3rd pilot; Flt Sgt S. B. Harbison, Flt Eng; wireless operators W/O W. C. Jenkins and Flt Sgt H. Gershenson; Sgt R. S. C. Proctor, Wom/AG; Flt Sgt F. J. Appleton, Wop/AG; and Flt Sgt A. I. Cregan, the rigger. This crew had been detailed for an A/S patrol in an area some 150 miles north of the Arctic Circle and to within about fifty miles of Lofoten Island.

After they had been flying for eight hours a radar contact was made fifteen miles distant: Cruickshank was then at an altitude of 1,500ft. He homed on to the contact, losing height to 200ft, and saw a vessel five miles dead ahead. At first it was thought to be a friendly destroyer and recognition signals were fired and the letter of the day flashed.

The vessel responded with a heavy box barrage, as it turned slowly to port. The Catalina now made a complete circuit two

miles from the target; the vessel was identified as a U-boat.

Cruickshank made a diving attack from 1,000ft to 50ft altitude and, when the range had closed to 1,000yd or less, his gunners opened up from the bow and the blisters. All of the depth charges failed to release and Cruickshank climbed to 800ft before turning to port for a second run.

By now the U-boat was stationary in the water and her AA fire was heavy and accurate. The Catalina suffered several hits; the navigator — F/O Dickson — was killed and Cruickshank, although seriously wounded, persisted in his second attack. With the Catalina flying at only 50ft, six depth charges were this time successfully released. They straddled the U-boat but, due to sea fog, it was difficult to determine the result.

The second pilot now took over the controls to fly the aircraft back to base. After reporting the attack, the wireless operators sent a further message reporting the death of the navigator and the injury to the captain, and requesting an ambulance on arrival. Thereafter, the wireless operators were busy attempting to obtain a fix on their position by land stations taking bearings on the Catalina's transmissions. They were given a series of bearings from Sumburgh and courses to steer.

An RAF Catalina equipped with Yagi aerials on the wings for ASV and a Leigh light suspended from the starboard wing.

According to the official RAF history[8], Cruickshank continued to command the aircraft despite 72 wounds, including two in the lungs and ten in the legs. The squadron record states that the second pilot brought the Catalina, *JV928*, back to base safely.

One may guess at the feelings of the crew of 'Y'. Any possible elation at overcoming an aggressive enemy would have been more than countered by the loss of their navigator and the injuries suffered by their captain.

In the one line devoted to this episode in the Coastal Command War Record is the remark: 'Pilot awarded V.C.'[9].

The U-boat proved to be *U-347* and was sunk in position 68°35'N 06°00'E.

The following day, Catalina 'Z' of 210 Squadron was detailed for an A/S patrol of an area similar to that given to F/O Cruickshank on 17 July. 'Z' was captained by F/O R. W. G. Vaughan and airborne at 06:35 hours.

By 13:53hr he had covered the area twice but had received a report of a U-boat at position 68°38'N 08°55'E. On nothing being sighted, he commenced a square search and, within eight minutes, while flying at 800ft, saw what was taken to be a ship, but through binoculars was identified as a fully surfaced U-boat. The vessel was heading south-east at 12-15kt. At three miles, while the Catalina was still closing to attack, the U-boat opened up with AA fire. Two of the Catalina crew were wounded — F/O K. S. Freeman and Flt Sgt J. Maule. Damage to the aircraft resulted in a petrol leak in the port tank of 100gal/hr, and a serious leak of lubricating oil to the starboard engine. Vaughan however, continued his bombing run almost down track of the U-boat, which was straddled by exploding depth charges.

As the Catalina turned to port, the aircrew saw the remains of the submarine disappearing below the sea. A number of small yellow dinghies were then seen, together with thirty to forty survivors from the U-boat and a large oil patch, which must have been from *U-742*.

About an hour later, Vaughan signalled that he was losing oil rapidly and, after another thirty minutes, that he was returning on one engine. The remaining 500 miles were flown on the port engine and it was over six hours before the Catalina was waterborne and beached.

These successful engagements by 210 Squadron during this period represent part of what the American historian Professor Morison states as 'the most effective air offensive in the anti-submarine war, relative to the means employed'[10]. Captain Roskill[11] gives 32 U-boats being based in Northern Norway during that time, while Morison refers to some fifteen U-boats sunk by Coastal Command in two months.

210 Squadron's final successful Catalina attack against a U-boat was on 7 May, ie, the eve of VE day.

Catalina 'X', captained by Flt Lt K. M. Murray was airborne at 03:30hr from Sullom Voe. While flying at 500ft just over an hour later, they obtained a radar contact at a range of two miles and, in another two minutes, a schnorkel, periscope and wake was sighted from a vessel heading north-west at 7-8kt.

Murray attacked with four depth charges a minute later and just five seconds after the U-boat had submerged completely. A pattern of sono-buoys was now laid and, meanwhile, a large patch of oil appeared on the surface, later developing into two long streaks. The sono-buoys transmitted hammering noises and later that of an engine, but the hammering continued.

Murray's attack had been at 05:20hr it was not until over ten hours later that he set course for base from position 61°38'N 01°58'E, having maintained contact with the U-boat during that period. The Catalina was waterborne again at 16:50 hours.

This engagement was notable in three respects: making a radar contact with a schnorkel at two miles (with the apparatus then available this was no mean achievement, even in a calm sea); the effective use of sono-buoys; and making a kill, with what were probably 250lb depth charges, after the U-boat had submerged.

Captain Roskill[12] gives this submarine *U-320* as being the last of 699 German U-boats claimed by Allied ships or aircraft in World War 2, adding that she was scuttled due to the damage sustained in the attack by the Catalina. Alfred Price[13] gives *U-320* as having foundered with all its crew. The American list of U-boat losses credits 210 with sinking *U-320* on 7 May in position 61°32'N 01°53'E. It does not appear in the American list of those scuttled.

P/O Dennis Briggs broadcasting an account of the *Bismarck* sighting at the BBC.

Leigh light operations over the Atlantic

The Leigh light was a searchlight adapted by Sqn Ldr H. de v Leigh of Coastal Command to be fitted to aircraft in World War 2. Its purpose was to enable aircraft to attack U-boats at night, and ultimately it was used by the RAF in conjunction with improved radar and a radio altimeter.

By 1944, radar giving 'blips' and 'sea returns' on a cathode ray tube with fixed aerials in the system, were being displaced by a CRT known as the PPI (position plan indicator), which gave a trace of coastlines and objects such as vessels in sea areas; a rotary scanner replaced fixed aerials. By 1944 also, German U-boats were using schnorkels which enabled them to operate with diesel engines below the surface.

Earlier, in 1942, following successful trials by Sqn Ldr Leigh, Air Chief Marshal Sir Philip Joubert had asked for six Wellingtons and six Catalinas to be fitted with Leigh lights[14].

No 202 Squadron, after operating from Gibraltar, moved to Castle Archdale, Lough Erne in August 1944, and undertook intensive training in the use of radar and the Leigh light.

Some training was undertaken over Lough Neagh at night with practice homing on oil drums in the centre of the Lough. When contact was made at a distance of one mile, an approach was made at 100ft altitude with the searchlight switched on. This was later followed by exercises with a submarine of the Royal Navy. Although practice was given in all weathers, the procedure to be followed proved very different if you were in a storm over the North Atlantic.

A Catalina captain with 202 Squadron from November 1944 to June 1945 was Flt Lt Charles Page, who gives this account: 'Following sighting at patrol height — usually 1,000ft — altitude would be dropped to 100ft with the pilot taking directional instructions from the radar operator. A black cloth screen could be pulled to a degree around the pilot who would fly entirely on instruments and watch the radio altimeter like a hawk.

31

'At one mile the searchlight would be switched on — hence the screen to help avoid the intense glare. At this stage the navigator/bomb aimer would be in the nose of the aircraft and would take over from the radar operator in giving final approach instructions towards the target.'

One trip Page recalls was the long haul out to escort RMS *Queen Mary* coming in from the USA with thousands of troops. The first aircraft to meet her would spend only about an hour on escort duty before a long flight back.

Before leaving, he would ask permission to take photographs and, as he writes: 'Everywhere there were faces looking at us and I could not help but feel that morale must have been boosted at the first sight of Great Britain in the form of the RAF roundels. The crew on the bridge would salute our farewell — as did all the Navy crews.'

In addition to escort duties there were anti-submarine patrols; these were given by Flt Engineer F/O Jack Chandler as being within the area off the Shannon, or 12° west of Land's End, with the object of intercepting U-boats out of Brest, and with care being taken to keep outside the Irish three-mile limit.

For Jack Chandler the trips involved taking on about 1,500 gal of fuel for a take-off at 16:30hr returning at 12 noon the next day. Their armament was 0·303 Brownings, 0·5 Brownings in the blisters, and bomb racks under each wing modified to take three or four depth charges each. The radar was on the whole time and was a considerable drain on electric power which was conserved by dispensing with electric hot plates and using a Primus stove for cooking — with a fire extinguisher to hand!

After four hours' flying to reach the search area, they flew for endurance rather than range with everything cut back to just above stalling speed, 'just hanging in the air': light boost with low revs, engine carburettors set at 'auto-lean', and air speed at 90kt or less. The signal 'Action Stations' came frequently, due to the sensitive radar picking up returns from oil drums, rafts, rainstorms and Irish fishing boats. In the latter case there would be much waving of torches from the fishing vessels.

The entry of the *Bismarck* sighting in Capt Briggs' log book. It is dated 26 May 1941.

On sighting a U-boat the drill was for the front gunner to aim at the conning tower while blister gunners aimed fore and aft of the conning tower with their armour-piercing 0·5s, and hopefully before the U-boat could train its guns on the Catalina. A crew member would be ready to drop either a flame float or smoke float according to conditions to mark the location.

All too often, the weather proved to be the most dangerous enemy for aircrew, as Chandler relates: 'An equally considered enemy of the lone patrolling Catalina was the weather. I recall we were patrolling off St George's Channel at night on a routine trip when we were hit by a terrific snowstorm and were diverted to Pembroke Dock. Flying fairly low and with the landing lights now on — not that they were of much use — we intended to be waterborne south of Milford Haven, an area thick with moored shipping. While straightening up the Cat for a night landing, we failed to see a moored ship that had swung on its buoy and we flew down and between the fore and aft masts of the ship — very hairy. However, we made it and taxied on the step to meet the RAF power boat to lead us on to a buoy. We were "trapped" there for the following three days.

'A stiff broom was used to sweep frost or snow from wings: dicey because always one float was in the water and one out. When one moved over the float which was out of the water, it would suddenly lurch down with the extra weight and sling the man into the water if not prepared against it.'

While most of 202 Squadron's Catalina losses occurred while they were based at Gibraltar, F/O Chandler does recall hunting for an overdue aircraft. After searching an area near the Sligo border, the Catalina was discovered crashed on a hillside. The Air Ministry list records Catalina *JX208* as having crashed near Castle Gregory, Tralee Bay on 19 December 1944.

1 *Ibid* Page 68
2 SWR, Vol 1, p379.
3 In his book *Battleship Bismarck*, p169, Triad/Panther, 1982 edn.
4 SWR, Vol 1, p415 (WSC, Vol III, p283 gives 10:40hr when 'it turned over'; Baron von M-Rechberg gives '10:39hr'.
5 Hudson 'H' of 53 Sqn.
6 SWR, Vol 1, p533.
7 'Press on regardless' was a common RAF aircrew expression in WW2.
8 Vol III, p125.
9 See also reference to David Hornell, *Ibid*.
10 SEM, Vol X, p309.
11 SWR, Vol III/1, p157.
12 S.W.R., Vol III/2, p300.
13 *Aircraft versus Submarine* p229
14 *The Flight Avails*, Vol II, p102.

Chapter 5
Iceland

September 1939-September 1941[1]

Winston Churchill was fully aware[1] of the strategic importance of Iceland, flanking as it does the great circle route from Halifax in Nova Scotia to Scottish ports: many wartime convoys were routed from Halifax. At the time of the Norwegian campaign he indicated that assurances of Allied protection would be given to Iceland. In a directive dated 28 April 1940 addressed to the First Sea Lord, Churchill proposed that a base be set up in Iceland for flying-boats and for the refuelling of ships.[2]

The Royal Air Force must have anticipated such a move as the first RAF Catalina, a PBY-4 *P9630* was flown by Wg Cdr L. K. Barnes on 25 September 1939 from Pembroke Dock when the aircraft was with 228 Squadron[3]. His route to Iceland was via Invergordon and he had been briefed to undertake a reconnaissance of Icelandic fjords for German shipping. Due to fog, the Catalina was forced down in Iceland on the 26th. Following some diplomatic exchanges, Wg Cdr Barnes returned to Britain on 28 September.

It was believed that Hitler intended occupying Iceland as an advanced U-boat base. However, such a move was forestalled by British troops entering Iceland on 10 May 1940, and these were reinforced by Canadians in June and July. In August No 98 Squadron RAF, equipped with 'Battles', were sent. They were followed by Hudsons and Sunderlands.

The importance of aircraft operating from Iceland was to assist in closing the 'Atlantic Gap', an area which was lacking in close support for convoys due to the limited range of aircraft and some escort vessels.

Shortly after Hitler had announced that waters surrounding Iceland would be a war zone where neutral ships would be sunk, President Roosevelt ordered a Naval reconnaissance of Iceland. On 10 April 1941 the American destroyer *Niblack*, while deployed for that mission, picked up survivors from a Dutch ship which had been torpedoed. During the rescue an Asdic contact in *Niblack* indicated a potentially hostile submarine. Depth charges were released and the U-boat withdrew. It was believed to be the first act of war between American and German forces in World War 2[4].

In 1940 the Royal Navy had been able to escort convoys in the Western Approaches to 17°W, but in April 1941, when their escort vessels were able to use Hvalfjordur as a base in Iceland, their range was extended to 35°W[5]. This, according to Professor Morison[6] 'filled the mid-ocean gap', albeit by surface craft.

Following pressure from Churchill, Iceland 'invited' the Americans to become responsible for the defence of that strategic island, and when intelligence reports indicated to Churchill that Hitler intended invading Russia, American Marines who had been scheduled for the Azores defence were diverted to Iceland. There was an awareness that Iceland might well be used as a supply route to a potential ally.

The United States Navy had aircraft based on the tender AVD-5, USS *Goldborough*, flying patrols from Reykjavik during the period 4-17 July and intended to cover the landings of the US Marines in Iceland, which began on the 7th and were completed on the 12th. For the strongly nationalistic Icelanders this was 'Hobson's choice'!

In that same month, the USN Atlantic fleet was ordered to support the defence of Iceland. This involved escorting convoys of American or Icelandic shipping, and included ships of other nations electing to join such convoys.

34

PBY-5As of VP-84. This squadron of the US Navy, while under RAF Coastal Command control, sank three U-boats and damaged two others.

VP-73 with Catalinas and commanded by Lt Cdr James E. Leeper moved from Argentia, Newfoundland to Reykjavik on 6 August and was joined by VP-74, equipped with 'Mariner' flying boats. They initiated patrols for the USN from Iceland over the North Atlantic convoy routes.

Attack on *U-452* by Catalina *AH553*

The move by the US Navy squadrons to Iceland coincided with that by 209 Squadron of the RAF, which was equipped with Catalinas.

On 25 August 1941, Catalina 'J' of 209 Squadron was able to claim the first anti-submarine success for Coastal Command while operating under the control of AHQ Iceland. This was the sinking of *U-452* in position 61°30'N 15°30'W, and the victory was shared with the trawler HMS *Vascoma*. It was to be the first out of 31 U-boats sunk by aircraft controlled from Iceland listed by Coastal Command and, of the 31, the only one to be given as 'shared'. There were to be, in addition, another thirteen U-boats so damaged

by Iceland-controlled aircraft that they had to return to base.

Catalina 'J' *AH553* was captained by F/O Jewiss who was airborne at 16:30 hours on 24 August detailed for a U-boat hunt. After 3½ hours' flying the search area was reached. Shortly afterwards signals were exchanged with an Icelandic trawler and the search was then continued.

The weather in that area was obviously deteriorating. Initially there was 10/10th cloud at 300ft, showers and sea fog with visibility 3-6 miles. Later the visibility was reduced to a mile or less with cloud down to 200ft; the wind had increased from 18 to 25kt and had veered from 60° to 115°. Nevertheless, six or seven hours after they had passed the trawler, a surfaced U-boat was sighted half a mile away from the aircraft.

Jewiss made a diving attack on the submarine releasing four depth charges. The squadron record states that the U-boat was blown to the surface before sinking stern first. Despite the weather, F/O Jewiss remained in the area of the attack for three hours before returning to base — a round trip of twenty hours.

35

Captain Roskill, in a brief account of this episode[7], states that it was one of eighteen attacks on U-boats made by Coastal Command aircraft in the month of August.

1941-42

On 4 September 1941 an event of great significance occurred in the Battle of the Atlantic. Until that date, captains of American ships were uncertain of what action to take on encountering a German ship or aircraft. *U-652* clarified the issue by launching two torpedo attacks against USS *Greer* which was en route to Iceland. Thereafter, according to Professor Morison[8], America was 'de facto' in a war in the Atlantic with Germany.

'Routine' operations for anti-submarine aircraft of Coastal Command were not without hazards. On 20 January 1942, Catalina *73-P-8* of the US Navy but working with Coastal Command, was airborne at 10:15hr to provide air cover for convoy UR29.

After flying for 3½ hours under the command of William Cole, *73-P-8* was above cloud at 3,000ft when a radar contact was made. Aircraft would normally avoid flying over a convoy, making instead a wide circuit, and even that following the transmission of recognition signals with an Aldis lamp plus 'the colours of the day' from a Very pistol.

Cole, however, spiralled down on instruments to arrive over the convoy UR29, which promptly opened fire. Four direct hits were scored on the Catalina and six out of nine in the crew were wounded, two with chest injuries. One engine and the rudder control were put out of action. When sixty miles from Kaldadarnes, the second engine cut but seemingly recovered as the crew managed to beach the aircraft before it subsequently sank a mile off shore.

A second PBY — *73-P-9* with Lt W. L. Brantley — arrived having sighted *P-8*. Lt Cole's crew had been able to use their dinghies and, on reaching shore, the wounded were taken in carts for medical treatment.

More U-boat sinkings

Lt Robert B. Hopgood, commander of Catalina *73-P-9*, was airborne at Reykjavik at 02:54hr on 20 August 1942, detailed to escort convoy SN73. After just over two hours' flying, an Icelandic fishing vessel was sighted, and then the second pilot, Ens Bradford Dyer, saw what he thought was a destroyer, and a recognition signal was fired. Visibility was 1-5 miles with 10/10th cloud at 800ft and a wind of 35kt from the east.

The Catalina closed to about a mile from the vessel which ignited a flare near what was now seen as the conning tower of a submarine, just four miles ahead of the convoy.

Hopgood lost height in his attack releasing five depth charges[9] spaced at 45ft intervals. They must have straddled the vessel as, during a climbing turn, two columns of water 70-100ft high were seen on either side of, and just abaft the conning tower. The Catalina crew opened fire with machine-guns and hits were seen on the U-boat, which replied with both cannon and machine-guns.

During a second circuit of the area, Hopgood could see that the U-boat was badly damaged; a large amount of oil had been released, she was blowing air and water like a geyser, her steering was erratic and a list to starboard was developing. With the U-boat out-ranging the aircraft in gunfire, the Catalina radioed for help, circling the area meanwhile.

At 06:00hr a rain squall resulted in loss of contact with the U-boat, but after a search the convoy was located and signals were passed by Aldis lamp. Hopgood remained with the convoy until 07:15hr and then searched again for the submarine, ultimately finding an oil-slick and then sighting the Icelandic fishing vessel with the submarine alongside. The U-boat crew were making for the fishing vessel, but some opened fire on the Catalina. Its crew did not respond because of the Icelanders' presence, but simply returned to the convoy.

A destroyer was led to the scene of the attack, but the U-boat had gone — apparently scuttled. The destroyer fired a warning shot over the bows of the fishing vessel which hove to. The destroyer, I-23 HMS *Castleton*, lowered a boat and picked up 52 prisoners. Hopgood now returned to the convoy, but at 09:20hr set course for base due to lack of fuel. He landed at Reykjavik at 11:07. Twenty-five holes were found in the wings of Catalina *73-P-9* due, apparently, to spent shrapnel.

U-464 had sunk in position 61°25'N 14°40'W.

There is conflicting data concerning the demise of *U-756*. Capt Roskill credits VP-73 with the sinking on 1 September; Coastal Command's War Record gives *B/73* sinking *U-756* on the 2nd while escorting convoy[10] SC-97; but this sinking is not included in Prof Morison's and the USN Aviation History Unit's lists. A further American source, *United States Submarine Losses in WW2*, credits a 'British aircraft' with sinking the U-boat on 3 September in position 57°30'N 29°00'W. From the foregoing, in addition to VP-73's squadron diary, it appears likely that an attack made by Lt Odell on 1 September was responsible for the loss of *U-756*.

Odell was airborne at 14:26 hours detailed to escort convoy SC97 but, en route to the rendezvous four hours later, a submarine was sighted twelve miles away. When Odell had closed the distance to half a mile, the U-boat was submerging. Odell was, however, able to release five depth charges 75ft ahead of the swirl only ten seconds after the submarine had disappeared.

Although at the time, this attack was thought to have caused no damage to the U-boat, the collective series of sightings by aircraft of VP-73 were considered to have broken up a 'wolf pack' set against the convoy.

September-November 1942

During this early stage for the Americans in Iceland, the conditions for the two winters 1941-2 and 1942-3 were 'pretty grim'[1]. This was due to the lack of roads and provision for both personnel and machines, in addition to the very variable weather conditions.

By the time VP-73 moved from Iceland to Port Lyautey in October, facilities included a movie hall, gymnasium, bowling alleys, pool room, baseball fields and an Officers' Club. They had the ever-present advantage of proximity to the highly civilized city of Reykjavik, which contrasted so sharply in late 1942 with the remote Höfn where other American personnel were stationed.

VP-73 began their move to Port Lyautey on 28 October, touching down en route at Bally Kelly in Northern Ireland and Lyneham,

Wiltshire, and completing the transfer on 13 November following the 'Torch' operation landings in North Africa.

1942-43 Operations by VP-84 of the US Navy

Another PBY squadron of the US Navy — VP-84 — moved to Iceland between 25 September and 8 October, and in the following eight months were able to claim six U-boats sunk and two damaged.

The first of their successes was due to an attack by Lt R. C. Millard[12] who, while on an anti-submarine sweep flying at 2,000ft, sighted a U-boat four miles away. In the three minutes that the Catalina took to reach the area, the U-boat had submerged and then surfaced to periscope depth again. Four depth charges were released 150ft ahead of the swirl made by

The attack on *U-200* by Lt Beach of VP-84 in Catalina *P-7* on 24 June 1943 using depth charges and a homing torpedo.

P-7 attacking U-200. Lt Beach was awarded the British DFC by the RAF.

the then vanished U-boat. Subsequent analysis indicated that the vessel must have advanced 290ft, so that the depth charges set for 25ft depth detonated astern, but *U-664* is recorded as having been damaged by this attack on 1 November.

Four days later Millard was to improve on this. Again the distance was four miles when he sighted a U-boat heading northwards at 15kt. The U-boat commander must have been unprepared for the attack which was with four depth charges, two of 625lb and two of 325lb. When they were released, the conning tower of the vessel was awash and eight or nine men were seen on it. Although the U-boat had made a sharp turn to port during the attack, the charges detonated 40ft aft of the conning tower. The men there either jumped overboard or were blown off by the explosions of the depth charges. Wood, oil and various objects were seen in the water and an oil slick extended to 200ft in diameter.

The Catalina crew thought the markings on the conning tower were 'U-10', but in fact it was *U-408*, sunk in position 67°40'N 18°32'W; there were no survivors.

On 10 December, Catalina *84-P-8* was airborne at 05:00hr commanded by Lt Lowell Davis. There were squalls and cumulus cloud of 5-9/10ths at 2,200ft, and a westerly wind of 23kt. After flying for about nine hours just

below cloud, Davis sighted a U-boat six miles away. He immediately flew into cloud cover. He had made sightings earlier on this trip but had been unable to launch an attack — it was to be different this time.

He remained in cloud, but when the distance had been closed to two miles, made a run to attack. At 1,200yd the U-boat opened up with AA fire. The Catalina reached 190kt and Davis turned to starboard allowing his port gunner to open fire. The U-boat began blowing tanks to crash dive. At about 35yd from the conning tower the aircraft was down to 30ft altitude. Depth charges were released, one landing 10ft from the conning tower and only 3-4ft from the hull. The aft deck and 6ft of the conning tower were still visible when the release was made at 100kt. About three minutes later two survivors and five floats were seen. An oil slick extended for half a mile. It was the end of *U-611*.

April 1943 marked a turning point in terms of Allied shipping losses, with 53 lost due to enemy action compared with 112 in March. Against these may be set the enemy submarine losses of sixteen and seventeen in March and April respectively.

In April, VP-84 gained only one victory against U-boats. This was by Lt W. A. Shevlin while in command of Catalina *2459*. He was detailed for an anti-submarine sweep in connection with a Halifax-to-Liverpool convoy of 55 ships — SC127. In a flight of just under ten hours he made three sightings of submarines: the third was from a distance of four miles. In his attack he straddled *U-528* with four depth charges while it was still awash. There was no evidence of damage to the vessel at that time, but subsequently 'G' of the USN was credited with causing damage to *U-528*.

Lack of attention by some aircrews to apparently quite simple pieces of equipment could have quite serious consequences. I had such an experience in a Wellington[13] when the navigator's intercom plug became displaced, cutting off all communication during a bombing run.

A similar incident occurred with VP-84. One of their PBYs had Lt Joe Beach acting as navigator on an anti-submarine flight from Iceland. After four hours' flying a U-boat was sighted and the depth charges were armed for attack. At a critical moment, when the pilot was making a good bombing run, Beach moved forward and asked 'What is going on?' In so doing his jacket knocked off the arming switches and the depth charges were not released. On a second run, with the depth charges re-armed, again Beach moved forward with similar results.

Capt Gallery, the American station's CO in Iceland, on hearing of the incident closed the Officers' Club until such time as efficiency of aircrews improved. Two weeks later one of VP-84's crews made a successful attack resulting in a kill, and transmitted to base in plain language the message, 'Sank sub, open club'.

The Americans were operating under RAF Coastal Command control, and Coastal Command was jealous of its W/T procedure. The RAF called for an explanation from Capt Gallery. 'What is this — some kind of secret code?' Gallery explained the closing of the Club which was subsequently re-opened. As one of the squadron's plane commanders[14] now recalls, 'The RAF were invited with very good results for all hands!'

VP-84 did not have pilots specializing in navigation, the system being for all pilots to become proficient in navigation and then slowly to work their way up to become Patrol Plane Commanders (PPC). The squadron sometimes carried four pilots on long flights: one under training, one navigating part-time, one co-pilot part-time, and one PPC.

Their PBY-5As did not have heating systems, so the crews depended on layers of flying clothing, although towards the end of their time in Iceland some new aircraft had provision for the electrical heating of flying suits.

Of maintenance Jamie Stewart writes: 'It was done mostly in an outdoor stand. Our planes were old and parts were a great problem. We did have very dedicated and well-trained maintenance crews who had to work in the worst possible conditions and with very little to work with.'

With their PBY-5As having an all-up weight of 34,000lb, the minimum flying conditions were given as two miles' visibility and a ceiling of 600ft, although in practice, after a long flight the weather could change requiring a return at much lower altitude round the coast to find their way in. Flights were based on a fifteen-

hour endurance but scheduled to land after twelve hours, giving a three-hour safety factor. Be cause of the high winds, special battens were used to protect ailerons and elevators. Canvas covers for the wings proved impractical. To reduce the risk of release gear for depth charges being frozen up, the Aeronautical Bureau suggested sealing with Sellotape!

During World War 2 a number of squadrons equipped with aircraft which had limited forward armament attempted to improve matters. In the case of VP-84 this was done by fitting a 20mm cannon in the nose: it proved of limited success.

In the war against U-boats in the Battle of the Atlantic, May 1943 marked the turning point. According to Churchill[15], in April there had been 235 U-boats at sea and 41[16] were sunk. Numbers were now to decline. Of U-boats sunk in May, Coastal Command-controlled aircraft from Iceland could claim seven, and out of the seven, VP-84 Catalinas sank two.

The first of these was *U-657* which was sunk on 14 May by Lt P. A. Bodinet. He was airborne in Catalina *2457* at 01:10hr detailed for a convoy escort of ONS7 bound for Halifax from Liverpool with forty merchant vessels steaming at about 7kt. Bodinet reached the convoy after three hours' flying. During the next three to five hours he made two attacks on a U-boat, first with three depth charges which straddled the vessel while its

The award of British DFCs by RAF officers to patrol plane commanders of VP-84 in Iceland on 28 August 1943.

conning tower was still visible, and then just over a minute later a 625lb depth charge was released, two minutes after the U-boat had submerged.

During its eighteen-day crossing of the North Atlantic, convoy ONS7 lost only one ship (5,196 tons).

Lt R. C. Millard was detailed for an anti-submarine sweep on 25 May, but giving cover to convoy RU75. Less than two hours after leaving the convoy he sighted a U-boat on the surface. He made an attack despite gunfire from the vessel, but as three depth charges were released the U-boat made a tight turn so that they fell short. Millard now turned his aircraft through 360° and attacked again with a 625lb depth charge. After 33 minutes in the area there was little evidence of him having sunk U-467 — just a slight oil trace.

Iceland-based aircraft sank three U-boats in June, one by a 120 Squadron Liberator and two by Catalinas of VP-84.

The attacks by VP-84 proved exceptional in that Mark 24 'mines' were used by the Catalinas in addition to depth charges. There was the dramatic effect of the 'mine' on U-388 and also the attempted use of a 20mm cannon in the nose of a Catalina. The tactic adopted in releasing the Mark 24 'mine' (in fact an acoustic homing torpedo) was first to attack with depth charges and, when the U-boat was submerged, to release the 'mine'.

On 20 June there was 8/10ths stratus at 3,000ft with a wind of 13kt from 300° in the patrol area of one of VP-84's Catalinas. It was airborne at 04:00hr commanded by Lt Everett Wood, USNR, on a wide sweep mission thirty or forty miles west of a westbound convoy. After flying for almost five hours in what Everett Wood now describes as 'chief pilot's weather', his second pilot — Ens O. S. Siquardson — sighted a submarine fully surfaced but low at the stern and heading south-west at 10-kt about seven miles away.

As Everett Wood now recalls: 'We applied rated power and began an immediate dive in the hope of reaching the U-boat before she was fully submerged and release our three depth charges at approximately 35ft altitude.'

The Catalina had been flying at 2,000ft and in the dive was able to reach about 175kt IAS. At a distance of between one and two miles, the U-boat began turning hard to port and submerging.

Everett Wood continues: 'By the time we had reached her she was still partially surfaced and our airspeed was about 160kt. At what I hoped was the exact moment to straddle the disappearing target with our three depth charges (via intervalometer drop), I released the bombs, reduced power to idle thrust and made a 360° turn to the left. As we had half completed the turn we could see our 'stick', due to underwater travel, had landed a little long. The U-boat was now completely submerged, but her propeller wake still distinctly visible. We headed immediately for the wake and dropped our mine as close to the altitude and airspeed as instructed by Commander Gallery.

'During the next circle of the spot where we estimated the submerged U-boat to be, we noticed a sudden underwater burst. No water rose above the surface, but there had been an unmistakable under-the-surface explosion.

'I cannot remember the time sequence involved — perhaps two minutes later, perhaps four or five minutes during which time we were able to take photographs and the nose-down condition of the stricken sub increased to 30-40° — the sub sank slowly out of sight.'

Air and oil bubbles appeared and two-thirds of the vessel broke surface at an angle of 30°. It was seen to have been split open with 10-15ft of its interior visible for many minutes.

Wood remembers, 'the embattled crew doing everything possible to raise the conning tower above the surface to allow those inside to escape. And they almost did so, but not quite . . . the sub sank slowly out of sight. We were convinced the U-boat had been destroyed and, with no more bombs left under the wings, started our return to base in Reykjavik.

'For all of us it was an unforgettable return to base. We had all seen shattered and burning merchant ships which had been torpedoed by enemy subs. Now (after three failed attempts by my crew to sink a surfaced U-boat), we had succeeded in our mission to sink one.

'Yet the elation was mixed with sadness. For the brave men in U-388 (however horrible the regime they represented and fought for), what we had just witnessed was a hell of a way to die.'

Four days after Lt Wood's success using the Mark 24 'mine', Catalina 84-P-7 was airborne on an anti-submarine sweep commanded by Lt J. W. Beach. With him in addition to other crew members were Lt Slingluff as second pilot, and Lt E. T. Allen as navigator.

P-7 had been fitted in the nose with a 20mm cannon taken from an AAF fighter. After the Catalina had been flying for just six hours, it was Slingluff who sighted a U-boat six miles away and heading west at 14kt.

Beach immediately closed the range and at a distance of three miles two men were seen in the conning tower. There was AA fire from the submarine to which the Catalina responded with 0·3 and 0·5 calibre machine guns. The 20mm cannon in the nose of the aircraft failed after only one round was fired, due to a broken gas jet.

During a bombing run by the Catalina, the depth charges failed to release electrically, but in a second run were released manually. They fell 40ft dead astern of the U-boat which straightened on course, perhaps due to the explosions.

On a third bombing run from 700ft altitude and 1½ miles' distance there was a further exchange of fire and again difficulty with the bomb release mechanism, but the 'mine' was dropped twenty seconds after the U-boat had submerged. It fell 250ft short of the estimated position, but a shock wave was seen from half a mile away.

Lt Beach circled for twenty minutes but saw no evidence of damage to the U-boat and dropped an RAF flame float to mark the position. He returned to the area 1½ hours later to find the float still burning and just a yellow board about 9ft long — the only evidence of the demise of *U-200*.

A series of photographs had, however, been taken of the attack and subsequent analysis suggested that the 'mine' was within 260ft of the U-boat and possible lethal range of the shock wave, with 50-60 seconds a reasonable time span for the mine to have been detonated by the vessel.

It was in June that VP-84 lost one of its aircraft and most of the crew in an attempted rescue mission. On the 11th Lt Douglas S. Vieira, USNR, while attempting an open sea landing to pick up the RAF crew of a Flying Fortress, hit a high wave and the aircraft sank. The Catalina crew of nine were able to use

U-200 framed by the hull and wing of *84-P-7* of the US Navy.

their dinghies but five days later there was just one survivor — Lionel F. Pelletier; the others had died of exposure.

RAF Coastal Command give its accolade to VP-84 with a paragraph in *Coastal Command Review* dated August 1943, which reads: 'No 84 has been co-operating with us from Reykjavik for eleven months in which time it has made 31 attacks and killed five U-boats, a really magnificent record for one squadron in Iceland. We see them and their old PBYs go with real regret.'

Air Chief Marshal Sir John Slessor, who as Air Marshal had become C-in-C of Coastal Command in February, sent the following telegram: 'I am very sorry to hear that VP-84 are ending their tour of duty in Iceland on 4 Sept. They have had a really splendid record of success against the U-boat and their co-operation with the RAF in Iceland has been so close and cordial that we had come to look on them as one of us. Please give them the thanks of Coastal Command and our best wishes for success in association with 128.'

Individual officers of VP-84 received British DFCs at a ceremony held in Iceland when Lts Allen, Millard and Wood gained the award from the hands of an RAF Air Commodore. Lt Allen gained a further distinction as he, together with Lt Stewart, was one of two bridegrooms at a double wedding held in New York: the brides were from Iceland.

Later that year, Beach, who had countered the daunting fire of *U-200*, crashed two miles from Beaufort Field in USA on 28 November in aircraft *7261* and was killed. Only three crewmen survived the crash.

VP-84 of the US Navy, 7 November 1944.

A rescue mission

Joseph Higbee joined the USN in 1934, became a Naval Air Pilot, and in 1937 took part in the search for Amelia Earheart who was lost in the Pacific.

In the winter of 1942-3 he was deployed in Iceland with Headquarters Squadron 7 detachment (Hedron 7). His official duties were supervising the Inspection and Test Dept of Hedron 7. This made him responsible for checking all aircraft on landing, and re-checking them before they were returned to the operational squadron, which in this case was VP-84. He undertook the air tests and, because of the very short days during the winter months in those latitudes, many of the air tests involved night flying.

On 23 October he made an open sea landing off the Westmann Islands to pick up Laufey Sigurdardottir, who had suffered a heart attack.

For such mercy missions he needed a co-pilot and, on 29 November, gained the help of a Hudson pilot who apparently 'had no sea-plane time'. This was to take a little girl of eleven years — Halla Gudmundsdottir — who was very ill after a bout of measles. Higbee touched down during a snowstorm in Patreksfjord near the shore where there was a house named 'Merkisteinn'.

As Higbee recalls: 'He [the Hudson pilot], did not seem to be worried on the landing, full stall, but when the seamen were loading in rough water, I had to keep engines running to avoid being blown ashore, he got a little worried and during the take-off into wind and

swell. We went through the first one with water over the top of the wing, causing the abort and making it necessary to take off downwind. He never said a word going home.

A letter from Harold S. Hadley RN one of, initially 42 survivors in an open boat, who was rescued by a VP-84 Catalina after eight days in the Atlantic.

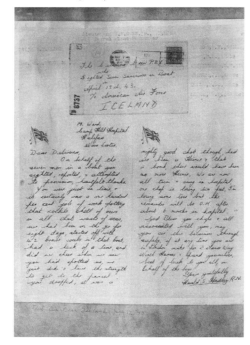

L/Cmdr J. Higbee's aircraft Bu.No. *08095* of the Rescue Utility Unit, Reykjavik. Circa 1986, Joseph Higbee was awarded the Icelandic Service Medal in recognition of his missions for Icelanders.

The boatmen were outstanding in loading in that water not to damage the plane. The plane captain [Flight Engineer] in the tower never flew again. Can't blame him. In the tower then he must have thought we were going to the bottom when I chopped for the abort.'

Higbee himself was no less alarmed but, as he concludes: 'By the Grace of God we made it.'

It was due to the Icelandic historian Ragnar Ragnarsson that these missions were brought to the notice of the President of Iceland, and recently, Lt Cdr Joseph Higbee was awarded the Service Medal of the President of Iceland.

He has been described by one of his friends as a modest, superb pilot and one who was referred to by VP-84, jokingly and affectionately, as 'the only real American in Iceland', due to his American-Indian background.

1 WSC. Vol III, p120.
2 WSC. Vol 1, p687.
3 DR. RAF 1939-45, Vol 1, p222.
4 SEM Vol 1, p57.
5 SWR. Vol 1, p451.
6 SEM. Vol 1, p58.
7 SWR. Vol 1, p467.
8 SEM. Vol 1, p80.
9 Mark 17 Mod 1 with Mk 24 Mod 1 fuses set at 25ft, released at 140kt.
10 Two cruisers, four destroyers and four large MVs.
11 *See* Capt Gallery, USN.
12 Capt R. C. Millard, DFC (Br), USN, + ca 1985.
13 Wellington *HF348*, 29.1.45.
14 Cdr Jamie B. Stewart, Sr, USNR (Ret).
15 WSC. Vol V, p8.
16 SWR. Vol II, p368 (map 39).

Chapter 6
Norway

1939-40

Norway was to prove of great strategic value in the Second World War. Of paramount importance to the Germans was the supply of high-grade iron ore obtained from both Sweden and Norway. According to Denis Richards[1], as much as two-thirds of Germany's requirement came from Scandinavia. Transit ports were Lulea, Oxelosund and Narvik, with four-fifths passing through Lulea and Narvik. However, with Lulea closed under winter conditions, the Norwegian port of Narvik was vital. A coastline of either a neutral Norway, or one controlled by Germany thereafter, provided a protected route to Germany.

The coastline extending from the Skagerrak to North Cape, with the ports of Narvik, Trondheim, Bergen and Stavanger, could provide anchorage for both U-boats and battleships. The Norwegian terrain provided natural cover and protection for such as *Tirpitz* anchored far inland up Trondheim fjord, bounded by mountains on which batteries could be sited. Enemy aircraft would suffer only disadvantages; in clear weather they would be 'sitting ducks' for both AA fire and fighters, in cloud, there would be the hazards of high land. Even if they made an approach to the Norwegian coast at low level to avoid radar detection, there would be rocky outcrops to avoid.

The Norwegian coast provided another route, other than the Bay of Biscay, to the Atlantic, and for Britain, those vital northwestern approaches. During Allied convoys to Russia, merchant ships could be subjected to attacks from aircraft based in Norway, in addition to attacks from both surface vessels and U-boats.

Just one battleship, such as *Tirpitz*, nestling

in Trondheim fjord would constitute much more than a 'vague menace'.

Churchill was acutely aware of these facts as shown by his memos of as early as 19 September 1939 when he was First Lord of the Admiralty[2]. It was to be April 1940 before his advice was heeded.

The enemy was no less aware of the Scandinavian potential, and Admiral Raeder proposed to Hitler on 3 October that bases in Norway should be acquired[3]. The Norwegian traitor — the notorious Quisling — met Hitler on 14 December and discussed the political situation, and it was on that day that preparations were made for the German invasion of Norway[4].

While, in March 1940, the Allies were still discussing what action if any should be taken concerning Scandinavia, the Germans had by the 26th decided to invade Norway and Denmark — operation 'Weserübung'. Enemy transports sailed for Narvik and Trondheim on 6 April and on the 8th a Polish submarine sank a German transport en route to Bergen. Rescue of German troops from this vessel gave a further, but belated warning to both Norway and the Allies, but it was unheeded. On the same date German forces reached Narvik and others were in Oslo fjord. There was time for both the Norwegian royal family and government to escape.

The following morning the surrender of Norway was demanded. The precise movements of King Haakon are not known but Capt Roskill states that he left Tromsö in the cruiser HMS *Devonshire* on 7 June[5]. Many of his loyal subjects also escaped; some to form Norwegian units which became integrated into RAF Coastal Command, such as 330 and 333 Squadrons.

Denmark had also been invaded by 9 April, and with negligible opposition.

44

While German transports were approaching Norway, the Royal Navy had been pre-occupied with engagements with warships, fighting many gallant actions as exemplified by HMS *Glowworm*; 'North Star' would surely have been a more fitting name!

Norwegians with Coastal Command

In May 1942 I was posted to a Coastal Command squadron which had suffered heavy losses on operations to Norway, filling just one place out of hundreds of aircrew[6].

Following the German occupation of Norway which began on 8 April 1940, many Norwegians escaped to British territory and became integrated in our services. An officer in the Norwegian Naval Air Service — Cdr Finn Lambrechts — was one of those who escaped to the United Kingdom in 1941. Before the war he had been a pilot with the Norwegian Airline DNL.

When in Britain, Lambrechts proposed that a unit be formed equipped with flying boats to operate along the Norwegian coast. Initially, the unit was a detachment from 210 Squadron RAF, and it became based at Woodhaven near Dundee on 8 February 1942 with about fifty men. It was designated No 1477 Flight, but gained squadron status on 10 May 1943. Their two flying boats, Catalinas *W8424* and *FP121* were named 'Vingtor' and 'Jøssing'.

One of the first to fly in 'Vingtor' was Egil D. Johansen who writes: 'I escaped from Bergen in August 1941 by fishing boat to Lerwick, Shetlands and joined the RNAF on 29 September and was scheduled for duty with the unit which became 333 Squadron.

'After training as a mechanic with 240 Squadron at Lough Erne, I was selected as aircrew in February 1942 and was lucky to be with a crew which was sent to Battery Park, Greenock to collect our first Catalina — W8424 which was named 'Vingtor'. My first operational flight was on 17 April, an armed reconnaissance to the Norwegian coast.'

This flight of just over ten hours was captained by Lt Cdr Jörgensen with Egil as Flight Engineer. The latter's log book remarks are terse: '*Operasjon-flygning Norge*'. They were airborne from Sullom Voe at 05:55 hours and after making a landfall south of Ålesund, flew parallel to the coast to the Isle of Vega.

At position 61°N 2°E they encountered a German Blohm & Voss 138 which opened fire on the Catalina, scoring a hit in the starboard wing.

A later, unconfirmed, report suggested that the German pilot was wounded by return fire from the Catalina and that the B&V 138 landed at Illsvika near Trondheim with the German navigator at the controls.

In addition to routine Coastal Command sorties, 333 Squadron undertook special duty operations. These involved putting agents ashore in Norway, picking them up from the enemy-occupied territory, and periodically taking supplies to agents.

Search for the *Tirpitz* by a Catalina from 1477 Flight

Hitler had an intuition that the British intended invading Norway and, on 12 January 1942, gave orders for the battleship *Tirpitz* to sail to Trondheim. Its route was via the Kiel Canal and thence to Trondheim. The following involvement of a Catalina from 1477 Flight of the Royal Norwegian Naval Air Service is related by Capt Carl Krafft:

'A navigator friend of mine in 333 Squadron, a Flt Lt Kirsebom — a most reliable navigator who acted also as Chief Navigator for the whole squadron — had a story to tell when they were ordered to search for the German battleship *Tirpitz* in the Norwegian fjords on her way northwards, with a Catalina flying boat armed with two torpedoes, one under each wing.

'At the beginning of 1942 *Tirpitz* was ready for operations and she was the first of the large ships to move north. The network of Norwegian agents which were later to prove invaluable had not, early in 1942, been fully established or trained and equipped. Submarines were stationed off the Norwegian coast, to report and attack if possible, but theirs was a difficult and dangerous task, especially as the nights grew shorter. A possible source of information was the link established by the British Naval Attaché in Stockholm, with the Swedish Secret Service.

'By *Tirpitz* sailing from Wilhelmshaven on 12 January she avoided inquisitive eyes in the Kattegat and managed to reach Trondheim early on 15 January. *Tirpitz*, together with other large German Naval units, was to leave Trondheim and proceed to Narvik and later to attack the Murmansk convoys.

'I seem to remember that this was one of Lieutenant Kirsebom's first navigational experiences along the Norwegian coast and fjords. Kirsebom was in the Catalina's front turret to observe better the course along the shipping lane. The weather was foggy with occasional rain and it was difficult for this reason to follow the marked lanes around the small islands, bends, boatsheds, headlands and fishing boats.

'In the tiresome and cramped position in the turret, Kirsebom knelt down and told us he prayed: "Please God, do not let us meet the *Tirpitz!*" Whether this is a true story or not it would by hindsight be characterized as a crazy idea to attack *Tirpitz*, one of the German Navy's biggest battleships, with two torpedoes attached to an attacking Catalina flying boat?!'

1942-43 Special duty operations

The first operation rated as 'special' undertaken by the unit was on 1 May 1942. 'Vingtor' was airborne from Woodhaven captained by Cdr Lambrechts. With him as crew were 1st pilot Lt H. Offerdal, 2nd pilot Lt B. Tingulstad, navigator Lt K. Stenwig, flight engineer H. Rønningen, wireless operators J. Roe, C. Christiansen and A. Ness, plus mechanic F. Christiansen. Flying with this crew as passenger but to observe, was the Norwegian author Nordahl Grieg.

After flying for just over 6½ hours, the Catalina touched down at Vikten near Rørvik. Two agents, Sverre Granlund and Odvar Röstgård, were set ashore at Kvaløy near Vikna. Weapons and supplies as well as a radio were unloaded before a return flight of about six hours to Woodhaven, where Cdr Lambrechts touched down at 11:00hr.

In May, Cdr Lambrechts was on a visit to Coastal Command headquarters in London. While there, an urgent message was transmitted by a secret radio station at Vestlandet in Norway. The message was a request to rescue some Norwegians from a fjord near Stavenes in Askvold. Lambrechts received the message just before midnight on the 22nd and returned immediately to Woodhaven.

After taking off in Catalina 'Vingtor', Lambrechts headed for Norway, making a landfall at a point only fifteen minutes' flying time from the German air base at Herdla near Bergen. Three men, a woman and a child were picked up at the last moment, only just ahead of the Gestapo. The men included two agents — Ole Snefjellå and Eivind Viken.

Cdr Lambrechts received a telegram of congratulation from the C-in-C of Coastal Command at that time — Air Chief Marshal Sir Philip Joubert. The telegram read: 'Good work — Joubert'. Subsequently, in London, Cdr Lambrechts was awarded the Norwegian 'Krigskorset med Sverd' (War Cross and Sword) by King Haakon, the Norwegian monarch who took an active interest in maritime warfare, and who, a few weeks earlier, had visited Area Combined Headquarters at Liverpool.

Catalina 'Vingtor' *W8424*, which had been used by Lambrechts on the first two special operations flown by the Norwegians, was to complete four more trips in 1942, but this aircraft was taken out of service the following year.

Other special missions to Norway in 1942 included one by Lt Birger Grinde on 14 July when he flew an agent, Hugo Munthe-Kaas, to Langøy in the Lofoten Islands. Lt H. Offerdal made two trips in July and August, and the second of these, on 22 August, proved notable because of its outcome. It was to Sommerøy, Vesterålen where agents Peter Ravik and Ewald Knudsen were to be set ashore. There was a struggle between Ravik and a German soldier with the former being killed. The other agent, Knudsen, escaped through to Sweden.

Lt Cdr H. Jørgensen was detailed for the next three special missions, the third one being on 14 May 1943. Weather conditions were described as 'good' for such as operation with 10/10th cloud down to below 1,000ft and no wind.

Jørgensen was airborne from Woodhaven in Catalina *FP183* ——'Vingtor II' at 18:55 hr. On board with a crew of eight were two agents — Ole Snefjellå and Erling Moe. Taken with the agents were about 1,000lb of equipment including radios, a petrol engine with six tins of petrol, and food. For Norwegian patriots there were 25 bags containing pamphlets, coffee, cigarettes and tobacco.

Commander Lambrechts, CO of 333 Sqdn with Air Chief Marshal Sir John Slesser during an inspection of the Norwegian squadron while serving with RAF Coastal Command.

Landfall was made at 66°23′N 12°20′E the following morning at 01:55hr near Lovunden. The Catalina was flown so low to drop the bags that the aircrew were able to see some heads 'sticking out from bedroom windows'!

Shortly after reaching position 66°33′N 13°21′E Haakon Jørgensen touched down in the sea near Lines, and at about 02:30 hours two dinghies were launched and the agents rowed away towing their supplies in the second dinghy.

The Catalina taxied out into the fjord for take-off and the engines were opened up. Suddenly, at that moment, a German guard ship appeared straight ahead. The enemy challenged with a signal lamp, but instead of aborting the take-off, Jørgensen instructed his second pilot to respond by flashing an answer with the Aldis lamp. By the time that was done, 'Vingtor II' was airborne. The response had been enough to confuse the Germans and they did not open fire.

When safely away from the guard ship, Jørgensen asked what signal his second pilot had sent. He answered: 'I sent "H" for "Hitler" and it certainly worked well!' They returned safely to base at 10:35hr: the mission had taken rather less than sixteen hours.

On 19 June Lt H. B. Anonsen was detailed to fly up to the Arctic Circle to land agents on the shore of Nordland at Alderen (66°26′N 12°48′E). He took off in Catalina 'Jøssing' FP121. On reaching the target area however, the Catalina was caught in the searchlight of a German guard ship. With agents Jon Kristoffersen and Odd Jønland to set down rather than pick up, it was too dangerous to attempt a landing and they returned to Woodhaven.

On 11 August, the same two agents were airborne again en route for Norway. Their aircraft was 'Viking' FP314 captained by Haakon Jørgensen. The load taken with them included a radio with engine and fuel, rations for six weeks and tents and dinghies. As in some other operations, bags containing coffee, tobacco, etc, were to be dropped.

With 10/10ths cloud at 2,000ft, showers and a light wind, the weather was again 'good'. Landfall was made at Lovunden, and at 03:18hr the Catalina taxied to Svartskaer,

Lurøy island, where it stayed thirty minutes — time enough to see the agents paddle away in dinghies.

After a return flight of about eight hours, Jørgensen was back at Woodhaven.

Catalina 'Jøssing' versus U-668

Catalina *FP121*, an ex-202/210 Squadron aircraft, was taken over by the Norwegian Flight 1477 of Coastal Command; it was given the letter 'C' and dubbed 'Jøssing'. On 16 May 1944, then with 333 Squadron, 'Jøssing' was detailed for an anti-submarine patrol, captained by Sub-Lt Harald Hartmann.

Weather in the operational area was reported as fair with 3/10ths to 6/10ths cloud at 2-3,000ft, visibility of twenty miles and wind blowing from east to north-east at 15-25mph.

Hartman took off from Woodhaven with a crew of eight on the 16th. Meanwhile, *U-668* had left the port of Bergen which it had been visiting after initially sailing from Kristiansand. En route, the U-boat crew had suffered a number of alarms due to the presence of both Sunderlands and Catalinas. Early on the 17th *U-668* must have been about 125 nautical miles south-west of Ålesund, following an order to sail parallel to the Norwegian coast with another boat and await a convoy. From the German account, there was a slight swell with a force 4 wind from the north.

Harald Hartmann's sighting of *U-668* was '. . . on the port side just after midnight . . . Although the nights in May in this latitude are comparatively light, nevertheless, visibility was quite reduced. What I discovered first was not the U-boat, but a foam cap which seemed to behave differently from the big pattern of foam caps on the ocean surface. When I turned to port to investigate I was not able to identify the direction in which the suspicious foam-cap was moving, and could not therefore at that stage manoeuvre into a favourable attack position.

'With the reduced visibility we could easily lose contact. When we got a clear view of the U-boat, we were in fact already on our bombing run with both sides firing at each other. I well remember passing over the U-boat deck at a height of about 50ft. The angle of attack must have been about 75-70° which is not the most favourable one.'

As far as the U-boat commander was concerned, the Catalina had appeared suddenly from low cloud and, while sounding the alarm, he ordered his crew to counter the attack on the surface since it was too late to dive[8]. He responded to the Catalina's attack with 37mm cannon fire and twin 20mm guns; while six depth charges were being released from the aircraft, Wolfgang von Eickstedt, the U-boat commander, applied hard rudder.

On board *U-668*, one gunner was wounded in the hand by a bullet, and there was some damage to the radio direction finding apparatus. However, the vessel escaped damage from the depth charges.

For Catalina 'Jøssing' and its crew, matters were different. As Hartmann relates: 'We were hit by a shell which entered the aircraft in the navigation compartment and passed aft before it exploded with the tragic effect that one of the gunners, Kyrre Berg, was killed. Both engines were working well after the attack. The gyro compass had been hit, but we had no problems in navigating back to base. The landing as such was rather unusual with the big hole in the bottom, but we felt confident that we could handle the situation and everything went well in as much as nobody was hurt during the landing, although the aircraft suffered.'

The hole in the Catalina's hull was about 30cm × 20cm and, on reaching the river Tay and touching down, Hartmann immediately opened up the engines again and beached the aircraft. *FP121* was found to be damaged beyond repair. The one casualty in the Catalina — Kyrre Berg Danielsen — was found to have been hit in the heart and he must have died instantly.

Von Eickstedt continued on course to Hammerfest where he arrived with *U-668* on 25 June. Later in the post-war years, Hartmann was able to contact his former adversary von Eickstedt, who by then had entered the priesthood in Hamburg. They were to become friends, and it is as a result of this liaison that I have personal accounts from the two former antagonists — unique in my study of eighty or ninety such combats.

More special duty operations

In addition to the Coastal Command Catalinas of 333 Squadron undertaking special operations over Norway, there were those land-based aircraft of the Special Operations Executive. These included Whitleys, Halifaxes, Stirlings and Liberators and were flown by such squadrons as Nos 161 and 138 of the RAF, with some B-24s of the 8th AAF. Such aircraft listed covered the period 1940-45 and in that time 1,200 sorties were undertaken out of which 704 were completed. In addition to 187 agents being dropped, almost 11,000 packages and containers were released'.

It was left however, for pick-ups from Norway to be carried out by the 333 Squadron Catalinas. These machines continued to cover the dual role of maritime patrols and special operations. In addition, 333 Squadron operated a flight of Mosquito aircraft.

The dual role of the Catalinas is indicated by successful attacks on U-boats being interspersed with special operations. Thus, following Harald Hartmann's attack on *U-668* in

May, Lt Anonsen was on a trip in June to Futøy, Lurøy, Nordland. This was on the 5th, when he captained 'Viking II' to pick up agents Erling Moe and Jon Kristoffersen.

When 'Viking II' reached the area, three men, rather than two were sighted in a boat. However, Anonsen decided to land. It was found that the third occupant of the boat was a young man with the first name Lars, who was being actively sought after by the Gestapo due to his work with the Norwegian resistance forces. All three were flown to England.

The one confirmed U-boat 'kill' by a 333 Squadron Catalina was now to follow.

The sinking of *U-423* by Catalina *FP183*

The weather for Saturday 17 June 1944 off the Norwegian coast was reported as being fair or fine with a northerly wind, but with much cumulus cloud at 2,000ft. Catalina *FP183* took off from Sullom Voe at 13:20hr on a special Ålesund-Faeroes patrol which began at 16:15

Vingtor of 333 Sqdn. This Catalina was flown on six special missions to occupied Norway between May and December 1942.

hours. The aircraft, captained by Lt Carl Krafft, was armed with six 250lb depth charges set to explode at 25ft depth and for release at 60ft spacing.

Krafft was on a course of 87° and flying at 1,200ft when, at about eighty miles from the Norwegian coast, his second pilot Karl Gilje sighted the periscope and conning tower of a submarine about ten to twelve miles away. The vessel was heading north at 12kt in position 63°06′N 02°05′E and the Catalina was following the procedure so often used in anti-submarine patrols, ie, flying just below cloud.

Krafft immediately prepared to attack. When he was still four to five miles from the submarine it opened fire with both cannon and machine-guns and Krafft flew into cloud to gain a better position for a bombing run.

His wireless operator K. Svendsen was also active, as he states: 'I sent the sighting signal "0 0 0" immediately to 18 Group Headquarters and received confirmation at once. I then followed with "465" and exact position, which means "enemy submarine sighted in position . . .". Group was continuously kept informed, followed with homing signals, as laid down in Coastal Command procedure.'

When the Catalina emerged from cloud, the U-boat was seen to port three miles away. Krafft altered course and dived from 1,500ft to attack. From two miles away, the U-boat opened fire again, and some shells exploded 50-60yd ahead of the Catalina. Krafft zig-zagged while his gunners responded with machine-gun fire, scoring hits on the conning tower of the U-boat. When the distance had closed to 800yd, firing from the U-boat ceased.

When the Catalina was over the vessel, six depth charges were released from 30-50ft altitude. The U-boat was straddled. Two of the charges were seen to explode on the starboard side, and three to port. Due to the explosions, water rose about 400ft. When the scene had cleared, the vessel was sinking slowly at the stern, the bow rose up out of the water, and two minutes later it was lost from sight.

The Catalina flew over the area and about forty of the U-boat crew were seen in the water. There were very mixed feelings and thoughts for both Carl Krafft and Gilje (the latter's brother had been shot down earlier in the war by a German aircraft).

Carl Krafft says, in retrospect: 'I will not forget the U-boat captain . . . who, together with the living members of his crew, waved to us in the Catalina when I flew over very low at the position of the "kill" . . . The captain[10] was fair-haired, he seemed to have lost his officer's cap and in the split seconds this lasted I imagine he had his naval insignia on the shoulders which showed at least two stripes. When passing, we saw some of the crew were already dead as their legs were the only visible part of their bodies.'

Both Gilje and Krafft were moved emotionally. When the latter, attempted to analyse his feelings his reactions were: '. . . first of all, full of thankfulness for having carried out the attack so successfully without any damage to either my crew or aircraft . . .' and then; '. . . great relief! A relief which felt like something loosened up within me and I had difficulty in keeping my tears back. I was indeed thankful for that we all lived — in spite of the terrible shooting at us with small and heavier guns. We were *alive* . . . the two engines were purring smoothly and we still had 104ft of wing-span intact.

'We were in good shape and were ordered back to base — Sullom Voe!' It was a trip of just 5 hours and 30 minutes. 'A deep-felt inner feeling was distinctive and prevailed in me.'

Lt Krafft realized fully that his fellows in the Mess would expect a celebration and made suitable provision. But he concludes; 'I myself went early to bed — without being able to sleep.'

This attack by one of Coastal Command's No 18 Group Catalinas was one of six successes achieved, according to Capt Roskill[11], by 18 Group between 11 and 17 June against enemy submarines patrolling off Norway, with three U-boats sunk and three damaged requiring them to return to base.

1944 Catalinas *FP183* and *F9754*

By their action on 17 June 1944, the Norwegian crew of Catalina 'D' *FP183* gained a one-line entry in Coastal Command's War Record, albeit for the aircraft and not themselves! Just a week later, the same crew's dedication, flying the same aircraft, resulted in a landmark in World War 2 history; not for the Royal Norwegian Air Service, but for the Royal Canadian Air Force.

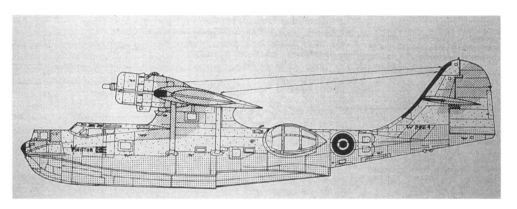

Section drawing of *Vingtor W8424* one of the first Mark 1 Catalinas (PBY-5s) to operate with the Norwegians in Flight No 1477.

The crew of 'D' on both occasions was captained by Lt Carl Krafft, with navigator Sub-Lt J. Johansen, and Petty Officers K. K. Gilje, T. F. Johannessen, A. M. Fritzvold, A. L. Bjerkseth, R. K. Hauge, E. Vetvik, and K. Svendsen. Svendsen was the first wireless operator and played a significant role.

Catalina 'D' *FP183* took off from Sullom Voe in the Shetlands at 19:30 hours on 24 June to undertake an anti-U-boat patrol 130 miles north of the Shetlands. On that same date, the Canadian squadron No 162 based at Reykjavik had six aircraft on operations, including Canso A *F9754*.

The Canadians reported the weather for that day as bright and clear with a slight overcast. The Norwegian Lt Krafft reached his patrol area at 21:16hr. After flying for another hour and a half, his gunner stationed in the port blister reported over the intercom some red-coloured tracer coming up from the sea. The cloud base at that time was 800ft, and there was a calm sea but dim light.

On the way to the patrol area, wireless operator Svendsen had maintained a listening watch, and shortly after leaving Sullom Voe he had intercepted signals from 18 Group calling a Canadian Catalina which was on patrol in the area. On hearing no response from the Canadian, Svensen tried transmitting to the Canadian, but again there was no answer.

Following his air gunner's report, Lt Krafft flew to the area of the red tracer which was

about two to three miles away, and there a dinghy was sighted. He flew low enough to count seven men whom he identified as wearing RAF uniform together with some flying kit including Mae Wests. Two appeared to be seriously wounded or dead, and two were out-board of the rubber dinghy.

Catalina 'D' was equipped with Bendix radio and, as Svendsen recalls: 'A signal was sent immediately to Group, who at once replied, and communication was established . . . instructions were received for Catalina 'D's' further action.' This was to circle the dinghy and remain in position until a rescue boat arrived. A smoke float was released from the Catalina to mark the position. Two to four miles away, Krafft located an oil slick which had spread over an area covering a mile. Within this oil slick ten to fifteen men were swimming; there were also 25 corpses floating in the oil.

After releasing another smoke float, the Catalina returned to the dinghy occupied by the Canadian aircrew. No 18 Group instructed the Norwegian crew to transmit homing signals while circling the dinghy.

The weather was rapidly deteriorating, and after some hours there was continuous rain and the cloud base dropped to as low as 50ft. The sea developed a heavy swell and sight was lost of the dinghy two or three times, but regained after some searching.

In his official report at the time, Lt Krafft made no mention of what must have been a very severe strain for the man at the controls. To circle a convoy at a 'safe' height under good weather conditions for a few hours would be taxing enough for most men. One may reflect on the difficulties in banking an aircraft having a 104ft wing-span with a cloud base down to 50ft and a heavy swell! In heavy rain some tight turns would be required not to lose sight of an aircraft dinghy.

With a strong wind blowing now, and a heavy swell, it was out of the question for Krafft to attempt a landing to pick up the Canadian survivors, and he was very aware of how short a time the ditched men might remain alive in such conditions. To assist in keeping track of the dinghy's position, he took a bearing from the extensive oil slick which had spread from the sunken U-boat.

After some time circling the dinghy, 'D' was informed that Warwick aircraft equipped with an airborne lifeboat had been dispatched, but when the first Warwick approached the scene it was unable to locate the dinghy due to exceptionally bad visibility and radar equipment which had failed. In addition to these aircraft a high-speed launch had sailed and was scheduled to arrive at 07:00hr. With the wind increasing to 50kt and high waves, the estimate was optimistic!

For Carl Krafft in the Catalina, the weather at 09:30hr was so bad that he had a Mae West fastened to his own emergency radio and it was dropped near the Canadians' dinghy. It fell about 50yd away from them and was not recovered.

At this stage, a patrolling Liberator which had homed on to the Norwegian Catalina's signals arrived but rapidly lost sight of the dinghy and disappeared. Krafft sighted a second Warwick aircraft at 11:00hr; the airborne lifeboat was released. Although it fell near the dinghy, strong winds prevented the Canadians from boarding and it was rapidly swept away.

Krafft's own translation of his official report sums up the situation at this point thus: 'The Germans floating in the oil seemed to be gradually disappearing. When 'D' had to return through shortage of fuel to Sullom Voe, there were two or three corpses and some pieces of wreckage remaining. The last that was seen of people in the dinghy was four or five men. Two corpses were seen a short distance from the dinghy. At 12:50hr a signal was heard from the Liberator to 18 Group. It indicated that the Liberator had seen the fast rescue launch some miles from the position of the dinghy. When 'D'/333 landed at Sullom Voe, a message was received that all the men in the dinghy had been rescued.'

One of the survivors from the Canadian Canso A *9754*, after being discharged from the Naval Hospital in Lerwick, wrote from RAF Wick to Lt Carl Krafft. He was the Canso's second pilot F/O B. C. Denomy. His letter dated 6 July 1944 reads:

'Dear Friends,

'On June 24-25 you and your crew were instrumental in the rescue of our crew 'P'/162. Words cannot express the deep feelings of gratitude and appreciation that we, the crew and myself, would like to convey to you. We owe our lives to your amazing ability and flying skill to keep us in sight. Through you unwavering doggedness to do your best — our rescue was effected. It is indeed a very great credit to you and your crew and we are most thankful. We also wish to thank you for the great part you played at the scene of the U-boat kill. It was cheering news when we read it on the Aldis lamp. It will be the major factor when our attack is assessed.

'Unfortunately I did not have the opportunity to get to Sullom Voe to thank you personally. We are now all out of hospital and doing very well. Unfortunately we lost three members of our crew due to exposure. At the earliest possible moment we intend to have a photograph taken of the survivors and I shall pass on one to you as a souvenir. In this closing paragraph the boys again join with me in saying many thanks. The best of health to you always — and good hunting.

Yours truly,
B. C. Denomy F/O'

Lt Krafft's flying log entry for 24 June is illuminating in its terseness:

'Catalina *FP183* . . A/S patrol; Air/Sea rescue; Cat P162 Canadian had U-boat kill.'

The mission took 17 hours 40 minutes which included thirteen hours circling a small rubber dinghy in a very large stretch of water. Krafft's wireless operator was fully occupied in radio transmissions for twelve of those thirteen hours.

Woodhaven to Graznia

Sub-Lt Harald Hartmann, who in May had attacked *U-668*, was in December assigned a special duty which he relates thus:

'Reports of fighting in the north on the Russian front showed that the Germans were retreating in Finmark and that the Russians were moving in. There were also reports of the Germans adopting the so-called scorched earth tactics. Consequently our Government wanted information on what was going on and wished to comply with a request for medicine, etc, for the Norwegian population.

'Originally we were to have flown a small Norwegian contingent to Kirkenes, but the contingent did not get ready in time, the trip was postponed and bad weather followed. However, on 6 December everything was clear. The aircraft[12] was loaded to maximum capacity with serum and other medical supplies. We were told that an American colonel by the name of Boyd was to come with us together with a man who wore Norwegian uniform but carried a Russian name. We were given little information on why these two passengers were to come along. Looking back they were obviously sent with us to get as much information as possible. We were not told however, and this gave the trip a certain mysterious character, particularly so when just before take-off I was told that the gentleman with the Russian name must under no circumstances be put ashore in Norway. To this day I do not know why.

'The weather outlook was not good. We first flew to Shetland where we could replenish our fuel supply. Just after nine o'clock in the evening of 6 December, we took off from the Shetlands in rather poor weather conditions but with hopes of better weather further north. It did not clear up.

'Life on board settled down to the routine we knew so well. The night was dark but pleasant. In the north, the northern light began to spread, on the starboard side was our own country, the war was drawing to its end, we were headed for Norwegian territory. Surely there was enough to give our imagination wings.

'However, the night wore on, the fatigue began to make itself felt and we longed for the day which would bring some, if not much, light. Gradually we turned more east as we started to fly along the coast of Finmark, but at a very good distance from the coast because of the possibility of German night fighters. We carried on until we had — or assumed that we had — Vardø about 60 miles to the south. Then we turned straight south and excitement began to make itself felt on board.

'We had two navigators. The aids to navigation along our route were rather poor. Would we make landfall at Vardø as we planned? What a triumph for navigators when in the faint grey light of day Vardø appeared dead ahead!

'Our orders had been altered just before take-off so that we were to proceed to Linahamri near Petsamo in Finland. It has a fairly wide but sheltered harbour. We were now sure of our position and in a very good mood. Soon we could see Linahamri below us with a few Russian warships anchored there.

'At this stage I should recall that the Russians were our allies. We were friendly and enthusiastic towards them and expected them to be the same towards us. On the background of the present east-west conflict it is strange to recall the rapid cooling down of our enthusiasm after landing.

'We rather expected a motor boat to come out to assist us and to indicate where we should moor. However, we continued to taxi on the water for what to us seemed a considerable time without any sign of life ashore, although there must have been many Russians there.

'Finally a boat came out. Rather than waving arms and smiles, the soldiers on board carried Sten guns and stony faces. We were taken to a buoy and moored there after which I went ashore with Colonel Boyd and our navigator.

'No sooner had we stepped ashore than soldiers turned up on both sides of us with guns and we were marched off down the road. We were taken to a house where there were military officers and shown into a room. The last thing I saw as the door closed was a soldier taking up his position there with his gun. We were received by an officer whose looks reminded me of a well-known actor at the time — Peter Lorre who always played the wicked gangster in crime films.

'Conversation was not lively. In fact it was non-existent, the Russian said not a word. The room was very hot. We were tired and a

53

certain drowsiness set in. I could well do with a few quiet minutes.

'Not so Colonel Boyd. As the meeting dragged on nothing happened, nothing was said, no smiles exchanged, he grew restless. So he tried the standard American soldier's approach: "Say, do you want a Camel?" The Russian shook his head to answer "Njet". Colonel Boyd lighted his cigarette and then — we could hardly believe it — the Russian pulled out a Russian cigarette and lighted it.

'Shortly thereafter, the door opened and a Russian Navy officer came in, smiling, shaking hands cordially and the ice was broken. Poor "Peter Lorre". His problem was that he didn't know a word of English.

'We now received all the help we wanted including a car to take our supplies to Kirkenes where we proceeded in the afternoon. My main recollection from the trip is my irritation with the very bumpy road as I tried hard to sleep.

'Kirkenes looked grim in the Arctic night, only a few houses left, the remainder were all in ruins. We met a few Norwegian officers in Kirkenes and spent the night there. There were few civilian Norwegians, but the presence of Russian soldiers was obvious. Colonel Boyd was active and we collected information concerning the situation.

'Next morning we went back to Linahamri, flew back to the sea and passed east of the Kola Peninsula. From now on we were most careful to follow closely the instructions we had received as to the route to follow, the signals to be given, etc. We were after all, close to the front and there had been accidents with Allied aircraft. However, we came safely down to Kola Inlet which had opened up into a large bay full of merchant and Navy vessels belonging to Allied convoys.

'We were well received by the Russians. The technical equipment on our aircraft was rather commonplace and we had no restrictions on showing it to the Russians. This made our relations happy and friendly. After a day or two, we were ready for the return journey but the engines would not start. No reason to worry. We explained the problem to a Russian technical officer in charge. He asked us to go back to our barracks and sleep and the aircraft would be in order on the following day. The last thing we saw was Russians swarming over our aircraft. The next day everything was in order. We exchanged gifts with the Russians and agreed that we were great friends. We took off and carried on up the Kola Inlet and out to sea.

'Another night passed away, another night with powerful northern lights shooting like searchlights in many colours over the sky. We felt content and relaxed. We flew away the night until we landed next morning at Woodhaven.'

Catalina *Ulabrand* captained by Harald Hartmann had taken off at 16:35hr on 13 December near the Kola Inlet to touch down after a flight of 17 hours 55 minutes on the river Tay.

Special operation in Catalina 'Jøssing II'

Another aircraft captain with 333 Squadron was Finn Ferner. He had left Norway in the autumn of 1939 and at the time the Germans invaded his homeland in 1940, was a student at Harvard University. Following the establishment of a training centre by the Royal Norwegian Air Force in Toronto, Ferner joined the service in 1942. After further training with the RAF, he was posted to England at the end of 1943, but it was to be some time before he was detailed for a special operation.

This was on 26 March 1945, a trip to Sørøya in the far north. It was part of a project to evacuate several hundred Norwegians who had escaped from the Germans and hidden in Sørøya. The Russians had forced the Germans southwards, and the enemy in turn was pushing the Norwegian population ahead of them in their retreat, and as Finn Ferner recalls: '. . . burning everything behind them. At Honningsvåg only the church was left standing, and in other places, not even that.'

Being flown to Norway in 'Jøssing II' were agents Lt Jansen, Lt Danielsen and Andersen. Andersen was a quartermaster wireless operator who, it is believed, was subsequently able to home in by radio on some Canadian vessels to evacuate the Norwegians who were hiding in the mountains.

Finn Ferner gives the following account of his mission: 'On the flight from the Shetlands we flew at about 2,000ft and when we were nearing Sørøya, we were supposed to approach the coastline at 90° and fly at deck level or about 50ft to avoid German radar.

'In the Shetlands the aircraft had been loaded with coils of wire and without our knowledge some of the coils had been stowed close to the compass. The result was that we made our landfall 100 nautical miles southwest of Sørøya, at Loppehavet. When Lt Danielsen, who had been in and out of northern Norway several times, recognized this, he told us to turn round immediately, as this region had heavy radar cover.

'Out we went, and some time later landed at the end of Sandøyfjorden. Our trip into Loppehavet had apparently been noticed by the Germans, because when we landed our freight and agents, we saw two Messerschmitts passing over us. Fortunately we had camouflage paint on our upper side, and having tied up to the shore we blended into the terrain and were not observed.

'After we were airborne again, we saw the Messerschmitts return, but they were probably low on fuel because they didn't follow us. At Vadsø we were supposed to land as the first Norwegian aircraft on Norwegian soil,

but unfortunately it was blowing so hard that we decided to go to Graznaya instead. We realized that the war was going to end soon, and we didn't want to knock in the bottom of our craft at this stage.

'After several attempts we gave up trying to get permission to land and decided to go in below radar cover before our fuel ran out. We managed to get in unnoticed but were met by a launch with guns pointed at us. After some discussion we were accepted as friends, and they beached our aircraft very quickly and efficiently. To do this they used far more manpower but less time than we were used to.

'The Russians had two squadrons of Catalinas of a later mark than we had. Their flying boats had a solid nose without the bomb-aimer's window — more sensible for Arctic warfare. The ground crew were very friendly and agreed to change one of our generators which had been causing us some trouble. They were very interested in our radar, but we had strict orders from the RAF not to let anyone inside.

'We learned that the day before we landed, Major Allen from Bernt Balchen's Liberator

Three PBYs of 333 Sqdn in formation over the River Tay 24 July 1943; *Vingtor* leading with *Jøssing* to port and *Viking* to starboard.

squadron had come in from "drops" in Norway and asked for permission to land as one of his engines was on fire. In answer, he was shot down and only a gunner survived.

'We also asked the Russian squadron commander why they didn't help escorting the Murmansk convoys around northern Norway, as these convoys were for their benefit and they could be on the job much longer than the Shetland-based aircraft could. He answered that they didn't have either the armament or the range. It became obvious that they were saving their war material for some other time and letting the Allies do the job in this theatre.

'Due to 60kt headwinds we spent a week up there waiting for the wind to die down. We spent our time ski-ing around, and on one of our trips we discovered twenty to thirty Airacobra aircraft that were not even unpacked, obviously also being saved for some future purpose. On our ski-ing trips we also noticed mounds of earth with some smoke rising from them. Every morning out of these mounds would crawl prisoners, in grey padded clothes and with grey expressionless faces, carrying picks and shovels on their shoulders: a sight one will never forget.

'Finally the wind decreased and we could take off. The Norwegian Military Attaché in Moscow, General Steffens, had come up from Moscow and wished to fly home with us. There was ice on the bay and I asked the squadron commander where was the best place to take off and if he could clear the ice for us. I don't remember exactly how many, but at least fifteen Catalinas took off, and with their steel reinforced bows, landed in the ice. A launch escorted us to an ice-free channel and we took off without damage.

'After an hour's flight an oil leak developed in one of the engines and we debated whether to go back or to land at sea for repairs. None of us, including General Steffens, wanted to go back, and when our two flight engineers felt sure they could fix it, we landed with full tanks. The sea was still fairly rough after the high winds, but we found a smooth place behind some islands and got down safely. The crew did their job and we continued to Woodhaven without further complications.'

Special operations

A flight of great significance to Norwegian patriots took place in April 1945. It was the first Norwegian aircraft to land in free Norway — Catalina 'Viking II' *JX582*.

At that time hostilities had not ceased, and there were still many thousands[13] of German troops in other parts of Norway, but some areas had been liberated. To avoid being evacuated by the Germans, the Norwegians in the Sørøya area had fled to the mountains and had lived under very grim conditions. Many civilians were evacuated by British destroyers, but the situation in Norway during late April and early May was confused.

'Viking II' was airborne from Woodhaven on 26 April with Lt Kjell Garstad as 1st pilot but with Cdr H. Jørgensen as the senior officer from 333 Squadron. Also on board was the Norwegian Admiral Danielsen as observer and agent Odd Heløe, who also served as wireless operator. The aircraft landed at Sandøyfjord, Sørøya where Heløe was put ashore together with supplies. Thirteen Norwegian civilians were then taken on board and flown to Kirkenes in the far north.

Sørøya at that time was virtually in the front line between Norwegian and German troops and as the Germans were withdrawing, they attempted to take Norwegian civilians with them. There was also some uncertainty concerning the possibility of German Naval units landing more troops.

Thus, while Sørøya had been freed, there were still potential hazards for the lone Catalina which, however, returned safely to Woodhaven from Kirkenes on 27 April. This was Cdr Jorgensen's last 'special op'. In his report on special duties he specified three important aspects which contributed to success:

1) weather conditions with essential cloud cover;
2) good navigation;
3) lack of interference by the enemy.

The return to Norway

On 2 May 1945, troops of the Western Allies had linked up with Russian troops at Lübeck, thus cutting off German troops remaining in Norway and Denmark. On the 6th, cruisers of the Royal Navy HMS *Birmingham* and HMS *Dido* sailed for Copenhagen from Rosyth together with destroyers and minesweepers.

Hostilities against Germany were considered to have ceased on 8 May, but on that day I was recalled from leave, ostensibly to fly to Norway, where the situation was still considered potentially dangerous due to the large number of German forces there. My flight did not materialize.

For the two Norwegian squadrons, Nos 330 and 333, it was different. On the 6th General Hjalmar-Riser-Larsen, the C-in-C of the Norwegian Air Forces, instructed 333 to have a Catalina operational, and 330, then at Sullom Voe, was to have a Sunderland aircraft flown to Woodhaven. The two aircraft were 'A' and Sunderland *ML827* 'G', both airborne from Woodhaven on 8 May. Cdr Jørgensen left at 11:50hr in the Catalina, while Capt S. Björnbye followed five minutes later. Their duties were to take a military commission to Oslo. The commission was led by Brigadier R. Hilton with Colonel R. Hay, and included Cdr Per Askim of the Royal Norwegian Navy, Sqn Ldr C. P. Bennet and Sqn Ldr Hancock.

The two aircraft touched down in Oslo fjord at 17:20hr. The duty of the commission was to accept the German surrender in Norway. This was an exceptional task as the Germans would be expected to disarm themselves in their own camps. There were then 360,000 German troops in Norway, but to enforce the surrender were 14,700 Norwegian police and 40,000 of the Norwegian Home Forces (the underground forces).

For the two aircraft captains there had been a definite procedure to follow: they rendezvoused at the entrance to Oslo fjord near Ferder lighthouse before flying down the fjord at 3,000ft and landing at Fornebu, Oslo. At Fornebu, the commission was properly received by the Germans before being taken in open cars by Norwegian forces to the Grand Hotel in Oslo which was to be their first HQ. It was a journey of triumph, followed by a balcony appearance at the hotel where they were treated as 'kings and heroes'. That evening, the commission left by car for Lillehammer which had been the location for the German HQ in Norway. There the commission delivered its instruction to the German commander — General Böhme.

The Catalina and Sunderland aircraft flew to Stavanger the following day and on the 10th. The cruiser HMS *Devonshire* left Rosyth on 11 May escorted by destroyers, including the Norwegian *Arendal* and *Stord* en route to Oslo. On board the cruiser was Crown Prince Olav. One of 333 Squadron's Catalinas serving as escort was 'B', captained by Sub Lt Finn Ferner and with 2nd pilot Sgt Blystad. They completed a 15¼-hour flight on the 12th.

Of this trip Ferner adds: 'We were at that time detached to 210 Squadron in the Shetlands and were ordered to join the convoy of British and Norwegian warships outside Christiansand. The Crown Prince was on board the destroyer *Stord*, well known from the sinking of the *Scharnhorst*. The weather was beautiful, and after leaving the convoy outside Lyngør, we flew low over the coastline and enjoyed all the Norwegian flags flying from every flagpole in celebration of the liberation. I remember particularly circling low over Stavanger in the beautiful spring weather with the leaves just turning green: a perfect background for the red, white and blue flags.'

Throughout the war years King Haakon of Norway had sent Christmas messages to such as 333 Squadron, and he had visited this unit at least once. On 5 June King Haakon sailed in HMS *Norfolk* for his homeland. The Royal Navy, mindful of history, arranged that HMS *Devonshire* should act as escort, this cruiser being the one which had taken him from Norway following the German invasion in 1940.

Post-war flying of the Norwegian Catalinas

No 333 Squadron returned to Norway on 10 June 1945, with the Catalinas based at Fornebu and technical facilities at Gressholmen. Duties involved transport assignments over the whole of Norway, with details from both civil and military authorities. One route was along the coast from Oslo to Tromsø and this was flown two or three times per week. If weather conditions permitted, a flight was made to Kirkenes every Sunday.

In October 1945, 333 Squadron flew escorts for ex-German aircraft to the RAF station at Hamburg. In late 1945 and early 1946, the unit moved to Sola which was to serve as a base for some time. Some of the squadron's wartime aircraft were flown back to RAF Wig Bay on Loch Ryan, Scotland.

57

By 1950 there was the prospect of the squadron being stood down and of some aircraft being sold to Indonesia. The advent of war in Korea resulted in 333 Squadron being responsible for surveillance in the northern territory within Nato and the unit moved from Sola to Skattøra. Following the end of the Korean war, 333 moved back to Sola.

Six PBY-5A Catalinas were received by the squadron in 1953 under the American aid programme. During the period 1944-45 they had received in total nineteen Catalina IVAs. In the period 1956-7 the squadron had a detachment in Bodø and, under winter conditions, used the wheeled landing gear to touch down at Svalbard. There was a fire at Sola in June 1960 and the remaining five aircraft were returned to the USAF at Wiesbaden, West Germany during June and July of the following year.

Catalinas had been operated by 333 Squadron over a period of 20 years in war and peace, with an overall total of 38 aircraft. Fifty per cent of these were the Catalina Mark VIAs which served from 1944-54.

1 DR, *RAF 1939-45*, Vol 1, p76.
2 WSC, Vol 1, p480.
3 WSC, Vol 1, p483.
4 *Ibid*, p484 (DR, Vol 1, p77 gives 12 Dec).
5 SWR Vol 1, p197.
6 See the author's *Seek and Strike*, Appendix N.
7 On 10 June of that year Hudson *T9428* of 48 Squadron flew up Trondheim fjord in a search for *Tirpitz* and the cruiser *Hipper*, albeit without a torpedo. At least one of the crew expressed similar sentiments.
8 'Wegtauchen wäre zu spät gewesen und hätte den sicheren Verlust des Bootes bedeutet!'
9 Based on data given in 'Slipp over Norge' from *Norsk Flyhistorisk Forening*.
10 Captain of *U-423* — Hackländer.
11 SWR, Vol III, Pt 2, p59.
12 Catalina 'Ulabrand' *FP222*.
13 Churchill quotes a figure of 40,000 German troops in Norway for as late as July 1945 (Vol VI, p581).

Chapter 7
Gibraltar

September 1939-42

Gibraltar had been acquired by the British in 1704. In World War 2 it became a fortress with Army units represented by such as the Devon Regt and the Royal Engineers, the latter constructing a runway by blasting former spoil from the rock face and using this to extend the land area westwards into the harbour. By May 1943 there was an excellent runway with a tarmac surface. For the Royal Navy, Gibraltar was a base for 'Force H', whose movements were readily reported in the *Gibraltar Chronicle*.

In 1939 it had been agreed that the French should have responsibility for the Western Mediterranean, but with the collapse of France in 1940, the Royal Navy had not only to fill that gap, but to contend with the threat of potentially hostile heavy French units.

The RAF Hudson and Catalina aircraft which became based at Gibraltar, were to suffer the retrograde activities of the Vichy French planes. Initially the RAF deployed London flying boats operating from Gibraltar harbour, but in 1940 it had Swordfish aircraft on loan from the Fleet Air Arm.

During the Second World War, AHQ Gibraltar of RAF Coastal Command were to control successful operations of 202 Squadron Catalinas and Sunderlands, Hudsons of 48, 233, 500 and 608 Squadrons, 179 Leigh light Wellingtons, Catalinas of VP-63, USN, and also at least one Catalina of 240 Squadron. Their total recorded score was 24 enemy submarines sunk and ten U-boats damaged; Catalinas were involved in eleven out of the 34 successes, while the Royal Navy took part in eight of the 'kills'.

As well as being the base for Coastal Command aircraft which undertook anti-submarine patrols and convoy escorts operating from Gibraltar, 'The Rock' served as an important staging base for aircraft en route from the United Kingdom to Africa and the Far East. It was perhaps most congested at the time of the 'Torch' landings in North Africa during November 1942. The Rock also served as an assembly point for Spitfires, and their packing cases — 'Spitfire Boxes' were a common sight in 1942-43.

After a week or so at Gibraltar, service personnel came to know what their diet would be just so long as they were with 'Fortress rations': 'M & V' sausages made from soya flour, tinned herrings and corned beef stew with tinned potatoes. There were compensations for those from rationed Britain with the open shops of Main Street, where tinned salmon representing a month's 'points' ration could be purchased, as well as sherry at 4 shillings per bottle. The civil population of Gibraltar had been evacuated, and those in need of feminine company were able on occasions to visit Algeciras or La Linea. Sunshine and sea bathing probably did much for both morale and general health, particularly in view of the crowded conditions and limited sanitary facilities.

Landing and take-off at Gibraltar were not to be considered lightly. The natural hazards of the Rock itself, with the turbulence it created, were added to by the Spanish guarding their 'neutrality' against British infringement. For both flying boats and land-based aircraft Gibraltar was a congested area, and to watch a Catalina attempting to take off or land, or to view the wrecked aircraft at the eastern end of the runway was warning enough. The Catalina adage — 'Airborne; waterborne; submerged' — could well have been coined at Gibraltar!

Some experienced Catalina pilots have referred to what they called a 'Gib landing' which they needed at Gibraltar due to heavy swells, and which must have been a form of fully stalled landing with the tail well down at the point of touch-down. A similar technique was used in some 'Dumbo' missions and in the special operations by 240 Squadron in the Far East.

Anti-submarine operations

No 202 Squadron began operating Catalinas from Gibraltar in April 1941, when their outdated London aircraft were replaced. One of their first successes recorded by Coastal Command occurred on 25 October.

Sqn Ldr Eagleton, the captain of Catalina *AH538*, was on a creeping line-ahead search in advance of convoy HG75. At 10:41hr he sighted a submarine in position 37°06'N 14°20'W when it was on a northerly course at 18kt. Nine minutes later he attacked with machine-guns and two depth charges which failed to explode.

While circling the area he signalled the escort vessels of the convoy and at 12:25hr HMS *Lamerton* attacked the submarine with gunfire. The crew of the submarine, later identified as the Italian vessel *Galileo Farraris*, scuttled it at 12:35hr in position 37°38'N 14°26'W. The Catalina returned to the convoy.

On 6 December there were two further attacks on enemy submarines by Catalinas of 202 Squadron. The first was by Flt Lt Garnell, captain of *AH562*, who took off at 06:01hr. At 22:15hr he sighted a submarine which crash-dived before he could attempt an attack, but just over three hours later, he made another sighting. This was in position 36°04'N 07°33'W, where the vessel was on the surface steaming at 12kt. The Catalina closed to attack and released depth charges which dropped 33-40yd ahead of the swirl left by the now submerged submarine.

Flt Lt Stacey in Catalina *W8424* at 15:45hr sighted a submarine stationary on the surface in position 36'45°N 09'25°W. It crash-dived and was fully submerged by the time Stacey released three depth charges 45 seconds later. They fell 80-100yd ahead of the swirl. The squadron was later credited with having caused damage to *U-332* in one of these attacks.

Dennis 'Bismarck' Briggs' second flying log book has a terse remark against an entry for 4 March 1942 — 'Intercept two Fw 200s and had combat, slight damage to Cat. E/A abandoned attack'. He was then on a convoy escort in *FP172*. While with the convoy he became aware of one enemy 'Kondor' about to attack the ships. He immediately headed his Catalina to place it between the convoy and the hostile aircraft. He then noticed a second 'Kondor' in the vicinity. Despite the odds against him, Briggs, much to the chagrin of another pilot with him, was fully prepared to attack the enemy aircraft and was successful in driving them off. He returned to base after a flight lasting 18 hours.

Catalina *AJ162* 'C' of 202 Squadron took off from Gibraltar at 02:36hr on 2 May captained by Flt Lt R. Powell. He and his crew of nine had been on patrol for over ten hours when a radar contact of a convoy was obtained eleven miles away. Then, a minute later, a U-boat was sighted. Powell was then flying at 3,000ft and the U-boat was seven miles away. He approached to attack at 45° to the vessel's port quarter and reached the U-boat ten seconds after it had submerged. He was then flying at 50ft and seven 250lb depth charges were released. No oil or air bubbles were seen as a result of the attack, but Powell remained in the vicinity.

Ninety minutes later, two destroyers arrived — HMS *Wishart* and HMS *Wrestler*. Powell then left the area returning to base 2½ hours later. The submarine was sunk and 202 Squadron was credited with sharing the kill with HM ships in position 37°32'N 00°10'E. There were no survivors from the vessel — *U-74*.

Support for the 8th Army

Earlier, on 12 November 1941, Powell was detailed to fly direct to Cairo from Gibraltar with a ton of anti-tank ammunition for the 8th Army, together with a bag of diamonds which he carried in his pocket; the diamonds were for the British Embassy in Cairo. The normal route at that time would have been over the Mediterranean to Malta and then on to Cairo. Powell had with him however, the HQ navigation specialist — Flt Lt Chapman — who had devised a new route and was on the flight as navigator.

Catalina *AX-L* of 202 Sqdn RAF, Gibraltar 1941. While operating from Gibraltar, 202 was credited with nine successful attacks on enemy submarines.

Their take-off was in *W8415* at 16:40hr, timed to reach the border between Algeria and Morocco at nightfall. They flew south along the border for an hour before heading east along the Atlas Mountains to Sfax, then over the sea to the Egyptian coast. All went well until they were over the Atlas Mountains at 11,000ft, aware of the range rising to 8,000ft. Powell shone an Aldis lamp on to the wings, saw that it was snowing, and then both engines cut. He asked his engineer Sgt Straker what was wrong and received the answer that they were going to try the hot air control. Much to their relief, the engines came to life again.

After crossing the Tunisian coast near Sfax, they ran into an electrical storm. There were only light clouds and no turbulence but there was lightning in all directions, both above and below them. St Elmo's fire appeared at every metallic point such as guns, pitot head and navigation light shields; the propellers were discs of flame. There was concern that the aircraft might be struck and catch fire, but two

hours later they were clear of the storm and, after 15½ hours in the air, they were waterborne on the Nile.

On the following day, the 14th, they went aboard for the short flight to Aboukir, but the starter motor for the port engine would not move. There was no maintenance base near at hand and with a lightly loaded aircraft it was decided to take off with just the starboard engine functioning, expecting the port engine to be started easily when they were airborne. However, with a completely calm river surface it still proved impossible to take off with only 40kt being reached.

They then attempted to start the port engine on compression, involving priming the engine while turning the propeller and then using the booster coil. To turn the engine, one man sat on the cowling and used his feet on the propeller while a second man stood on the hull to reach the tips of the blades as they came round. Both had to stand clear when the booster coil was used. At a third attempt the engine sprang into life and they were away.

61

On the 18th they took off for Malta at 22:00hr for a three-hour flight during which they suffered a complete electrical breakdown with not even the cabin lights functioning. Even the competent wireless mechanic, Flt Sgt Harvey, was unable to trace the fault.

As Sqn Ldr Powell now recalls:
'I considered three alternatives:

'1. To return to Aboukir, but we were not expected and had no means of identification. We would risk being shot down by Beaufighters.

'2. We could wait until daylight and then return to Aboukir. This was the safest course but I did not like it.

'3. We could proceed to Malta eight hours away, but we had no flame floats to determine our drift and if we missed the island we would finish over enemy territory in daylight.

'I decided on a mixture of 2 and 3. If one hour before dawn the sky ahead was clear, we would press on for Malta, but if it was cloudy, we would turn back.

'In the event, the sky was clear and at dawn we went down to 50ft. I got a good star fix using the maritime sextant which I always carried. From this accurate position and in daylight it was easy to navigate the last part of the journey with confidence. The remainder of the trip to Gibraltar was routine.'

Powell may have served as a guinea pig, since Churchill later followed the same route to Cairo.

Catalina *AJ158* shot down by French fighters

At Gibraltar in 1942-43 I was warned to beware not of German, but of Vichy French aircraft, and with full justification! No 233 Squadron lost a number of Hudsons to the French, but the shooting down of a Catalina by our Allies must have been one of the first of such incidents and gained the attention of Winston Churchill[1].

On 18 May Catalina *AJ158* of 202 Squadron was on a patrol eastwards from Gibraltar. It was captained by a Canadian, Flt Lt Bradley, who had as second pilot F/O Sisney — at that time wicketkeeper for the Australian cricket team.

As Sqn Ldr Powell recalls:
'When attacked, Bradley flew close to the water. The French fighters came in on the beam firing into the sea and raising their sights when the splashes were right. Thus both pilots were hit but little else. Bradley had a cannon shell burst in his guts but managed to put the Catalina down safely before he collapsed. Sisney had several bullets through his neck.

'I was sent in *Z2147* at 12:45hr with P/O Herrington and Flt Lt Le Couteur, a New Zealander, as second pilots with Flt Lt A. M. Ruston as spare captain to fly *AJ158* back. Nearing Algiers I was contemplating how to transfer Ruston to the other aircraft when we were ordered to return to base. I had previously noted a destroyer speeding west. When we caught up with it again, I asked by Aldis lamp if they had the crew of a Catalina on board. The messages were terse. "Yes." "How is Bradley?" "When do you reach Gib?" "Dusk." "Can you take the stretcher case and orderly?" "Landing". I then did a wide circuit to drop the depth charges — live and all together!

'The destroyer — HMS *Ithuriel* — went to action stations thinking we had attacked a submarine. Nevertheless, by the time we landed, a boat had been launched and I asked about Sisney and was told his case was not urgent.

'Bradley was soon on board. I stepped on the gas and, when well away from the destroyer, sent a message to Gib requesting immediate hospital facilites.

'An ambulance was waiting on our arrival and Bradley was speeded to the operating theatre. For three days his life was in the balance — a bit of shrapnel had been left in his bladder and he was too weak for a second operation. However, using the bed-bottle, there was a clink and the offending shrapnel had found its own way out!

'When I was allowed to see him, Bradley pulled out a match-box and in cotton wool was a jagged piece of metal a full ½in long. He recovered rapidly and went home to Canada with a DFC.

'Some years later, Sqn Ldr Boore of 'P' staff, Coastal Command, told me he got a rocket for sending Sisney to an operational squadron,.but he said with the Australians he couldn't do otherwise — they would not have it.'

The following day Churchill sent a memo to the Foreign Secretary concerning this attack by French aircraft on a Catalina, using the term 'wanton' and asking if something could be done about it.

Such attacks were to be repeated, the victims including 233 Squadron Hudsons'.

1942-44 Anti-submarine operations

Despite such incidents, squadrons continued to fly anti-submarine sorties from Gibraltar. On 9 June Catalina Z2143 of 240 Squadron was airborne at 01:00hr captained by Flt Lt Hawkins, DFC. Exceptionally, the squadron record is definite in stating that a U-boat was attacked and sunk, in the approximate position 38°03'N 4°E. Also airborne at the time of the attack was another Catalina of 240 Squadron — VA726 captained by F/O Godber, who at 12:00hr intercepted Hawkins' sighting report.

The submarine sunk by Flt Lt Hawkins was in fact the Italian vessel Zaffiro. According to the official Italian history[3], the Zaffiro was commanded by Ten Vasc Carlo Mottura who had been assigned to the area fifty miles south of Cape Solinas in the Balearic Islands, but on the 9th was sunk in position 38°21'N 03°21'E as the result of the attack by an aircraft.

Hawkins attempted an open sea landing to pick up survivors from the Italian submarine Zaffiro but his Catalina was damaged as a result and he returned to Gibraltar, touching down at 18:50 hours.

Aircrew of Coastal Command were always fully aware of possible hazards, even during the course of a 'routine' trip. Once such hazard was anti-aircraft fire from 'friendly' ships, both merchant vessels and warships. On approaching an Allied convoy, recognition signals were given using a signal cartridge giving the 'colours of the day', and the 'letter of the day' was flashed using an Aldis lamp. Exceptionally, should it be desirable to fly close to a vessel, permission was first requested by means of morse signals using the Aldis lamp.

Understandably, escort vessels although not 'trigger happy' were certainly quick off the mark. I can recall during a trip in Hudson EW930 giving the signal for 13:59hr, but the destroyer captain apparently expected signals for 14:01hr and a warning shot was fired!

For Catalina FP153 it was rather different. It took off from Gibraltar at 07:45hr on 20 November 1942 captained by F/O O'Connor. With him in the crew were P/Os Macarthur, Campbell and Pollock, and Sgts Drywood, Fletcher, Sanderson and Laverty. They had been detailed to carry out an anti-submarine escort to a convoy. This was during a period of intense activity following the 'Torch' operation landings in North Africa.

Not all the details of the last flight of Catalina FP153 are known, but from the Ministry it is understood that this aircraft was shot down by anti-aircraft fire from ships of the Royal Navy. There was later no trace of the aircraft or its crew, and it is therefore believed the aircraft sank with no survivors.

Sqn Ldr W. E. Ogle-Skan was one of four Catalina captains of 202 Squadron who were airborne from Gibraltar on 10 February. His duty was to undertake a creeping-line-ahead patrol to the south-west of Gibraltar. He took off at 04:06hr and just over six hours later sighted a U-boat on the surface ten miles away. He was then flying at 2,500ft and lost height as he turned to attack. The submarine had submerged when the Catalina was still four miles away, but two depth charges were dropped ninety seconds later, ahead of the swirl.

After flying for another six hours, Ogle-Skan was at 3,500ft and made a second sighting, again from ten miles distance. He turned to attack but this time using cloud cover which was 10/10th at 4,000ft. He was within a mile of the U-boat when it dived, but he was able to release four depth charges 100ft ahead of the swirl. The outline of the vessel was visible and two explosions appeared to straddle its stern. This was in position 32°15'N 15°53'W. According to Coastal Command records U-108 was damaged by the Catalina's attack.

'J' of 202 Squadron was one of a number of aircraft to escort convoy KMS9. This Catalina was airborne on 13 February at 09:58hr captained by Flt Lt H. R. Sheardown. The convoy was detected by radar about 4½ hours later when it was on a southerly course at 7½kt. After searching for two destroyers, the Catalina was back with the convoy at 17:18hr.

At 22:40hr a U-boat was sighted a mile away, but it submerged before any attack could be made. Fifty minutes later a radar contact was made on a U-boat nine miles distant. Sheardown attacked, releasing five depth charges which exploded 57yd from the vessel between its stern and conning tower. The Catalina crew then opened fire with machine-guns, but within 25 seconds the U-boat had submerged.

In the early hours of the following morning, a U-boat was detected on the radar at 3½ miles distance in position 39°27′N 11°34′W. An attack was made with the last depth charge which exploded near the stern of the vessel as it was submerging. The Catalina crew opened fire on the conning tower with machine-guns and scored hits. Flt Lt Sheardown now returned to the convoy and reached base in 'J' after a trip lasting 21 hours. He and his crew made no claims other than having scored a few hits with machine-gun fire. Both British and American lists, however, credit 202 Squadron with having sunk U-620 on 14 February; the Americans give the position — 39°27′N 11°34′W — which coincides with Sheardown's report.

Sheardown's attack may be compared with that of Powell in 1942: in neither case was there evidence of a 'kill'. Taking into account the number of depth charges used, time and distances, one might well wonder whether Powell's attack on U-74 was lethal without the follow up by two destroyers a considerable time later.

Flt Lt Powell's record was not yet complete. On 8 July he was detailed for a patrol west of Gibraltar in Catalina 'G' FP322. After flying for 10½ hours he was in position 42°05′N 13°40′W when he sighted a fully surfaced submarine. An attack was made at 40° to the starboard bow of the U-boat with gunners firing from the front turret and port blister. The vessel was still surfaced when the depth charges were released and the U-boat lifted at the bows before disappearing a minute later. The only evidence of the attack were some air bubbles and a small quantity of oil on the surface. This action was confirmed, however, as having damaged U-603.

The two final successful anti-submarine operations for Catalinas of 202 Squadron based at Gibraltar occurred early in 1944. Both were captained by Flt Lt J. Finch with largely the same crew.

On 8 January F/O N. H. Anyon, captain of Catalina 'K', while on an anti-submarine patrol east of Gibraltar was ordered to search an area within 33 miles radius of position 37°27′N 01°15′W. He reached the area at about dawn and after searching for over ten hours without seeing anything, Anyon returned to base.

Flt Lt Finch in 'J' had taken off from Gibraltar 4½ hours later than Anyon and was on a westerly patrol. He had been flying for twelve hours when his wireless operator intercepted a message giving the position of a U-boat. This sighting report was probably from the Wellington aircraft 'R' of 179 Squadron which was on a night patrol and equipped with a Leigh light. Although it was by then night-time, Finch gives the visibility as ten miles, with 5/10th cloud at 1,500ft and a calm sea.

At 22:40hr both Finch and his second pilot, F/O B. J. Goodhew, saw AA fire six miles away. This almost certainly was from U-343 and directed against the Wellington.

Finch closed the range in his Catalina and at 700yd was himself subjected to AA fire from what was thought to be 30 or 40mm cannon and four machine-guns. As the Catalina passed over the conning tower of the U-boat, depth charges were released. These were thought to have slightly overshot in what was nevertheless a straddle of the submarine.

The Catalina suffered damage to the port wing, both petrol tanks were holed in addition to the hull, what is described as starboard superstructure was torn away and the air speed indicator was put out of action. Of the Catalina crew, the engineer was wounded by flak splinters in the shoulder and nose. Finch returned to Gibraltar despite the damage to the Catalina, landing after a trip of almost 15 hours.

The Wellington and Catalina crews were credited with causing damage to U-343 which later on 10 March was sunk in position 38°07′N 09°41′E by HMS Mull.

VP-63 anti-submarine operations and MAD

Anti-submarine operations by the Royal Air Force aircraft from Gibraltar successfully began with, appropriately, Catalinas A and B of 202 Squadron; Flt Lt Finch in 'G' represented the RAF in final stages from Gibraltar involving HM ships and Catalinas of the United States Navy.

VP-63 of the US Navy was commissioned on 19 September at Alameda under Patrol Wing 7. On 15 March 1943 the squadron moved from Alameda to San Diego. It was at San Diego that Lt Cdr Edwin Wagner observed an experimental detection installation and subsequently three of the squadron's PBY-5As were equipped with the device, designated 'Magnetic Anomaly Detector' (MAD). MAD was essentially a sensitive magnetometer installed in a cone in the tail of the aircraft and able to detect anomalies in the Earth's magnetic field.

The range of MAD was 400ft regardless of the proportions of intervening air and water. Although of low range, it was accurate and able to determine the position of an object to within a few feet.

Used in conjunction with MAD were retro-bombs of 65.5lb filled with 25lb of Torpex. The bombs were rocket-propelled at a speed coinciding with the forward motion of the aircraft, being released rearwards from rails fitted to the wings of the aircraft. Thus they should fall directly on to the target detected, and were designed to detonate on contact. They therefore possessed two advantages

over depth charges: no presetting for depth was required, and the enemy would be unaware of attack if hits were not scored. VP-63 Catalinas carried 24 to 30 such retro-bombs which were released in groups of eight or ten each.

Because of weight factors, VP-63 favoured PBY-5s rather than PBY-5As and with a fuel load of 1,600gal.

During the period 1 January-1 March 1943, fifteen PBY-5s were converted for MAD.

Used in conjunction with MAD were propulsive float lights which were mounted in the tunnel hatch and which could be fired with MAD or manually. Release of a series of these floats effectively indicated the track of a U-boat which had been detected.

On 6 April the squadron sent a detachment to Quonset Point from Elizabeth City for anti-submarine operations. While there, coverage was given to RMS *Queen Elizabeth* and RMS *Queen Mary* which were bringing and returning Winston Churchill for his conference in Washington with President Roosevelt.

Seven Catalinas were sent to Bermuda on 2 May following reports of a U-boat pack of about 12 off Bermuda. While on patrol 250 miles from Bermuda on the 9th, Lt Kauffman in *63-P-6* made an open sea landing to pick up men from a life raft. They had been torpedoed 38 days earlier in the *Melbourne Star*.

FP191 at Gibraltar in September 1943. It crashed while landing at Redhills Lake on 16 May 1944.

On 27 June VP-63 moved to Reykjavik with fifteen aircraft, their heavy gear being shipped in the tender USS *Rockaway*. While in Iceland, in addition to anti-submarine sweeps, the squadron undertook reconnaissance flights to check the effect of magnetic disturbances on MAD. A number of crews crossed the Arctic Circle and thereby became 'Bluenoses'.

VP-63 became the first US Navy anti-submarine squadron in the United Kingdom when they moved fifteen aircraft to Pembroke Dock in July and became operational on the 15th. They came under 19 Group, Coastal Command, RAF control, and while there completed 338 sorties averaging 11.8 hours.

Lt Sam R. Parker in *63-P-12* sighted two submarines on 28 July but rightly refrained from attacking until two RAF flying boats were homed in to the area — at which point both U-boats promptly dived.

On 1 August PBY-5 *08231 P-10* was being flown by Lt William P. Tanner Jr at 5,000ft in scattered cloud when enemy aircraft were sighted five miles away. He was unable to escape into cloud cover and was attacked by eight Ju 88s. They first made individual runs at 6-700yd range, followed by runs from both sides at 100-200yd. Rudder cables were shot away, the fuel tanks were set on fire, the trailing edges of the wings were in flames and the starboard engine was put out of action. The wireless operator, Arthur Rittel, was able to transmit long enough for shore stations to gain a bearing before he was killed.

Fortunately, the PBY was heading into wind when it crash-landed in the sea. The aircraft water-looped to starboard and split at the waist, but the bow remained afloat long enough for the two pilots, Lts Tanner and Bedell, to escape. A third survivor, Douglas C. Patterson, was thrown through the port blister. All three had been wounded but Bedell swam to a dinghy which, although damaged, was floating and he was able to inflate it.

Others in the crew had either been killed during the attacks or at the time of the crash. Some were seen face down in the sea surrounded by burning petrol. Two of the Ju 88s had been damaged in the fight, one of these going down into the sea.

There was a 40kt wind and sea broke over the dinghy which was kept inflated by Bedell. The three were picked up by HMS *Bideford*

on 2 August and were in port on 4 August.

Lt/Cdr Curtis E. Hutchings relieved Cdr E. O. Wagner as CO of VP-63 on 23 September. On 16 December the squadron moved from Pembroke Dock to Port Lyautey, a base which had been captured from the French in November 1942. Two of their aircraft remained in the United Kingdom for some secret experimental operations.

It was realized that U-boats were leaving French ports and tracking down following closely, if not in, territorial waters of Portugal and Spain. Then, from a point 36°N 06°W, they were attempting to cross the Straits of Gibraltar at night with the moon down or obscured, and using a current of about 2kt flowing into the Mediterranean Sea.

Although there is a stretch of 35 miles across the Straits of Gibraltar, from the 100-fathom lines the gap is reduced to seven or eight miles. It was in forming a 'barrier' across this gap that the MAD-equipped aircraft of VP-63 proved their worth.

Their procedure was to use two aircraft flying legs four miles long and ¾ mile apart at an altitude of 50-100ft, enabling them to detect U-boats at 200-300ft depth. The barrier began with Catalinas *P-12* and *P-8* leaving Port Lyautey at 08:20hr on 18 January 1944 and returning to base at 18:17hr. As datum points they used Point Caraminal, Spain, and Point Malabata, Morocco.

Their first kill was in February. Much of the credit for it should go to the VP-63 plane commanders Lts Woolley and Baker, although the kill was 'shared' by the Royal Navy and the RAF.

After leaving Brest, *U-761* followed the coastal water boundary but was attacked by 'B' of 179 Squadron RAF on 19 February with six depth charges which overshot in position 38°55'N 09°31'W. The average cruising depth of the U-boat (according to VP-63's war diary) was 50m.

At 15:59hr on the 24th Lt jg T. R. Woolley in *63-P-15* obtained a MAD signal and released float lights. *P-14* with Lt jg H. J. Baker then joined in, forming a cloverleaf pattern to cover the area. HMS *Anthony*, two miles away, then approached and scattered the lights which had been laid, also preventing the aircraft from proceeding in their tracking procedure. A spiral search was undertaken by Woolley who then regained contact with the U-boat and released more floats. With the destroyer again making an approach, Woolley decided to attack using 23 retro-bombs, one failing to fire. Baker then fired 24 retro-bombs. These were followed by ten depth charges from HMS *Anthony*. The conning tower broke surface at 17:02hr before the U-boat sank stern first a minute later.

HMS *Wishart* now arrived and dropped more depth charges, followed by HMS *Anthony*. At 17:10hr the submarine surfaced again, its crew abandoned ship and the destroyers opened fire, scoring hits on the conning tower. At 17:17hr Lt Holmes in *127-P-46* straddled the U-boat with six depth charges, then two minutes later Flt Lt John Finch in 'G' of 202 Squadron did likewise. At 17:20hr the U-boat's bows rose 40° before sinking. HMS *Anthony* and HMS *Wishart* picked up 48 survivors, but one died on HMS *Anthony*.

It was later confirmed that the first retro-bombs from VP-63's Catalinas had caused such serious damage to *U-761* that it had had to surface with 'now or never'. Closer liaison and co-operation was to follow between the Royal Navy and VP-63, with some officers of the Royal Navy being 'checked out' in respect of MAD procedure at Port Lyautey.

In the following month of March, contacts by aircraft on the 14th and 15th in the area 36°N 07°W suggested that a U-boat was about to attempt a run through the Straits of Gibraltar reaching the MAD area on the 16th. To counter this, VP-63 had three PBYs land at Gibraltar on the 15th to avoid the possibility of being grounded by fog at Port Lyautey. They arranged also for an additional barrier between Europe Point and Point Alimina.

Two aircraft, *P-8* with Lt R. C. Spears and *P-1* with Lt van A. T. Lingle, formed the first barrier while Lt M. J. Vopatek in *P-7* provided a 'fence' at the eastern outlet.

A U-boat reached the barrier at 08:53hr on the 16th and was detected by Lt Spears at position 35°54'10"N, 05°45'30"W, and Lt Lingle was notified. Due to the arrival of two French vessels, contact was lost but regained at 09:35hr by Lt Spears who seven minutes later made a bombing run, releasing 24 retro-bombs. Lt Lingle followed with another 23 retro-bombs. Three from each aircraft were heard to explode by HMS *Vanoc* which was

standing off. *Vanoc* then moved in to fire 24 hedgehog contact bombs whereupon three more explosions were heard followed by a large underwater explosion. HMS *Affleck* launched a boat and picked up locker tops from the attack area. Human remains were also visible. Credit for a kill was given by the Admiralty to Lts Spears' and Lingle's aircraft, assisted by Lt Vopatek in *P-7* with HMS *Vanoc* and HMS *Affleck*. It was the demise of *U-392* and her crew.

Although Spain was officially 'neutral' it was suspected that some of her shipping served to screen U-boats. Two Spanish fishing vessels were being investigated by Lt Vopatek and Lt H. L. Worrell north of Point Malabata on 15 May when, twelve minutes later, Vopatek in Catalina *P-12* gained a MAD signal at position 35°55'N 05°45'W. After Worrell also made contact, a cloverleaf pattern was flown, and float lights released indicated the track of a submarine. Vopatek called in surface vessels and, after he had released a sono-buoy, Worrell's radioman heard propeller noises. Both aircraft then tracked the U-boat and, at 15:30hr, Vopatek made a run, releasing thirty retro-bombs in three groups of ten each.

Explosions were heard by HMS *Blackfly* from some miles away, but the cloverleaf pattern was continued. At 15:52hr Worrell released 24 retro-bombs in groups of eight. A large piece of wood was seen and the speed of the U-boat was reduced. HMS *Kilmarnock* and HMS *Blackfly* were now instructed to attack but they had no success due to bubble targets released by the U-boat. When, however, HMS *Kilmarnock* used the MAD position rather that Asdic, a hedgehog pattern attack resulted in underwater explosions and two great air bubbles. A modified spiral search by the Catalinas after a cloverleaf run showed only pieces of floating wood. However, relief aircraft detected an oil slick which by the next day had extended to a mile long by 200yd wide. The kill then deduced by the Admiralty was later verified as *U-731*, sunk in position 35°54'N 05°45'W.

Following the sinking of *U-731*, a report from HMS *Blackfly* mentioned that the task of the Royal Navy had been made easy due to the continuous accurate marking of the detected U-boat's position by the Catalinas.

By this time, U-boats were being withdrawn

from outer areas and concentrated in Biscay and Norwegian ports in anticipation of an Allied landing in Northern Europe. By D-Day, 6 June 1944, there were 22 U-boats in Norwegian bases and 36 in Biscay ports[5].

Admiral Dönitz had intended keeping twelve U-boats at Toulon to cover the Straits of Gibraltar, but of 27 which attempted to enter the Straits between September 1943 and May 1944, only fourteen succeeded — seven were lost and the others withdrew[6]. Toulon was lost to the enemy by 19 August as a result of the invasion of Southern France.

In July, VP-63 had two aircraft making open-sea landings due to engines cutting. They were *P-3* commanded by Lt Vopatek, and *P-15* flown by Lt Head. Although *P-3* sank, all the crew were rescued; *P-15* remained waterborne and was towed into Gibraltar. On 13 October Catalina *34013 P-20* was lost together with a crew of six and plane commander, Lt Bedell. Wreckage of the aircraft was located 24 miles from Port Lyautey. By 6 December, the squadron had been reduced to a 12 aircraft unit.

On 9 January 1945, the squadron's PBY-5As were moving from Port Lyautey to Dunkeswell, Devon. This movement began with aircraft *33964* and *48318* serving as an attachment to Fleet Air Wing No 7 and RAF Coastal Command with, as the detachment CO Lt Cdr C. A. Benscoter.

On 11 January, Catalina *46518* commanded by Lt F. G. Lake was damaged by flak from German-occupied Jersey, and Lake had to make an emergency landing at Lessay in France. Another of the squadron's aircraft — *7295* — with Lt Cdr D. L. Russell Jr, acted as ASR cover in the Azores for President Roosevelt's trips to and from the Yalta conference which took place in February.

From Dunkeswell, VPB-63 (as it had by now been designated) began a trial barrier patrol from Cape Barfleur to St Catherine's Point with a flying distance on both sides of latitude 50°N. Their first anti-submarine patrol in the English Channel was flown on 4 February.

On 11 March the squadron was inspected by Air Chief Marshal Sholto-Douglas with Air Vice-Marshal Maynard of No 19 Group, RAF. The 'MAD' gear was explained to those officers.

At this stage VPB-63's PBY-5As were being operated with a cruising speed of 95kt and an endurance of fifteen hours, but with patrols averaging eight to ten hours.

A submerged U-boat was attacked in position 50°24'N 05°25'W on 23 April by Lt jg R. E. Aspen in Catalina *34047*, but there was no evidence of damage to the submarine. The last confirmed kill by the squadron occurred on 30 April in position 48°00'N 06°30'W when *U-1055* was sunk by Lt F. G. Lake commanding Catalina *48318*. At 18:06hr he was flying at 2,000ft when he sighted a schnorkel and periscope two miles off the port beam.

Lake made a diving attack, releasing 24 retro-bombs on a MAD signal from 100ft, when the aircraft's ground speed was 107kt. The schnorkel of the U-boat was then six feet out of the water. One explosion was observed and the schnorkel disappeared, but with oil,

63-P-18 of VP-63 US Navy, equipped with MAD gear in the tail; retro-bombs are visible on the starboard wing. They proved successful under the conditions which prevailed in the Straits of Gibraltar.

wood, and other debris coming into view. An oil slick 2,700yd long developed.

Lake made a series of MAD passes but there was no further signal from the now stricken U-boat, and he returned to base. It was *U-1055*[7] which had, between 9 and 11 January, sunk three ships in the Irish Sea, and was one of six which had entered that sea, following the sailing of twenty U-boats from Norwegian ports.

One of the final involvements with U-boats by VPB-63 came when W. D. Ray accepted the surrender of *U-541* in position 36°N 11°W on 11 May. Surface vessels were homed in to the area and a guard crew was put aboard the submarine which was then escorted to Gibraltar.

The last 'fence' of the Gibraltar Straits was flown on 8 May. The Dunkeswell detachment returned to Port Lyautey on 2 June and orders were received on the 4th for VPB-63 to return to Norfolk, Virginia, under Fleet-Air-Wing-5 for decommissioning.

Between 6 December 1941 and 15 May 1944, aircraft under AHQ Gibraltar had been directly involved in the sinking of 25 enemy submarines and inflicting damage on ten more. Catalinas were involved in eleven of these episodes. Captain Roskill, in his summing up of U-boat activity in the Mediterranean, gives the loss of 68 U-boats set against 95 merchant vessels sunk, in addition to the sinking of 24 British warships including HMS *Barham* and HMS *Ark Royal*. The total of 68 U-boats includes six sunk in the approaches to Gibraltar[8].

1 WSC, Vol 4, p773.
2 See the writer's *Seek and Strike*.
3 *I Sommergibili In Mediterraneo*, Vol 2, Cap Vasc M. Bertini.
4 *Ibid*. Page 132
5 SEM, Vol X, p323.
6 SEM, Vol X, p252.
7 SWR, Vol III-2, p291.
8 *Ibid*, p108.

Chapter 8
Operations in the Far East

The first RAF squadron in Malaya

In 1939 No 205 Squadron was based at Seletar and equipped with Singapore flying boats, but in April 1941 it received its first Catalinas. Prior to open hostilities by the Japanese, agreement had been reached between the Far East Command and the Dutch to share reconnaissance duties, with the Dutch providing three Catalinas of their Naval Air Service at Seletar. The RAF become responsible for an area bounded by a line from Kota Bharu to Cape Cambodia, thence down to Great Natuna Island then westwards to Kuantan.

There was an awareness of hostile movements by the Japanese and, on 1 December 1941, 205 Squadron was brought to a 2nd degree of readiness.

On the 4th, Flt Lt Stilling was captain of Catalina FV-Y which was airborne at 23:30hr from Seletar en route for Manila. He had, as passengers, Admiral Sir Tom Phillips and two of his staff, who were scheduled to meet leaders of the American defence forces.

On 6 December, Hudsons of No 1 Squadron RAAF sighted a Japanese convoy of 22 merchant vessels escorted by a battleship, five cruisers and seven destroyers; there was a second convoy of 21 merchant vessels escorted by two cruisers and ten destroyers. The convoys were then 300 miles from Malaya.

On the following day, Catalina FV-S was airborne from Seletar captained by Flt Lt Atkinson who had been detailed to patrol the Gulf of Siam, south of Cambodia. Only two merchant vessels were sighted, and the Catalina returned to base at 00:30hr on the 7th. Meanwhile a relief aircraft, FV-W, had taken off at 17:30hr on 6 December. This Catalina was in radio contact at 01:00hr when it should have been in the area of the enemy convoy.

The crew were posted as missing[1].

The loss of a 205 Squadron Catalina on 7 December is recorded as perhaps being the first warlike act against the Commonwealth by the Japanese in WW2[2].

Churchill states that both London and Washington were aware on 6 December that a Japanese fleet of transports and warships was moving across the Gulf of Siam, but Air Chief Marshal Sir Robert Brook-Popham's terms of reference inhibited him from taking the initiative in forestalling Japanese aggression. The aircraft available to him on Singapore Island and Northern Malaya on 7 December totalled 164 first line with reserves of 88, including Blenheims, Buffalos and Vildebeestes in addition to Hudsons and eight Catalinas.

At 21:30hr on the 7th, a Japanese bomb struck 205 Squadron's Airmen's billet, but without casualties; Japan declared war the following day.

Sqn Ldr Jardine captained FV-Z on the 8th, patrolling the Gulf of Siam in conjunction with the Far East Fleet. Nothing of importance was sighted and the Catalina returned to base at 14:07hr after a flight of just fifteen hours. That same day, HMS *Prince of Wales* and HMS *Repulse* sailed from Singapore but without air cover, commanded by Admiral Sir Tom Phillips who had earlier been flown by a 205 Squadron Catalina to Manila. Both ships had been sunk by 13:20hr on the 10th in a series of attacks by 84 Japanese bombers and torpedo aircraft.

Sqn Ldr Jardine in FV-Z, which had taken off at 06:35hr on a screening mission for HMS *Repulse*, later found a Walrus amphibian from *Repulse* down through lack of fuel. Food and water were dropped to the aircraft.

By 12 December two Catalinas, Y-52 and Y-53 on loan from the NEI Naval Air Service, had arrived at Seletar. They had been flown in by skeleton crews captained by Flt Lt Stilling and Flt Lt Atkinson. The same day, two Singapore flying boats *K6912* and *K6918* flew south for service with the RNZAF, ceasing to be attached to 205 Squadron.

FV-S was in air-to-air combat with Japanese aircraft on 14 and 17 December, captained by Flt Lt Atkinson. In the first engagement there was neither damage to the Catalina nor injury to the crew. On the 17th however, there were bullet holes in the hull; and one of the crew, Sgt Allen, suffered a scalp wound. The enemy aircraft was seen disappearing with smoke issuing from its port engine.

Rescue by submarine *K-12*

On 24 December, Catalinas 'X' and 'V' of 205 Squadron were detailed for a diverging search between bearings of 017° and 037° from a datum of 02°20′N 104°08′E to a depth of 247 miles.

They took off from Seletar at 22:37hr and 22:46hr respectively, briefed to leave the datum point at 23:15hr with 'Z' captained by Flt Lt R. A. Atkinson taking the eastern section. The object of the sorties was to seek an enemy convoy and then shadow any group of transport vessels located. At 04:35hr Sqn Ldr Jardine, the captain of 'X', returned to Seletar having sighted nothing and without incident.

At 07:15hr, however, a signal was received from Catalina 'Z' that it was being attacked by enemy aircraft, and then nothing more was heard. The attack on the Catalina came from a large twin-engined Japanese aircraft which circled at about 600yd and which was apparently armed with cannon in addition to machine-guns.

Hits were suffered by the Catalina on the forward turret and the port wing, setting fire to a fuel tank. Atkinson dived for the sea and ordered the crew out. In a very short time the aircraft blew up. There had been no opportunity to launch a dinghy, and three of the crew were without their Mae Wests. However, they had all managed to escape from the aircraft and formed a circle supporting those crew-members who needed aid.

Early next morning, Catalina *FV-W* captained by Flt Lt Stilling took off from Seletar

JX281, a Mark IVB, after crashing during take-off at Koggala on 19 May 1944 while operating with No 413 Sqdn RCAF.

and made a square search of the area where Flt Lt Atkinson was thought to have been attacked.

At 08:09hr, an oil patch was sighted and then, as the aircraft headed towards it, a number of small objects were identified as human heads. Catalina 'W' dropped two dinghies together with food and water. Conditions were unsuitable for an open sea landing to pick up the survivors, and the Catalina remained in the area until dusk. By that time the survivors, now in the dinghy, had drifted 25 miles from their former position and flame floats were dropped together with marine distress signals — the latter for the survivors to release as necessary.

After 'Y', flown by Sqn Ldr Stilling had returned, Sqn Ldr Jardine took off in 'X' on a square search for the survivors, intending to lead either the destroyer HMS *Thanet*, or the Netherlands submarine *K-12* which was in the vicinity, to the site of the dinghy.

Three hours after 'X' was airborne, base was notified that submarine *K-12* had picked up the survivors, and at 04:45hr a pinnace met the submarine in the Straits of Johore to bring the survivors ashore. They had been recovered at position 04°43′N 105°57′E at 20:30 hours on Christmas Day.

All were suffering from burns caused by the fire and exposure to the sun. The second pilot, P/O Scales from New Zealand, had severe burns on his body, the navigator D. Babineau from Canada, severe burns to his arm, Sgt

Borchers of Australia a bullet wound in the wrist in addition to chest burns, Sgt Smith three bullet wounds, while Sgt Morris, Petty Officer Heath and Cpl Wyant all had burns. Borchers and John Wyant survived the war, but Flt Lt Atkinson was killed in action on 13 December 1944.

K-12, with sister submarines *K-9*, *K-10* and *K-13*, was under operational command of the C-in-C Eastern Fleet from 8 December and was detailed to guard lanes between Natuna and Anambas Archipelago in the South China Sea against a possible attack by Japanese Naval forces on the Malay Peninsula.

At 12:40hr on 25 December, Lt Cdr C. J. Coumou, commanding *K-12*, was signalled to pick up survivors reported in position 04°29′N 106°03′E where he made a ten-mile square search. He stopped engines at 03:30hr to pick up the nine aircrew. Only two pieces of roller bandage were available for first aid to their serious burns and flesh wounds.

205 Squadron operations from Singapore

By Christmas Eve 1941, squadrons which had been in airfields near the Thailand border were being re-organized further south. No 205 Squadron, with their few Catalinas, shared reconnaissance duties with the RAAF Hudsons.

On 30 December, however, Catalinas 'V' and 'S' were detailed to bomb Sungei Patani, the former base of 21 Squadron RAAF and 27 Squadron RAF, but now occupied by the enemy. It had been at Sungei Patani that

Battle honours of the 'Tusker' Sqdn No. 413 RCAF including the celebrated operations from Ceylon in 1942.

200,000gal of petrol had been left intact during the evacuation.

The two Catalinas were each armed with fourteen 250lb bombs with instantaneous fuzes and were airborne from Seletar at 10:08hr and 11:25hr respectively, captained by Sqn Ldrs Stilling and Jardine. It was intended that their attack should be synchronised with a raid by three Blenheims but, according to the 205 Squadron records, the raid was of very limited success.

The year closed for 205 Squadron with the arrival at Seletar of three new Catalinas from England, a fourth aircraft being retained at Koggala. The replacement officers arriving included Sqn Ldr Max F. C. Farrar, DFC and P/O Stephen P. Wilkins.

On 1 January 1942, 205 Squadron operations staff recorded receiving a message regarding the disposition of AA guns at Gong Kedah. As the Catalinas were the only aircraft available with sufficient range to attack northern fields occupied by the Japanese, they were detailed to make night raids on both Gong Kedah and Singora.

From 205 Squadron's operations room log, names given at the Singapore War Memorial and an Air Ministry list of Catalina aircraft, it would appear that Catalina 'Q', which was airborne at 18:37hr from Seletar on 12 January, was *W8409* captained by Sqn Ldr M. F. C. Farrar with a crew of seven. By 13:10 hours on the following day W/T transmissions to 'Q' had been 'called off'. *W8409* failed to return.

At 11:10hr on the 17th, two Japanese aircraft — probably Zeros — attacked the Catalinas at their moorings, and 'P' and 'Y' are given as having burst into flames before sinking. Two others, 'T' and 'W' (ex-Netherlands *Y-54*), were damaged. Sgt Joseph H. Arch in 'Y' continued to fire his gun although he had sustained a fatal wound.

By 28 January most of the squadron must have moved to Java, but on 31 January Catalina 'N' is given as taking off for Batavia with 'remnants of 205 Squadron still left at Seletar'.

In Batavia (now Jakarta), 205 Squadron officers were billeted in the Hotel der Nederlanden and airmen at the Wielriders Club, but on 1 February a move was made to Oosthaven, where accommodation was obtained in Soerabaya Hotel, Hotel Wilhelmina and Hotel

JX431 a Mark IVB off the Ceylon coast in 1945 while operating with No. 205 Sqdn RAF

Empress. The CO, Wg Cdr Councell, made a contract with Weng Kie at a nearby Chinese restaurant to provide meals for 105 men for 95 Guilders per day.

For the aircraft, there were three buoys in Oosthaven with one of these located at Telek Betong on the other side of the harbour. Refuelling was from 64gal drums taken out on rafts, with transfer made by hand pumps.

Withdrawal from the Dutch East Indies

Following a report that Palembang had been taken by the Japanese on 15 February, evacuation was arranged and 205 Squadron moved to Tjilatjap on the southern coast of Java. Here, thanks to the courtesy of Lt Cdr Pratt, USN, 205 Squadron enjoyed the hospitality of the tender USS *Childs* which provided accommodation for personnel. The three Catalinas 'V', 'R' and 'W' were joined on the 17th by 'N', and regular patrols were resumed. In addition to the men on USS *Childs*, some personnel were billeted on the USS *Pecos*, while others, due to the efforts of a Dutch liaison officer with 205 Squadron —

Cdr Swaab — were housed in the Dutch Naval barracks. Arrangements for dispersing the Catalinas were made in conjunction with Lt Burgeraut of the NEI Air Force.

On 18 February Catalina 'R', captained by Flt Lt Graham, flew to Colombo via Emmahaven for refuelling. It carried dispatches together with, as passengers, Gp Capt Chappell, Brig Austice and Capt Taylor. It was to be 30 March before notice of its safe arrival was received.

Following orders from Bandoeng HQ, all non-essential personnel embarked on two American destroyers on the 21st, later to transfer to USS Holland at sea, arriving at Fremantle on 3 March.

On or about 1 March, F/O Jefferies arrived at Tjilatjap with 35 airmen. The ship *Tungsong*, which at one time had served as a tender for 205 Squadron in the Andaman Islands, commanded by Capt McNabb, was used to evacuate some personnel from Tjilatjap. It arrived in Fremantle about 12 March.

On 3 March at Tjilatjap a strafing raid was made by six Japanese Zeros with all the Allied aircraft at moorings or on land destroyed.

73

VA723 an RAF Mark IIA at Redhills Lake. As 'F' of 240 Sqdn it had flown on special duty operations 'Lunch' and 'Siren VA'.

According to the squadron record which was written some time later, Flt Lt Garnell and three of his crew were killed, P/O Singh was drowned, and two others were wounded.

Early on 4 March, 205 Squadron personnel together with about sixty from the Netherlands Navy[3], embarked upon *Nickel Bay* which sailed for Port Hedland in Western Australia, arriving on the 6th. The men from 205 were transferred by air to Pearce. In the second half of March, 112 men from 205 Squadron were at No 1 Embarkation depot, Melbourne, while about 75 others with two Catalinas were in Colombo.

After a number of signals to the Air Ministry in London, it was decided to retain some of 205 Squadron for service in RAAF squadrons, although most were sent to India for posting to GR squadrons and for the return of time-expired men to the United Kingdom.

As a result of enemy action at Broome and other locations, all of 205 Squadron's records were lost.

Maritime operations in the Far East

No 191 Squadron re-formed at Korangi Creek near Karachi in May 1943 and was equipped with Catalinas until June 1945 when it was disbanded.

One of the Catalinas to be ferried out in May was *FP117*, captained by Sgt Hitchlock. With him as second pilots were Wg Cdr Cornabe and Guy Collings. *FP117* was collected from Scottish Aviation at Gourock. They flew down to Plymouth on the 20th and left the United Kingdom two days later for Gibraltar. Their route to the Far East was via Cairo, Habbania and Bahrain, arriving at Korangi Creek on 1 June.

Guy Collings found his duties to be anti-submarine patrols around the Persian Gulf and approaches to Karachi and Bombay. There were also various convoy escorts and trips to places such as Masirah and Muscat. On 4 December, Collings was in the crew of *FP307* which flew some senior officers of Group HQ to Bangalore, Madras, Koggala and then to Cochin and back via Bombay, returning on the 14th.

Robert Cole was another pilot who was posted to 191 Squadron in early 1944. Much of his flying was in *FP315*, captained by an Australian — Flt Lt Hortle — although he had some trips with a New Zealander, F/O Vowles in *JX369*.

A flight engineer, Jack Whitley, was apparently selected to fly in Catalinas because of his experience with Pratt and Whitney engines in Hudsons at Silloth. He left Oban on 11 June 1944 in *JX347* captained by Flt Sgt Williams, and reached Korangi Creek on the 27th. En route to India via North Africa they passed over some former 8th Army positions, and saw obvious signs of the desert war battles with burnt-out tanks, aircraft, tank tracks and positions, and Tobruk harbour full of capsized shipping. In addition to doing some Met flights, Whitley was with a crew engaged in anti-locust patrols from Korangi Creek during the period 16 May to 2 June 1945. On leaving 191 Squadron, some of these aircrew converted to other aircraft, such as Sunderlands and Liberators.

Kenneth Emmott, another pilot who flew with 191 Squadron, trained with the US Navy at Pensacola, had further training at Killadeas in Northern Ireland, and then ferried *JX319* to Korangi Creek. A month later he took the same aircraft to 262 Squadron based at Durban. Emmott rejoined 191 Squadron as a captain. After the war he became a captain in civil flying, ultimately completing over 20,000 hours.

After operating from Korangi Creek, Karachi, with detachments at places such as

Bahrain, 191 Squadron moved to Redhills Lake, Madras, in November 1944. In May 1945 the unit moved to Koggala, Ceylon, and the squadron was disbanded in the following month.

Special operations in the Far East

No 240 Squadron began to leave the United Kingdom for the Far East at the end of March 1942, with ground staff such as Ralph Parker embarking on the *Capetown Castle*; aircrew were to fly out a month later. The squadron was based at Redhills Lake, about ten miles from Madras, and initially flew patrols over the Bay of Bengal and the Indian Ocean.

A pilot with 240 Squadron who flew on eight of their special ops was Nic Dewdney, his first being on 1 December 1944 in *FP304* with P/O Brooks as captain in operation 'Biff'.

As Dewdney recalls: 'The objective of these operations was similar in all cases, ie, to fly from base at Redhills Lake, or another location on the eastern seaboard of India, carrying half-a-dozen passengers, to a pre-arranged rendezvous off the coast of the Andaman Islands, Burma, Siam or Indo-China, perhaps

FP152 which had served with Nos 212 and 270 Sqdns was here, at Hong Kong in September 1945 operating with 240 Sqdn RAF.

Malaya, there to alight on the sea by moon-light and put off the passengers, and return to base. Alternatively, one would fly empty to the rendezvous and take up passengers.

'Some six crews were engaged in this work which was carried out by a separate unit until shortly before my involvement, when the work was absorbed by 240 Squadron.

'A flight of 24 hours duration was normal, which, if successful, would include about an hour of intense activity on the sea at the rendezvous. The flying kit worn was uncon-ventional with such as W/O Frisby in jungle overall, carrying a machete for chopping one's way through the jungle, stiletto for those wishing to impede progress, 0·45 revolver and a survival kit. None of us was required to prove our skill in the use of these accoutre-ments.

'Four extra fuel tanks were installed in the hull, and on occasion, extra supplies were carried in cans.

'Take-off was generally scheduled for early afternoon to allow for arrival at the rendez-vous in the early hours of the morning in conjunction with the phase of the moon, the only external aid to alighting on the sea; thus the operating period was restricted to a few days/nights in every month.

'With a heavily loaded aircraft a take-off run at Redhills commonly lasted two minutes and the longest straight stretch on the Lake was about six miles.

'Soon after becoming airborne, one crossed the Indian coastline when the skipper would open the envelope given him in the Ops room to find out where we were going.

Z2146 with 240 Sqdn at Redhills Lake in 1944. It was one of fifteen Mark 1s in the 'W' series of Catalinas (PBY-5s) received by the RAF in 1941.

'The navigator was kept continuously busy from the time of take-off to eventual return. Navigators became extremely proud of their profession, preferred not to have a substitute on board, and even looked askance at the idea of a 2nd pilot, also trained as a navigator, taking an astro shot. These navigators there-fore worked for the entire duration of the trip and produced exemplary feats of DR naviga-tion, mostly over the sea for 24 hours or more, at a maximum height of 2,000ft with, apart from heavenly bodies, only one reliable source of bearings — the transmitter in Ceylon.

'For maximum range one flew out fast and returned slowly. As we approached to enemy radar limit, the aircraft making a steady 85kt, we descended to as near sea level as was prudent, when for the pilots, flying became more interesting under manual control.

'Thus we would proceed to the Andaman rendezvous, or, if going further afield, to the coast of Burma, up over the hills on the peninsula and down the other side and across the Gulf of Siam. I recall the beauty of the landscape in the moonlight and wondering what was going on down there.

'Arrival at the rendezvous was announced by flashing in morse by torchlight from the ground. A — it was safe to alight, B — alight with caution, C — it is not safe to alight, D — I am under enemy control.

'The commonest signal was 'B'; sometimes no signal would be received in which case, after a reasonable wait, the crew headed for home not knowing the reason why.

'Alighting on the sea at the rendezvous was the exciting climax of the trip, when one recalls that the technique of putting a Catalina down on calm water during the day or in all conditions at night, was to start some miles downwind, set the props in fine pitch, revs at 2,300rpm, descent at 200ft/min, no flaps to worry about, point in the right direction and wait; until with a murmur the aircraft touched the water, then to ease back the throttles and settle like a feather, if all went well.

'Thus would begin the approach at rendez-vous with the skipper looking outside to see as much as possible, and the 2nd pilot calling out airspeed at intervals. Contact with the water was generally announced by an almighty bang and immediately the aircraft would become

FP301 'R' of 205 Sqdn RAF on 25 September 1944, one of 170 Mark 1Bs.

airborne again, whereupon the skipper would change to a stall landing technique which entailed engines off, and with the 2nd pilot pulling with all strength on the control column, while murmuring the Lord's prayer to themselves.

'A second bang followed soon after and the aircraft would be wallowing in the water more or less stationary. The first bang produced the danger of sprung rivets.

'Further assistance to reduce the danger in alighting at night was alleged to be provided by one of the crew standing in the front turret who would call out over the intercom "fishing stakes", if a forest of these vertical bamboo poles appeared in the alighting run. I heard this cry only once, and it coincided with the first bang — we missed the obstacles.

'On anchoring, members of the crew would hop out onto the wings with Sten guns, others

would hold on to their 0·45s, while the passengers disembarked in collapsible boats as carried to Andaman, or into boats provided by the reception committee, which at Koh Kut amounted to a fully lit launch, using engine signal bell with abandon, undecipherable Asiatic lettering on the prow — we were unhappy at the noise. More was to come when, after pulling away some distance, the boat returned at speed. Relief came when we heard the committee had forgotten to unload a crate of beer for us.

'The return trip was as for the outgoing but in reverse, characterized however, by growing fatigue, relieved to some extent by the Catalina's cooking facilities, a two-ring electric stove, which was soon in use for brewing up tea.

'We held little conversation with our passengers, either going out or bringing them

The RAF base at Koggala, Ceylon taken from Catalina *JX342* which was being delivered to No 205 Sqdn.

Addu Atoll in the Maldive Islands 600 miles south-west of Ceylon which served as a secret Royal Navy base in early 1942.

W/O Frisby, aircrew, but dressed and equipped for special duties flying with 240 Sqdn RAF.

back, and so knew nothing of the purpose of their journey. Some were clearly natives of the area visited, while others were obviously British or American. An interesting aspect of our charts was that there were three or four islands marked where rescue and survival equipment could be found in the event of disaster.'

Dewdney's final special op was 'Balmoral 5A' on 2 March 1945 in *VA723*, a 25-hour flying trip.

Flt Lt John Ayshford, DFC, was one of 240 Squadron's Catalina captains. Part of his training was at 131 OTU in Northern Ireland with his Catalina crew, followed by further experience at 302 FTU at Oban in Scotland.

It was at Oban in 1944, while I was 'on rest' between tours of operations, that I met some of Ayshford's crew, Sgts Coates, Shirt, Thistlethwaite, and their navigator, my brother Don Hendrie. It proved to be the only time Don and I met while on duty.

John Ayshford and crew completed about 90 hours' flying together before ferrying Catalina *JX342* from Oban to Koggala in Ceylon. They were airborne from Oban at 22:10hr on 23 May and, after a series of stops en route and with a further 65 hours' flying, reached Koggala at noon on 21 June.

Ayshford and his crew now undertook a series of training exercises with 240 Squadron before proceeding on operations in the Bay of Bengal. Sorties at this stage comprised convoy escorts, anti-submarine patrols and Met flights.

Their first special duties operation was coded 'Balmoral VI' and extended well into a second day. It was captained by their Flight Commander, Sqn Ldr Parry with whom they took off in *JX311* from Redhills Lake at 2' March 1945. After 15 hours' flying they landed at China Bay, refuelled, and after about two hours were airborne again. They were in company with another Catalina and at Chance Island fifteen Burmese fishermen with an escort were evacuated. *JX311* returned to Redhills Lake after a total flying time on this operation of 29 hours.

On a trip extending over 25/26 April my brother was navigator to Wg Cdr Robinson who was on operation 'Nickel II' in *JX311*. This mission involved the dropping of leaflets over north-east Sumatra. At one stage Don asked some of the crew what all the disturbance was about, and then realized that a bullet had come right through the table on which he was working. Tragically, there were other

JX328 an RAF Mark IVB *(PB2B-1)* which served with 191 Sqdn. It broke adrift during a gale at Redhills Lake and was wrecked on 26 October 1944.

bullets and one of the crew, Flt Sgt Shirt, was killed. After first landing at Kyaukpyu, they returned to Redhills Lake. This was my brother's last special op; thereafter he flew with the Catalina Ferry Flight (CFF).

Two Catalinas of 240 Squadron, 'F' and 'X', were airborne from Redhills just after 05:00hr on 21 May. Their intended operation, 'Lunch 1', was to land two men with two tons of freight on the east coast of the North Andaman Island and evacuate four members of operation 'Bacon'. The aircraft were captained by Flt Lts Ayshford and B. M. Ridgway with the loads being shared, each taking one ton of freight, a conducting officer and an agent on the outward run and returning with a conducting officer and two agents.

After almost six hours' flying they were in position 12°31′N 90°00′E and had lost height from 800 to 50ft to avoid radar detection. At 12:22hr they were in the target area and received a green signal flashing 'A'.

Ridgway released a flame float and was the first to touch down, followed by Ayshford

who taxied about 50yd away from Catalina 'X'. A kayak came from the shore and, after the exchange of passwords, three trips were made by kayak and a dinghy to each aircraft for unloading and loading. After the conducting officers had gone ashore to confer with the reception party, two agents were taken aboard and the Catalinas took off again, returning safely to base shortly before midnight on the 22nd.

Ayshford was detailed for another operation in the following 24 hours. This was 'Siren V, A&B' which he shared with Flt Lt Turnbull: they were required to take three agents and half a ton of freight to position 12°32′N 101°30′E, from where seven agents would be evacuated.

Ayshford and Turnbull were both airborne at about 02:30hr on 23 May in *VA723* and *W8405* respectively. Each carried 600lb freight, a conducting officer, and one agent with Ayshford, two agents with Turnbull.

After crossing the Bay of Bengal together they reached Landfall Island at 09:48hr, went down

JX328 being re-fuelled on Redhills Lake from a scow.

to 100ft and set course for Owen Island in the Mergui Archipelago. While climbing over the isthmus at 3,500-4,000ft, they lost contact with each other, but it was regained over the Gulf of Siam. They went down to 500ft for their datum point — position 11°45′N 101°00′E — then altered course for the target area, which Turnbull reached at 15:23 hours. After sighting the agent's boat showing two white lights and flashing 'TTT', he touched down. There was a moderate sea with a 4ft swell and the launch was unable to come alongside the Catalina. Rubber dinghies were used, two of which were damaged, one by a packing case. Both foundered but the loads were saved. Ayshford was by now waterborne. With unloading and loading completed, there was difficulty in hauling in the anchors and one was cut loose. On the return trip, Ayshford refuelled at Coconada but both Catalinas reached Redhills before 07:00hr on 24 May.

John Ayshford, captain of *FP308* on the port engine nacelle; in the foreground is the radio mast and loop aerial.

The crew of *FP308* when with the Catalina Ferry Flight at Dzaoudzi.

A trip for Geoff Myers on 19 June was ostensibly straightforward. This was operation 'Lunch III' to deliver 1,585lb freight to a Met party on the North Andaman Islands.

He took off in *FP152* with the Flight Commander — Sqn Ldr Parry — as screen captain. En route the weather was good, but on approaching Landfall Island there was heavy rain and low visibility. He made four runs over the target area at position 13°30′N 93°03′E before any sign of the reception party was seen and then a torch flashing 'A' from the beach was noted. There was continuous rain, lightning and with 10/10th cloud down to 600ft. The moon which should have provided their 'flare path' was completely obscured but gave a little diffused light. A smoke float was dropped and Myers touched down to anchor 100yd from the beach. He stayed there about 45 minutes, during which time a kayak from the shore took the freight and brought an agent with two conducting officers back to the Catalina.

Geoff Myers, a Pensacola-trained pilot, had earlier in his service gained experience on Loch Ryan, the Cromarty Firth and Lough Erne. A ferry trip to Korangi Creek *FP246* for 212 Squadron was to follow 'Lunch III' with more 'special ops' as Catalina Ferry Flight having completed an operational tour.

In operation 'Paddle' on 20 June, *FP182* captained by John Ayshford was the support aircraft to Flt Lt Dennis Turnbull in *FP152*. They were both airborne from Redhills at 04:50 hours and followed a route via Little Andaman and Auriol Island to the target area at Goh Kam Yai. Turnbull had on board three conducting officers with 716lb freight, and while he searched for the reception party, Ayshford circled at 800ft.

As no recognition signal had been seen after half an hour, a conducting officer flashed the name of one of the party towards the beach but, getting no response, he asked Turnbull if he would be willing to land. Turnbull said no and the search continued. Later, a faint blue light was seen and, although this was not the pre-arranged signal, Turnbull landed for the conducting officers to investigate.

After touching down north-east of the island, the Catalina was taxied about two miles round to the bay from which the light had been flashed, and the signal was repeated as the aircraft was being anchored 100yd off shore in 12ft of water. A dinghy was launched from the aircraft and loaded. It returned later with the three agents and, after it had been stowed, the engines were started and Turnbull taxied northwards for take-off. They had been down

An engine check of *FP308*, a RAF Mark 1B, at Diego Suarez.

in the pick-up area for over an hour before returning to Redhills, arriving the following morning at 08:25hr.

Turnbull captained *W8405* on 26 June in operation 'Obstacle', which was to take three agents and 250lb freight to position 06°57'N 100°52'E between Singora and Pattani on the east coast of the peninsula in the Gulf of Siam. The Catalina took off from Redhills at 03:14hr and en route a climb was made to 7,500ft to cross the isthmus, with many deviations to avoid large cloud formations.

Turnbull crossed into the Gulf of Siam south of Lakon Roads and his navigator, Flt Lt H. de Vere, obtained a pinpoint on Koh Kra Island from which course was set for the target area. After touching down seven miles from land the Catalina was taxied until it was five miles east of the coast at Pulo Chelai. A powered dinghy had been brought with the aircraft, and it took twenty minutes to assemble the craft and another thirteen minutes to load passengers and freight. The dinghy was left with the agents, and Turnbull took off at 17:33hr. Course was set from Koh Kra en route for Redhills, but for Rangoon, where *W8405* was waterborne at 02:38hr on 27 June.

A drop by parachute of almost a ton of freight was arranged for the 28th. The mission was to be flown by Geoff Myers in operation 'Priest/Rayon 1' which included a drop of five packages of matches. (Matches had been chosen as most suitable for diversionary drops as they survived the impact, were attractive to finders, and served also as a means of propaganda.)

Myers was airborne from Redhills at 07:59hr and en route flew via Sandy Point, Chance Island and South Island in the Sayer Islands, Ko Mak Nui and Ko Song Phinong. At the latter, a pinpoint position was obtained due to two rocks projecting 100ft from the water. The target at position 08°27'N 98°36'E was located by three nearby streams and a track running north-east from Ban Khao Thao. When the Catalina arrived over the dropping zone, the pre-arranged signal fires in the form of a 'T' were seen in addition to a flashing light.

Three runs were made with six packages released in each of the runs made from about 600ft. All packages fell within 250yd of the 'T' and the drop took just over twenty minutes.

Myers then flew towards Ban Kralai and Ban Chiangmai, where hut fires and lights were seen.

Up to the end of June 1945, 240 Squadron had flown 73 special operations, and 51 of these were undertaken in 1945. Only nine out of the total of 73 were abortive, and it is doubtful whether any of these nine could be attributed to a fault of the squadron. The figures give a success rate of 88 per cent. Seventy agents were infiltrated, together with over fifteen tons of freight, and 108 agents were evacuated plus fifteen native fishermen. Nine aircrew were lost on special operations, but only one aircraft.

On 1 July, 240 Squadron was disbanded and its special duties flight joined 212 Squadron, which was renumbered 240.

A regular Army officer, Major Guy Peace, became directly involved with special operations for the Siam area. He was called to the War Office just before D-day, for work with the Special Operations Executive which in the Far Eastern area became known as 'Force 136'. In remarks concerning these special ops Major Peace has spoken of Mountbatten's wish to bypass Siam, avoiding sabotage but obtaining military intelligence.

Of the aircrew with whom he worked, Major Peace states that they were the best pilots and 'certainly the best navigators that anyone could ask for'. Of the pilots he added, '. . . they would try anything, not only within reason, but almost without reason'.

1 W8417 or W8423.
2 Gillison, p201.
3 Described by 205 Sqn as a 'pearling lugger'; Gillison, p464, refers to Nickel Bay as a 'refuelling lighter' with Capt H. Mathieson as master.

Chapter 9
South Africa

1940-42

The Mediterranean Sea was closed to Allied shipping in May 1940; Italy declared war on France and the United Kingdom on 10 June, and France surrendered to Germany on 22 June. The Mediterranean was opened again to shipping in 1943 following the landings in Sicily and North Africa. Closure of the Mediterranean had made the long sea route round the Cape of Good Hope increasingly important to the Allies.

By the middle of 1940, the SAAF had 549 pilots, 500 air gunners and 249 administrative officers. The force adopted the RAF system of squadrons comprising two flights and equipped with sixteen aircraft. Ultimately, the SAAF had 35 squadrons.

The initial lack of bases and the high cost of constructing airfields favoured the use of flying boats, particularly Catalinas which, unlike the Sunderland, could be literally dropped down in any clear stretch of water. They proved suitable not only in the Pacific, but also for the Indian Ocean.

1942-44 RAF Catalina squadrons move to South Africa

No 209 Squadron RAF left the United Kingdom for East Africa on 30 March 1942 and it appears likely that Catalina 1Bs of this unit were operating from Langebaan on 19 October. Earlier, on the 13th, they must have suffered one of their first losses in the area when *AH543* was ditched in a storm and abandoned five miles north of Lourenço Marques.

Unsatisfactory operating conditions at Langebaan, plus the presence of enemy units off the east coast of South Africa, promoted a move of the Catalinas to Congella, Durban, in November 1942.

The smallness of Congella for heavily loaded Catalinas resulted in a further base north of Durban — Lake St Lucia — being used for refuelling after a comparatively light take-off from Congella. When the water of St Lucia was too low another lake, Lake Umsingazi, was used.

No 262 Squadron began their move out on 29 September 1942 to arrive at Congella on 12 November. They had as CO Wg Cdr G. E. Wallace.

In February 1943 there were fifteen Catalinas operating in South Africa. It was in this month that 259 Squadron was re-formed at Kipevu, Kenya. In March, 259 Squadron had a detachment at Congella, and in June they sent a detachment to Langebaan.

On 29 October 1942, the first recorded Catalina encounter in the South African area with the enemy was in an anti-submarine search off Cape Agulhas. This was the sighting of *U-159* which was later to be sunk by a USN plane[1].

One of those to join the re-formed 259 Squadron was a wireless operator/mechanic, Dai Thomas. He sailed from Glasgow on 27 August 1942 in SS *Nia Hellas*, which two weeks later bunkered at Freetown for 24 hours. Due to U-boat activity, he and others were disembarked at Cape Town instead of Durban, the journey to Durban being completed by train. At Durban, Thomas was billeted on the SS *Manila* which was shared with 209 Squadron personnel.

Thomas was later sent to 207 Group HQ in Nairobi, Kenya, due to a shortage of wireless operators. He later returned to 259 Squadron at Mombasa and was then detached to Kisumu on Lake Victoria, where major inspections on Catalinas were undertaken.

A Catalina which was flown out from the United Kingdom to serve with 262 Squadron was *FP322*. Captained by Flt Lt McKirdy, it was airborne from Oban on 18 June 1944 on what proved to be the longest leg — 13hr 40min — to Gibraltar. It was then flown via West Africa, East Africa and Madagascar to Durban, arriving there on 16 July, with a total flying time of 85hr 40min. From Durban this aircraft was operated on patrols lasting over eighteen hours, but typically of about twelve hours' duration. It was struck off charge on 12 July 1946.

No 265 Squadron RAF in the South African area

An aircraft for 265 Squadron was flown out by F/O Temple-Murray from Pembroke Dock on 30 April 1943. This was *FP263* which was airborne at 20:55hr en route for Gibraltar. Following a similar route, Temple-Murray reached Mombasa after total flying of 79 hours 15 minutes. *FP263* was subsequently captained by P/O Pinkard of Tasmania and operated from Madagascar. Flying with Pinkard as second pilot was George McKendrick[2], who had trained at Pensacola and No 4 (Coastal) OTU, Alness. He had flown out to 265 Squadron at Diego Suarez in July 1943. They shared a series of convoy escorts and anti-submarine patrols, and were detached to other areas such as Masira, the Seychelles, Mauritius and Aden.

On 27 December McKendrick was seconded to the Royal Netherlands Naval Air Force as second pilot to Ovl II Willi Aernout on a trip to Karachi in the Dutch Catalina Y-57, which had been used in the escape from Java in March 1942 and later served with 321 Squadron at China Bay. They returned to Masira in the same machine on 3 January 1944.

Writing about his flights in this area, McKendrick states, '. . . they were mostly convoy escort. We operated from a number of detached bases from Aden to Durban, migrating with the convoys. They were mostly tankers bringing oil from the Persian Gulf to the United Kingdom via the Cape. We considered ten to be the full complement for long trips, usually with the addition of a rigger and a third pilot to help the navigator by taking sun sights, drifts etc. Apart from being an air gunner, the rigger was traditionally in charge

of mooring operations and was expected to cook a hot meal on the Primus stoves. The only airframe work he would find to do on board would be to plug rivet holes after a heavy landing. The plates on the bottom of the hull would sometimes give enough to cut off the heads of some rivets during a stall landing.

'Navigation was perhaps our biggest problem in the Indian Ocean. There were almost no radio aids, so it was all DR and astro. With prolonged cloud cover, it was all DR, and whilst finding Africa was not to difficult, the small island bases were a problem after ten or more hours without a fix.'

The demise of *U-197* off Madagascar

On 19 August the possibility of a U-boat operating about 250 miles off Cap Ste Marie on the southern tip of Madagascar was reported. Three Catalinas took off to search, and one of these was captained by Flt Lt O. Barnett of 259 Squadron from St Lucia.

At 12:10hr on the 20th, he was flying at about 2,000ft on a southerly course when he sighted a large white-cap. On using binoculars, a submarine was observed sailing at about 10kt. Barnett made a diving turn to port and closed the distance for an attack. The submarine opened fire and the Catalina responded from the forward and port blister guns. During his bombing run, Barnett released six depth charges from 50ft altitude. These were followed by flame and smoke floats to mark the position.

At 14:28hr the submarine surfaced and fired every time the aircraft approached. The Catalina's wireless operator, Sgt Metcalfe, homed in a second Catalina which arrived at 17:05hr. This was *FP313* from 265 Squadron and captained by F/O C. E. Robin.

The two Catalinas now made a series of strafing runs to silence the U-boat's AA fire, followed by Robin making his depth charge attack. Six charges were released and they straddled the submarine: it disappeared for the last time, leaving debris and a large patch of oil.

According to US Navy records, this was the sinking of *U-197*, captained by Bartels and lost in position 28°40'S 42°36'E, which is southwest of Madagascar.

Catalina 'K' of 209 Sqdn at Khartoum when the unit was based in East Africa during the period 1942-45.

On 3 September, an armistice was signed with Italy, and the importance of the Allied sea route via the Cape of Good Hope was diminished.

Catalina search for a U-boat supply vessel

On 11 February, Catalina *FP263* of 265 Squadron took off from Mauritius with three other Catalinas. All had been briefed to fly together to a datum point 1,000 miles south-east of Mauritius, and then to follow a special search pattern to locate a U-boat supply ship.

After ten hours' flying they had reached the datum point. The search was commenced and 1½ hours later Catalina 'F' of 259 Squadron ex-Dar-es-Salaam, captained by Bob Dutton, broke radio silence. Dutton was flying at about 2,000ft above 4/10ths strato-cumulus when the ship was seen through a break in the cloud. As the vessel gave no sign of having noted his presence, he circled above cloud, watching and radioing a report.

To his surprise, a submarine surfaced and closed with the tanker. The Catalinas had been equipped for maximum endurance with overload tanks and were not armed with depth charges or guns. Dutton did his best by making a dummy attack. The U-boat crash-dived and the ship took evasive action. When no real attack followed, the tanker headed south-east.

'F' then shadowed the vessel and, on reaching PLE, gave a final course, speed and position of the enemy ship before returning to base, reaching Mauritius after almost 30 hours' flying. Catalina *FP263*, captained by F/O Pinkard, following instructions, had returned to base after receiving Dutton's sighting report, but even so was airborne for over 21 hours.

The supply vessel — *Charlotte Schlierman* — was sunk by HMS *Relentless* on 12 February 1944. The position given by the Catalina to the Royal Navy proved to be within sighting distance. The Catalina captain and navigator were awarded the DFC.

The South African Air Force and RAF Catalina squadrons

No 262 Squadron RAF was established at Congella, Durban in November 1942 with personnel drafted from the United Kingdom. It received its first Catalinas in February 1943.

BOAC had been operating a flying boat service to South Africa with a terminus at Congella in Durban Harbour, and with developed facilities including a hangar and slipway. With only a narrow channel for flying boats to take off and land, in addition to much shipping, Durban was not considered a satisfactory base for heavily loaded operational Catalinas, so additional bases were made at Lake St Lucia, a crocodile-infested lake in Northern Natal, and at Saldahna Bay about 120 miles north of Cape Town.

During 1943 the SAAF had been planning to form its own flying boat squadron and a number of its aircrew were selected for training. About six South African crews were sent to the United Kingdom, led by such as Lt Col Ron Madeley and Capt Maxwell in late 1943.

In February 1944 six additional future flying boat captains assembled in London. Their flight engineers and radio operators were drawn from South African Airways and the remainder of the crews of eight came from the SAAF. The intended flying boat captains were Capts D. Broadhurst, D. Eden, J. Spoor, C. A. Smith, M. Mitchell and J. Winning. Most had come from operational tours on Marylands or Bostons with the Desert Air Force and were unaccustomed to auto-pilots, 2nd pilots and flight engineers. They trained at 131 OTU Killadeas before transferring to No 302 Ferry Training Unit.

Des Eden[3] ferried an aircraft out to Durban from Oban on 17 June and en route was diverted to Mauritius to join a search for a U-boat before arriving at Durban on 16 July.

Of about fifteen crews in 262 Squadron during July and August 1944, about half were from the SAAF. Capt Mitchell ferried a Catalina IVB to Korangi Creek and from there collected a Catalina for delivery to 262 Squadron in Durban, where he arrived in August.

Mitchell found Col R. Madeley as CO with Sqn Ldr E. S. S. 'Gar' Nash, RAF, as Flight Commander: Nash was a South African commissioned in the RAF. Towards the end of 1944, Col Madeley and Capt Maxwell rejoined

South African Airways, Col Madeley being replaced by Wg Cdr E. S. S. Nash, DFC, as CO, with Mitchell and Eden promoted to Majors in the SAAF as 'A' and 'B' Flight Commanders respectively.

It was not until 15 February 1945 that 262 Squadron RAF was disbanded and 35 Squadron SAAF took over its base and aircraft, as well as its duties. When Wg Cdr Nash was posted to Ceylon in April, Col Danie du Toit, DFC, who had commanded a SAAF Boston squadron in the Western Desert, became OC of 35 Squadron SAAF.

Attacks on U-boats off South Africa

In early March of 1944, reports indicated that *U-178* and a former Italian submarine — *Alpino Attilio I Bagnolini* redesignated *UIt-22* — might rendezvous in the area south of Cape Agulhas. In addition to Naval forces, South African Venturas and RAF Catalinas were involved in an intensive search operation. On 8 March, seven Catalinas of 262 Squadron were detached from Congella to Langebaan, and on that day *U-178* was attacked by a 25 Squadron Ventura, but without damage. Radio and weather conditions precluded other aircraft being homed on to the position.

Catalina 'D' (*FP279*) of 262 Squadron was airborne as 04:30hr on 11 March captained by Flt Lt F. J. Roddick. At 10:20hr he had reached his datum point to begin a patrol just below cloud base. He was about 600 miles

'L' of 209 Sqn beached in East Africa, January 1943.

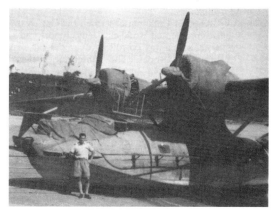

209 Sqdn servicing a Catalina at Mombasa, January 1943. A propeller and bomb trolley are in the foreground; an improvised awning is over the starboard engine.

south of Cape Point when he sighted a submarine steaming at 10kt on a westerly course. To attack from astern, Roddick made a diving turn to port. The submarine made no attempt to submerge but opened fire, whereupon the Catalina crew retaliated.

In his run at 10-15° to the line of the vessel, Roddick released five depth charges, and in a second run, the final charge which had previously hung up, exploded 5yd from the U-boat's port bow. It had a heavy list to starboard and lost way, but after 12 minutes it submerged.

Another Catalina, captained by 'Gar' Nash, had intercepted Roddick's radio report and at 10:48 hours was patrolling over the oil slick from the U-boat. The submarine surfaced again at 11:30hr and Nash attacked at 60° to the starboard bow with six depth charges which straddled the U-boat forward of the conning tower.

A third Catalina captained by Flt Lt A. H. Surridge followed by attacking the submarine with machine-gun fire. When the water subsided there was no sign of the U-boat, apart from the oil patch.

As a result of the attacks by the three Catalinas, the former Italian submarine, *UIt-22*, was sunk in position 41°28'S 17°40'E while

under the command of Kapitänleutnant Wunderlich.

When *U-178* arrived at that position on the 12th it found only an oil slick and headed for Bordeaux.

After ground stations had obtained a D/F fix on a U-boat giving a position of about 300 miles south-west of Durban, a series of air patrols was laid on to cover the area.

Catalina 'D' of 262 Squadron, but now with the SAAF, was airborne from St Lucia at 04:05hr on 5 April captained by F/O Cover, and was followed twenty minutes later by Flt Lt Fletcher in 'L'. The squadron was following a procedure used by Coastal Command, ie, to arrange take-off times for aircraft so that they would arrive over the appropriate area by first light. Both had been detailed to undertake a creeping line-ahead, anti-submarine sweep along parallel tracks of 100 miles.

At 13:11hr Flt Lt Fletcher had just reached the limit of his patrol and was about to turn when he sighted a U-boat surfacing. The Catalina was then at 3,000ft altitude and with the submarine four miles away. While losing height to attack, and closing the distance, the aircraft suffered AA fire from light cannon and at 1½ miles the port wing was hit, the hull was damaged by shrapnel and the air speed indicator became inoperative. Despite rapid changes of course by the U-boat, Fletcher was able to release depth charges, and one was seen to detonate about 12ft to port and forward of the conning tower. One depth charge hung up and could not be released.

Meanwhile F/O Cover's wireless operator had intercepted Fletcher's sighting report and Catalina 'D' homed on to the scene, but at 15:38hr found only an oil patch.

The following day Flt Lt Surridge in Catalina 'K' located an oil slick which extended for twenty miles. It was evidence that *U-859*, commanded by Korvettenkapitän Jebson, had been damaged.

From the data given for this attack, and about sixty others made by Catalinas against submarines, it is evident that 'L' would have been equipped with 250lb depth charges and not those of 650lb used by the US Navy. The latter have been shown to be lethal at a distance of 12ft.

Later that year on 23 September off Penang (05°46'N 100°04'E), *U-859* was sunk by HMS *Trenchant*.

1   *U-159*, sunk 15.7.43 by *VP-32*, 15°58'N 73°44'W.
2   Flt Lt G. G. McKendrick, DFC, RAFVR
3   Major D. Eden, SAAF (Ret).

Chapter 10
The Atlantic Ferry

1940-44

Early in World War 2 it was realised that there were serious disadvantages in shipping aircraft from America, 'the arsenal of Europe', to Britain. Machines had to be dismantled for transit, valuable shipping space was used, there was a very real risk of ships being torpedoed or bombed, re-assembly was necessary should they reach delivery stage, and the whole procedure could take up to three months.

However, if aircraft were flown across the Atlantic, they could reach operational squadrons of the RAF in as little as ten days.

Two of the first Catalinas to be received in Britain were *P9630*, a PBY-4, and 'Guba II', a PBY-2 (*P9630* in July 1939 and 'Guba II' in October 1940). These movements, however, were not part of the established Atlantic Ferry Service.

This service was organised by the Canadian Pacific Railway with headquarters at Montreal and with technical assistance provided by British Overseas Airways. Trained pilots were

A Catalina with Russian markings at Reykjavik in August 1945 en route to the USSR.

obtained with little difficulty, but there were a limited number of radio operators. For the latter, radiomen with ground experience were recruited, and then trained for their role as aviators.

The first scheduled ferry flights were from Gander, Newfoundland, on 10 November 1940 to Aldergrove, Northern Ireland, by seven Hudsons[1]. They were successful in inaugurating the Atlantic Ferry, and certainly, in early 1942, Hudsons were still being flown across. While based at Limavady, I was asked by a Hudson pilot who had obviously just made such a crossing, 'Where am I?' The alternative way of checking one's position under such circumstances was to enter the Mess and observe the heading of 'DROs' (Daily Routine Orders), a method frowned upon by the Air Ministry but 100 per cent reliable.

For some Catalinas Bermuda proved to be an acceptable staging post, and a former British Airways manager, Sqn Ldr G. J. Powell, was transferred from Newfoundland to Bermuda to organize the base. Seven PBYs arrived there in January 1941 and the first flight to Britain was by Capt Fleming with Capt Meikle as co-pilot. For crew members they had two radio operators and two flight engineers.

While they were flying at 18,500ft, six hours out from Bermuda, the auto-pilot jammed, the starboard aileron went full down, and the aircraft went into a spiral dive. Due to the force of the dive, the ailerons fluttered and were torn away, but some control was regained just a few hundred feet above the sea. It proved possible nonetheless to slowly get back on course, and the Catalina touched down at Milford Haven, South Wales, after a trip of 28hr 50min.

The fastest Catalina flight listed up to June 1944 from Bermuda to the United Kingdom — a distance of 3,400 statute miles — was in 19hr 50min by Capt R. E. Perlick. In the summer of 1944 it was said that Catalinas were having their endurance raised to 32 hours by the addition of fuel tanks located in the fuselage.

In June 1941, the first flying boat left Gander Lake, which was about a mile from the land-base at Gander, Labrador. From there they might have flown to Reykjavik, Iceland, direct to the United Kingdom, or down to Bermuda.

To comply with conditions set by President Roosevelt, the ferry organization was changed from a civil to a military one, and on 20 July 1941 Ferry Command of the RAF came into being under Air Chief Marshal Sir Frederick Bowhill, the Coastal Command officer who in May had made the right decisions concerning Catalina searches for *Bismarck*[2].

It was Sir Frederick Bowhill who suggested that newly trained crews in Canada should undertake the delivery of aircraft from North

America to the United Kingdom, and in fact these crews often ferried aircraft to other areas, such as North Africa.

At about the time of the 'Torch' operation landings in North Africa, it became undesirable to use the North Atlantic route to Britain, ferrying aircraft down across the Bay of Biscay, with the very likely hazard of encountering enemy aircraft. A South Atlantic route was followed instead, with its advantages of more favourable weather and a shorter hop across the ocean. A series of variations appears to have been applied according to conditions on the two main routes, for example, shortly after the North African landings, I met one of a Catalina crew on the Rock who had flown direct from Bermuda to Gibraltar, a trip taking 24 hours.

Canso *JX327*, a PBY-5A, flew from Elizabeth City, North Carolina, to Bermuda on 14 April 1944. Two days later it left Gander and then, on 17 April, completed the longest leg in just under fourteen hours with Capt Giffin to Largs in Scotland. *JX327* was later flown to the Far East.

A mixed Russian/British crew including 1st pilot Harry Buxton, RCAF 2nd pilot — the Russian Leonov, at San Juan, Puerto Rico, 4-5 November 1944 with PBN-1 *02897* being ferried under 45 Group control to the Middle East en route to the USSR.

On 11 April 1943, after the formation of Transport Command, Ferry Command was designated No 45 (Ferry) Group. It was then to have four wings: No 112 covering North Atlantic operations; No 113 the South Atlantic; No 216 for the Middle East; and No 179 Wing in India.

Figures given in the official 'Atlantic Bridge' for the years 1940 to 1943 inclusive, for all types of aircraft ferried by air across the Atlantic Ocean, are: North Atlantic 1940 — 26, 1941 — 722, 1942 — 1,163 and 1943 — 1,450 aircraft. For the South Atlantic, there were 127 aircraft ferried in 1942 and 1,336 in 1943.

Catalina *FP261* took off from Montreal on 17 September 1943 captained by P/O Lonsdale and with Jack Campbell as navigator. En route to Gander, they were forced down by bad weather and touched down at Stephenville after a seven-hour flight. *FP261* created a minor sensation as apparently, it was the first seaplane to land there. After two days they were airborne again and 'Bradshawed', following the rail road to Gander. After two more days of rain, although the weather was still considered too bad by some civilian pilots, P/O Lonsdale took off in *FP261* on the final leg of his ferry trip, from Gander to Largs across the North Atlantic.

For navigation, Campbell used what he describes as 'the old drift system', dropping flame floats to determine drift and thus the wind. He obtained also some fixes by astro-nav, but depended on the astro-compass to back up the magnetic compass by sighting the North Star.

The weather forecasts they had received proved to the reliable and they made landfall on Ireland before heading for Largs in Scotland, arriving there after a flight of 16 hours 10 minutes including eight hours flown at night. *FP261* was later destined for 302 FTU and East Africa.

The NC-4 re-enactment flight by Catalinas

On 17 May 1919, three NC flying boats of the US Navy were near the Azores after fifteen hours' flying from Trepassey Bay, Newfoundland. They were *NC-4* with Lt Cdr A. C. Read, *NC-1* commanded by Cdr J. H. Towers, and *NC-3* with Lt Cdr P. N. L. Bellinger.

Only Lt Cdr Read commanding *NC-4* was able to complete the two final legs of the journey, which was via Lisbon and terminating at Plymouth, England, on 31 May 1919. This was the first transatlantic flight completed by the US Navy. The three flying boats

Connie Edwards' PBY at Pensacola on 4 May 1986. It was one of two Catalinas flown to Plymouth, England in the NC-4 re-enactment flight.

'X' of 321 (Dutch) Sqdn in East Africa 1943. The possible Dutch serial No Y-82 conflicts with other data received.

had begun the trip at NAS Rockaway, New York, on 8 May and routed via Halifax, Nova Scotia; Trepassey Bay, Newfoundland; the Azores and Portugal to England.

Photographs taken subsequently show, in addition to Lt Cdr Read, Assistant Secretary to the Navy, Theodore Roosevelt, and Lt Cdr P. N. L. Bellinger. The latter had begun his career in 1914, and in 1940 became Commander of Patrol Wing 2 at Pearl Harbor.

Aviation for the US Navy had begun officially in 1911 and its diamond anniversary was celebrated with the re-enactment of the NC-4 flight by two Catalinas. One of these, a PBY-6A, was at Pensacola on 3 May 1986 with a number on the bow *TX 3317 DW* which, as Robert Gregory, an ex-PBY pilot himself suggests, was probably a State of Texas BOAT registration. Gregory spoke to the pilot of the Catalina — Wilson 'Connie' Edwards — on the 4th, just before he took off for a local photo flight to celebrate the 75th anniversary of the US Navy, and with the Catalina marked '75th'. What was, perhaps, the second Catalina, made a forty-minute flight over Washington DC.

Preparation for the arrival of the Catalinas in England included a 'notice to Mariners'

published on 15 May and issued by the Plymouth harbourmaster. Three landing areas were designated, but with moorings at RAF Mount Batten. Surface craft were instructed to keep 200m clear ahead and 100m clear astern of the Catalinas. The final sentence warned that 'Catalinas have NO astern power'.

The touch-down was officially scheduled for 11:00hr on 31 May to music provided by the band of the US Navy's 6th Fleet. British press and television reports gave emphasis to the waterloop made by the second Catalina, piloted by Louis Petersen. It was seen to strike a buoy and a float was torn off with part of the wing before the aircraft began sinking rapidly, nose down. All eight on board were rescued although one — Cdr Howard Wheeler — was injured and taken to the Royal Naval Hospital.

The *Western Morning News* of 2 June reports Wilson 'Connie' Edwards achieving a 'perfect touchdown', this in the apparently unscathed PBY-6A *TX 3317 DW*, but without that identification given.

After speeches made by the Lord Mayor of Plymouth, Councillor Bill Glanville, Vice Admiral Robert F. Scoultz, USN, Deputy

Commander in Chief of the US Naval Forces in Europe, and pilot 'Connie' Edwards, the band played 'Navy Wings of Gold' and 'Rule Britannia'. The crashed aircraft was destined for a hangar at RAF Mount Batten; the serviceable amphibian to the Naval Air Station, Yeovilton.

The Royal Air Force had been represented quite unofficially by some of its former 'Cat men', such as George Speers, an ex-628 Squadron W/AG who obtained a permit to go aboard the Press tender. Of the Catalina men he met, one proved to be another from 628 Squadron and from P. McKeand's crew whom he'd last seen in World War 2 at Redhills Lake in the Far East.

Catalinas to Russia

Of the 156 PBN-1s which were built by the US Naval Aircraft Factory, 137 were delivered to Russia. Routes used for ferrying were via Iceland, the Aleutians, and also the southern route across the South Atlantic.

Two RAF pilots who captained some of these aircraft for delivery to Russia were F/O Harry Buxton and Flt Lt Eddie Miles. They were both with 45 Group, Ferry Command based at Dorval and, during the period November 1944 to March 1945, each delivered three Catalinas to Habbaniyah in the Middle East.

As Harry Buxton now writes: 'The route which we followed was from Elizabeth City, North Carolina, to San Juan, Puerto Rico, thence to the USN base in Trinidad, from there to Belém, Brazil, landing on the Amazon, then to Natal, Brazil.

'The longest hop followed, across the South Atlantic to Bathurst, British West Africa, and from there to Port Lyautey, Morocco. On the first of the three deliveries which I undertook, we stopped at Port Etienne between Bathurst and Port Lyautey. The reason may have been to ensure clearing of the stages.

'From Morocco we crossed the Atlas Mountains en route to Djerba — the first two trips; on the third trip we went to Augusta, Sicily, rather than to Tunisia. Then on to Kasfareit on the Great Bitter Lake, Egypt, and thence to Habbaniyah. The Russian crew then carried on into the Soviet Union. Overall the delivery flight represented about 70-80

hours flying time, with about a third of it night-flying.

'Several of the stops in this delivery route had limited capacity for handling these transit aircraft, and could take two only. Thus deliveries were in pairs, and an advance to the next stop required the base to be cleared — a kind of musical chairs progression. Each aircraft carried a full Russian Navy crew with three English-speaking crew added between Elizabeth City and Habbaniyah — a first pilot who was captain, a radio navigator and a flight engineer.

'Each aircraft had Russian markings and was provided with a small 15 x 30in Russian Navy flag. At the conclusion of one trip the flag was given to me, on it a number of the crew names were inscribed. I had also a one Rouble Russian note signed on the reverse by four of the Russians on the second trip.' (PBN-1 02879.)

Before delivering 02879, Buxton's first trip had been with Catalina 02897, having as 2nd pilot the Russian officer Leonov. His final delivery to Habbaniyah was of 02930 with Iakoulev as 2nd pilot.

Flt Lt Eddie Miles in the same period delivered three other PBN-1s, 02900, 02896 and 02929. Russian officers who acted as 2nd pilots on these flights with him were Capt Checkov, Capt Pogordski and Lt Slyusarev.

Relations between the crews and nationalities involved were sufficiently cordial for a group photograph to be taken of two British and two Russian crews together with an American liaison officer at San Juan during an overnight stop there on 4/5 November 1944.

Following the deliveries of the PBN flying boats, 44 PBY-6A amphibians were sent to Russia during the summer of 1945. These Catalinas were taken on the strength of the Russian Naval Fleet. Their duties included anti-submarine patrols, surveillance of enemy maritime communications, and air-sea rescue operations for ditched aircrews. They also undertook ice patrols and meteorological flights. Patrols in the north were largely involved in counter-measures against U-boats.

In the summer of 1944 the German-Russian front extended south-east to the Black Sea. Romania and Bulgaria were effectively on the

German side; the former with its valuable oil fields at Ploesti, the latter officially neutral in respect of German-Russian hostilities although, following Pearl Harbor, it declared war on America and Britain.

In August 1944 the Russians began what was for them, the Jassy-Kishinev campaign. The campaign, in addition to the deployment of 18 armies, involved 891 aircraft of the Black Sea Fleet out of a total of 2,650 machines[3]. An unknown number of Catalinas from the Black Sea Fleet were deployed off the Bulgarian ports of Varna and Burgas in September; they were PBN-1s and used to counter German anti-shipping measures.

Russia declared war on Bulgaria on 5 September; there was no resistance and an armistice with a new Bulgarian government was declared on the 9th.

The PBY-6As were deployed during August 1945 in the liberation of the island of Sakhalin by supporting the landing forces. It was the recovery of Sakhalin that Stalin (*vide* Churchill[4]), at the Yalta conference, made one of Russia's conditions for entry into the war against Japan.

1 See the author's *Seek and Strike*, pp91-5.
2 See DR, RAF Vol 1, p226.
3 *The Soviet Air Force in WW2*, MOD USSR, p301 (David & Charles).
4 SWC, Vol VI, p341.

Chapter 11
No 321 (Dutch) Squadron

1940-58

Although formed at Pembroke Dock in June 1940, 321 Squadron became effective as a Catalina-equipped unit in March 1942 with its main base in Ceylon.

Following the Allied defeat in the battle of the Java Sea and the Japanese invasion of Java, the Governor-General of the Dutch East Indies ordered Admiral Hellfrich and part of his staff to evacuate and prepare for the continuation of the war with what was left of the Dutch Navy.

Some Dutch Catalinas had escaped Japanese attentions and they were to be used for withdrawal, with Lt Cdr W. van Prooyen detailed for the operation on 1 March 1942. Of the Catalinas which were hidden from the Japanese in mountain lakes in the interior of Java, some were scheduled for Colombo, and others for Australia. Three of the Catalinas, *Y-55*, *Y-56* and *Y-57* arrived in Ceylon on 3 March, while a fourth, *Y-64*, made a forced landing on a small lagoon in the Pondicherry area. The lagoon was subsequently dubbed 'Lac Venema' after the name of the aircraft's captain.

Another section of the Royal Netherlands Naval Air Force (RNNAF), flew to Australia. One of these was *Y-70*, captained by Lt Cdr A. J. de Bruijn. On 1 March he was ordered by the commandant of the Marine Luchtvaart-dienst (MLD) in the NEI from Surabaya to Loeloeng Agoeng, an artificial lake near the south coast of east Java, to await further instructions. On 2 March a phone call came from Cdr Broesder ordering the Dutch Catalinas to take off from Toeloeng Agoeng and fly to Broome in Western Australia. Passengers were to include a few staff officers with their wives. On board *Y-70* were Capt and Mrs Hendrikse, Cdr and Mrs. A. A. C. Kramer,

Cdr Broesder, and Lt Cdr de Bruijn, Mrs de Bruijn and her two sons.

During the flight, Cdr de Bruijn, aware of limited re-fuelling capacity and of a number of American aircraft already at Broome, advised Capt Hendrikse, the senior officer on board, to divert to Geralton. Capt Hendrikse declined. On arrival at Broome early on 3 March, Cdr de Bruijn found many other Catalinas already moored and, while waiting for the motor launch, some of his passengers were sea-sick.

As Capt A. J. de Bruijn now recalls: 'All of a sudden, Japanese Zero fighters started to attack the aircraft in the bay. We fired at them with our machine-guns. I told one of the crew to make the inflatable dinghy ready for use and went down in the aircraft, instructing passengers and crew to go into the dinghy as soon as possible. Some passengers reacted hardly at all because of sea-sickness. When I came back on deck of the Catalina, I saw our dinghy drifting away with only one of the crew who had failed to fasten the dinghy line.'

Cdr de Bruijn swam out to the dinghy to help to tow it back for the passengers and crew. While he was with the dinghy, his Catalina was strafed by Zeros, set on fire and sunk. After some time, the motor launch arrived and towed the dinghy to the jetty.

Capt de Bruijn continues: 'In the afternoon of the same day I assisted in recognizing the victims the Japanese had made by attacking eighteen Catalinas at anchor. Amongst the victims were Capt and Mrs Hendrikse, Cdr and Mrs Kramer, and several other passengers who the day before had gone to Toeloeng Agoeng hopefully.'

In addition to Catalina *Y-70* three others, *Y-59*, *Y-60* and *Y-67*, arrived in Australia together with five Dornier flying boats,

Do24K, X1, X3, X23 and *X28*: these were German machines in Dutch service. All four of the Catalinas were destroyed by the Zero fighters and there were 11 casualties with *Y-59*.

The serviceable Dutch Catalinas now remaining in Australia were *Y-49, Y-45, Y-62, Y-69* and *Y-71*. They were ordered to Ceylon on a direct flight of nearly 3,000 nautical miles.

The Dutch now had nine Catalinas at Koggala, and No 321 (Dutch) Squadron, RAF, was effectively re-formed on 1 July 1942, but with less than a hundred ground personnel.

Y-69, which had been returned to San Diego for a refit and then ferried to Australia, was flown to Koggala by Cdr de Bruijn on 31 May. Concerning subsequent missions he writes: 'According to my log book we used the month of June mainly for instruction to newly formed aircrews. In July we started flying operational patrols.' His first sortie was an anti-invasion patrol on 5 July coded 'gang-smasher'.

In the middle of July, 321 moved to China Bay, Trincomalee. From there further 'gang-smasher' and cross-over patrols were undertaken in anticipation of approaching Japanese ships, including a cross-over patrol of 250 nautical miles west of Port Blair, Andaman Islands, on 31 July in a flight lasting 19½ hours.

A detachment of six aircrews was sent from Australia to America to ferry six amphibians (PBY-5As) *Y-74-Y-79* inclusive, which left San Diego in September. They arrived in Ceylon on 5 January 1943. In September also, another 100 men reached the squadron from Australia.

Operational flights in October included one by Cdr de Bruijn from China Bay to the Seychelles on the 11th, which was followed by a search for what was believed to be either a raider or a vessel supplying enemy submarines.

American ferry pilots flew into Ceylon with five PBY-5As, *Y-83* arriving on 1 November, four others following in the same month; a sixth *(Y-81)*, was damaged in transit.

Initially, 321 Squadron Catalinas had major overhauls undertaken at Bangalore by an American company — the Industan Aircraft Factory which employed Indian labour. At China Bay, however, 321 undertook to have its own workshops, beginning with almost nothing. They made tools but bought others from Ceylon, India and Australia. There was a strong desire by the engineering officer, Lt Cdr A. Everaars, to acquire a workshop lorry, and this was achieved in March 1943. When the AOC, ACM Sir Arthur Peirse, inspected the unit about six months later, he was so impressed that he ordered a second workshop lorry for the squadron.

The unit employed Sinhalese, Tamils and Indonesians, but of particular value were fifteen ex-KLM technicians. While 70 per cent serviceability was considered normal, following a request for an extreme effort by the AOC of 222 Group, AVM Sir Alan Lees, 100 per cent serviceability was achieved for a short time with nineteen Catalinas airborne, and the 20th on standby at the moorings in China Bay.

In late 1942 and early 1943 it was apparent that U-boats were being transferred from the Atlantic to South African waters, and there were losses of Allied ships which were unescorted.

In January 1943, 321 Squadron sent a detachment of six Catalinas led by Lt Cdr W. J. Reynierse and Lt Cdr A. J. de Bruijn. They were originally based at Durban, Port Elizabeth, and Darling near Cape Town. As Durban proved unsuitable for night take-offs and landings, Lake St Lucia was used as an alternative. In April, Lt Cdr de Bruijn returned with his flight to China Bay while Lt Cdr Reynierse's flight remained at Port Elizabeth.

Besides providing escorts for convoys, the squadron undertook many hunts for U-boats which were reported by shipping. On one such trip, Lt J. Vonk was the captain of *Y-84*, flying about 400 miles south of Cape Agulhas at night.

There was a rapid change of wind direction which increased to gale force. It precluded a safe return to the coast, but fortunately a British destroyer was sighted. Vonk set the Catalina down near the vessel, and all on *Y-84* were rescued despite the rough sea. The aircraft could not be taken in tow and was sunk by gunfire.

On the night of 23 May, Lt Vonk took off from Port Elizabeth in *Y-85*, detailed for a convoy escort. At 06:30hr the following morning his radar operator saw a blip on the screen which indicated something about 1½ miles to starboard. Later, in the area of Algoa Bay, a wake was sighted near, and approaching the convoy.

The wake was that of *U-178*, which was about to attack the convoy. *Y-85* was subjected to AA fire, but suffered no hits. The U-boat submerged but, at about 07:00hr, a periscope was seen a mile away. Vonk attacked with four depth charges. Some oil and a few planks were seen and it was thought at the time that there had been a 'kill'. In fact, *U-178* had an oil leak which was made worse by the attack. It could be deemed an Allied success in that the enemy was thwarted and the Merchant Navy were reassured by the vigilance of their escorts.

From June onwards, enemy submarines were directing their intentions towards the Arabian Sea, and in the latter half of 1943, following the re-opening of the Mediterranean, a 321 Squadron detachment moved up from South Africa to Socotra Island, east of Aden. At the same time, two of their Catalinas were detached from China Bay to Masirah on the south coast of Arabia.

Of this move, the squadron history records: 'This transfer from Cape Town, Durban, Port Elizabeth and Johannesburg to stations like Socotra and Masirah made all the difference in the world to the crews. They left Heaven and landed in Hell.

'For eight months in succession their spare time had been very enjoyable indeed with every thinkable diversion available. In their new stations there were rocks, sand flies in plenty, but nothing else, not even trees or grass.

'Water had to be imported by ship and they received two bottles a day, one for drinking, the other for cleaning purposes. The temperature rose to unknown heights and it was no use looking for shade because there was none. Aden is not much of a civilization centre, but the crews were in high spirits when maintenance or repairs to their aircraft caused them to call on that place.'

In addition to the detachments to South Africa, Socotra Island and Masirah, there were others from China Bay to Madras, Cochin, and to the Maldive Islands. They were of shorter duration and smaller in number. As a rule, they did not comprise more than three Catalinas, and did not exceed one month from base.

On the night of 9 December, 'N' *Y-78* a PBY-5A, was airborne from Minneriya, an RAF base in Ceylon. It was scheduled for a reconnaissance of about eighteen hours and had a very full load. About thirty minutes after take-off, one of the engines failed while the aircraft was still at a low altitude. It thus became necessary for a forced landing to be made, and with a tail wind. To add to the difficulties, it was raining. Nevertheless the pilot was able to touch down without injury to any of the crew in the Bay of Bengal. All eleven boarded one of the two dinghies — the other was lost during landing. The Catalina sank about an hour later, the crew eventually reaching the coast fifty miles south of China Bay near Batticalca.

During 1943, the squadron had escorted 333 convoys, flown 5,110 operational hours and completed 2,551 hours on non-operational flights. The latter included several return trips from Ceylon to Australia including one undertaken by Lt G. R. Rijnders in *Y-57* to take Admiral Hellfrich on an inspection tour. For the return flight from Perth to Ceylon he covered 3,156 nautical miles in 28½ hours.

Another inspection tour was by the AOC of 222 Group, AVM Sir Alan Lees, who flew with the squadron's CO Cdr W. van Prooyen in their converted Catalina dubbed 'Sky Sleeper', visiting Bombay, Karachi, Masirah, Aden, Nairobi, Pretoria, Cape Town and Port Elizabeth.

One of 321's more experienced pilots was Thijs de Liefde. He began flying in 1937 and was posted to the Dutch East Indies which he left in August 1941 to join 320 Squadron, where he was involved in Hudson shipping strikes.

The contrast in operating conditions is indicated in his letters: 'The Cats were used operationally for A/S patrols in the Gulf of Bengal, also for convoy duties between Karachi, Bombay and Colombo, Madras and Calcutta. These jobs were not dangerous with regard to flak or fighters. The main "enemy" was the extreme bad weather one could encounter in the Bay of Bengal, or in the SW Monsoon in the Arabian Sea between Karachi and Bombay. No decent weather forecasts whatever.

'The other enemy was fatigue, as the Cat could fly fully loaded with DCs for more than

24 hours, with extra tanks built in, but a take-off for miles. The engines were marvellous, they never failed. The PBY was an easy one to fly. The longest patrol I made was 22 hours in the Gulf of Bengal. I had never before seen so much lightning and rain.'

De Liefde, on a trip to the Cocos Islands from Trincomalee, found the weather clear on the way out and DR navigation was used, 'flying the wind triangle every hour' with sunshots taken through the blister. A radio beacon was picked up a few hundred miles from the Cocos Islands. It was different on the return flight as there was no weather forecast and conditions deteriorated rapidly with heavy rain storms so that good DR navigation proved impossible. Bad visibility prevented sunshots during the day and star shots during the night. Added to these problems, the beacon at Trincolamee was u/s. Ultimately, bearings obtained from Bangalore and Madras showed them to be a long way off course and they touched down with very little fuel left.

In 1944, 321 Squadron provided escorts to 233 convoys, flew 194 anti-submarine patrols, and undertook 32 searches for enemy submarines. Their role became increasingly one of air-sea-rescue, giving cover for both RAF and American AAF operations, in addition to directing rescues of merchant seamen who had been torpedoed.

As early as 1943, 321 Squadron had requested Liberator aircraft and in October 1944 received six B-24s which proved to be incomplete in equipment. Partly due to the condition of the Liberators and the need to train crews, it was not until July 1945 that Lt Cdr de Bruijn led a detachment of Liberators to the Cocos Islands.

Cdr W. van Prooyen was relieved by Cdr H. Schaper as CO of 321 Squadron in September and joined the Naval staff in Batavia. The Liberator detachment which had been on shipping strikes to Sumatra and Java until the end of the war, returned to Java in March 1946.

When the war was over, Cdr de Bruijn was sent to Calcutta to take the Governor General of the NEI and also General ter Poorten back to the Netherlands. The latter had become a prisoner of the Japanese on surrendering to them at Tjilatjap on 8 March 1942.

After this trip, Cdr de Bruijn returned to Batavia and later to Surabaya, where he became CO of the Dutch Marine Vliegkamp, Morokrembangan until the middle of 1947.

No 321 Squadron returned to the Dutch East Indies in 1946 and was designated Eastern Reconnaissance and Transport Squadron. No 7 Squadron, which was formed on 23 December 1949, left for Dutch New Guinea with six Catalinas. On 1 February 1951 No 7 became 321 Squadron and continued operations in New Guinea.

Of six amphibians which had been flown from USA to Valkenburg in the Netherlands in 1951, two were used for training and ASR operations.

In 1958 on Biak Island off the Dutch New Guinea coast, Catalina Y-79 321/0 was left to serve as a monument to the Royal Netherlands Naval Air Service.

A restored PB2B-1 Bureau No 46521 is on display at the Military Aviation Museum, Soesterberg, Holland.

The Dutch Catalina with markings 18-215. This PBY-5A 46883 was received at Valkenburg on 27 April 1951 and scrapped at Biak on 14 June 1956.

Chapter 12
Canadian Squadrons

During the Second World War thirteen squadrons of the RCAF were equipped with Catalinas or Cansos, and after the war such aircraft continued to be operated by eight RCAF squadrons.

At the outbreak of war in September 1939, Squadrons 4, 5, 6 and 120 were mobilized. Initially these units operated out-dated machines such as Supermarine flying boats, Blackburn Sharks and Tiger Moths. In the summer of 1941, the two auxiliary squadrons 116 and 117 were re-formed; 117 was equipped with Stranraer flying boats, but 116 was probably one of the first units to obtain Catalinas, which it received in July.

Following the Japanese attack on Pearl Harbor on 7 December, two more maritime squadrons were brought into service; they were No 7 equipped with Blackburn Sharks, and No 9 operating Stranraer flying boats.

Two overseas squadrons were formed and were initially at Coastal Command, RAF bases. They were 413, formed at Stranraer on Loch Ryan in Scotland during July 1941 and, in the following April, 422. No 422 was on Lough Erne in Northern Ireland using Saro-Lerwick flying boats on a non-operational basis, but it received Catalinas in July 1942.

No 162 Squadron formed at Yarmouth, Nova Scotia, on 19 May 1942, was to prove exceptional in more ways than one. It was equipped with the Canadian version of the Catalina amphibian — 'Canso A' — and was later seconded to Coastal Command, RAF.

In late April/early May 1943, when the anti-U-boat war in the Battle of the Atlantic was reaching its peak, two more maritime squadrons became operational, 161 at Dartmouth, Nova Scotia, and 160 at Vancouver.

1939-45 Western Command reconnaissance

For the Canadian home defences, there was the western coastline to the patrolled with surveillance of all shipping movements; these operations became increasingly important following Japan's entry into the war. Canada was acutely aware of the constant threat posed by German U-boats in the Battle of the Atlantic, and this threat was enhanced by the Allied decision to use Halifax, Nova Scotia, as a terminus and assembly port for vital trans-atlantic convoys.

When No 4 Squadron RCAF was redesignated No 4 (BR) Squadron in October 1939, it was based at Jericho Beach, British Columbia, and equipped with Canadian Vickers Vedettes and Supermarine Stranraers. It received Canso As in December 1942 and some Catalinas from April 1944. The squadron moved to Ucluelet, BC, in May 1940 but also used Coal Harbour and Tofino. It was from Tofino that Canso *A11016* completed the unit's last sortie on 31 July 1945. It was disbanded on 7 August following anti-submarine duties off Canada's west coast.

In April 1943, four squadrons of the RCAF's Western Command received Canso amphibians; they were Nos 6, 7, and 9 with the auxiliary squadron No 120. All four were based in British Columbia, with No 6 at Alliford Bay, No 7 at Prince Rupert, No 9 at Bella Bella and No 120 at Coal Harbour.

What must have been typical of their operation is shown in the log book of a pilot with No 7 Squadron. His operational flights were in Cansos lasting up to about thirteen hours on anti-submarine patrols. This pilot, McGregor Knight, had completed his training with David Hornell at No 31 GR School. They became friends, and as McGregor Knight states: 'Our common bond was over air-sickness . . . at one time we both thought that we might have to give up flying.'

Don Dickson was one of many Canadians who trained as observers. Their instruction covered the dual role of navigation and bomb-aiming. After completing about 100 hours' flying on navigation exercises, he had six weeks at a Bombing and Gunnery School. This was followed by a month largely devoted to astro navigation with the use of a bubble sextant. After two years as an instructor he was posted to No 6 (BR) Squadron in Western Command when the squadron was deployed at Alliford Bay in the Queen Charlotte Islands. At that time they had just one Stanraer flying boat reserved for pilot training in water take-offs and landings.

No 6 Squadron moved to Coal Harbour on the northern tip of Vancouver Island in April 1944 and at about that time they were receiving Consolidated Canso As. Don Dickson however, recalls that Catalina flying boats were generally used for operational patrols. He gives the following account:

'A typical patrol was to fly a given course out over the Pacific, usually south-westerly for a given distance or a given time, and our assignment was to locate, intercept, and challenge any shipping that happened to be in the area. The ships were required to show flags for the signal of the day, which we would verify and take photographs. Our crews consisted of eight men; two pilots, three W/AGs, two flight engineers, and one navigator. One of the W/AGs looked after the radar which was only ASV, but quite useful in pin-pointing positions on our way home, as there were a number of radar beacons along the coast which could be picked up within fifty miles or so.

'Our patrol duration was normally from twelve to eighteen hours but the weather was generally atrocious and we rarely came to complete our assignments. With heavy overcasts and lots of rain we generally would fly at an average of 300ft altitude — we had cause for celebration when the ceiling ever got to be 1,000ft. As the only navigator in our crew, I was usually busy checking drifts and wind speeds — overcast meant no astro and our radio compasses were not powerful enough to pick up transmissions beyond 100 or 200

miles, and often times we would be over 1,000 miles out in the Pacific.

'I took drifts with a drift recorder, and of course, with the help of white caps, of which there were always plenty. I would also get the pilot to fly a vector triangle to check myself, but I found that if I checked the wind every 15 minutes I could keep pretty close check on position and generally make a landfall within ten miles when we got back to the coast. The radar beacons proved very helpful too, and it was always a relief to get a radar fix when we got close enough to the coast — particularly after twelve or fifteen hours of flying over nothing but water.

'We had both gas and electric ranges on board and the flight engineers were our cooks. We were always allowed to draw steaks as our rations, so the one good thing about having to fly was that you were going to be well fed.

'Aside from that though, it was generally rather frustrating, the weather was always against you and we really could not see that we were playing any great part in the war. It was something that had to be done, but to a man, I think we all felt that the risks were too great for the accomplishment. The Japanese did occasionally throw a few shells into the west coast but I don't think any of the squadrons on the coast ever saw them, or had a chance to do anything about it.'

The last sortie flown by No 6 Squadron was with Catalina *FP290* captained by F/O Erickson on 1 August 1945 from Coal Harbour. The squadron was disbanded on 7 August.

Canadian Eastern Command

No 5 Squadron RCAF received its first Catalinas in June 1941, at which time it was based at

Amphibians of No 5 Sqdn RCAF at Dartmouth, Nova Scotia.

Dartmouth, Nova Scotia, with Stranraer flying boats. In October some Canso As came into service. From 2 November 1942 until 9 May 1943 the squadron was operating from Gander, Newfoundland, and it was from there that one of their aircraft claimed their first kill. This was a Canso A *9747 W* which was captained by Sqn Ldr B. H. Moffit who, while on a convoy escort, attacked and sank *U-630* in position 56°38'N 42°32'W on 4 May 1943.

The auxiliary squadron, No 116, followed No 5 in July 1941, being equipped with Catalinas and Canso As in September, using bases in Nova Scotia and Newfoundland. No 116 provided a nucleus of crews and aircraft for the reactivation of No 117 Auxiliary Squadron at Sydney, Nova Scotia, on 28 April 1942. Initially, 117 flew Canso As, but in March 1943 it also received Catalinas, and operated both types until August 1943 in the region of the Gulf of St Lawrence and Cape Breton Island on anti-submarine missions.

After a short time with Canso As in Western Command, No 160 Squadron moved to Yarmouth, Nova Scotia, with Eastern Command from July 1943. In August 1944, the squadron moved to Torbay, Newfoundland, but continued to operate Canso As until June 1945.

No 161 Squadron, which was formed at Dartmouth in April 1943, used Douglas Rigby aircraft initially, but received Canso As in October. It came under No 5 (Gulf) Group the following year, but operated again under Western Command from Yarmouth during the period November '44-May '45, with a detachment at Sydney, Nova Scotia.

Another Eastern Command squadron — No 162 — gained its distinguished record while serving under RAF's Coastal Command, and its successes are recounted in the following pages.

No 162 Squadron RCAF with Coastal Command

No 162 Squadron was formed at Yarmouth, Nova Scotia, on 19 May 1942 and was equipped with Canso As. They were deployed initially on anti-submarine patrols off the east coast of Canada, but in January 1944 they were loaned to Coastal Command, RAF. To cover the mid-section of the Atlantic they were stationed in Iceland.

With the invasion of western Europe by the Allies in June 1944, No 162 (as also the Norwegian squadron No 333), was deployed to cover the north-west approaches to prevent the break-out of German U-boats into the Atlantic by that route.

While under the control of AHQ Iceland, Canso S *9767* captained by F/O T. C. Cooke sank *U-342* in position 60°23'N 29°20'W. This was during a sortie covering a convoy on 17 April.

In June, however, while with a detachment at Wick, 162 Squadron achieved a record which must be unique. Between the 3rd and the 30th they sank four U-boats and shared a fifth with 86 Squadron.

At 02:11hr on 3 June, Flt Lt R. E. McBride was flying 'T' *9816* at 1,700ft on a course of 180°, when he sighted a U-boat four miles away. The vessel was heading north at 15kt. McBride reduced height and at 1,000yd range his front gunner opened fire, scoring hits on the conning tower of the U-boat. The vessel altered course, but the Catalina continued down and attacked with four depth charges up track at 60ft. The U-boat was straddled and completely enveloped in plumes. About 15 seconds later, the Catalina crew saw the vessel lift bodily, swinging to port and losing all forward movement before submerging. At least five survivors were seen in the water. In less than four hours a small patch of oil had spread to a mile long by 400yd wide.

U-477 had been sunk in position 63°59'N 01°37'E.

The sinking of *U-980*

F/O L. Sherman was captain of Canso 'B' *9842* which was one of three aircraft from 162 Squadron operating on 11 June. The sky was overcast with slight occasional drizzle. At 15:15hr Sherman was off south-west Norway patrolling the north-west transit area when a surfaced U-boat was sighted on the starboard bow. Sherman lost height from 1,000ft and as he turned to starboard his gunners opened fire at 800yd range. The vessel responded with light but accurate AA fire, but seven minutes later the Canso released four depth charges from 50ft while tracking over the U-boat from port quarter to starboard bow. They straddled the vessel — two were seen on the port side, while one fell midway between bow and conning tower.

The vessel continued to circle but at slow speed and it was lower in the water with a spreading oil trail. There was a short gun duel before the U-boat sank, leaving about 35 survivors on the surface in position 63°07'N 00°26'E.

Two days later F/O Sherman in the same aircraft sent a flash report from position 64°10'N 00°11'W of attacking another U-boat, but nothing more was heard and he was reported missing. On the 19th, notification of the award of a DFC to Sherman was announced.

1944 The demise of Canso *9816* and *U-715*

Canso *9816* was on a north transit area patrol east of the Faeroes on 13 June. At 10:12 hours the aircraft was being flown by Wg Cdr G. C. Y. Chapman at about 750ft when the feathers produced by two periscopes from one vessel were sighted three miles away. Chapman lost height to 50ft and attacked with four depth charges from 30° to starboard of the submarine. Three depth charges were seen to explode and, after twenty seconds, the U-boat surfaced turning from a westerly to a northerly course. Chapman circled at 1,000ft from two to three miles distant.

After travelling about 400yd, the U-boat stopped and began to settle at the bows, the conning tower disappeared and the stern rose to show motionless screws. Many of the vessel's crew were in the water.

While making a run over the U-boat to take photographs, the Canso suffered AA damage to its port engine, which lost much oil and belched smoke. The propeller could not be feathered and altitude could not be maintained; the aircraft hit the waves at 45kt. With large shell holes in the hull, the amphibian sank within twenty minutes.

None of the Canso crew had been wounded, but they found that one dinghy had two holes in it and the other dinghy exploded. Only two of the eight in the crew managed to board the holed dinghy — the others clung to the sides.

After first a Liberator then a Sunderland had arrived and disappeared, a Warwick made two runs and dropped an airborne lifeboat

A Canso A of No 7 Sqdn RCAF in December 1943.

which fell downwind over 100yd away. The navigator, P/O Waterbury, stripped, and keeping only his Mae West, swam out and after more than an hour brought the lifeboat to the survivors. Meanwhile, flight engineer Flt Sgt H. C. Leatherdale lost his hold and was gone. The seven now boarded the lifeboat and placed the dinghy in its centre as the lifeboat was damaged. Another Warwick now dropped Lindholme gear, and the Canadians managed to recover one section but it was damaged, while the other section drifted away.

Two of the wireless operators, F. K. Reed and G. F. Staples, were now suffering from exposure, sitting on the floor of the lifeboat in sodden suits with water up to their armpits.

When an air-sea-rescue launch arrived, all seven were taken aboard. Artificial respiration was given to Reed and Staples, but it was too late. Five from the crew of eight were landed at Lerwick and taken to the Military Hospital. Canso 'T' was credited with sinking *U-715* in position 62°45'N 01°69'W; on the 18th the squadron was notified of the award of the DSO to Wg Cdr Chapman.

David Hornell, VC

Of the six aircraft from 162 Squadron airborne on operations on 24 June, one was Canso A *9754*, captained by Flt Lt D. E. Hornell. At 19:00hr he was north of the Shetlands on an anti-submarine sweep when a fully surfaced U-boat was sighted. Hornell closed the range and at three-quarters of a mile, the vessel opened up with accurate AA fire. At 800yd the starboard engine was hit and, although the propeller was feathered, the engine fell off.

Hornell continued with his attack and straddled the U-boat with depth charges. He was however, unable to maintain altitude and ditched the Canso about a mile from the U-boat's position.

By chance, a Catalina from the Norwegian 333 Squadron, captained by Carl Krafft, sighted both the survivors from the U-boat and the Canadians from the Canso, and sent a radio report to Group HQ[1].

Hornell and his crew managed to get into their aircraft dinghy which was circled by the Norwegian Catalina for many hours. By the time an ASR launch arrived, the two flight engineers, Sgts R. G. Scott and F. St Laurent had died from exposure, and the navigator, F/O S. E. Matheson, was suffering from a shrapnel wound to his head. David Hornell died shortly after the arrival of the launch and his body was taken to Lerwick for burial.

The survivors — co-pilot F/Os B. C. Denomy, Matheson, and wireless operators F/O G. Campbell, Flt Sgt I. J. Bodnoff and Flt Sgt S. R. Cole — were taken to the Naval hospital in Lerwick suffering from eighteen hours' exposure[2].

The submarine U-1225 had been sunk on 24 June in position 63°00′N 00°50′W. Flt Lt Hornell was awarded the first VC of the RCAF during the war for 'inspiring leadership, valour and devotion to duty'. Against an entry for the sinking of U-1225 in Coastal Command's War Record is the terse remark: 'Posthumous VC'.

No 162 Squadron RCAF

By the end of June the bar stock in 162 Squadron's Officers' Mess was becoming depleted — understandably so! In that one month they had sunk four U-boats and were to share the sinking of a fifth with 86 Squadron.

The 30th was bright and clear with scattered clouds at Reykjavik when Canso A 9841 took off to patrol the north transit area, north of the Shetland Isles. Captained by Flt Lt R. E. McBride, the crew sighted a U-boat which submerged before an attack could be attempted. Later in the day, following a second sighting, McBride's depth charges hung up during his attack. The RCAF official history however, states that U-478 was damaged in position 63°27′N 00°50′W. Liberator 'E' of No 86 Squadron was homed on to the scene by the Canso, and the U-boat, U-478, was sunk by the Liberator.

By early August, crews were flying up to seventeen hours on patrol, having eight hours rest and then being required to fly again. Ground staff had the problem of maintaining aircraft with some on detachment at Wick. Nevertheless, on 4 August, ten aircraft were airborne on operations. One of these, captained by F/O W. Marshall, attacked a U-boat. Another aircraft flown by F/O C. H. Leech homed on to the scene. The action by 162 Squadron resulted in such serious damage to U-300 that it had to return to base[3].

The exceptional record of the squadron was endorsed by a visit to their base by the AOC together with the Under-Secretary of State for Air on 5 August. On this same day, a Liberator arrived with 8,000lb freight from Canada and, as passenger, the Personnel Counsellor, Flt Lt R. D. McLeod of Eastern Air Command. Their other links with Canada were maintained by ferry flights of Cansos.

No 162's last sortie was by Canso 11074, captained by F/O R. J. Mills from Iceland on 31 May 1945.

They had lost nine aircraft, six of these on operations, with seventeen men killed and seventeen missing; eight had been killed on non-operational flying. In June the squadron was with Canada's Eastern Air Command again until 7 August 1945.

The sighting of the Japanese Fleet SSE of Ceylon

On 3 March 1942, 413 Squadron was based at Sullom Voe in the Shetland Isles, but between the 4th and the 29th personnel and aircraft were en route to Ceylon. Four of their machines arrived on 2-4 April.

At this stage in the Far East war, the Japanese had gained control of the East Indies, Malaya, Siam, and Southern Burma with the fall of Rangoon. Ceylon and India now threatened, and on 28 March Admiral Sommerville received an intelligence report of the enemy's intention to attack Ceylon about 1 April. The enemy intended deploying two fleets — one major force to engage and destroy the British fleet, while a second naval force would be free to attack merchant shipping in the Bay of Bengal and the Indian Ocean.

When Admiral Somerville, C-in-C Eastern Fleet, received intelligence of the imminent attack on Ceylon, he learned that the enemy forces were greatly superior to those available to him. The British fleet was deployed at Addu Atoll in the Maldive Islands about 600 miles south of Colombo, from where Somerville planned to launch night attacks by carrier-borne aircraft. His success depended on accurate reporting of enemy movements, and in this, the Catalinas played a crucial role.

Four of 413 Squadron's aircraft arrived at Koggala at about this time captained by Wg Cdr J. L. Plant, Sqn Ldr L. J. Birchall[4] and Flt Lts R. G. Thomas, DFC, and O. G. Roberts. Thomas arrived on 28 March, Birchall on 2 April.

Thomas flew a patrol south-east of Ceylon on the night of 2-3 April for more than seven hours, but sighted nothing.

A change in an aircrew flying detail often proved fateful — and there was no exception for Sqn Ldr Birchall. Instead of flying to the Royal Navy's secret base in the Maldives, at about midnight on the 3rd he was asked to undertake a reconnaissance and agreed.

Birchall was airborne in Catalina AJ155 at 00:52hr on 4 April in search of the Japanese fleet. This hunt was to be in the form of a cross-over patrol 250 miles south-east of Ceylon, and flown at about 2,000ft. His crew comprised another Canadian — W/O G. C. Onyette — and seven RAF aircrew. Reaching the patrol area at first light they found a clear sky, with not a scrap of cloud cover. With overload tanks in the cabin, the Catalina's endurance could be increased to 32 hours, and it was with the rise of the moon that they came to their final cross-over.

The navigator obtained a fix and, just as they were on the final leg and about to make a turn for base, something was sighted on the south horizon. There was only just time to identify the enemy and send a sighting report, before AJ155 was attacked by fighters.

Without cloud cover there was just no chance for a Catalina. A shell exploded putting the radio out of action, fuel tanks were holed, and flaming petrol poured into the cabin. Two of the gunners were severely wounded and, as Birchall made for sea level, Mae Wests were put on the two wounded men.

The aircraft had even in the air begun to break up; on reaching the sea, those who could attempted to swim away and avoid the strafing by the Japanese fighters. Eventually they were picked up by the destroyer Isokaze[5]. There were now six survivors out of the crew of nine, and three of these were badly

Canso A, possibly 'G' 9773 of No 5 Sqdn RCAF at Dartmouth, Nova Scotia.

wounded by shells and bullets. Birchall, being the senior officer, was beaten. The six were then put in a paint locker in the forecastle with little ventilation, room for three to lie down, and no medical treatment whatsoever. It was not until the 7th that they were let out of the paint locker and taken to the aircraft carrier *Akagi*[6], where treatment was slightly less inhumane.

The aftermath of the Birchall sighting

Following the sighting report transmitted by Birchall's Catalina just before it was shot down, Admiral Layton, who was responsible for the defence of Ceylon, had harbours evacuated of all shipping. Naval units in Ceylon included the cruisers *Dorsetshire* and *Cornwall* at Colombo, with the carrier *Hermes* at Trincomalee.

Carrier-borne aircraft[7] attacked Colombo at 08:00hr on 5 April and were countered by Hurricanes and Fulmars. By 09:30hr the raid was over. The Allies lost nineteen fighters and six Swordfish of the FAA which had made an untimely arrival during the raid. The Japanese losses (see Roskill) were seven aircraft.

In the afternoon, the two cruisers which had sailed on the 4th to rendezvous with the main British fleet were attacked by carrier aircraft east of the Maldives, and sank in about fifteen minutes; 1,222 survivors were picked up on the 6th.

Admiral Somerville was warned by Layton of the greatly superior enemy fleet and, on 8 April, the British fleet was at Addu Atoll having escaped what in Churchill's opinion would have been a disastrous action[8]. A patrolling Catalina captained by Flt Lt Thomas reported on the 9th sighting the Japanese fleet before being shot down — there were no survivors. By then enemy aircraft were approaching Trincomalee. Twenty-two British fighters were deployed against 120 aircraft of the Japanese: the enemy lost ten, the British nine. Just over an hour after this raid, the carrier *Hermes* was sunk together with four ships.

The other Japanese naval force under Admiral Ozawa had free rein in the Bay of Bengal, attacking unescorted merchant vessels and sinking 23 in five days. Churchill sums up the shipping losses resulting from attacks by both

Japanese fleets as nearly 116,000 tons. Thereafter the enemy directed his attentions to the American fleets.

By this time, lone Catalinas with their vigilant crews had twice demonstrated the crucial part they could play in the war; first in May 1941 it was *AH545* of the RAF captained by P/O Dennis Briggs sighting *Bismarck*; Sqn Ldr Birchall in *AJ155* with the RCAF had become 'The Saviour of Ceylon'; and Jack Reid a month later was to represent the USN at Midway in this distinguished triad.

Writing in retrospect of the two sightings made in April 1942, Lawson Randall[9] says: 'Given little or no publicity, was the loss of Flight Lieutenant Rae Thomas and crew . . . in the opinion of many officers Thomas, a South African in the RAF, but an original 413 Squadron captain, was our most skilful pilot, and most experienced captain. Birchall and Thomas and their crews — half of our squadron strength in Ceylon at the time — was a tremendous loss.'

Randall had joined 413 at Stranraer, and served continuously from the time it formed, on 1 July 1941, until September 1944, first as captain of aircraft then as Flight Commander, and from 21 June 1943 when he relieved Wg Cdr J. C. Scott he was Squadron Commander until 14 September 1944, to be relieved in turn by Wg Cdr S. R. McMillan.

From 9 April until 25 May 1942, the squadron had only two Catalinas and crews. On the 25th four more aircraft were flown in by Randall, Scott, Flt Lt R. J. Furzman and W/O D. S. Martin. Ground staff which had embarked in *Nieuw Holland* at Liverpool on 17 March arrived on 29 May at Colombo.

The 'Tusker' Squadron in the Far East

Madagascar was another part of the world controlled by the notorious Vichy French, and with the lack of Allied surface escorts for shipping Catalina detachments were made by 413 Squadron to Mombasa and the Seychelles, with Scott at Mombasa from June to August, and Flt Lt Fursman in the Seychelles from June until 7 July 1942.

John Gowans was one of many Catalina pilots who, after completing a captain's course at Killadeas in Northern Ireland, was posted to a Ferry Training Unit. Subsequently he took command of Catalina *FP282* at Beaumaris and on 25 March 1943 was posted to 413 Squadron. The flight to Ceylon terminated on 20 April at Koggala with a total flying time of 86 hours. En route it was necessary to fly south, avoiding the Tunisian war zone.

His first trip was on 26 April down to the Malacca Straits on what was to become a 'milk run' — an anti-Japanese invasion patrol which on this occasion was a 20½ hour flight. As he remarks, he 'picked up high-flying experience in the monsoon weather'.

With an operational tour of 1,000 hours, and varying operational requirements, there were times when there was little respite from flying, with missions clustered into a few days. The sorties included ship detector patrols, convoy escort, anti-submarine, and search-and-rescue after a sinking had occurred, in addition to non-operational training.

On 3 November, Gowans was detailed for a night convoy escort with P/O Armstrong as second pilot in Catalina 'Y' *FP282*; this was for a convoy en route to Bombay in the nine degree channel. On reaching the convoy flying at 2,000ft he was ordered by the Senior Naval Officer (SNO) to give extra cover to a ship having engine trouble and straggling behind the convoy.

As Gowans recalls: 'We had the old Mark 1 ASV, time-base-line radar, and decided we should practise reading blips as we went astern of the convoy. We varied the time of our patrols as we knew that enemy subs timed them. After some runs the W/Op informed me there were two blips instead of one, astern of the main convoy.

'We headed down moon and found the sub full on the surface closing on the ship. We turned in on the sub and went to 100ft. On nearing the sub heavy gunfire was seen directed towards us, but as we got nearer, the sub veered to the right out of the moon's wake and we lost sight of it. I turned around the left to come in again when heavy fire struck the tail section.

'As we proceeded astern again, my rigger Sgt Lynam from the blister swept tracer across the point of origin of the enemy's tracer. It stopped their fire. We attacked again from 50ft or less. I thought we would strike the conning tower, for the altimeter was registering below zero. The pressure had changed.

No 31 GR School, RCAF class 19, December 1941. David Hornell, the first RCAF VC of WW2 is in the front row, 4th from left.

There was fire at times as we approached. My crew said the depth charges had straddled the sub, but of course that then became the dark side of the sky and, at night, vision was now difficult. We dropped a flare but could not see anything. It would have been good to have dropped two deep setting depth charges if the sub had been visible. We didn't know how damaged the tail section was. I flew around for a while before proceeding to the convoy to report by R/T to the SNO of the attack.

'We had sent out attack signals and had asked for relief. A Liberator was to have relieved us, but none arrived so we covered the convoy from the 10.30pm attack until morning and daylight landing at Cochin.

'There were small fire holes in the tail and some about 40mm in diameter. Cables were damaged. Our blister gun fired 0.5 calibre. The sub did not show again. The convoy did not realize it was endangered. It was tacky flying that low visually in a 30° half moon. I don't know why we weren't blasted out the first run in as fire was heavy and we were a large target at 100kt. I was advised it was a Jap sub but received nothing in writing about it.'

On touching down at Cochin, Gowans had completed 18¼ hours flying, 12 hours of those at night. After refuelling and debriefing, *FP282* returned to Koggala on 4 November.

The skill of the Catalina crew, exhibited by the radar operator, the gunner and the captain, is obvious. An apparently successful attack at night by an aircraft not equipped with a Leigh light and with early-type radar was a rarity. In

107

the November-December 1943 period[10], a number of Japanese submarines were listed as sunk by causes 'unknown'. John Gowans released two Torpex-filled depth charges with probably a 25ft setting. With a 'straddle' they should have at least damaged the submarine.

The *Jean Nicolet*

Don Wells was one of 413's Canadian pilots. He joined the RCAF in July 1941 and completed his training at No 1 GR School, Prince Edward Island, in December 1942. He embarked for Liverpool in the RMS *Queen Elizabeth* and, after a crossing of four days, was posted to Oban. He served as a 2nd pilot with 422 Squadron Sunderlands before undertaking a captain's course at Killadeas. In December 1943 he was back at Oban, but with 302 FTU, where he met his own crew. This newly formed crew was then instructed to ferry Catalina *FP159* out from Fort Matilda, Gourrock, to Karachi.

On arriving at Korangi Creek on the river south of Karachi, their aircraft *FP159* was taken away, the ferry crew split up and assigned individually to others and, now at Koggala, Ceylon, Don Wells became a 2nd pilot again for about ten trips with his new unit — 413 Squadron.

As he recalls: 'The following months were the most interesting time to be in Ceylon as we did some long trips to the island bases, were visited by Lord Louis Mountbatten, and saw the decline of the Japanese presence in the Indian Ocean.'

By 2 July 1944 he was again captain of a Catalina (*JX276*) when, as he writes: 'We were dispatched from Addu Atoll in 'Z' to do a submarine patrol in the area to the east. We took off just about dusk and after two hours into the patrol the radio operator picked up an SOS with a position perhaps 100 miles to the south. We altered course and about 30 minutes later saw a light on the horizon. The light brightened as we approached and eventually we came right up to the ship which was afire from end to end.

'Thinking about submarines we started an expanding square search around the ship. About an hour later, when on a westerly leg, we had a near radar blip, indicating that a submarine had surfaced.

'We were too near to dive in time but dropped a flare from 800ft. One crewman in a blister said he thought he saw a sub, but I did not see it. In any case the blip did not reappear and we continued to search.

'When the dawn came, we could see the pillar of smoke from the ship which was about seventy miles away. We arrived back just in time to see the hulk turn over and sink. There were quite a number of survivors in the water, some on rafts but many clinging to debris. There were no lifeboats.

'We had of course, radioed the position asking for help and we knew that one or more aircraft were on the way. The sea was too heavy for a landing but we dropped our Mae Wests, dinghies and emergency rations. We were also informed that the Navy was sending a sloop and, as our fuel was getting dangerously low, we turned for home as soon as a relief aircraft appeared.

'A few days later some of us went to visit the survivors at a makeshift hospital across the bay at Addu Atoll. The younger ones seemed to be recovering but the older chaps, those over forty, were in very poor shape. At one bed I was told a story that was right out of the *Boys' Own Annual*. This seaman swam back to the ship and climbed a davit rope in order to retrieve a life raft. The ship was burning and he had to run across the deck which was hot and his feet were bare. But he made it and after releasing the raft dove over the side again. His feet were now bandaged and he seemed quite chipper. He was an American from San Francisco about 19 years old.

'Some of the 23 survivors (out of a total of 103), talked about the submarine captain who spoke English and had lived in Brooklyn. This fact seemed to them positive proof of Japanese culpability. My strongest recollection of the sinking now is the sight and extent of the debris floating on the sea, scattered little sticks which I learned later were baseball bats.

'One sailor told me he had used one to discourage a shark. Our flying time on this sortie was sixteen hours exactly.'

Don Wells' navigator on that trip was Jack Campbell who had no difficulty in locating the stricken vessel, with as he says, 'very basic nav'.

Campbell's recollections are: 'As we

approached we saw tracer bullets and found out later that the sub had fired on the lifeboats. We actually saw the sub dive but were too far away and high to drop depth charges.

'It is an unforgettable sight to see a ship on fire from stem to stern. Going up-moon we could see survivors in the water but were not allowed to land.

'At first light a sailor went up the side of the ship and threw down some floats. We met him later in Colombo and I think his nickname was "The Goon". We could see sharks amongst the men but none was attacked. We dropped our dinghy and container of water. The ship suddenly rose on the stern and slipped quietly under the water.

'We heard later that, after the ship was struck, all the men got into the lifeboats. They were then ordered by the sub to approach it. When the first man climbed the ladder he was shot by a mess boy. Others had their hands tied, were taken behind the conning tower and struck over the head. It is said that one of the survivors swam with his hands tied until rescued 20 hours later.'

According to a published account, the ship sighted by Don Wells was the Liberty ship *Jean Nicolet* which, while bound for Bombay, was torpedoed by *I-8*. After *Jean Nicolet's* master — Capt F. E. Nillson — had given orders to abandon ship and the hundred crew were in lifeboats or on rafts, *I-8* surfaced and shelled the stricken vessel. The Americans were then ordered on to the deck of the Japanese submarine which then sank all the lifeboats and rafts.

Thereafter the surviviors were subjected to brutality and torture. A few took their chance with sharks as the lesser of two evils and jumped into the sea.

The same Japanese submarine, *I-8*, had earlier on 29 June sunk the P&O liner, *Nellore* with 341 on board. Survivors from *Nellore* were sighted by Flt Lt J. F. Irvine, RAF, resulting in 234 being saved.

I-8 was itself sunk on 31 March 1945 off Okinawa[11] by the USS *Morrison* and USS *Stockton*. Prof Morison's account gives the Commander of *I-8*, Tatsunosuke Ariizumi, as having massacred 98 survivors of the Dutch merchant vessel *Tjisalak* on 26 March 1944 and of committing suicide in August 1945[12].

While based at Koggala, Ceylon, 413 Squadron had detachments at Addu Atoll, the Seychelles, Mombasa, Bahrain, Langebaan and Aden. Squadron personnel returned to England during January and February 1945.

In the immediate post-war era, No 13 squadron was re-numbered 413. This squadron used some Canso As, in addition to other aircraft, from April 1947 until October 1950.

Canso *11087* in the camouflage employed by No 162 Sqdn RCAF during their service with Coastal Command, RAF.

Canadian detachment to Russia

No 422 Squadron was formed at Lough Erne, Northern Ireland, in April 1942, and until November its operational aircraft were Catalinas. From Lough Erne their sorties would have comprised escort and anti-submarine patrols over the North Atlantic.

At the end of August three of their Catalinas 'A', 'B' and 'C', *FP103*, *FP105* and *FP106* respectively, were scheduled to transport key personnel and spares for Hurricane aircraft from Sullom Voe in the Shetlands to Grasnya near Murmansk, and other personnel with equipment to Lahkta, Archangel. In addition to ferrying personnel and equipment to Russia, their duties included acting as escorts to convoys PQ18 and PQ14.

At that time, pilots and navigators on the squadron were largely Canadian, but there were some experienced British and Commonwealth pilots. The flight engineers and wireless electrical mechanics were mainly British.

For two who were involved in the Russian expedition — Keith Patience and Bill McEwen — it began on 27 August at Lough Erne. Patience, a New Zealander, was initially 3rd pilot to *FP105* captained by a Canadian, F/O J. W. Bellis, but was later 2nd pilot to a South African — Lt. H. N. Honey in *FP103*. McEwen became flight engineer on *FP103*, which took off from Lough Erne at 14:00hr on 27 August for Invergordon. Both the Group Captain and the Wing Commander saw them off, but it was not until they reached Invergordon that the final destination for the three Catalinas became known, when a packing case was seen marked 'SNSO Archangel'.

Due to bad weather, they were delayed at Invergordon, but were airborne for Sullom Voe on the 29th. From Sullom Voe the Catalinas took off on consecutive days with Sqn Ldr Hunter leading on the 30th in *FP103*, with Patience as 2nd pilot.

On the way they flew nearer to the Lofoten Islands than was wise, but rounded North Cape on a calm morning. Murmansk was found bombed and burned, but a Junkers 88 at an airfield put out by the Russians as a bait was recognized. They fired off the colours of the day before landing near a Russian destroyer, and were then guided down river to Grasnya where the aircraft was taken ashore. The flight had lasted 15hr 40min. W/O Limpert

in *FP106* followed on the 31st, flying direct to Lahkta, Archangel, and on 2 September F/O Bellis was airborne from Sullom Voe in *FP105*. The latter encountered violent magnetic disturbances en route and a front extending from the White Sea inland to Russian Lapland, so Bellis flew round the coast to Lake Lahkta, taking 21½ hours.

Because of enemy activity, Sqn Ldr Hunter also flew on to Lake Lahkta on 1 September. It was a beautiful area and deep in forest. They were quartered in a convalescent home and very well looked after. McEwen was given the opportunity of making two expeditions through the forest. These were in a truck to deliver papers and mail to Red Army units and he was accompanied by a pretty parachutist nurse. Russian Security took care, however, to keep RAF crews away from local people.

While McEwen was working on the aircraft one evening, three Russian officers offered to help him, apparently wanting to examine the radar equipment. However, McEwen had orders to keep them out of the Catalina and he had to refuse their kind offer!

The RAF crew were permitted to visit the city of Archangel travelling by train. It had been bombed the night before and was still burning. After visiting the Navy's headquarters the aircrew returned to their forest billet.

At 15:00hr on the 4th, *FP103* was airborne for a patrol over the White Sea. It was whiter than expected — the Catalina ran into a blinding snowstorm and the patrol was abandoned! Clear weather was found on return to Lake Lahkta; in fact it was such good weather that the crew bathed from the flying boat. On the following day they returned to Murmansk to refuel in preparation for the flight back to the Shetlands.

422 Squadron detachment — return from Russia

All three aircraft were airborne on 7 September between 16:00 and 19:00hr with 'A', 'B' and 'C' captained by Lt Honey, F/O Bellis and W/O Limpert respectively. As passengers were Lt Ryan, RN, in 'A' and the British Vice-Consul General to the USSR in 'C'.

W/O Limpert in 'C' *FP106* landed at Sullom Voe at 07:30 hours on the 8th, apparently

Canso *9750* of No 161 Sqdn RCAF which operated over the Gulf of St Lawrence on anti-submarine patrols with Cansos from October 1943 until May 1945.

without incident despite bad weather conditions, while F/O Bellis was diverted to Invergordon. But for *FP103*, captained by Lt Honey, the situation was very different.

When just north of the Shetlands, the Catalina ran into very severe rain squalls. Lt Honey tried to climb steadily through the weather and was able to reach 7,000ft. The crew were considering which base to make for — Sullom Voe, Invergordon or Castle Archdale. It was at this point that the aircraft went into a spin. It was pulled out, but then spun the other way.

McEwen was by then checking the dinghy and, on looking out at the wings, as he now writes, 'saw the ailerons blow up and lose their fabric'. The Catalina regained its natural stability and began flying straight and level. It hit the sea at high speed with the floats still retracted and ran ashore at Whalsey.

McEwen cleared one blister of the gun installed there while another crew member fired bursts from the other gun to attract attention. Crew members forward in the aircraft were able to walk ashore along one of the wings. McEwen was less fortunate — he was

pushed out on the seaward side and had to swim for it. When all were ashore, the crew were taken to a signal station and given rum and hot drinks. Later, an ASR launch took them to Sullom Voe.

In the Catalina on the return trip from Russia (see McEwen), were two passengers; one was a merchant navy captain said to have been torpedoed two or three times while with convoy PQ17. It was thought easier for him to return by aircraft!

The other passenger was a Russian diplomat who, not having been killed, was pleased to recommend the crew. Although no award was forthcoming, a letter of congratulation from the Air Minister at that time — Sir Archibald Sinclair — was received, but with a rider to the effect that it was not policy to accept what the diplomat had offered.

W/O Limpert had another trip to Grasnya on 15 September in *FP106* with a crew of only three, according to the squadron record which must surely be wrong. The British Vice-Consul was again a passenger.

While operating from Russia on the 17th, Limpert was tailed by a Dornier 18 for ten minutes; icing at 300ft was reported. On the 20th there was again icing at low altitude and a 75kt tail wind. Then on 22 September, Limpert landed at Grasnya during an air raid with bombs dropping around the Catalina during his approach.

W/O Limpert returned to Sullom Voe on the 24th in only 12¼ hours. He had as passengers Rear Adm Miles RN and Lt Cdr Palmer. His experiences were such as to be reported in *Coastal Command Review* No 7 of November 1942.

In November 1942, No 422 Squadron became based at Oban, Scotland, and their Catalinas were replaced with Short Sunderland flying boats, which they continued to operate until 1945.

1 See 162 Sqn operational record, p8.
2 *Ibid*.
3 RCAF official history credits F/O W. O. Marsh in Canso (ITON9759 'W'.
4 Air Cdre L. J. Birchall, OBE, DFC, CD, RCAF.
5 *Isokaze*, 1,900 tons, sunk by US carrier a/c 7.4.45, 31°N 128°E.
6 *Akagi*, 36,000 tons, sunk by US carrier a/c 4.6.42, 30°N 179°W.
7 SWR, Vol II, p26, gives 91 bombers & 36 fighters; WSC, Vol IV, p158, gives 'about 80 dive bombers'; Gillison, p496, '50+ bombers & about 35 Zeros'.
8 WSC, Vol IV, p158.
9 Gp Capt Lawson H. Randall, DFC, RCAF (Ret).
10 SWR, Vol III, Pt 1, p374 (I-39, I-21 & RO-38).
Author's Note: the type of altimeter used measured changes in atmospheric pressure and would normally be set at sea level before take-off, or for the barometric pressure of the base at which the aircraft was due to land. A change in barometric pressure during flight would result in a false reading for altitude.
11 25°29'N 128°35'E (ref SWR & Japanese Naval & Merchant Shipping Losses, p23).
12 SEM, Vol X p300.
For further references to these sinkings see SWR, Vol III, pt 2, pp205/6 and *Canadian Flying Operations in SE Asia*, p67.

Chapter 13
Pearl Harbor and the Japanese Advance

7 December 1941

'They have attacked us at Pearl Harbor. We are all in the same boat now.' (President Roosevelt to Churchill.[1])

By the end of July 1941 Russia was under attack by Germany. The Japanese, following a pact with Vichy-France, had occupied Indo-China. Allied fleets in the Pacific, while slightly numerically superior to the Japanese, were widely dispersed and, with many nations involved, were not a cohesive force.

Oahu in the Hawaiian Islands had six airfields on 7 December in addition to US Naval air bases at Pearl Harbor and Kaneohe. Neatly arranged around Ford Island in the harbour were 94 ships, including eight battleships of the US Navy. The latter were the main target of a Japanese task force led by six aircraft carriers supported by battleships, cruisers, destroyers, submarines, tankers and supply ships. The three aircraft carriers which the Americans had in the Pacific were at sea.

Admiral Richardson, C-in-C US Fleet, was opposed to deployment of the fleet at Pearl Harbor, but had been relieved of his command on 1 February. Admiral Stark, USN, had forecast a Japanese attack on the Netherlands East Indies as a result of the American oil embargo and, on 27 November, sent a 'war warning' anticipating Japanese attacks against the Philippines, Thai and Kra Peninsula, possibly Borneo, and General Marshall had warned Hawaii of a possible raid from the west.

The first indication of the raid came at 03:42hr when USS *Condor* sighted a periscope while on a routine patrol outside Pearl Harbor, and signalled USS *Ward*.

That morning seven Catalinas were airborne: four from VP-24 at Ford Island had left at 06:00hr on a refuelling exercise at Lahaina Roads between Molokai and Kuai; while three PBY-5s of VP-14 from Kaneohe were on a surveillance mission and armed with depth charges. One of the latter was Catalina *14-P-1* piloted by Ens William Tanner who at 06:33hr sighted a submarine and dropped flame floats to mark the position. USS *Ward* opened fire on the vessel, and both *Ward* and the Catalina released depth charges.

Air searches at that time were being undertaken west and south of Oahu, but the Japanese launched their air attacks from position 26°N 258°W about 275 miles from Pearl Harbor, after heading south from a northerly point — 31°N 158°W.

The first enemy bomb dropped at 07:55hr and at 07:58hr Cdr Logan Ramsey, the operations officer for Rear Adm P. M. L. Bellinger of Patrol Wing 2, broadcast from Ford Island, 'Air raid Pearl Harbor — this is no drill'.

Skilful and effective attacks were made by Japanese torpedo aircraft from between 40

The *Honolulu Star Bulletin* of 7 December 1941 announcing war with Japan.

and 100ft altitude, and these were followed by bombing and strafing aircraft. At Kaneohe, 27 Catalinas were destroyed and six damaged; but at Ford Island, four Catalinas were made airworthy shortly after the raids. Of the main enemy target — battleships — five were sunk but four of these were later recovered and returned to the fleet, together with three which had been damaged. Fuel dumps and other important shore installations had been left intact.

The success of the Japanese may be attributed to: a) surprise and lack of preparedness of the US Forces; b) the effective use of strike aircraft from carriers with highly trained crews; c) torpedoes which were designed for the task and had a high degree of reliability.

The aftermath

The United Kingdom declared war on Japan on 8 December. That evening HMS *Prince of Wales*, HMS *Repulse* and four destroyers sailed from Singapore, but without the intended air cover. The battleship and battle cruiser were sunk off Kuantan on the 10th as a result of Japanese air attacks: the maritime initiative in the Far East was now with the Japanese.

Churchill had been elated at America's entry into the war following Pearl Harbor. He was aware that the resources of America, Russia and the British Commonwealth assured the Allies of ultimate victory. The loss of HMS *Prince of Wales* and HMS *Repulse* was no less a shock, however.

While Allied governments had closely followed political moves, and service chiefs had been able to forecast military deployments, the efficiency of Japanese aircraft and air crews had been grossly underestimated. As Capt Roskill suggests[2], the Japanese may well have learned a lesson from the Fleet Air Arm's success at Taranto.

The key to the American defences in the Pacific (see Craven & Cate[3]) had been specifically Pearl Harbor, but the American military leaders considered that the Philippines could not be 'profitably defended' with the forces then available against Japanese attack. Nonetheless, on Luzon in the Philippines, the Army Air Force had a major air base at Clark Field plus eight other airfields. The US Navy

had bases at Olongapo and Cavite, also on Luzon.

As for Pearl Harbor, and later Midway, Catalinas of the US Navy were in the front line when the Philippines were attacked. Patrol Wing 10 had been formed in the Philippines in December 1940 from a nucleus of fourteen PBYs of VP-21 which had left Pearl Harbor on 21 September 1939.

In December 1941 Patwing 10 comprised VP-101 and VP-102, with the tenders *Childs, William B. Preston, Heron* and *Langley* (AVD-1, AVD-7, AVP-2, and AV-3 respectively).

The two squadrons under Lt Cdr J. V. Peterson and Lt Cdr E. T. Neale were equipped with 28 PBYs. Although their main base was Cavite, Luzon, at the time of the first Japanese attacks, both planes and tenders had been dispersed with some as far south as Davao on Mindanão with the tender *William B. Preston* under Lt Cdr E. Grant. Of the three or four planes with this tender, *101-P4* and *101-P-7* were destroyed at their moorings during an enemy dive-bombing attack.

The main Japanese thrust was at Luzon with heavy bombing raids on AAF bases such as Clark Field, where Japanese bombers were strongly supported by fighters. The Naval bases at Cavite and Nichols Field were systematically bombed on the 10th.

Following a sighting report from a Patwing 10 aircraft of an enemy force 250 miles off Luzon, a strike force of five VP-101 PBYs were homed in on to the enemy. A bombing attack was made, despite very heavy AA fire, and it is recorded that some damage was caused to a warship. Other PBYs armed with torpedoes near Cavite were caught in a raid, but two managed to take off and proceed on a search.

Olongapo where seven other PBYs were based, was attacked on 14 December and it was on this day that Patrol Wing 10 began withdrawing from the Philippines to operate from various bases, such as Balikpapan, Surabaya and Ambon. By 23 December ten PBYs were operational at Surabaya and four of these aircraft moved down to Ambon. From there a counter-attack was mounted.

In their drive south towards the Netherlands East Indies, the Japanese occupied the island of Jolo in the Sulu Archipelago between

Kaneohe 7 December 1941 with damaged PBYs in the foreground. Three PBYs were airborne during the raids on the Hawaiian Islands and escaped the bombing and strafing raids by Japanese aircraft.

Borneo and the Philippines. At that time the Japanese forces in the area would have included the 23rd Air flotilla of the 11th Fleet.

At about 23:00hr on 26 December, six Catalinas of Patrol Wing 10 were airborne from Ambon about 800 miles away to attack shipping of the enemy which must have arrived in Jolo only a day or so earlier. With an indicated cruising speed of 80kt, the formation of the PBY flight was ragged.

At 07:00hr on the 27th, the first section of the Catalina flight was 30 miles south of Jolo with the second section ten miles ahead. All suffered heavy and accurate AA fire from shore batteries until Japanese fighters moved in to engage the Catalinas.

Each of the PBY-4s was carrying three 500lb bombs and enough fuel for sixteen hours' flying. Their leader — Lt B. R. Hastings in *101-P-1* — was seen from *101-P-9* commanded by Ens E. L. Christman, to dive towards the vessels in Jolo harbour; *101-P-1* did not return to base.

The first fighter to attack *101-P-9* was shot down by one of the waist gunners. Christman went into a 60° dive at 200kt and released his bombs against a cruiser from 5,000ft. He was then attacked by another fighter in a running battle lasting twenty minutes. One cannon shell opened up a fuel tank and petrol poured into the flight engineer's section. Another shell exploded inside the aircraft near the radio and set fire to the plane. Two of the crew jumped by parachute and landed safely, followed by a third. Christman touched down with three others in the plane — Ens W. V. Gough, NAP D. D. Lurvey and a radio operator, R. L. Pettit.

The four swam towards an island although Pettit could not see as he had been seriously burned. Gough proved an able swimmer and went ahead in the hope of finding a boat. Christman and Lurvey were picked up by natives on 28 December, and Gough was rescued later.

Ultimately, survivors from Christman's aircraft with those from *101-P-6*, met at the Philippine Constabulary camp on the island of Siasi. The crew of another Catalina — *101-P-11* — were also rescued; two aircraft returned to base.

US Navy reinforcements to the South Pacific

By 15 January ABDA command had been formed. This comprised officers from American, British, Dutch and Australian forces, but under the overall command of General Sir Archibald Wavell. Within the command was a Patrol Aircraft division commanded by Capt F. D. Wagner, USN. The ABDA area included Burma, Malaya, Borneo, Sumatra, Java, Dutch New Guinea and Northern Australia. The adjacent Anzac area covered Papua, the Solomon Islands, Fiji Islands and the North Island of New Zealand.

On 11 January, VP-22 joined Patrol Wing 10 at Ambon, bringing twelve PBY-5s with them. They were the first aviation reinforcements of the US Navy from the Central Pacific to oppose the Japanese advance in the East Indies.

At this stage, the Japanese intention was to attack bases on the east coast of Borneo and to occupy Menado, Macassar and Kendari on Celebes. At the time VP-22 reached Ambon, the enemy was occupying Menado and Tarakan. High-level bombing sorties by the AAF B-17s were largely unsuccessful against the advance, while Patwing-10 PBYs made a strike against the Menado landings.

One of the Catalinas, *101-P-7* flown by Ens Jack L. Grayson, was attacked by fighters and forced down sixty miles south-east of Menado. All the crew made it to the dinghy and after five days went ashore on Magole Island. From there they were taken by natives to Sanana. Following a radio signal by the Dutch at Sanana, a VP-22 PBY came to pick them up on 20 January.

Lt D. G. Donaho[4] in *22-P-7* was one of those to arrive at Ambon in January. While making his approach he was attacked by Zero fighters. The Catalina caught fire, as also a second PBY accompanying him. Donaho was able to beach his aircraft, and the following day all the crews and aircraft moved to Surabaya in Java. The Japanese made air attacks against Ambon on the 23rd and it was taken on 31 January[5].

On 1 February six Catalinas became based on the small seaplane tender USS *Heron* (AVP-2) located in the Kai Islands west of New Guinea. Lt Richard S. Bull, while flying one of these aircraft (*22-P-6*) on reconnaissance in the Ambon area, radioed sighting a

Japanese force which included carriers, and then reported a fighter attack. It was learned later from the sole survivior, his co-pilot Ens Hargreaves, that he was shot down.

The CO of Squadron VP-22, Frank O'Beirne, in a letter dated 8 February, reported having two serviceable aircraft out of 12 brought out by VP-51. Two more were being repaired by the Dutch at Surabaya, one was on a reef, and the rest had either been destroyed or damaged beyond repair due to enemy action.

In his letter, Frank O'Beirne recorded contacting the tender *William B. Preston* at Kendari in Celebes with the object of establishing a base and, 'I arrived with the first two planes at Kendari just five minutes behind a Jap scout which may have seen us. Jimmie Grant had his ship so well hidden that even I could hardly find it. We decided Kendari was not very healthy . . . we stayed one night, started our patrol to the Molucca Sea area and retired south. Since then I've been in one place no longer than five days.'

Although based most of the time with the tender USS *William B. Preston*, he used also the tenders USS *Heron* and USS *Langley*. He reports six aircraft of VP-101 and VP-102 making a dawn attack on Japanese positions at Menado while operating from Ambon and with the loss of four or five out of six, although most of the crews were recovered.

Of the Catalinas, O'Beirne wrote: 'They are effective only for patrols in areas where the enemy do not have strong aerial concentrations. Even then, if any enemy planes are present, they cannot outrun or outfight the attackers. Power and speed limitations are almost non-existent.

'So far only 92 octane fuel is available, but we find that we can use 48 in safely, even so, without overheating or detonation. When we are attacked, only the stops hold you down. One PBY-4 was flown for one hour at 2,700rpm and 50in Hg manifold pressure in escaping from Cavite! . . . what that has done to the engines with 800 hours since overhaul; 200 hours since checks on spark plugs, etc!

'Plenty fail, sometimes at crucial moments, but they still patrol if they can stagger off — they may sound like threshing machines and pop all over the place while they take a couple of miles to get off in a 20kt wind, but they usually smooth out at cruising speeds. Fortunately there are only about five of these planes left. A few PBY-5s have been obtained from the Dutch, who dislike them now and scarcely fly them, to give us a total complement of almost a squadron, but all scattered out . . . everyone is enthusiastic about the performance of our 0.50 calibre guns in the blisters. They can be fired effectively in a 200kt power dive with the plane being slipped at the time. Jack Davis in 22-P-1 was doing just that while being attacked by a Zero fighter, and the waist gunner shot the fighter down on his second attack . . . At least three other fighters have been shot down by PBY gunners, but cloud cover is considered the best defence.

'At first the Japs did not strafe personnel who abandoned a shot-down boat; of late however, they have not been so punctilious.

'. . . We're rolling up time, 150-200 hours a month . . . the high command is realizing the extent of usefulness of the PBYs now, so there is little rash work ordered . . . The Japs probably will keep on pushing down this way. I look for more air attacks on every Allied base down to and including Darwin. Their planes are within striking distance in large numbers.'[6]

The battle of the Java Sea

Japanese bombing attacks began against Java on 3 February and, by the 11th, Patwing 10 was left with ten aircraft out of a total of 45 which included those of VP-101, VP-102 and five planes from the Dutch.

A series of enemy successes followed: Singapore capitulated on 15, Palembang on 16, Bali on 18 and Timor on 20 February.

On 26 February, Patwing 10 had three aircraft at Surabaya but none serviceable. Others had already reached Australia. At 18:30hr an Allied naval force of cruisers and destroyers sailed from Surabaya under the command of Admiral Doorman to counter a reported Japanese convoy. In the battle of the Java Sea which followed, the Allies lost five cruisers and six destroyers. It began at 16:16hr on the 27th and was effectively over by 22:50hr. Although it seemed as though the opposing forces were evenly matched, the Japanese had the advantage of critical air support; Admiral Doorman had a mixed force

with overworked crews who lacked the close integration enjoyed by the enemy. The Japanese lost just four transports.

On that same date, the seaplane tender USS *Langley* AV-3, a former carrier, was sunk 74 miles from Tjilatjap. She, with 32 AAF fighter aircraft on board, was one of two vessels taking in a total of 59 aircraft as reinforcements; planes from the other ship could not be landed.

Lt Gen Hein ter Poorten of the NEI Army commanded the ground forces for ABDA and his interest lay in defending Batavia. Japanese landings were made west of Surabaya on 1 March. The Dutch withdrew from Batavia on the 5th and it was taken by the Japanese, together with Bandung, on that day. On the 8th, Tjilatjap was captured and ter Poorten surrendered Java to the enemy; he had under his command about 38,000 Allied servicemen[7].

The surviving Catalinas of Patwing 10 had moved to Tjilatjap when enemy troops landed on the northern shore of Java. Some PBYs were flown back from Broome, Australia, to assist in the evacuation; the Wing's CO — Capt F. D. Wagner — had left on 2 March, on the last USN PBY to fly out.

Return flight, Australia to Corregidor

Following the withdrawal from Java, Catalinas operated by both the Dutch and US Navies suffered further attacks and losses in Australia. Patwing 10 was left with three

The blister positions of a USN PBY; drogues may be seen on the fuselage ready for deployment.

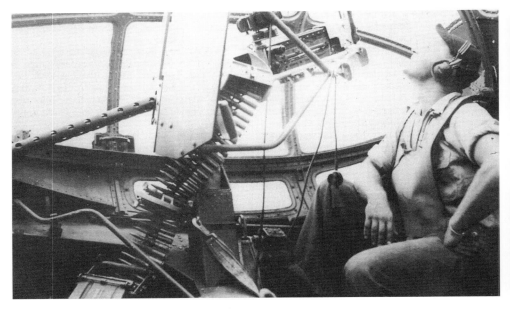

A blister position in a US Navy PBY armed with a ·5 calibre Browning.

PBYs, but continued to operate from Australia. Following a decision by President Roosevelt, Gen MacArthur was flown to Australia from the Philippines, having escaped from Corregidor by surface craft.

In April the remaining defenders of Corregidor were in need of supplies for their rearguard action. Two Catalinas of Patwing 10 were ordered to fly from Australia to the island of Corregidor, lying south of the Bataan peninsular on Luzon. The two pilots were Lt jg L. Deeds and Lt jg T. F. Pollock, who took off from Perth on the 27th and were refuelled by the tender *William B. Preston* at Shark Bay.

At Darwin, in addition to fuel, supplies were taken on board for the defenders of Corregidor. They were airborne again on the 28th, planning to reach Timor at night. En route, they skirted enemy bases at Kendari, Ambon, Menado and Davão; and, following pre-arranged recognition signals, touched down on Lake Lanão, Mindanão.

The Catalinas were hidden and camouflaged, then refuelled for take-off at 18:45hr. They touched down again off SE Corregidor in

an area which had been swept and with two lighted buoys set as markers: it proved to be Emperor Hirohito's birthday, and the enemy must have been less vigilant. Officers of Gen MacArthur's staff and Army nurses were taken on board — thirty passengers in one PBY, 25 in the second.

On its return to Lake Lanão, one of the Catalinas was damaged on a reef and, although the aircraft was patched up, some of the passengers had to be left behind. Both Catalinas returned safely to Australia; Lt Pollock in the damaged one on 3 May. On that day, 27 more passengers were taken from Corregidor by the submarine *Spearfish* which surfaced outside the minefield.

Corregidor was surrendered by Gen J. Wainwright on 6 May.

1 WSC, Vol III, p 538.
2 SWR, Vol 1, p5.
3 C&C, Vol 1, Chap 6.
4 Capt D. G. Donaho, USN (Ret), +c 1983 (see Capt L. Lampman, USN (Ret)).
5 DG. *RAAF 1939-42*, pp370, 374.
6 From the copy of a letter to C-in-C Pacific Fleet, March 1942 (courtesy of Adm J. S. Russell).
7 WSC, Vol IV, p133.

Chapter 14
Midway, Guadalcanal and the Bismarck Sea

Midway

Since the Hawaiian Islands represented in World War 2 by Midway Island and Pearl Harbor, lay approximately mid-way between Tokyo and San Francisco, they posed a potential threat to either Japan or America, depending upon the nationality of the occupying force. Similarly, to the north lay the Aleutian chain extending from Alaska, but here the potential bases were of limited value due to extremely harsh climatic conditions.

Admiral Nimitz at Pearl Harbor was aware on 15 May as C-in-C of the Pacific Area that intelligence indicated likely Japanese attacks against Midway and the Aleutians. His three aircraft carriers, *Yorktown* with Rear Adm Fletcher, and *Enterprise* and *Hornet* with Rear Adm R. A. Spruance, were by 2 June deployed north-east of Midway.

The Japanese fleets had sailed between 24 and 27 May; their Admiral, Yamamoto, intended sending a diversionary force to the Aleutians while directing his main forces to Midway. Yamamoto hoped that the Americans would be drawn to the Aleutians, allowing the main force to occupy Midway Island. The Japanese forces included four fleet carriers, *Akagi, Hiryu, Kaga* and *Soryu;* seven fast battleships, and other vessels. There were, in addition, 12 transports carrying about 5,000 troops.

At Midway there were aircraft of the 7th AAF and aircraft of the USN, including thirty Catalinas. Although correctly forecasting the intentions of the enemy, the American admirals needed to know the position of the Japanese fleet if they were to counter vastly superior forces.

Searches by Catalinas began from Midway in May with 22-24 aircraft deployed, each covering an arc of 8° and extending to the west for 700 miles.

One of the Catalina commanders on 3 June was Ens Jack Reid of VP-44, whose account is now given unchanged, at his request:

'Patrol squadron VP-44 arrived at Midway May 22 1942 and the crews were briefed on the possibility of the Japanese trying to take Midway Island during the first week of June. We had a twelve-plane squadron and started a pie-shape vector search to the west on the morning of 24 May to 700 miles. My crew and I flew almost every day for two weeks, approximately eleven hours each day, plus briefing and debriefing on each flight. For the first week we lived in the BOQ when we were not flying and then moved into dug-outs, which were very inadequate for rest and sleep after long flights. We were briefed that our primary objective was to spot and report the Japanese fleet without being seen. At no time were we told of the possibility of two Japanese fleets approaching Midway.

'As June 3 approached, we were very excited by the possibility of being the first to sight the enemy. During our search missions, I worked out a plan mentally, what I would do when we spotted the Japanese fleet, so I could make my report without being seen. I am not clairvoyant, but I had an intuition that my crew was going to spot the fleet on their approach to Midway.

'On June 3 we were briefed that the Japanese fleet was due to hit Midway on the 3rd or 4th. During our search mission on the 3rd we were excited about the prospect of sighting the enemy on this flight. Our patrol was uneventful the first 600 miles, however my radioman, Chief Musser, was guarding Midway radio frequency and listening to transmissions on another receiver of Japanese traffic. He told my navigator, Ensign Swan, "The Japanese ships using the low short range frequency are very close to our position". He suggested to my navigator that we should search an additional thirty miles with a good chance of spotting the Japanese fleet. With this information, my co-pilot and I kept a sharp lookout to the west.

'We were flying a heading of 270° at an altitude of 1,000ft, visibility was over thirty miles with a few scattered clouds. At the end of our 730-mile search, just before I was to turn to a north heading, I spotted what at first appeared as specks on the horizon or dirty spots on the windshield. After a second look, I shouted "Enemy ships thirty miles dead ahead".

'My co-pilot, Ensign Hardeman, snatched the binoculars and after looking shouted, "You are damned right, they are enemy ships". I immediately dove the airplane to a low level skimming the whitecaps and turn to a north heading.

'I did not try to ascertain the number or type of ships. There were three columns of ships steaming on an eastern heading and I wanted to prevent being sighted by the Japanese, as we were converging on the enemy dead ahead at approximately 3 miles per minute. The best way was to stay with the fleet, make my reports, but remain unsighted.

'During our flight on the north heading at low altitude, I requested my navigator encode and have the radioman send to Midway, "Sighted main enemy fleet, course 90°, range 730 miles". We flew on the north heading for twelve minutes, then turned to a heading of 270° and flew on this heading for 25 miles, which put us abreast the enemy fleet.

'We climbed to 900ft and spotted the three columns of ships at a distance of 25 miles to the south. I informed Midway the enemy fleet consisted of one small carrier, one seaplane carrier, two battleships, several cruisers and destroyers. I immediately dove the plane to the water and continued on a heading of due south and flew for 25 miles. At this time we sighted three large wakes made by several ships in columns.

'I turned the plane to the heading of the enemy ships and climbed to 800ft and spotted more enemy ships that consisted of transports, fuel tankers and supply ships, astern and to the south of the previous ships reported. This information was sent to Midway.

'It was talk around the squadron that to spot the Japanese fleet would be suicide. The Emperor's little men would send up everything they had to shoot you down, so the plane wouldn't return with a comprehensive report. With this in mind, I requested my navigator give us a heading to Midway but scout to the north of any enemy ship. We had spent over two hours within 25 miles or less of the enemy and had not been "sighted". Also we were closer to Tokyo that the Japanese fleet we were tracking.

'On returning to Midway, we were informed to land on the water, due to several B-17s, B-16s and other planes that arrived from Pearl Harbor, which left no parking space available. We landed on the water and after touch-down, one engine stopped due to starvation of fuel. Just as we made the buoy, the other engine quit. My flight log shows we were in the air for 14.3 hours.'

Capt Reid's Aviators' Flight Log Book had the following entries confirmed by the CO of VP-44 — Lt Cdr R. C. Brixner, USN:

'June 3: On routine patrol out of Midway sighted first body of Japanese fleet in the battle of Midway. Fleet consisting of 17 ships, battle-ships and cruisers, destroyers and troop transports. Tracked for two hours and returned to Midway.

'June 4: On patrol out of Midway sighted same force as above. Fired on by eight cruisers. Tracked and returned to Midway.

'June 5: On patrol out of Midway, sighted Japanese force consisting of 2 battleships, 4 heavy cruisers, 4 destroyers and a burning carrier. Fired on battleships' AA battery.

'June 6 & 7: Searched and rescued survivors shot down during the battle of Midway.'

An attack was made on the enemy fleet at 16:23hr on 3 June by nine B-17s of the AAF using 36 x 600lb bombs released from 8,000ft. There was perhaps one hit[1]. This was followed by four PBY-5As whose crews had just completed a ten-hour flight from Pearl Harbor. Their aircraft were armed with single 2200lb Mark VIII Mod 1 torpedoes which in evaluation were shown to be 31 per cent effective, and needed to be dropped from 60ft or less.

The flight of four Catalinas was led by Lt W. L. Richards with Ens G. D. Propst, Lt D. C. Davis and Ens Alan Rothenberg. They all took off from Midway at 21:15 hours in *24-P-12, 24-P-7*, and *51-P-5*, respectively.

A radar contact from a single vessel was reported at about midnight by *24-P-12*, but at 01:15hr there was a further contact from about ten ships to port. Lt Charles Hibberd with Richards then sighted two columns. Two of the Catalinas had become separated, but Richards looked for the largest ship and a run was made just above the surface at 100kt. The torpedo was releasd at 800yd distance — there was a flash.

Davis in the second plane made two runs due to the ship's evasion and, as he released his torpedo, was subjected to severe AA from several ships. Propst now arrived and attacked a vessel at the end of the column; no evasive action was taken. The time was 01:43hr. There was a big explosion. Of the three torpedoes launched, the third struck *Akebono Maru*, killing or wounding 23 men and slowing down the vessel which ultimately rejoined the enemy force.

On returning to Midway after about thirteen hours, the Catalinas found an air raid in progress and touched down at Laysan Island about 350 miles further on, after first trying Lisianski which was overcast. Propst, however, had to land in open sea through lack of fuel, to be rescued by a VP-23 Catalina three days later.

The main battle of Midway was on 4 June when US Navy dive-bombers sank three Japanese carriers. There had however, been the sacrifice of 35 out of 41 American torpedo-bombers which had attacked without waiting for their support aircraft. Later, the enemy lost a fourth carrier and a heavy cruiser. The American carrier, although damaged in the confrontation, was reluctant to sink, but was finished by a torpedo from a Japanese submarine. Catalinas were now being used on rescue missions and in ten days picked up 27 survivors.

Samuel Morison[2] and Winston Churchill[3] in their accounts refer to superior American intelligence and the rigid planning of the Japanese, who readily withdrew if thwarted. Morison politely contrasts the high level bombing by B-17s with the carrier-based dive and glide bombers. The less dramatic role of the Catalina was a vital sighting 700 miles west of Midway Atoll, enabling the American admirals Fletcher and Spruance to act. Morison pays tribute to the latter.

George Favorite's PBY of VP-33 being hoisted aboard the tender USS *Tangier* at Morotai.

For Churchill, the Japanese carrier strength was broken irretrievably; for Australian historian John Robertson[4], Midway ended Japanese naval dominance and was more important for Australia than many battles involving Australians. For Captain Roskill[5], six months' Japanese Naval dominance was destroyed in a few hours.

With the four carriers and a cruiser, the Japanese had lost 258 aircraft with experienced aircrew against the American losses of *Yorktown*, the destroyer *Hamman*, forty shore-based and 92 carrier aircraft. For the US Navy it ended the success of the Japanese offensive in the Pacific and turned the tide of that war.

Guadalcanal

In 1942, while General MacArthur's aims were directed northwards towards the Philippines, the Japanese intended extending their influence southwards and cutting off communications with Australia and New Zealand. Both sides proposed occupying the Solomons and, by 3 May, the Japanese had taken Tulagi in the Solomons group.

On 4 July an Allied aircraft reported that the enemy was constructing an airfield on the largest island in the Solomons — Guadalcanal. The airfield was later to be known as Henderson Field. Guadalcanal and Henderson Field were later to become famous or notorious, according to one's point of view. Of the many

121

battles which were to be fought over this disputed territory, a major one involving land, air and naval forces took place in October 1942.

Following the report of an airfield being constructed by the Japanese, 11,000[6] American marines were landed in that area of Guadalcanal on 7 August and it was occupied the following day.

The tender, USS *McFarland*, moved to Ndeni in the Santa Cruz islands on 5 August from which five Catalinas of VP-11 and VP-14 could extend their operations by 300 miles. USS *Mackinac*, as tender for nine PBYs from VP-23, became based in the Marasike estuary on the south-east coast of Malaita island east of Guadalcanal, and their range was effectively extended for searching between the Japanese base of Truk and Guadalcanal by 500 miles.

The Japanese vital sea lane between Rabaul and the Solomons, known as 'the slot', was covered by B-17s of the AAF. Other long-range searches were undertaken by PBYs covering arcs with a radius of 6-700 miles from Espiritu Santo and Nandi in a north-westerly direction. These searches, begun on 8 August, were supported by sightings of enemy units by submarines and Hudson aircraft, but a section in 'the slot' was missed by the B-17s and the Japanese gained initial surprise and success in the naval battle of Savo Island on 9 August.

In the battle of Savo Island, which Captain Roskill refers to as a 'disastrous episode' due to losses of Allied warships, the transport vessels of the Allies were not attacked, and they were unloaded in support of the Marines.

To supply their troops in the Solomons, the Japanese ran the 'Tokyo express' — fast naval vessels which steamed down 'the slot' at night carrying both equipment and reinforcements.

Five more naval battles for Guadalcanal were to follow with a major ground battle in which American Marines and the 64th Infantry Regt held Henderson Field at the end of October.

At 09:50hr on 23 August a Catalina from USS *Mackinac* at Ndeni reported sighting enemy transports escorted by two cruisers and three destroyers on course for Guadalcanal at 17kt. Bad weather thwarted an attack by US Marine aircraft from Guadalcanal and others from the USS carrier *Saratoga* group. Five Catalina strike aircraft were ordered out

at night, but the enemy had reversed course.

The battle of the Eastern Solomons which followed on the 24th prevented the landing of 1,500 Japanese troops and further reduced their air forces. Estimated losses of Catalinas in the area for one month given by Morison were almost 25 per cent. Increasingly, they appeared in the role of strike aircraft in addition to flying routine patrols.

The battle of Cape Esperance on 11-12 October resulted in the Japanese losing a heavy cruiser and a destroyer, but they had been able to land some heavy artillery against the American Marines.

In the following days, Catalinas made a series of sighting reports, although one aircraft failed to return on the 14th and two more were shot down on the 15th. Torpedo attacks were made by others, such as a PBY from VP-51 commanded by Lt A. Rothenberg on the 16th, who probably scored a hit on an enemy cruiser.

A USN patrol plane commander who was in the South Pacific area at the time of the battles for Guadalcanal was V. Jack Coley Jr of VP-11 and, as he recalls: 'VP-11 commenced deployment to the South Pacific on 3 July 1942, three PBY-5s each day on four consecutive days. I flew No 2 in the first section. July 3 Kaneohe to Palmyra, July 4 Palmyra to Canton Island, July 5-6 Canton to Suva. The squadron regrouped at Suva and made preparations to operate from a new seaplane facility being prepared at Nandi.

'On 12 July, three planes and crews deployed to Noumea to be based on the AVP *Mackinac*. Mine was one of these; Joe Cobb had the lead, I was No 2 and Charlie Muckenthaller was No 3. We flew patrols to the northwest from Noumea.

'In the meantime, the rest of the squadron moved from Suva to Nandi and flew patrols to the west. At that time patrol aircraft were scouts rather than attack aircraft as they were later used . . . But the patrol aircraft continued to be used as scouts keeping large areas of the ocean under surveillance. They carried bombs with selective fuzing or depth charges for targets of opportunity — hopefully just submarines — but their numbers were too few to risk such valuable resources unless the stakes and pay-offs were very high, as for example, the battle of Midway.

'On August 1 1942, VP-11 regrouped at Segundo Channel on Espiritu Santo where we based on the AV *Curtiss*. There were detachments of several other squadrons based there also. This move coincided with the invasion of Guadalcanal and brought the PBY base closer so as to be able to scout the large ocean areas and prevent any surprise attack by the Japanese . . . A PBY was not expected to survive daylight sweeps where the Jap Zero fighters still disputed control of the air. B-17s with their defensive turrets could and did survive, but not with impunity.

'On 15 August I was assigned an afternoon mission to fly up the slot past Guadalcanal about half-way to Bougainville, or as far as I could go and still return to land at Tulagi before dark.

'The purpose was to detect the "Tokyo express" — the Jap cruisers which steamed down at night and shelled Henderson Field and then retired before daylight. As luck would have it, the Tokyo express did not run that night, and in my eagerness to sight them I pressed on too far and so it was after dark when I got back to Tulagi.

'I had been briefed on the USS *Curtiss* that Tulagi was secure and that Florida Island would be secured in a few hours, so I expected no problems of that sort. It was a clear dark night but there was enough light from the stars and a crescent moon to make out the hills and the water in the bay. There was a large fire on the east end of Tulagi Island and that helped. To show the Marines I was friendly I turned on all my running lights and circled over the hills to make a night blind-landing on an easterly heading.

'In the PBY-5 this was an air speed held at 60kt with rate of descent held at 300ft per minute. There would be a slight cushioning from the ground effect just before touchdown, and when the hull touched the water, the pilot would chop the power and hold the nose up while it slowed. The landing was routine but when I turned to taxy back to get my bearings, we were surrounded by boats shining bright floodlights on us. An officer demanded to know who we were and what we were doing there!

'I had been briefed to use a mooring buoy at an abandoned Jap seaplane base, but the officer said "Hell, you can't go there; that is still Jap territory!" It turned out the Marines held only half of Tulagi Island and none of Florida Island.

'We spent the night moored to the end of a finger pier in Marine territory. My crew were loaned rifles by the Marines and set up a watch to guard against swimmers with evil intent. Fortunately, that area was quiet. I was led through many challenges to the command post and met the General commanding the Marines in Tulagi. He did not know what to do with us and recommended we not stay any longer than necessary.

'So the next morning as soon as it was light, we took off, searched the area between Florida Island and Guadalcanal. It was empty of ships and quiet so we headed home to Espiritu Santo.

'The big advantage of the seaplane in those early days of World War 2 was its basing flexibility. With a tender for fuel, food and sleep — or even just a pre-positioned mooring buoy with a 500 or 900gal rubber gasoline tank and a handy billy pump — any reasonably protected water could be used for operations.

'The tenders we had in addition to the USS *Curtiss* were USS *Kenneth Whiting*; at Segundo Channel were the USS *Mackinac*, USS *Ballard* and USS *McFarland*. The latter two were converted four-stack destroyers. With their support during 1942, PBY detachments operated out of Noumea, Vanikoro, Grasiosa Bay on Ndeni and Maramasilke on Malaite.

'On some sectors our patrols overlapped those of the long-ranged Jap seaplanes out of Truk. I remember on one occasion I sighted a Jap Mavis and started in pursuit. I had 137kt indicated air speed, but the Mavis could do 150kt so we could not close. We fired a couple

PBYs of VP-33 over the South Pacific. Catalinas of VP-33 were credited with damaging or destroying 197,000 tons of Japanese shipping.

of bursts from the bow 0·3 calibre gun, but got only splashes in the water at about half the needed distance. The Jap fired a few rounds from his tail turret 25mm gun, but got only splashes half way to us.

'On this particular flight I had departed Segundo Channel on an extra long-range search which would terminate at Vanikoro, which made the extra-long-range search only routine distance. However, shortly after giving up pursuit of the Mavis we received instructions to return to Segundo Channel. Now I was worried about our fuel. In addition to the longer track flown, I had burned some additional fuel chasing the Mavis. We were still far enough out that I could gain some fuel economy by climbing to 10,000ft. It would be dark before we could make a landfall so we needed that much altitude to clear the island peaks.

'As it got dark our flight path took us under a high thin overcast so we couldn't use stars and we were uncertain of the winds aloft, so very soon we were lost. We maintained our DR navigation, but with a total blackout that existed, how could we find it?

'Shortly after out ETA we sighted the lighted torches of some natives night-fishing on a shallow reef. With the lighted torches as a fix I circled. I had the radioman signal the base asking for a bearing. I was not the only one lost that night and the staff were getting worried. They gave me a course to steer, and the other lost planes the same assistance, and as we approached, they had all the ships in the harbour turn on their lights and the tender showed a searchlight straight up. With this help we could not miss, and all landed safely amongst the crowded ships in the dark harbour.'

For Jack Coley, the first night harassment raid against Japanese troops on Guadalcanal was on 18 October. He had with him Max Ricketts as co-pilot and O. A. Patterson as navigator. Their PBY was equipped with radar and, at about 22:00hr, his radioman reported a blip at 5 miles to starboard. It proved to be from a barge loaded with aviation fuel and towed by a tug en route for Henderson Field which was then in Allied hands. Coley turned to investigate and found himself over an enemy submarine, at full speed on the surface heading for the barge.

The PBY was turned again to attack but enemy contact was lost, and Coley circled the area for ten minutes before contact was regained. A further attempt to attack the sub was made but it submerged, having apparently decided to withdraw. The tug and barge later arrived safely at their destination.

Coley continued to Guadalcanal, arriving at midnight, with his load of two 500lb bombs under the wings, twelve 100lb bombs within the aircraft and about twelve parachute flares.

He had been briefed that the front line between the Marines and the Japanese was perpendicular to the shore line, just about at Point Cruz, an easily identified landmark. The entire Marine area was dark, all the way from the front line to past Henderson Field to the east. On the Japanese side were many watch fires scattered through their area, and the plan of the PBY crew was to locate targets using flares and then release bombs followed by strafing of personnel areas.

To ensure that the flares reached ground level before illuminating, they were set at maximum delay and dropped from 1,000ft instead of the usual 3,000ft. A supply dump was located and set ablaze, burning for about two hours. The 100lb bombs were released through the rear tunnel hatch; finally the 500lb bombs were dropped in the enemy's supply area before the PBY headed for base. In the raid the Catalina had been subjected to much small-arms fire and some heavy AA, but suffered only two hits from spent rounds aft.

On the night of 22 October, Coley led a three-plane night torpedo raid against the Japanese fleet anchorage at Tonelei harbour on the eastern end of Bougainville Island. Flying the second and third PBYs of VP-11 were George Poulos and Charles F. 'Whiskey' Willis; Coley's lead navigator was Joe Deodati. With a flight radius of 900 miles from Espiritu Santo, they proposed returning to Tulagi to refuel independently. At Tulagi, then safely under US control, there were mooring buoys in addition to one from which they could refuel.

A coast-watcher had reported an aircraft carrier anchored at Tonelei and it was to be the PBY's prime target. Coley flew the last 100 miles at 50ft to avoid detection and was successful in making a surprise approach, pulling up over a picket destroyer guarding the south entrance to the Japanese anchorage. The PBYs made individual runs seeking the carrier, but by now the enemy was alarmed and Coley sought the largest target available. He released his torpedo just as a searchlight beam caught him. He turned to drop the remainder of his load — two 500lb bombs — from the other wing on to a large merchant vessel.

As Captain Coley now recalls: 'We were caught in several searchlights at once and every ship in the anchorage was firing at us. It looked like a tremendous 4 July fireworks display with us in the centre. I turned that PBY every way but inside-out, evading the gunfire. There are several islands to the east of the main anchorage, and I tried to get behind one to escape the searchlights, but each one I approached had a ship anchored nearby which started firing at us. Finally I got far enough out that I could get behind an island . . . while we were evading, the sights were spectacular.'

Coley's aircraft suffered several holes, the worst being from heavy AA shrapnel which hit the bottom of the starboard wing and went right through, leaving a large hole and puncturing the fuel tank. Because it was the one self-sealing tank in the aircraft, most of their fuel had been reserved there. The hole was so large, that the self-sealing did not function, but there was enough fuel left in the port tank to reach Tulagi and make for their base. None of Coley's crew was wounded and all of the Catalina flight returned to Espiritu Santo. It is not clear if any of the shipping then at Tonelei was damaged or sunk, but some damage appears possible.

On 23 October an enemy carrier was sighted by a PBY. That night a strike force of Catalinas was sent out but there was only one attack. That was by Lt G. A. Enloe of VP-11 who released a torpedo against a cruiser.

Further attacks were made by Catalinas on Japanese warships on the 25th and 26th. They included the battleship *Haruna*, carrier *Zuikaku* and a destroyer, *Isokaze*. The date given for the naval battle of Santa Cruz Islands is 26 October, when 32 PBYs formed part of the American task force No 63 under Rear Adm A. W. Fitch which included Hudsons of the RNZAF – 12 at Espiritu Santo and 13 in New Caledonia. A Catalina from VP-91 flown by Lt Melvin K. Atwell attacked a destroyer, –

A PBY of the US Navy armed with a torpedo. The USN torpedoes used at Midway needed to be released from 60ft or less altitude and were 31% run effective.

Teruzuki, with four 500lb bombs from below 600ft. Two hits were scored, but the aircraft suffered damage from shrapnel with a number of holes, and the wing was distorted by blast. The destroyer retired to Truk on 27 October.

In the battle of Santa Cruz Islands, the Americans lost the carrier USS *Hornet* but the Japanese fleet suffered damage to many ships, and their air strength was further reduced.

Two more naval battles followed in November — Guadalcanal during the 12th to the 15th, and Tassafaronga on the 30th. The Guadalcanal naval battle was notable not just because of the Japanese loss of two battleships and eleven transports, with further destroyer losses, but as another turning point when the Americans switched to the offensive. At Tassafaronga the Americans were outfought by ostensibly inferior forces. But the Guadalcanal issue was decided.

On 13 December a Catalina began attacks on the Japanese airstrip at Munda in New Georgia. On 8 February 1943 American ground forces found only empty boats and abandoned Japanese supplies. By 16:25 hours on the 9th the enemy was reported defeated in Guadalcanal.

Morison gives figures of 60,000 US Army and Marine Corps committed to Guadalcanal against 36,000 Japanese. The US Army and Marines lost 1,592 killed in action, while Japanese casualties were 25,800 killed, missing or dying from disease. Both sides lost 24 warships, of 126,140 tons and 134,839 tons respectively.

In the south-west Pacific the Allies were no longer fighting a rearguard action but were taking the initiative in offensive operations. The offensive is reflected in the role of Catalinas deployed by both the Americans and the RAAF. For the Americans, their PBYs became patrol bombers armed with machine guns, bombs and torpedoes; with the RAAF, mine-laying was developed. The mercy, or 'Dumbo', missions applied to both.

Shipping strikes over the Bismarck Sea

In late 1943 VP-52, which had earlier been operating over the North and South Atlantic, moved down to Australia. Fifteen of their PBYs were flown from Bermuda to Perth, Australia, via Norfolk, San Diego, Kaneohe Bay, Midway, Johnson Island, Kwajlein Atoll, Suva and Adelaide.

They became one of three Catalina squadrons to operate under Fleet Air Wing 17 commanded by Cdre T. S. Combs, FAW 17 having been commissioned on 15 September at Brisbane for operations in the SW Pacific area. From Perth, VP-52 PBYs patrolled the Indian Ocean as far north as Madang in New Guinea. On 20 November they moved from Perth to Namoia Bay, near Samarai, New Guinea with, as CO, Lt Cdr Harold A. Sommer. Their route was via Adelaide and Palm Island, and it was at the latter that one of their plane commanders — Lt Lahodney — experimented successfully with a modification to his Catalina.

This involved fitting a group of four 0.5 machine guns in the nose of the aircraft, similar in nature to the armament seen in B-25s. After removal of the bomb-sight and bow plate window from the Catalina, the four guns were bolted to the keel in two pairs, one above the other. It proved unnecessary to remove the existing two 0.3 machine guns.

The squadron role, although it included convoy escorts, daytime patrols and air-sea rescue, was notable for its anti-shipping strikes. These took place in the Bismarck Sea along the south coast of New Ireland or the north coast of New Britain, but usually in the region of Rabaul.

One of their first actions was by Lt Lahodney who dive-bombed a destroyer. Later, on 22 November in St George's Channel, he attacked an enemy barge with his four 0.5s, leaving the vessel burning.

Just after midnight on 25 November, Catalina No 55 of VP-52, flown by Lt Cdr H. Sommer, was ten miles from New Britain cruising at 800ft when a radar contact indicated a convoy fifteen miles away. Sommer closed and attacked a destroyer from 700ft against heavy AA, but his attack proved abortive. He called up a second Catalina, commanded by Lt Lahodney, which arrived in thirty minutes but, on sighting no ships, Lahodney undertook an expanding square search.

After five minutes flying at 1,200ft, a radar contact was made and then, at a distance of two miles, the zig-zag wake was seen of a ship steaming at about 30kt. Lahodney set his bombs at 75ft spacing and made a deep diving run from stern to bow, with co-pilot Ens H. M. Halstad releasing the load from less than 150ft at 140kt. The gunner in a blister was able to identify the details of a large superstructure, several masts and a gun turret — they were those of a heavy cruiser, contrasting with the destroyers in the convoy.

Lahodney made a slow climbing turn. The ship's wake had almost disappeared and black smoke was coming from it. While he was on a second run at 400ft to drop flares and fragmentation bombs, a shell from intensive AA fire blew the tunnel hatch out, rudder control was lost and the aircraft banked steeply and lost altitude. Boost and revs were increased to 50in-Hg and 2,850rpm, but one engine had to be cut back to keep the wings level. They were now in the searchlights of several ships and subjected to more AA fire. All free equipment was jettisoned.

It seems likely that Lahodney must have flown directly over Rabaul, with all that that entailed! After heading south, Lahodney's crew examined the damage. The port rudder

The crew which reported the Japanese fleet off Midway on 3 June 1942. Their commander was Ensign Jack Reid (back row, 4th from left).

cable, the rudder trim cable and Sperry cables were severed, and the elevator cable was almost cut. At one stage they flew into a front with an upward current giving a rate of climb of 3,500ft per minute.

After thirty minutes, the rudder cable was repaired with three lengths of rudder trim cable, and the engines were adjusted to normal setting. In the last half-hour of flight they flew at 80kt with 24inHg boost and 1,500rpm, using 60gal/hr. Earl S. Tilley had been one of those involved with the rudder cable repair.

They landed safely at Samarai, ten miles from their tender. The squadron recorded that two of the 500lb and one of the two 1,000lb bombs carried by Lahodney's aircraft had hit the Japanese cruiser. The Catalina had 187 shrapnel holes in the tail section as evidence of the affray. Lt Lahodney was awarded the Navy Cross in addition to his DFC.

On the night of 30 November, Lt William J. Pattison was flying south of Kavieng, New Ireland, when a radar contact of a convoy was obtained at 19 miles. Heading the ten merchant vessels escorted by two destroyers was a tanker of 10,000-15,000 tons, and this was selected as a target. In a bombing run made at 500ft, Pattison released his bombs manually. Despite evasive action by the ship, two hits were scored, one with a 1,000lb another with a 500lb bomb. Within thirty seconds, the ship was completely ablaze.

The Catalina was now subjected to intensive AA fire, which included some heavy-calibre shells. The aircraft suffered many hits on the starboard wing and fuselage, but the only man wounded was the wireless operator. Pattison was decorated with the Silver Star for this strike; an award made for gallantry in action.

On that same night, Lt Kunkle, having sighted no enemy shipping, bombed the harbour at Garove Island north of New Britain, after first releasing flares. Fighters were detected on the radar screen, but Kunkle escaped their attention. It was on either 30 November or 1 December that another Catalina, commanded by Lt Charles J. Schauffler, scored hits with 500lb bombs on two Japanese destroyers.

VP-52's record over the next fortnight would have been exceptional even if they had been equipped with an aircraft designed for offensive operations, but they were still using the pre-war designed patrol plane, the PBY Catalina.

While on patrol over the Bismarck Sea on the night of 9/10 December, Lt Rudy Lloyd sighted an auxiliary cargo vessel of 8,000 tons between New Ireland and Dyaul Island. He made a 30° dive from 1,200ft at 150kt and attacked the ship with four bombs. Three hits were scored, one with a 500lb, and two with 1,000lb bombs. The vessel was seen to sink stern first with the bow projecting at 60°.

Two nights later, Lt Flenniken sighted three cargo vessels escorted by a destroyer steaming south, probably for Rabaul, along the New Ireland coast. After circling to get down-moon, Flenniken could see the ships in line ahead spaced at 200yd. As he approached from the port quarter they broke formation. Flenniken attacked the first cargo vessel, which was of about 4,000 tons, in a shallow dive from 600ft at 130kt and with his bombs spaced at 75ft. A 1,000lb bomb struck the vessel amidships and there was an explosion, but no fire. At this stage there were indications of three enemy aircraft in the vicinity, and the Catalina moved out seawards.

Flenniken later detected a large oil slick, and after the convoy was shadowed for 2½ hours there was no trace of the fourth ship and it was recorded as sunk.

The following night, Lt Lloyd was flying east over the Bismarck Sea south of New Ireland when he sighted an enemy cruiser. It was anchored 16 miles south-west of Kavieng between Teclampin and Bandissin Islands. Although the Catalina would have been clearly visible to both the cruiser and shore batteries in the bright moonlight, Lloyd decided to attack.

He made a climbing turn to 1,500ft and then put the aircraft into a 20° dive with 55in Hg boost and 2,100rpm. At three miles there was intense AA fire but, at 300ft altitude and

180kt, Lloyd released his bombs manually, attacking from port bow to starboard quarter. There were two direct hits on the stern of the vessel with 500lb and 1,000lb bombs.

Since aircraft were indicated on the radar, he made for cloud cover, but still remained in the area for another 45 minutes. From observations made by two of the crew, the stern section of the cruiser must have been blown off the vessel for it was seen floating 30ft away from the rest of the ship.

VP-52 is credited with two successful attacks on Japanese submarines. The first of these was by Lt C. Schauffler, who straddled an 'I'-type vessel with four 650lb depth charges on 15 December.

On the 17th, Lt 'Pat' Flenniken was on patrol over the western Bismarck Sea when a radar contact was made five miles to port. At one mile, a fully surfaced 'I' class submarine was sighted on a course of 300° and travelling at 15kt. Flenniken attacked with four 650lb depth charges which were released from 100ft. The charge straddled the vessel and the explosions covered the aft section, which was blown to the right and stopped dead in the water. It began to sink stern first and, after one minute, the top of the conning tower and 25ft of the bow were above water. When another flare was dropped, 10ft of the bow was visible at an angle of 45°, and the submarine disappeared within a further four minutes. There was an oil slick and what appeared to be about 15 survivors.

Twenty minutes later, aircraft No 41 of VP-52 released two 500lb bombs with a four-second delay on the oil slick and wreckage, which by then covered an area 125yd x 50yd. The submarine was thought to have been returning from the eastern Pacific. A kill has not been recorded by the US Naval History Division[8] for this date, but two 'I'-type submarines were given as 'Probable marine casualty' in early 1944 (*I-11* and *I-171*).

On the night of 19/20 December, Lt Cdr H. A. Sommer and Lt A. N. McInnis both located an enemy convoy of fifteen ships. Sommer homed on to a group of four of the vessels by radar, and from two miles' distance, flying at 800ft, he selected his target visually and put his Catalina into a glide. At 440yd the ship opened fire, but Sommer still set his bomb release for 45ft spacing and went in at 130kt. A 1,000lb bomb exploded inside the vessel between amidships and astern. Clouds prevented a visual check on results, but radar now showed only three out of the four in the group of ships attacked.

Lt McInnis made a radar contact at fourteen miles, but on dropping below cloud in his approach was caught by a searchlight and suffered intense AA fire before returning to cloud cover. When estimated to be 440yd away, McInnis, while flying at 1,800ft, put the aircraft into a steep dive passing over a ship at 180kt with, according to his crew, masts of the ship on either side. The explosion of a 1,000lb bomb set fire to the vessel and the fire spread rapidly: these results were confirmed by crews of other aircraft.

Two more enemy ships were either damaged or destroyed by VP-52 at about that time. The attacks were made by Lt Lahodney and Lt W. B. Squier, with Lahodney scoring a hit on a 5,000-ton merchant vessel and Lt Squier setting fire to a 5,000-ton auxiliary transport.

Before the end of the year VP-52 claimed two more successful attacks. Lt Robert D.

Dilworth on the 24th bombed a 12,000-ton merchant vessel, and Lt R. John scored a hit on a destroyer.

In addition to individual awards, the Squadron gained a Presidential Citation for their exceptional achievements. They were followed in that area at six-week intervals by VP-34 and VP-33. During January and February of 1944, VPB-52 was on air-sea rescue and convoy escorts operating from Port Moresby. They were then deployed, after rest, to Seeadler Harbour in the Admiralty Islands.

1 C&C, Vol 1, p457/8. See also RK, Chap 4, JR, p23, & USNA, p113.
2 SEM, Vol IV, pp103-157.
3 WSC, Vol IV, p226.
4 JR, p23.
5 SWR, Vol II, p41.
6 D. Gillison, p578, & SWR, Vol II, p226 (but see also JR, p141, & WSC, Vol V, p17).
7 SWR, Vol II, p225.
8 Appendix to *US Submarine Losses in WW2*, Washington 1963.

Chapter 15
The Aleutians

May 42-Apr 44

The Aleutians, a chain of islands extending westwards from Alaska for 1,000 miles and bounded by the Bering Sea, were occupied by Japanese troops in 1942 as part of an overall expansion plan extending from the west islands of the Aleutians southwards to include Port Moresby and taking in Midway, Fiji and New Caledonia. Attu and Kiska were occupied by the Japanese on 7 June 1942. In battles which followed to regain US territory, many Japanese soldiers were lost, USN warships fired many rounds with little effect and most of the American aircraft losses were not in combat, but due to atrocious weather conditions.

Of all the theatres of war in which Catalinas operated, the Aleutians must have been one of the most grim. Naval historian Morison pays tribute to this fact, referring to the Catalinas of Patwing 4 flying in all conditions, the need to warm engines with blow torches, scraping ice and snow off wings, frozen spray and limited radio facilities. Of hanging on the props waiting for a hole in the cloud through which to land. On touching down helping with maintenance and an ultimate 'gipsy' existence.

Although naval 'patrol planes', the Catalinas were used in bombing raids on Kiska in mid-June with three aircraft lost. In August they sank the disabled *Kano Maru*[1] of 8,572 tons, and played a major part in the sinking of the Japanese submarine *RO-61*.

The first officially recorded move concerning Naval PBYs was the transfer of Patrol Wing 4 from Seattle to the North Pacific with the arrival of the CO at Kodiak on 27 May 1942. For the American Army Air Force, the Aleutians campaign effectively began on 3 June 1942 when the enemy launched carrier planes from *Ryujo* and *Junyo* against Dutch Harbour and ceased on 10 April 1944 following a Joint Chiefs of Staff decision. For both sides, the Aleutians campaign was a defensive measure, although the initial Japanese attack against Dutch Harbour in June 1942 was a diversion from their major attack on Midway.

VP-41 was one of two PBY seaplane squadrons, the other being VP-42, assigned to Patrol Wing 4 (subsequently Fleet Air Wing 4), based at NAS Seattle, Washington; the base known as NAS Sands Point — 'the country club of the Northwest'. This was in June 1941. At that time VP-41, equipped with PBY-3s, was commanded by Lt Cdr F. B. Johnson who was set upon qualifying all his pilots as Patrol Plane Commanders (PPC), and aided by the Flight Officer, Lt P. H. Ramsey, with over fifty flying categories to be completed. Joining the squadron at this time was Paul Foley, Jr[2] from previous service with USS *Northampton* and a tour with VP-1. Every two months VP-41's routine was interrupted by 'Advance Base Operations' which involved the whole squadron taking off for one or two weeks to an Alaskan base, the first being Sitka. Sitka was being gradually completed as a base with ramps for flying boats and docks for aircraft tenders. After operations at Sitka in August, they subsequently flew across the Gulf of Alaska to NAS Kodiak. Here, in addition to flying boat facilities, was an airfield with paved 5,000ft runways but with a very muddy area for living quarters, the mud referred to as 'Muskeg'.

The 'town' of Kodiak was ten miles away and described by Admiral Foley as 'like a typical Hollywood frontier town of the US West'. Seventy-five miles from Kodiak is the volcano Katmai which erupted in 1912 depositing five feet of ash and pumice. To the west 430 miles away was an AAF base at Cold Bay with a military port and good runways, useful to USN aircraft en route between Kodiak and Dutch Harbour. Dutch Harbour, a further 200 miles along the Aleutian chain, on Unalaska Island had, in addition to a small naval base, a fishing village with Aleuts.

It was to such bases that aircraft of VP-41 and VP-42 flew from Seattle in 1941 to become familiar with the conditions. In November VP-41 was deployed at Kodiak and it was in the latter part of this month that cessation of long-range radio from Japanese ships gave one indication of the enemy fleet being at sea, although there were other factors. On 6 December, Paul Foley was on temporary duty with VP-13 at San Diego. While on a visit to a relative the following day he switched on a radio and heard the news of Pearl Harbor. Although a blackout was ordered, the Consolidated Aircraft factory was exempted! In early January 1942, Foley was ordered to return to VP-41 which by then had returned to Seattle from where they shortly moved to Tongue Point, Oregon. Their aircraft, one or two at a time, flew south to NAS Alameda, California, to have British type ASV installed which was then checked over the sea on a suitable target at forty miles range before acceptance and the return to Oregon.

With cloud base of about 200ft and sea fog near the coastline, the aircrews became conditioned for Aleutian operations and, with the aid of radar with which all their aircraft were equipped by April, they learned to make accurate landfalls. At this stage, both VP-41 and VP-42 were re-equipped with new PBY-5A amphibians and aircraft were flown to Alameda for the change. When Commander F. B. Johnson was appointed Naval Air Attaché in London, Paul Foley succeeded him to command VP-41. While at Tongue Point, VP-41 pilots were logging 180-200 hours' flying per month. An airport was constructed there with 3,500ft runways which were then used by some AAF Hudsons in addition to PBY amphibians.

VP-42 was another of the four PBY squadrons of the US Navy to be deployed in Alaska in 1941. James S. Russell joined VP-42 in July 1941 when it was equipped with six Catalinas (PBY-5s). While one aircraft was left behind for gunnery school, the other five flew 600 miles in formation to Sitka where there was a newly constructed Naval seaplane base. As Admiral Russell now writes: 'This leg of our journey was accomplished in clear weather amidst beautiful mountainous scenery. Not yet qualified in Catalinas, I served as navigator in the executive officer's aircraft. We spent the night at Sitka. The next morning there was light rain falling. After taking off we

joined up in a five plane formation and started across the Gulf of Alaska. The further we went, the lower the ceiling became, and finally there was no ceiling.

'We continued on in the fog, flying very low in a tight five-plane "V" with our bellies just off the water. The only aid to navigation was an uncalibrated radio range station. It was emitting and I could take directional bearings on it with a loop antenna. The signal got louder and louder, and when the bearing started to change rapidly, I knew we were about to make a landfall on Kodiak Island, and so informed the executive officer at the controls.

'Shortly a rocky coastline with stunted spruce trees on it appeared on the starboard side; the squadron fell out of the air like a flock of wounded ducks. Three of us landed straight ahead, one took pains to reverse course and land into wind, the fifth, the squadron commander's aircraft, continued on up the fjord to the far end beyond which he found a bay and a dome in the fog. Fjords don't usually end that way!

'There he circled for the better part of an hour trying to punch his way out of the fog somewhere. Finally he turned back and joined us anchored in the lee of a small island. We had started up our little power units and were in communication with the Naval Air Station, Kodiak, our intended destination.

'Shortly after we landed a dory set out from the beach. As he approached I greeted him and asked if he could tell us exactly where we were. My duty as a navigator would require no less. As he neared our aircraft, he said, "Have you a chart in there?" I answered in the affirmative and we took him aboard. As we walked forward to the navigator's station he introduced himself as Mr. Nelson. As we leaned over the chart table to look at the chart I said, "Could you tell us the name of the little island in the lee of which we are anchored?" He smiled and said, "Oh yes. That is Nelson's Island!" He then put his finger on a small inlet or fjord just east of Woody Island and the village of Kodiak. It is not really an inlet but rather a narrow and long passage which separates Kodiak Island from Afognak Island to the east.

'We had a seaplane tender at Kodiak Naval Air Station. It was one converted from a pre-WW2 destroyer. Her two forward boilers had been removed and replaced by tankage for the stowage of aviation gasoline. This was USS *Gillis* and her captain was Johnny Heath . . . He radioed to us, "Stay where you are and I'll come tend you for the night". Several hours later he did come. We could hear his fog whistle blowing as he steamed gingerly into our little inlet. As he sighted us through the fog, he stopped and let go his anchor . . . A phenomenon of weather, not unusual in Alaska and the Aleutians, then occurred. The fog lifted about 300ft and underneath it one could see for miles. At this point all five of us started engines, took off, and proceeded to the NAS, Kodiak, leaving our inlet to Johnny and his seaplane tender.

'This was my introduction to flying Catalinas in Alaska and the Aleutian Islands, and I tell it to indicate the extreme utility of the type of aircraft it was. Flying cruising at 120kt, advancing two nautical miles every sixty seconds, it was slow enough to let the pilot execute an emergency measure when he saw something coming ahead in the fog which he didn't like.

'It could only be improved upon by the amphibious model, in which one could land ashore, if a field were available, and avoid the nasty water work in the stormy Aleutians. Something was sacrificed in the amphibian however. The wheel wells, recesses cut into the hull, reduced the buoyancy of the hull, and the wheel wells having filled with water, added to the take-off weight and were slow to drain, which continued for some time after becoming airborne. For a rescue at sea, for example, one would prefer to have had the added buoyancy and integrity of a complete hull, and the simple flying boat type was preferred.

'When WW2 broke out for us with the Japanese attack on Pearl Harbor, my squadron, VP-42, expanded from six to twelve aircraft. We also re-equipped with Catalina amphibians, changing from PBY-5s to PBY-5As. It was a joy to be able to use the airfields ashore with greatly simplified maintenance, yet we retained the ability to operate from the sea and our seaplane tenders.'

Dutch Harbour

'When the Japanese struck Dutch Harbour on 3 June 1942, the day before Midway Island in

the central Pacific; and struck again on the 4th, none of my aircraft was there. We used to service in Dutch Harbour or at one of our Army airfields in the area, then fly to a dispersion point in a bay, inlet, lagoon — even a lake — in the vicinity but far enough away not to be identified with our base.

'An aircraft from a sister squadron spotted what he thought would be a good dispersion point in a salt water lagoon one day. He landed and found that when his aircraft settled down off the step, he was hard and fast aground. A combination of high tide and jettisoning much of the equipment and he finally got off. Determined that such an incident would not happen to our squadron, we developed a way of sounding the depth of a likely body of water for dispersion *without landing*. We took a fathom, 6ft of twine. At one end of the twine we tied a chip of wood, at the other — a rock, with the rock large enough to sink the chip. Flying to the intended dispersion point we would fly across the body of water whilst the waist gunner dropped out chip and rock every five seconds. Returning to our track across the water and flying low we could see if all the chips of wood were under water — if so, it was safe to land. The water was 6ft or deeper.

'Something which made a vast difference in our flying happened in April 1942. We flew down successively in pairs to Alameda, California, where we installed the British ASV radar in our aircraft. While the radar was being installed, we in the flight crews, went to school to learn how to use it. Returning to the Aleutians, we looked much like porcupines — hay rakes under the wings and dipoles around the hull. Being able to see through the fog made a tremendous difference in our capacity as scouts.'

Of a former fellow pilot with VP-42 (Lou D. Campbell), Admiral Russell has written: 'There was no pilot in the squadron better than Lou. When the Japanese struck Dutch Harbour, he, his crew and airplane had gone to their dispersion point at Akutan Island, the next large island east of Unalaska, the location of Dutch Harbour. On news of the attack he took off and was the first to locate and report the Japanese carriers. A Zero fighter chased him into cloud and sprayed his airplane with machine-gun bullets, one of which severed the rudder wires of his airplane.

'Flying back to base with no rudder control and leaking gas tanks he ran out of fuel fifty miles out. At that point he made a let down through about 6,000ft of cloud, and sighted water at about 300ft just in time to pull up the nose of his plane and make a successful landing, without engine power and no rudder, in the open sea. He and his crew, one of whom was wounded, kept the plane afloat until rescued by a Coast Guard patrol boat. When he described this escapade to me, he said, "Skipper, I made a mistake". When I asked him "What?", he said, "When I ran out of fuel and my engines stopped, I forgot to cut the ignition".'

Japanese attack on the Aleutians

VP-41 flew via Sitka to Kodiak where they arrived on 26 May 1942. There they were briefed on the impending arrival of a Japanese Naval force, and moved on to Dutch Harbour. VP-42 went to Cold Bay. *United States Naval Aviation*[3] gives these moves as the transfer of Patrol Wing 4 from Seattle to the North Pacific. With the Wing Commander — Capt Leslie Gheres, USN — at Kodiak; Lt Cdr Foley at Dutch Harbour was designated 'Staff Advance Operations Officer' (ADSTOP) and directed to co-ordinate PBY forward operations in addition to the six attached seaplane tenders.

Foley had twelve amphibians at Dutch Harbour. They had patrols organised in a 'fan' of vectors centred on the axis of the Aleutian chain, originating at Dutch Harbour and extending out to 600 miles. He allocated aircraft and crews on a daily basis according to availability. He was conscious of the heavy losses suffered by PBY squadrons in the SW Pacific due to Japanese carrier aircraft; night patrols were therefore flown with take-offs just before sunset and relying on radar for contacts.

Normally, crews would breakfast at Dutch Harbour, where their aircraft would be re-fuelled and re-armed. They would then be dispersed following a short flight to a nearby fjord on Unalaska Island to anchor near a small seaplane tender (AVP), remaining there quietly during daylight to avoid being caught on the water. The tenders provided messing and rest facilities for the mechanics. Entire crews could be changed at intervals at Dutch Harbour thus easing the tension for pilots. With a customary low ceiling of 2-300ft with cloud on the hilltops, they felt reasonably secure against detection by the enemy.

In an attempt to divert American forces from Midway, the Japanese sent a force including the carriers *Junyo* and *Ryujo* supported by heavy cruisers *Takao* and *Maya* with three destroyers to raid Dutch Harbour. A PBY detected the carriers on 2 June, 400 miles south of Kiska but lost contact on being pursued by fighters. On the morning of the 3rd the enemy task force was sighted by returning Catalinas 210 miles from Dutch Harbour and ahead of a front. VP-41 lost two of their aircraft with sixteen men and officers, one of the latter being captured and returned to USA after the war.

In addition to PBYs of Patrol Wing 4, the Americans deployed P-40s, B-17s and B-26s of the AAF. In strafing and bombing attacks on Dutch Harbour some shore installations were damaged with casualties but the Japanese lost some bombers and fighters to the P-40s. Operations had been continuous for forty hours up to the 4th June and by this time the Americans had lost four PBYs[4], six were out of action, leaving fourteen serviceable. The second pair of Catalinas lost was not on patrol but in a bombing strike against the enemy task force on the 4th. No ships were hit but the two PBYs were shot down and then one was strafed by the Japanese when on the water, killing all of the crew.

Foley as ADSTOP at Dutch Harbour was initially in improvised quarters of an administration building at the NAS. After the first enemy raid, sites were hastily excavated on a nearby hilltop for three Quonset huts. These were then used by the Station Commander, Lt Cdr W. N. Updegraffe; by the submarine commander who was OC of six S-boats — Cdr O. E. Colclough — while the third hut was for Lt Cdr Foley. Outside his hut was installed a 40mm gun subsequently blown up with its crew in a Japanese raid.

After the Japanese task force had retired from the Dutch Harbour raid, 'Sea Bees' began constructing a landing strip on the slopes of Mt Ballyhoo adjacent to the seaplane parking apron. With dimensions of 3,000ft x 300ft it was enough for lightly loaded PBYs and was promptly used by P-38s.

133

It had been the Japanese intention not only to create a diversion at Dutch Harbour as part of their Midway Island plan, but also to invade the western Aleutians. Their task force was reinforced about 600 miles south of Kiska by *Zuiho*, *Kongo* and *Haruna* from Midway, and on 6 June, 1,250 men were landed on Kiska. On the 7th, there were landings on Attu.

It wasn't until the weather cleared on 10 June that Lt Litsey of VP-41, on flying over Kiska sighted enemy troops on land and many ships in the bay. By that time the Japanese had set up AA guns and were dug in. B-26s, B-24s and B-17s of the AAF initiated raids on Kiska, and were followed by PBYs operating from the tender USS *Gillis* in Nazan Bay, Atka Island. The Catalinas continued their raids over the three days 11, 12 and 13 June until petrol and bombs on Gillis were exhausted. This was the so-called 'Kiska Blitz'.

Around the start of the blitz, thirteen PBYs of VP-43 arrived, commanded by Lt Cdr C. B. Jones. They had flown in from San Diego and were deployed at Chernofsky, a small port on the northern side of Unalaska, from where they operated as flying boats. During the three-day blitz, AAF planes returned to Umnak; the USN PBY crews were accommodated on board USS *Gillis*, but for additional sleeping space, some were billeted in Aleut fishermen's shacks, pervaded by the smell of sea-lion blubber.

After the Kiska raids, the PBY squadrons withdrew; VP-41 to Dutch Harbour, VP-42 to Cold Bay, VP-43 to Chernofsky Harbour and VP-61 with VP-62 to the Shuagin Islands, all to resume routine patrols. For Lt Cdr Foley of VP-41, it was a welcome break, but he was conscious of the strain apparent in his aircrews. Only one form of recreation appeared possible — fishing — and arrangements were made for a crew to go up into the hills with rod and line, to seek out a stream or brook.

One rare clear day, a pilot returning from Kodiak to Dutch Harbour reported sighting a wrecked Japanese plane in the centre of Akutan Island. A party was sent and the Zero fighter found in marshy terrain was recovered intact. It was later flight tested at San Diego and then flight analysed at Anacostia, DC. Subsequently the Grumman F6F was designed to exploit the Zero's weaknesses.

The Americans, conscious of enemy occupation of their soil, sent a task force to bombard Kiska on 18 July. They were supported by the 11th Air Force under General William Butler. On the 19th the tender USS *Casco* (AVP12) established an advanced base at Nazan Bay, Atka, for US Navy PBYs. With rough water, fog and low cloud, effective operations were impossible. VP-41 aircraft were now reduced to seven, and when armed with a torpedo and a 1,000lb bomb, climbing was slow and tedious. In a squadron led by Foley, planes were kept together by shining Aldis lamps astern in the clouds and fog banks which they encountered. They had to jettison their loads before touching down in the dark at Nazan Bay which was unprotected and rough. Subsequently on 7 August, Kiska was bombarded by another force but under radar control without significant effect.

By September 1942, VP-41 crews were exhausted and were ordered back to Seattle from Dutch Harbour for rest and recreation. For Cdr Foley, the pleasure of meeting family and friends was countered by condolence calls to the families of five highly qualified plane commanders with their crews lost — three due to insidious weather conditions and two crews due to enemy action.

A fortnight later VP-41 assembled on the Sand Point apron and grouped their seven amphibian Catalinas which had been cleaned and re-equipped. They were airborne over Lake Washington and then in 'V's led by Cdr Foley, headed towards Sitka, 500 miles away. Half-way there, the overcast came down and by mid-morning was at 100ft, but they reached Sitka at 14:00hr, landing in the channel beyond Baranov Island.

Return to Kodiak and Adak

The following morning they crossed the Gulf of Alaska to Kodiak and found an addition — a 100ft water tower near the flying field. It was considered to be a possible aiming point for an enemy submarine; the tower was dismantled and a water catchment was constructed on a nearby mountainside.

VP-41 found VP-42 at Dutch Harbour and they themselves were ordered on to Cold Bay from where they were to operate using a landing strip. Although with fewer salt-water problems, the open wind-swept area was especially hard for ground crews. Their sole recreation was movie films. A ground staff officer sent to Seattle to arrange for some improvement, organised the shipment of six pianos but five of these were acquired by other units in transit. Their Quonset huts were heated by wood-burning stoves which proved inadequate.

At the end of October, VP-41 moved to a new base at Adak. Both messes and accommodation were tents. 'Flying control' was a Quonset hut equipped with radio, Aldis lamps and primitive field lighting but located 50ft above the lowest ground. About half the time, the runway was covered with three to four inches of water. With no tie-down points in volcanic ash and winds averaging 20-60kt, Catalinas were anchored by lashing three 1,000lb bombs which had been de-fuzed under each wing. The wings of the PBYs were still lifted as the winds picked up. The 'lows' over the Aleutians were generated by cold air from the Bering Sea meeting the relatively warmer air over the Japan current on the south side of the Aleutians, and were in a six-hour cycle. As the low passed over there would be a rapid reversal of wind direction.

From time to time, Catalinas of the US Navy, AAF planes and US submarines would encounter Japanese supply ships en route from Paramushiro to Kiska or Attu.

In November, VP-41's CO — Cdr Paul Foley — was ordered to Washington, DC, for duty in the Bureau of Aeronautics. He had been awarded the medal of the Legion of Merit for his services in the Aleutians campaign. Further recognition of Cdr Foley's North Pacific service was given by his wife naming a new escort carrier (Hull No 31), *Prince William* after an Alaskan sound. It was commissioned on 9 April 1943.

Aleutian attack — the sinking of *RO-61*

At the end of August, the CO of VP-42 was on duty at the Command Centre, Dutch Harbour, when he, James S. Russell was informed that their seaplane tender, USS *Casco*, anchored at Nazan Bay, Atka Island, had been torpedoed. Also at Dutch Harbour, heading a detachment of two PBYs from VP-43 was Carl

'Bon' Amme[5]. Amme had gained his wings at Pensacola on 16 February after 248 hours flying; he was posted to VP-43 at San Diego in March, and following Japanese attacks on Midway and Dutch Harbour in June, VP-43 was sent immediately to the Aleutians. On 12 and 13 June, Amme had been one of the plane commanders to attack warships of the Japanese task force at Kiska.

In August, USS *Casco* (AVP-12) was deployed incident to the US occupation of Adak Island, and was anchored awaiting further orders. A Japanese submarine had entered the bay intent on a torpedo attack, but when USS *Reid*, a destroyer stationed to guard the tender arrived, the submarine settled on the bottom to await a more favourable opportunity. It so happened that Army engineers had flown from Dutch Harbour to Adak, but found the bay too rough to land with a 40kt wind, and returned to USS *Casco* which was boarded with difficulty. It was then decided that the engineers should be taken by the destroyer to Adak, sixty miles away, thus leaving USS *Casco* unguarded.

RO-61, seeing the destroyer leave, surfaced and fired two torpedoes. One ran up on the beach, but the other struck the tender destroying one engine and killing five men. Aviation fuel tanks were opened releasing petrol over the sea, in addition to a flame float which ignited. The vessel was saved by one of the crew — Sam Cobean, who dived into the sea and kept the float away from the petrol until the flames died down. For this gallant action he was awarded the Silver Star. *Casco* got under way with one engine but it failed and the tender was beached.

During an intensive air-sea search, Lt Sam Coleman of VP-42 reported from his PBY-5A fog almost completely covering the area, followed by a sighting report. Coleman was over a hole in the fog in the lee of Atka volcano when *RO-61* surfaced beneath him. His crew raked the conning tower with 0·5 machine-gun fire and two quick runs were made releasing firstly two depth charges and then two 500lb bombs.

Amme at Dutch Harbour had organised a medical team and took off at first light. On arriving at Atka 3½ hours later, he found the bay blanketed by fog and flew on to Adak to await better weather. About an hour later with some clearing of fog at Atka, he was airborne and on rounding Mount Korovia, sighted the beached tender, and then due east of the volcano, his co-pilot Arnie Havu saw a surfaced submarine.

Amme made a diving turn to the right to gather speed and head for the vessel. He then sighted the other PBY on a bombing attack — Sam Coleman's. With no time to set up a bomb sight, Amme levelled off at 500ft and, at what he judged to be the right instant, pulled back the throttles to idle and nosed directly over the submarine, releasing two depth charges manually. Throttles were then jammed forward and the nose of the aircraft pulled up. In such a manoeuvre he says; '. . . we only lose about 200ft in altitude, but the accuracy can be great depending upon how many times the pilot has practised it'. One of Amme's crew reported a direct hit which bounced off the side of the submarine and also a close miss. The vessel dived but the PBY remained. The PBY crew saw an oil slick moving out to the east and then changing course to the north.

Amme flew about twenty miles north of the island and alerted USS *Reid* with an Aldis lamp and later indicated the estimated position of the submarine with smoke floats; the destroyer released a pattern of depth charges. When the Japanese submarine surfaced, *Reid* raked the deck of the vessel with 20mm cannon fire, and the submarine was then sunk with a broadside. About five prisoners were taken, the officers and NCOs of *RO-61* preferring to die in the Bering Sea. Amme, on returning to the tender USS *Casco*, found that the torpedo released by *RO-61* had gone right through the bunk room where he normally slept. Sam Coleman was later to be lost while attacking a destroyer in a Liberator, apparently shot down during his bombing run.

VP-43, which was commissioned on 21 July 1941, had by the end of that year six PBY-5 flying boats in Alaska. As with VP-41, they returned to Alameda, California, in September 1942 for a two-week stay during which time radar was installed in their aircraft. Up to that stage, their flying was notably lacking in navigation aids. As Capt Amme writes: 'We had no radio range or beacons along the [Aleutians] chain. Practically all flying was done near the surface. Weather was the most dangerous enemy. It was easy to get lost.'

As a typical example he quotes a 7.9-hour search north of the Aleutian chain on 13 July 1942. The weather was foggy and he flew at 100ft above the waves. Suddenly he saw a submarine 200yd ahead, and to starboard. By the time he had turned to attack, the submarine had dived and contact was lost. Of the radar which was fitted, he writes: 'It lacked precision but did warn us that we were heading perilously close to mountains when we were in fog or haze, skimming along the water'.

In March 1943, his crew was sent to Amchitka, where a short Marsden airstrip had been constructed. With two PBYs there were some P-40s of the AAF. On one or two occasions, the PBYs were used to decoy Zeros with floats out of Kiska, fifty miles away. On the first occasion, it was successful; on the second, the P-40 fighters did not appear and the PBYs sought cloud cover.

Carl Amme was ordered back to Whitbey Island in Puget Sound during May to take command of VP-45 which had been newly commissioned. It was on 4 May that the first regular patrols began from Amchitka and extending the search area of Fleet Air Wing 4 beyond Attu towards the Kuriles. By 8 July 1943 VP-45 was stationed at Attu which had been captured by the US Army[6]. On 10 July, Amme led the first bombing mission by PBYs over Paramushiro. It was after dark and the sky was overcast when the PBYs reached Paramushiro and their 500lb bombs were released by radar with unknown results. The procedure was repeated on the 19th.

At Casco Cove in Attu, there was not enough shelter for flying boats against prevailing winds, and VP-45's PBY-5s were returned to the USA for replacement with PBY-5As. On 20 December two Catalinas of VP-43 flew the first US Navy photo-reconnaissance and bombing mission over the Kuriles from Attu.

1 Kano Maru 8,752 tons, sunk 8.11.42, 51°58'N 177°33'E by AAF & surface craft.
2 Rear Admiral Paul Foley, Jr, USN (Ret).
3 *United States Naval Aviation 1910-70*, p113.
4 C&C, Vol 1, p469; SEM, Vol IV, p175 gives six out of ten lost.
5 Captain Carl Amme, PhD, USN (Ret).
6 28 May 43 Yamaziki was invited to surrender via a drop from a PBY — he refused. Attu was taken on 29th (Ref SEM, Vol VII, p49).

Chapter 16
Shipping strikes by the US Navy Catalinas

Attack on a Japanese convoy

VP-34 was one of three Catalina squadrons of the US Navy under Fleet Air Wing 17 which was formed on 15 September 1943 for operations in the south-west Pacific area. The Wing was commissioned in Brisbane, Australia, and commanded by Commodore T. S. Combs. VP-34 arrived in New Guinea in December and was based at Samarai on the southern tip of New Guinea. Their first operations were on the 31st and flown by the CO Lt Cdr T. A. Christopher, Lt V. V. Utgoff and Lt E. Fisher. Following a report of an enemy warship north of New Britain, Christopher located a Japanese destroyer there which he attacked and scored a direct hit with a 500lb bomb. The same night at about 02:00hr on the 1st, Lt Fisher sank a merchant vessel estimated at 9,000 tons in Hyane Harbour, Los Negros Island in the Admiralties.

On 11 January, Lt Utgoff flew along the north-eastern coastline of New Guinea. He first made bombing runs on an enemy airfield and then sank a lugger off the Sepik river, and by strafing with 0·5 machine guns, set a small tanker on fire. Lt S. B. Bradley, who was patrolling the Bismarck Sea, located two ships. One — a destroyer — was attacked from 300ft. He obtained a very near miss with a 1,000lb bomb which must have exploded below the vessel which was lifted out of the water and AA fire from the destroyer ceased.

A Japanese convoy was reported on 15 January[1] as having entered the Bismarck Sea en route from Truk to Rabaul. VP-34 laid on a strike of five or six aircraft, some armed with two 500lb and two 1,000lb bombs, others with two 500lb bombs and a torpedo. They were airborne from Samarai at 18:00hr. After seven hours' flying the convoy was sighted north-west of New Hanover steaming at 10kt. Lt

Fisher made three torpedo runs against one of the escort cruisers — all proved abortive due to the torpedo hanging up.

Lt S. B. Bradley in another PBY was more successful. In a dive-bombing attack on a tanker, his co-pilot released a 500lb and a 1,000lb bomb, scoring two direct hits. Flames from this vessel illuminated targets for other aircraft. As Captain V. V. Utgoff now writes: 'On my airplane I carried a torpedo under the port wing and two 500lb bombs under the starboard wing. Each of the five planes had an assigned sector to search. I found nothing in mine, but I intercepted a radio contact report from one of the others. Presently I saw distant AA fire and a burning ship. Seeing the other ships in the convoy I made a torpedo attack at 50ft altitude. There was no explosion so I concluded I had missed. I then climbed to 1,200ft and circled the convoy. The AA fire was continuing and the burning ship was clearly visible. I observed another of our Catalinas make an attack and then spotted a large freighter ahead. When one mile distant I pushed over in a shallow dive. At half-a-mile and 500ft altitude he took me under AA fire. I could see the black puffs of exploding shells directly in front of and above the cockpit. I pushed over further to get under the flak and released my two bombs at an altitude of 100ft. Both bombs found their mark and we left the ship in flames.'

The attacking PBY seen by Lt Utgoff was flown by Lt Cdr Christopher who released four bombs onto another ship which resulted in debris being blasted 200ft up and causing all AA from the vessel to cease. Reconnaissance by an AAF aircraft the following day confirmed one ship in the final stages of sinking, to be closely followed by two others. The *Meisho Maru* sinking was shared with AAF aircraft, the *Hozugawa Maru* and *Shunko Maru* are credited to Navy land-based aircraft.

Strikes and rescues by US Navy Catalinas

Another pilot with VP-34 at that time was Jules M. Busker[2] who had joined the squadron in March 1942 as an Ensign at the home port of Norfolk. For him, the squadron really 'went to war' when it moved to the South Pacific, and as he states: 'We became fairly accurate with our glide bombing'. Busker was one of three in the squadron who on the night of 18 January made successful attacks on Japanese shipping.

Lt Fisher located a 2,500-ton tanker between Manus and Los Negros in the Admiralty Islands. He scored a hit on the vessel amidships with a 500lb bomb which sank the ship. Lt Busker and Lt Cdr Christopher sank other vessels. According to Capt Busker, the shipping strikes undertaken by VP-34 were with their heavily laden Catalinas taking off at about 16:00-17:00hr on a lone night search lasting 14-15 hours. They carried two 1,000lb and two 500lb bombs with some fragmentation bombs within the fuselage, and cruised at about 800-1,500ft. After hopefully getting the enemy between the moon and the aircraft, they would glide down to about 50-150ft and release the bombs with four-second delay fuzes.

When VP-34's shipping strike role was taken over by VP-33, VP-34 became employed on air-sea-rescue missions. One of these was flown by Lt Nathan Gordon who on 15 February acted as cover for a B-25 raid on Kavieng, New Ireland. After first touching down and taking off near what proved to be an empty raft, he was directed to another dinghy close to the enemy shore by a B-25. Gordon landed despite the heavy swell and taxied to the dinghy which was under Japanese fire. He cut his engines so that the dinghy could come safely alongside. The enemy fire was shifted to the Catalina, but the engines were started and they were airborne.

A further call was made to him, and once again he touched down and picked up three more. He was by now overloaded, but when airborne, received yet another call. This time it was necessary to approach the ditched aircrew close to the beach and near enemy fire to rescue six more ditched aircrew. Two lines in *United States Aviation* are devoted to this incident. They read: 'Gordon, Nathan, G. Lt. (jg) USN 11421 Rescue of 15 officers and men under fire in Kavieng Harbour, 15 Feb 1944'. This entry comes under the heading 'Medal of Honour Awards' which is first in order of precedence for US Service awards.

By the end of February, Japanese Naval aircraft in Rabaul were ordered to Truk from which their fleet had been withdrawn. Allied orders to invade Seeadler Harbour in the Admiralties were made on 13 February and on the 27th, a USN Catalina landed a party of American soldiers on Los Negros. Although observed by the enemy, the Japanese commander had given orders not to fire to create the impression of the island having been evacuated, although there were 2,615 Japanese troops in the Admiralty Islands. Following a bombardment by cruisers and destroyers, Allied landings were made on 29 February.

Seeadler Harbour later served as a base for VP-33 and VP-52 with the tenders *Tangier* and *San Pablo*. Lorengau airfield on Manus was captured on 17 March and Emirau Island occupied on the 20th. Rabaul, with a Japanese garrison of about 80,000, could now be blockaded which was in keeping with MacArthur's leap-frog tactics. In addition to Seeadler Harbour, Langemak Bay south of Finschhafen in New Guinea was used by USN Catalinas, Langemak serving VP-34 for air-sea-rescue sorties. As part of operation 'Reckless', landings were made on Hollandia in Dutch New Guinea during 21-24 April.

On the 25th an exceptional rescue was achieved by one of VP-34's plane commanders — Jules Busker. As Captain Busker recalls: 'We had been alerted that an Air Corps craft with five crewmen aboard had to ditch after a strike on the island of Truk. My crew and I departed from the Admiralties on a day search in an area normally searched by Japanese "Bettys". About 350 miles out one of my crewmen spotted a lifeboat in the water, and also a PBY from another squadron going in for a landing. A few moments later, while circling, I noticed that the PBY was beginning to settle so I flew over low. The plane crew was signalling for me to land which I did.

'It was the best full stall landing I had ever

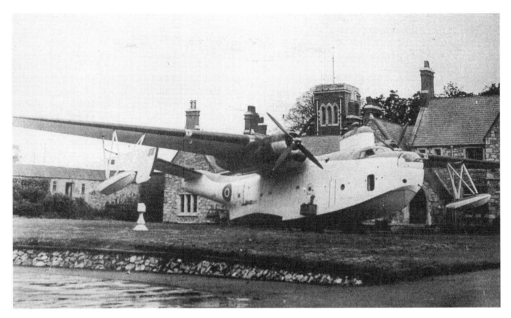

A Martin Mariner (PBM) flying boat such as succeeded PBYs in some US Navy squadrons. This RAF machine has the serial No JX103.

made. The Cat splashed down nicely into the sea which had about 8ft swells. Upon landing, we saw the other ill-fated Cat go down leaving the crew of fourteen plus the five Air Corps crew adrift in the lifeboat. I also had fourteen total in my crew. The rough landing of the lost PBY had broken open its hull and severely injured one of the crew. The five Air Corps personnel were in bad shape with broken arms and the fatigue from five days' exposure in a lifeboat.

'Now to get airborne! We drained about 1,000gal of fuel and threw a few unneeded items overboard. The wind was about 12kt so I elected to go into it directly. Up and down the swell we went, until finally a large swell threw our Cat violently into the air. I yelled for my co-pilot, Bill Syring, to give her hell! Bill actually bent the throttles in going for full power. Our trusty Cat slowly settled back down and just kissed one more swell — I knew we had it made. It was a great moment back at base when a medical team met us and gave the injured first aid. We silently thanked our Black Cat.'

From 1 April, searches had been undertaken from the Admiralties as far out as 1,000 miles to check for any Japanese shipping which might be sailing in reaction to the intended Hollandia landings. On 12 May, the tender San Pablo was at Hollandia to act as a base for a detachment of Catalinas which were detailed for night anti-shipping strikes. The tender Orca relieved San Pablo on the 22nd and meanwhile Half Moon had arrived on the 16th.

The occupation of the Marianas in the central Pacific area was to take place during the period 11 June to 11 August but American Marines went ashore on Saipan Island in the group on 15 June. Saipan had been an important Japanese base and its occupation cut the enemy sea communications to the south.

Between 18 and 21 June a major battle was fought between Japanese and Allied fleets west of Saipan in the Marianas. This, the Battle of the Philippine Sea, involved both land and carrier-based aircraft. In the engagement, the Japanese lost a carrier, two other warships and 402 aircraft. It is summed up by

FLYING CATS

Capt Roskill[3] with the comment that the Philippine Sea came firmly under Allied control, thereby sealing the fate of the Mariana Islands. Guam, south of Saipan, was taken by the Allies on 10 August.

In the US Navy, there was some redeployment of Catalina units and personnel. On 9 July, Rear Admiral Frank D. Wagner (who had commanded Patwing 10 at the time of the Japanese Philippines offensive) relieved Commodore Combs as Commander of the 7th Fleet aircraft. Fleet Air Wing 17 moved their headquarters to Manus, Admiralty Islands, on the 27th, and FAW-10 moved up from Perth, Australia, to Los Negros in the following month.

Operations by the US Navy 'Black Cat' squadrons

About this time, VP-34 returned to shipping strike operations with Lt Cdr V. V. Utgoff as their Commanding Officer. They had the tender *Orca* moored at Wundi (or Woendi) Island off Biak near Dutch New Guinea on the 30th. One of VP-34's first successes was achieved by Lt J. Ball while operating over the Ceram Island area, when he attacked a merchant vessel scoring four hits with bombs. The only Japanese ship sunk about this time by US Navy land-based aircraft was the *Seia Maru*, a passenger-cargo vessel of 6,659 tons lost in position 01°46′S 125°32′E on 1 August. However, on the night of 1 August, a Japanese destroyer must have had its steering gear damaged by a very near miss in an attack made by Lt Cdr Utgoff.

VP-11 joined VP-34 on the 6th at Wundi Island but later, on 22 August, both units moved up to Middleburg Island off the Vogelkop Peninsula of New Guinea. There, the squadrons were based on the tenders *Orca* and *Half Moon*. This move put part of Mindanao in the Philippines within range of the Catalinas. During the rest of August, VP-34 undertook a series of armed recces with apparent success against small enemy vessels[4] and on the 30th returned to Manus Island in the Admiralty group.

VP-11 were to continue their armed recces during the following months, initially from Middleburg, and subsequently from Morotai before their tour of duty in the Pacific areas ended in November.

During 1943, VP-33 had served initially in the Canal Zone, followed by duty in the central Pacific, and later in Australia. From October 1943 until February 1944, VP-33 had operated from bases at Perth, Exmouth Gulf and Darwin. While at Perth, their PBYs were converted to 'Black Cats' by the application of matt black camouflage, their bomb sights were removed, and the aircraft were fitted with radio altimeters. The latter were to enable accurate low level bombing attacks to be made in respect of altitude, alleviating at least one of the very real hazards of such sorties.

During this period in the Pacific war, the rapid advance being made by the Allies, and the earlier successes of other Catalina squadrons, limited the targets available to VP-33. According to the squadron record, however, while based at Samarai, the unit sank seven merchant vessels, damaged others and destroyed a number of enemy barges. In addition, raids were made into enemy-held territory as far as Hollandia.

On the night of 12 Match, PBY-5 No 08521 was airborne from Samarai Island at about 16:00hr. It was commanded by Lt Gates whose co-pilots were Lts George Favorite and Robert Hendrie. Crew members were J. B. Hawk, 1st mechanic, R. G. Diez, G. E. Delong and H. L. Heinrichsen — gunners; and R. Utterberg and L. T. Wentworth, radiomen. Their mission was to search for the crew and plane that was overdue from the previous night, but also to seek and destroy any enemy ships that could be found off the north coast of New Guinea. Their departure was timed so that enemy territory would be reached after dark, and they flew along the coast to Japen Island in Geelvink Bay, the area which the lost crew should have covered. There was no sign of either survivors or of Japanese shipping.

On the way back however, as Lt Cdr Favorite recalls: '. . . We spotted three coastal cargo ships which we estimated to be between 1,000-2,000 tons each, running close to the shore off Tanamarah Point. We attacked them with machine-gun fire and observed that their crews had run them up on the beach.

'We were back in that area several weeks later and saw and photographed the burnt out hulks. We continued our search on the way back with no success. Just north of Hollandia we spotted a 4,000-ton freighter and made a

140

low level glide bombing attack dropping a string of four 500lb bombs. We made no direct hit but believed it might have been damaged with a near miss.

'Having no more ammunition we had to withdraw. Near Aitape we suffered some intense AA fire, probably from a Japanese patrol boat. One bullet went through the forward cabin area, missed me at the navigator's station by about an inch, and hit and instantly killed out radioman, Dick Utterberg. Very sadly, we continued on our way, stopping at the Australian base in Finschhafen to refuel before arriving back at Samarai about 12:00 noon, a 19.8-hour mission.'

VP-33 was the first unit to operate Allied aircraft from Seeadler Harbour, Manus Island. From there daylight searches were undertaken as far north as Truk and Woleai in the Caroline Islands. On the night of 9 April, the first attack by Allied forces against the Japanese base on Woleai Island was made by Catalinas of VP-33. They were then based on the tender USS *Tangier* in Los Negros Harbour, Manus Island. The lead plane was PBY No *08254* commanded by Lt Gates with George Favorite as navigator.

Of this trip, Favorite's recollections are: 'This was difficult of course, we had no navigation aids and the sky was overcast, so we had to depend on dead reckoning to hit a small island five miles in diameter 600 miles away. Fortunately, we encountered two small breaks in the overcast and I was able to get a couple of star sights, and we hit the target on the nose.

'We each made two dive-bombing attacks on the ships in the harbour from 3,000ft down to mast-head level. The wings were really flapping. Our plane scored hits on a 9,000-ton ship and a 2,500-tonner. We encountered heavy AA fire and came back with over forty holes in the plane. The Japanese sent up nightfighters, but interestingly they flew around with their lights on and never attacked us!'

VP-33 moved to Humboldt Bay, Hollandia, on 18 May where there were the tenders *San Pablo* and *Half Moon*. The squadron was taken off shipping strikes to provide air-sea-rescue cover for the AAF strikes against Wewak, Wakde, Biak, Noemfoor and other areas as a prelude to Allied landings. Of a number of successful rescues one of the more

notable was by George Favorite on 14 July. He made an open-sea landing fourteen miles from Halmahera which was then held by the enemy, to pick up the crew of six from a ditched B-25.

Between 22 March and 30 April, the Americans had made strikes on Palau, Hollandia and Truk using carrier-borne aircraft, and on 30 March the AAF had attacked Hollandia. Landings had been made at Aitape, east of Hollandia, on 22 April.

Forming part of the American 7th Fleet at that time were PBY-5s of squadrons VP-33, VP-52 and VP-34. VP-33 and VP-52 became based with tenders *Tangier*, *San Pablo* and *Heron* in Seeadler Harbour, on the NE coast of Manus Island in the Admiralties, each with thirteen Catalinas. This followed landings which had been made in February. VP-34 with ten PBY-5s under Lt Cdr T. A. Christopher was based with the tender *Half Moon* at Langemak Bay, south of Finschhafen, New Guinea. Nos 11 and 20 Squadrons, RAAF, had become attached during 14-21 April to the Seeadler Harbour group. In addition to mining Balikpapan Harbour, the RAAF carried out patrols and strikes in the Arafura, Banda and Timor seas.

The Americans similarly were involved with searches and strikes to Truk, Woleai Atoll in the Carolines and rescue operations. From 1 April they had undertaken searches as far as 1,000 miles from the Admiralty Islands to detect any Japanese vessels. A detachment of PBYs was located at Hollandia to undertake shipping strikes in north-west New Guinea. The tender *San Pablo*, which had arrived on 12 May, was relieved on the 22nd by *Orca*, and was supported by USS *Half Moon* from 16 May.

Biak Island had been invaded on 27 May and in July the tender USS *Wright* moved to Owi Island off Biak. The former CO of Patwing 10 — Rear Admiral F. D. Wagner — relieved Commodore Combs as commander of the aircraft of the American 7th Fleet, and now to be with advancing rather than retreating forces. From Truk in the Carolines, to Mindanao in the Philippines, the western Pacific was covered by Allied air patrols.

VP-11, which had joined VP-34 at Woendi Island, near Biak, on 6 August, moved to Middleburg Island off the Vogelkop Peninsula on the 22nd and was served by the tenders *Orca* and *Half Moon*, as also was VP-34. During the following weeks of August and September, VP-11 received via their CO, Lt Cdr T. W. White, six despatches from the Commander Aircraft 7th Fleet congratulating them on their achievements.

Lt Nelson attacked a Japanese destroyer off Celebes on 29 August against intense AA fire from ships and shore batteries. About the same time Lt Cdr White sank two merchant vessels, one near Bangka Island, the other at Manado. At Davao Gulf, Mindanao, on 3 September, an air gunner in Lt Hine's crew set fire to a 7,500-ton tanker using a 0.5 machine-gun. In the same area but at Saragani Bay on the 4th, Lt Penfold attacked some small ships, sinking three and damaging two others. The despatch from the Fleet Commander dated 9 September reads: 'Congratulations on landing the big one at Zamboanga'. This must surely relate to a 10,000-ton tanker sunk by Lt jg J. D. Dyer on the 8th off Basilan Island which is south of Zamboanga, Mindanao[5].

On 9 September, FAW-17 moved to the Schouten Islands north of Dutch New Guinea to direct patrol plane operations in support of the intended occupation of Morotai. Following a bombardment by the American fleet and bombing by Allied aircraft, Morotai was taken on 15 September under MacArthur's direction and by-passed a strongly held Halmahera. Simultaneously, Admiral Halsey captured a base in the Palau group in the Caroline Islands deploying American Marines. These two moves, given by Churchill as of 'high importance'[6] were a prelude to the Leyte Island battle which followed in October.

On 1 September, VP-33 Catalinas began operating from the tender *Orca* (AVP-49), located off Middleburg Island north of the Vogelkop Peninsula. They were commanded by Lt Cdr Fernald P. Anderson who had earlier relieved Lt Cdr Bengston as CO. In the following weeks they were to sink over 100,000 tons of enemy shipping within the Mindanao-Celebes-New Guinea area.

Nine ships were sunk in the first four nights. One of the first missions was flown by Lt jg John R. Zubler who, on the night of 2 September, sighted eight coastal freighters of about 1,000 tons anchored along the eastern

shore in Davao Gulf, Mindanao. During his first run he released four 500lb bombs set at four seconds delay from about 300ft altitude. Strafing runs were made using 0·5 machine-guns in the blisters, but in their last run, the gunner damaged the tail section of the Catalina with about a dozen bullets. Zubler withdrew to assess the damage. En route to base, a small ship was sighted in Beo Bay, Talaud Islands, and further strafing runs were made until all ammunition was exhausted.

On the fifth night, Lt Cdr Anderson located two destroyers moored together and they were bombed from mast height. Direct hits were scored on both vessels which exploded and were left on fire. A 7,500-ton merchant vessel was set on fire by Lt Merritt on the 16th. He flew so low in his attack that his starboard wing struck part of the ship which became embedded in the aircraft and was brought back to base. The ship had been left in flames. Lt Sumpter, while over Davao Gulf on the 23rd, sighted two destroyers refuelling from a 10,000-ton tender. All three vessels received direct hits following the Catalina's bombing run. There were secondary explosions in the destroyers before they sank. The tender began listing and then rolled over. That same night, at Celebes, Lt Cdr Anderson sank a 10,500-ton tanker.

VP-33 rounded off this tour of anti-shipping strikes on the night of 3 October. One plane commander, Lt Sumpter, sighted two cruisers and two destroyers in Toli Toli Bay, Celebes. Instead of making a direct attack, he flew out to sea and then, using the terrain as cover, briefed his crew before moving in on a bombing run. When the aircraft was half-a-mile away from the warships, they all opened fire with both heavy and light AA. Sumpter headed for what was believed to be a 'Katori' Class cruiser and at 125ft altitude, released all his bombs as a salvo which struck the vessel. Sumpter escaped by taking the Catalina down to sea level and then making a sharp turn out of the bay. Fires were seen on the cruiser before Sumpter returned to base.

That same night Lt John Zubler also made a successful attack. As he writes: '. . . our mission was staged from the tender *Tangier* anchored off Morotai to the south-east of Celebes. We attacked a 3,000-ton freighter, dropping four 500lb bombs which exploded on the ship. Our plane was also hit by AA fire killing my radioman and wounding two other crew members. Our elevator control cable was severed which made control difficult since we were trimmed nose down position. We were about 650 miles from base and immediately began a return flight with no time to observe the damaged ship.' A Presidential citation later credited John Zubler with scoring two hits which probably sank the vessel.

VP-33 was given a short break from front-line operations by being withdrawn to a seaplane/patrol boat base at Woendi Island off north-west New Guinea before being ordered up to the Philippines on 23 October.

The Leyte Island naval battles

In addition to their anti-shipping forays, VP-33 flew some notable reconnaissance missions. These were during the naval battles of Leyte Gulf of 22-24 October. Three PBYs were airborne from Hinunangan Bay, Leyte, to search northwards for the Japanese naval units. According to Professor Morison's account[7] only one of these Catalinas could have encountered Admiral Kurita's ships, and this aircraft was flown by Lt Sillers who had as co-pilot, Lt jg Robert F. Hendrie. The latter's recollections differ somewhat from Colin Sillers'; as Hendrie recalls: 'We took off from Leyte Gulf around dusk of 23 October. As we were leaving the Gulf in pitch dark we were suddenly fired on by our friendly surface forces. Rather than try to run that gauntlet, Colin spiralled up to about 10,000ft and then we took off on our appointed patrol. That consisted of flying up, probably twenty to thirty miles from the Samar east coastline on our outward leg, the usual 500-600 miles, a right or left 90° turn, and then south, returning to our tender in the lower end of Leyte Gulf.

'We heard all the voice communications in the early morning concerning the Japanese force which had come through San Bernardino Strait but we located no Japanese ships either on radar or by sight. On arrival at Leyte, we could not locate our tender which unbeknown to us had moved to the northern end of the Gulf nearer Tacloban. As we searched for the ship we met up with Lt Maurice Moskaluk whose plane had been damaged by a large shell hole in the hull. As we joined forces,

suddenly we were attacked by a Japanese fighter from the rear. Just after that, the Army forces on the shore opened up on both of us. With that Moskaluk landed with us following. His plane sank and we picked them up.'

The Japanese fleet units were in fact detected by American torpedo boats.

It had been proposed by Admiral Halsey in September that Leyte Island in the Philippines be invaded. Bounded to the north by Luzon and Samar, two islands separated by the San Bernardino Strait, and to the south by Mindanao from which it is separated by the Surigao Strait, Leyte was known to be lightly defended by the Japanese. However, the enemy became aware of the American threat and decided to set a trap for the United States fleet by deploying a decoy force northwards as part of the 'Sho-Go' operation.

In the 'Sho-Go' operation, the Japanese intended luring the American fleet to the north while two more Japanese forces would enter the San Bernadino Strait and the Surigao Strait to attack the American invasion forces. Ultimately, it was the Japanese intention for their three main fleets — Northern, Centre and Southern under Vice-Admirals Ozawa, Kurita and Nishimura respectively — to engage and destroy the American fleets in a final 'show-down'.

Admiral Halsey, believing that the main enemy forces were off Luzon, ordered all his forces northwards. Meanwhile strong Japanese forces under Kurita entered San Bernardino Strait undetected. They were subsequently engaged by a comparatively weak American force of light carriers and destroyers. In this engagement, the Japanese lost three cruisers and a destroyer; the US Navy, two escort carriers and three destroyers off Samar.

The battle for Leyte involved three major engagements which were followed by pursuit operations. They were notable in the use made by the Americans of torpedo boats, destroyers, submarines and aircraft rather than the heavy guns of battleships. Accounts differ in respect of losses, but for the Japanese Churchill lists: three battleships, one fleet carrier, three light carriers, six heavy cruisers, four light cruisers, nine destroyers and one submarine[8]. These against the American losses of one fleet carrier, two escort carriers, three destroyers and one submarine.

After passing through San Bernardino Strait, Kurita was in a position to achieve a major victory against the American landings on Leyte but withdrew westwards. Captain Roskill in his account suggests reasons for this withdrawal; Churchill leaves others to form their own view[9]. American troops began landing in Leyte on 20 October, and by November (vide Churchill), 250,000 were there[10].

Prior to the troop landings on Leyte, Commander Parsons with Colonel Frank Rouelle of the US Army, flew from Morotai in a Catalina. Col Rouelle was landed on a beach south of Tacloban on 10 October to enable warning to be given to the native population via guerrilla headquarters of an intended pre-invasion bombardment.

At Morotai on 20 October, the date for the invasion of Leyte, the tenders *Tangier, Orca* and *San Pablo* served as bases for the PBYs. During rescue operations which followed the naval battles, PBYs based with the tender USS *San Carlos* at San Pedro Bay were engaged in searches for aircrew who were ditched. The CO of VP-34 at that time was Lt Cdr V. V. Utgoff, USN, who (as Captain), now writes: 'On 23 October 1944 I led a ten-plane flight consisting of five Catalinas from my squadron, VP-34, and five from VP-33, from Mios Woendi to Hinunangan Bay, Leyte.

'The next day I attended a conference on the USS *Half Moon*, a small seaplane tender. During the conference the ship was attacked by two Japanese twin-engined aircraft which made a strafing and glide bombing attack. They scored a few bullet hits and one man was slightly wounded. I observed a bomb which one of the airplanes dropped, enter the water short of the ship's stern, ricochet out of the water and fly over the stern, and re-enter the water on the other side. It failed to explode.

'During a second attack by the same two airplanes, the ship's AA battery hit one engine of one of the aircraft and set it smoking. That evening we observed the flashes of the engagement which was taking place at the entrance to Surigao Strait, while a number of our Catalinas were scouting the Japanese fleet.

'The next day the seaplane tender and the Catalinas moored nearby were attacked by Japanese dive bombers. The bombs missed,

but it was deemed advisable to move. We flew our Catalinas to San Pedro Bay, Leyte, and the tender joined us there later. That night, October 25, I set out to search for Kurita's northern force which was assumed to be retiring through San Bernardino Strait.

'Just after leaving Leyte Gulf I saw a life raft in the sea below with a man in it. I was reasonably certain that it was one of our aviators shot down by Kurita's forces earlier in the day. I radioed his position to our tender then continued on my search. It was unrewarding. Kurita's fleet had indeed passed through San Bernardino Strait as we learned later, but my own search was frustrated by thunderstorms covering the Strait. Our primitive radar was not up to "seeing" ships in the confines of a narrow body of water, and the thunderstorms inhibited visual search.

'After a frustrating night, at dawn, we started back towards Leyte Gulf. I deliberately flew back towards the position in which I had seen the life raft in order to ascertain whether the downed airman had been rescued. He was still there. I decided to try and make an open-sea landing and effect the rescue myself. There was little wind, but as I neared the water, I noted a heavy swell was running.

'I attempted a power landing, nose high, considerable amount of power on both engines, speed just above stalling speed. The aircraft hit hard, splitting open the bow and starting to take on water. I opened the throttles wide hoping to remain airborne but the airplane refused to fly; the right wingtip float caught a wave and slewed the airplane into a swell.

'The cockpit began to fill with water. The co-pilot and I opened our overhead hatches and started to climb out of the airplane. I noticed that the propellers were still turning — I had neglected to cut the magnetos, so I climbed back into the cockpit and killed the engines. Then I climbed over the top of the airplane and supervised the disembarkation of the rest of the crew.

'They broke out two life rafts and we all clambered aboard as the airplane assumed a vertical, nose down position with the bow under the water. Thirty seconds had elapsed.

'Don Wright, one of our mechanics, sustained a small cut over his right eye. Otherwise there were no injuries and we embarked dry shod into the life rafts. We paddled over to our would-be rescuee and took him into one of our life rafts. His name was R. B. Snell, and it turned out he had made an attack on a Japanese battleship the previous day and had run out of gas while trying to reach Tacloban airstrip. We then started paddling south towards the entrance to Leyte Gulf, keeping well clear of Samar which we understood was still occupied by the Japanese.

'We covered five miles in six hours and finally rounded the southern tip of Samar. Here we hoisted sail intending to sail into Leyte Gulf. At this time some Philippine natives arrived in their fishing boats and took us in tow. A Navy TBF spotted our rafts with the Philippine regatta and gave us air cover, chasing away a curious Jap airplane.

'The natives took us to their village and served fresh coconuts while preparing dinner. In the meantime, the TBF flew off and guided one of our Catalinas back to the village. The airplane landed in the adjacent lagoon, all of us embarked, and we were flown back to our tender. We had not stayed for dinner.'

On the night of 3 December, the destroyer USS *Cooper* was torpedoed by the Japanese destroyer *Take* in Ormoc Bay, Leyte. Some of the crew swam ashore but others remained to await rescue. This was undertaken by Catalinas, five from VPB-34 and one from the AAF which also provided fighter cover. The rescue took place on the 4th near Ponson Island and in sight of the enemy. One aircraft took 56 survivors in addition to its own crew of seven, another rescued 45, but 191 officers and men had been lost with the destroyer.

Mindoro and Luzon

At the end of November there were still Japanese troops on the western side of Leyte and General MacArthur planned to make landings at Ormoc Bay on 7 December when this objective was achieved. By the 12th, approaches were being made towards Mindoro by US Navy forces. In advance of the Allied warships on the night of the 14th-15th, were Catalinas patrolling twenty to thirty miles ahead. These aircraft had been airborne from Leyte, and at about 03:00hr on 15 December, one of them reported a surface contact. It proved to be a small merchant vessel which was sunk by a destroyer.

Landings were made on Mindoro that day and were a stage in General MacArthur's main objective — Luzon. In this Mindoro campaign, the Japanese lost 341 aircraft with fighters from American carriers giving blanket cover over Luzon.

Attention was now directed towards Luzon and on 2 January, Fleet Air Wing 17 HQ was based on the tender USS *Tangier* (AV-8) in San Pedro Bay to direct patrol plane support of the Lingayan Gulf operations. A task force was off the Lingayan Gulf on the 6th which was entered on the 7th. Two assault forces followed, and by 9 January, the day scheduled by MacArthur, 68,000 men had been landed. Thirty-four serviceable Japanese aircraft were found on Clark Field out of 243 which had been seen earlier.

Following the American landings on the 9th, Catalinas of VPB-71 which had been operating from Morotai Island moved up to undertake missions extending over the South China Sea. As bases they had the tenders USS *Barataria* (AVP-33) and USS *Currituck* (AV-7). During this period, VPB-71 was credited with sinking eight enemy ships and damaging nine others.

For the US Navy, the Luzon campaign was considered over on 20 January. Fleet Air Wing 17 had its headquarters established at Clark Field, Luzon, on 26 February. It was to be decommissioned the following January in Japan. Winston Churchill concludes his summing up of the Philippines campaign by the command of the South China Sea being lost by the Japanese and thus control of their supplies including oil. Catalinas of both the RAAF and the USN had played an active part including shipping strikes, reconnaissance and mercy missions. By now USN Catalina squadrons were converting to PBM Mariners on returning to the USA.

1 On 16.1.44 *Hozugawa Maru*, 1,925 tons, *Shunko Maru*, 4,027 tons, and *Meisho Maru*, 2,735 tons, are recorded as sunk at 2°25'S 149°42'E.
2 Capt Jules M. Busker, DFC, USN (Ret).
3 SWR. Vol III Pt 2, p196.
4 Vessels of less than 500 tons are not recorded in the Joint Assessment Committee's lists.
5 Listed for the 9th is *Kuniyama Maru*, 6°30'N 121°50'E.
6 WSC. Vol IV, p157.
7 SEM. Vol XII, p289.
8 WSC. Vol VI, p162.
9 SWR. Vol III Pt 2, p223.
10 WSC. Vol VI, p164.

Chapter 17
Australia and the South Pacific

Ferry flights to Australia

Following the collapse of France and the entry of Italy into the war, communications with Australia became restricted, and on 28 June 1940 when the French banned flying over their colonial territory, air routes between Australia and Britain were cut. Qantas Empire Airways were requested by the Australian Dept of Civil Aviation in September to initiate a Pacific Ferry Service from the USA to Australia, there being the advantage that a civil organisation would not infringe American neutrality. At that time eighteen Catalinas were awaited for the RAAF.

The arrangement made was for an American crew to fly the aircraft from San Diego to Honolulu where the Australians would then take over. The route was Honolulu-Canton Island 1,921 miles, Canton Island-Noumea 1,900 miles, Noumea-Sydney 1,236 miles. The first flight was on 25 January 1941, captained initially by E. J. Greer but apparently with Capt Brain of Qantas, who had been organising the ferry, also on board and who was to take command in the latter stages of the delivery. From the official list of RAAF Catalinas this aircraft was with the RAF serial No *AH534* when it left San Diego to arrive at Rose Bay, Sydney, on 2 February 1941. Its civil registration was *VH-AFA*.

Glen Mumford, a former Merchant Navy radio officer who joined Qantas, writes: 'A. S. "Pat" Patterson (ex-Imperial Airways), our senior radio officer helped in the QEA ferrying the first eighteen RAAF Catalinas from the USA. These machines were equipped with Bendix exclusively, including the RDF with indicators for homing, and with the facility to obtain good beam bearings. On these Pacific flights for the first time I found myself in aircraft with stable fixed frequencies using crystal control.

'After the Coral Sea battle stopped the Jap in his track we commenced the Indian Ocean project because Australia was cut off from the

Mother country, there was an urgent need for communication to Europe and our troops in North Africa. In these latter operations we began with five Catalinas which were equipped with both Westinghouse G-09 powerful transmitters and Bendix apparatus. Catalinas *G-AGID, E-AGKS* and *G-AGKS* were installed with Westinghouse G-09 transmitters which had been designed for small ships, but the receivers were Bendix RA-1B.

'Operating speeds for the Catalinas of 110-112kt were later increased to 115kt. Although designed for an all-up weight of 27,000lb, QEA increased the figure to 35,150lb but 35,400lb was not uncommon. Aircraft were fitted with eight auxiliary tanks and at take-off carried seven tons of fuel. To become unstuck required a special technique worked out by the pilots.

'Navigation was more difficult westbound as we rarely flew above 2,000ft and low cloud limited astro-navigation. Eastbound, we often flew at up to 18,000ft. Cocos Island was avoided because of Jap surveillance there. Even rain delayed departures because its weight seriously affected the take-off performance. QEA pilots found Koggala lake especially difficult because of its short perimeter.'

A list[1] prepared by the Pacific Islands Aviation Society includes with the eighteen PBY-4s, a ninteenth with a contract No 27 and civil registration *VH-AFB*. The last of the PBY-4s, Consolidated Models 28-5MA, was delivered on 23 October 1941. It was lost over the Coral Sea on 5 May 1942.

The delivery of *A24-1* from San Diego to Sydney.

A Catalina was airborne at 14:15hr on Wednesday 12 February 1941 from San Diego on the first leg to Honolulu, commanded by L. J. McMakin. In addition to his own Consolidated Aircraft Corporation crew, McMakin had on board five Australians giving a total of nine. McMakin was obviously concerned with flying for maximum efficiency taking account of range and endurance. After being airborne with an all-up weight of 33,000lb he levelled off at 5,000ft flying between two layers of cloud, and for the first seven hours it was not possible to take either regular drift sights or obtain an astro-fix.

His navigator, therefore, depended on D/F bearings from Los Angeles in addition to winds which had been forecast. When the alto-stratus above had cleared, astro shots were taken, and in the final stages to Honolulu, bearings were taken using the aircraft's loop aerial in addition to bearings received from a ground station. They touched down at Pearl Harbor on 13 February having covered a distance of 2,371 nautical miles in 23hr 40min. It is significant that the best fuel consumption for the ferrying was achieved on this leg — an average of 56gal per hour.

At Pearl Harbor, the Americans handed over to the Australians with a Qantas pilot, Capt O. D. Denny, in command. The next leg of the ferry flight was to Canton Island in the Phoenix Islands. Departure was on 15 February but when over 500 miles from Honolulu, the starboard engine cut. By using a cross feed in the fuel system it was possible for the port engine pump to supply both engines and the flight continued.

The crew encountered a warm front with heavy tropical rain and in the latter stage to Canton Island, the Catalina was flown blind with reliance placed on a homing beacon. They were delayed at Canton Island until the 25th due to cyclonic weather conditions. Despite running through several storms, Noumea in New Caledonia was reached after a flight of 15¼hr. At Noumea two of the Australians disembarked taking with them the only sextant available. They were to return to America for more ferrying.

Without a sextant and flying above strato-cumulus cloud, the final stage from Noumea to Sydney involved navigation depending very much on D/F fixes from Lord Howe Island, Brisbane and Sydney where a landing was made at Rose Bay on 28 February after a flight of exactly ten hours.

Perhaps the most notable aspect of this ferry flight was the use of radio communication and the reliance placed upon it for navigation by both the American crew who from the outset checked their track from D/F bearings obtained from San Diego and Los Angeles; followed by the Australians without a sextant. Taking drifts was difficult for the Australian navigator, the sight being fitted at the tail tunnel and not near the navigation table. The observer's compass had no sight attachment for taking bearings from the aircraft. A request was made that the Pioneer drift sight Mk VII as used in the US Navy's PBYs be fitted. An indication of what was expected of the radio was given by an attempt to 'raise' Sydney from Canton Island, a distance of 3,000 miles. The final delivery along this route was completed on 23 October 1941 when *A24-18* was brought on charge.

No 11 and No 20 Squadron, RAAF, Port Moresby

No 11 Squadron was formed on 21 September 1939 and on the 25th it became established at Port Moresby, commanded by Flt Lt J. Alexander. It was the first RAAF unit to serve in New Guinea and was initially equipped with two ex-Qantas flying boats *Centaurus* and *Calypso*, *A18-10* and *A18-11*. In October the squadron received Seagulls *A2-11* and *A2-12*. Their first Catalina — *A24-1* — arrived on 19 March 1941 piloted by Sqn Ldr E. L. Sims.

The duties of No 11 Squadron included reconnaissance of the Port Moresby area bounded by Rabaul in New Britain, Tulagi in the Solomons and Vila in the New Hebrides. They were also involved in establishing a radio network and a chain of refuelling bases. By June 1941, flying boats were able to use bases at Rabaul, Tulagi, Vitla, and Noumea in New Caledonia.

An officer who had served with the Australian squadron No 10 but under RAF Coastal Command for the first two years of the war, Sqn Ldr J. A. Cohen, DFC[2], took command of No 11 Squadron in August. In the same month, No 20 Squadron was formed and took over six Catalinas from No 11.

By 7 December, No 20 Squadron had seven Catalinas and 11 Squadron was operating four Empire flying boats. Their first encounter with the enemy was on the following day when three Japanese pearl luggers were ordered to Thursday Island. It was on 8 December also, when No 11 Squadron lost Catalina *A24-15*, which crashed near Port Moresby with the RAAF suffering some of their first casualties of the Pacific War.

Six Catalinas each with 11 and 20 Squadrons on 11 December 1941, with fourteen fully-trained crews, represented the only first line long range capability of the RAAF. Following the rapid Japanese southwards advances, the RAAF flying boats were used in the evacuation of civilians from Port Moresby, Rabaul and Samarai. The ex-Qantas flying boat *A18-11* was flown by Sqn Ldr Cohen to take personnel from Samarai.

On 2 January 1942, the Japanese captured Manila and Australian forces were attacked at Rabaul on the 4th. Following a reconnaissance flight by a Hudson pilot — F/Lt Yeowart[3] — six Catalinas from Nos 11 and 20 Squadrons were briefed for a strike on the Japanese base at Truk in the Caroline Islands. Three of the aircraft went to Lorengau and three to Kavieng for refuelling but exceptionally bad weather forced them to return to base.

Sqn Ldr Cohen, operating from Tulagi in the Solomons with Catalina *A24-1*, made a flight of 21 hours over 14 January. This was for a reconnaissance of the Gilbert Islands during which he took 100 photographs, covering nine islands. A further Catalina strike against the Japanese naval base at Truk was arranged for 15 January, again with three to Kavieng and three to Lorengau for refuelling. Sqn Ldr T. H. Davies crashed on take-off from Kavieng and he, together with his crew of six were killed. An American pilot seconded from Patwing 10 of the US Navy, Lt G. H. Hutchinson, made a rescue attempt in his Catalina from 11 Squadron, RAAF; it proved abortive. Only one of the Catalinas, *A24-14* captained by F/Lt E. V. Beaumont, was successful in making an attack. Beaumont reached the target when there was a break in the cloud. He made two runs releasing sixteen bombs but with unobserved results due to the weather closing in.

At that time Catalinas, slow and with little defensive armament, were the only aircraft available with the range and bomb load capacity able to make such a strike. The Australian War Cabinet placed an order for nine more Catalinas on 20 January.

Catalina *A24-9* of 11 Squadron failed to return from a mission over Salamaua on the 21st. It was captained by the American with the squadron — Lt Hutchinson. While there he reported being attacked by five enemy fighters to be followed by a second signal of 'On fire'. Wreckage of the aircraft was later located in the jungle between Salamaua and Lae. Six others were lost with Hutchinson, but there was one survivor — Corporal T. H. Keen. Keen arrived in Port Moresby ten days later. From Robert Piper's account published in *Wings*, Keen was able to shoot down one of the Japanese fighters despite the heavy odds. All of the others in his crew must have been killed by enemy fire before the Catalina crashed. Keen was fortunate in being near an open hatch and was sucked out by the airstream but complete with parachute. He was found by local villagers who took him to a missionary who tended his ills. His subsequent return was by a native canoe and a small rescue aircraft from a landing strip. *A24-9* was the first Catalina shot down by enemy fighters in the Pacific area.

A second Catalina was shot down only a few hours later. This was *A24-8* captained by Flt Lt R. H. Thompson of 20 Squadron. While on a northerly reconnaissance with Flt Lt P. M. Metzer as second pilot and operating from Gizo Island in the Solomons, he was attacked by four Zero fighters. There had been time for the Catalina crew to give warning of the imminent invasion of Rabaul and report four enemy cruisers south-west of Kavieng. They were in fact shot down by anti-aircraft fire, two of the crew were drowned, the others became prisoners-of-war after being picked up by one of the cruisers.

Bendix radio installed in a RAAF Catalina. Such apparatus had crystal controlled fixed frequencies.

Possibly *A24-56 'R'* a *PBY-5 Bu.No. 08286* which in 1943 was serving with No 43 Sqdn RAAF.

On 22 January Japanese landings were made on both Rabaul and Kavieng while Balikpapan was occupied. With another landing at Ambon Island on the 30th the enemy was in range of Darwin.

Shipping strikes by RAAF Catalinas

With a long range and yet able to carry a useful bomb load, Catalinas were now used as strike aircraft on Simpson Harbour, Rabaul. On 24 January the aircraft were captained by Sqn Ldr T. McB-Price, Flt Lts Beaumont and G. E. Hemsworth, and F/Os A. L. Norman and B. H. Higgins. Due to cloud cover, targets were pin-pointed by the AA fire. Two nights later, during a raid by Hemsworth, Higgins and F/O Duigan, two ships were apparently hit and set on fire. There was also a possible hit on an aircraft carrier.

Sqn Ldr Cohen, while on an armed reconnaissance to Kavieng at the northern tip of New Ireland flying Catalina *A24-10* on the 27th, was attacked by three Japanese fighters. He promptly jettisoned his bombs and escaped in cloud but still with a long haul back to Samarai.

The Australians made two more raids on Rabaul, the final one being on the 30th. This was by captains Price, Norman, Hemsworth, Higgins and F/O W. K. Bolitho. Despite

searchlights, heavy and accurate AA fire, a direct hit was scored on one of the enemy ships and it was seen to catch fire. During the months of December and January the two Catalina squadrons completed 427 sorties totalling, 3,764 flying hours.

They were flying an aircraft designed as a pre-war patrol plane covering territory with limited intelligence of what hostile forces might be encountered. Should they be lucky enough to survive AA fire and fighter attacks, there was still the return flight to be covered without the support of friendly fighters and an established rescue service. When the American Navy came to employ their PBYs in a similar manner, a report stressed the vulnerability of the aircraft due to integral fuel tanks (as opposed to self-sealing tanks), lack of defensive armament and nil visibility for the pilot in an aft direction.

At this stage in the South Pacific war at the end of January 1942, Winston Churchill[1] sums up the losses in the area with Kendari in Celebes, Balikpapan, Borneo; Ambon Island, Rabaul, New Britain; and Bougainville in the Solomons. These gains by Japan represented a threat to communications with Australia being severed. Attacks by the RAAF Catalinas on Rabaul were renewed in February. On the first, twelve ships were seen in the harbour, but the results of subsequent bombing were

149

not observed. Five Catalinas were there on the night of the 3rd, and for the first time night fighters were encountered. F/O B. H. Higgins, captain of *A24-3*, evaded the enemy by diving down through the smoke from an active volcano on Matupi Island. He had been able to release his bombs before the attack by fighters, but his wireless operator was wounded in both ankles.

Flt Lt G. E. Hemsworth in *A24-5* was also attacked during his bombing run. He had to jettison his load; the aircraft being holed in both port and starboard fuel tanks, which were not self-sealing. Other damage was to a propeller, the tail unit, an oil tank, oil feed line and wings. There was now petrol pouring into the cabin, and one propeller had to be feathered, but Hemsworth then flew the aircraft for another five hours to Salamaua on the Huon Gulf coast of New Guinea where he touched down in darkness lacking the aid of a flare path. After temporary repairs *A24-5* was again airborne, but once more the damaged propeller had to be feathered. Without a second engine, altitude was kept at 50ft round the coast to Port Moresby. In 20½ hours flying, 14½ hours had been on one engine. Over 150 bullet holes were counted in the aircraft.

The Japanese landed at Gasmata on the south coast of New Britain on 9 February. An attack was made that night by Australian Hudsons and Catalinas, and on the 10th Sqn Ldr Cohen in *A24-6* led another attack on surface vessels and landing forces in that area, but with unknown results. On 24 February three Catalinas, *A24-2*, *A24-13* and *A24-17*, captained by P/O W. K. Bolitho, Flt Lt Beaumont and P/O Norman, were detailed to attack two airfields at Rabaul. Bolitho had an engine failure requiring him to jettison his bombs, and nothing was heard from Beaumont in *A24-13* which failed to return. Norman however, was successful in making an attack.

Sqn Ldr Cohen was again over Rabaul on the night of the 25th using Catalina *A24-2* as a dive-bomber from 1,300ft to straddle a ship near a wharf. Two nights later the same aircraft was used by Sqn Ldr F. B. Chapman to bomb the same wharf. The attack started a fire which could be seen from thirty miles away. The Japanese retaliated the following day when Port Moresby was raided by eleven

bombers escorted by five zero fighters. In this raid three Catalinas were lost at their moorings with a fourth damaged, leaving only three operational aircraft — a Hudson and two Catalinas. One Zero was shot down and the pilot captured. Successive Japanese raids on Port Moresby rendered it suitable only as a staging post and on 7 May the two Catalina squadrons set up their headquarters at Bowen, Queensland.

Port Moresby and the Battle of the Coral Sea

The Allies were aware by 17 April that the Japanese intended an assault on Port Moresby in New Guinea together with Tulagi adjacent to Guadalcanal in the Solomons. The loss of such bases would have been a direct threat to Australia and its communications with America. Admiral Nimitz, who had been appointed Commander in Chief of the Pacific theatre, endeavoured to deploy forces in the Coral Sea to counter such moves. The Japanese had made landings at Lae and Salamaua in New Guinea on 8 March, and Lorengau in the Admiralty Islands had been taken on 8 April. Using bases at Rabaul in New Britain and Truk in the Caroline Islands, the Japanese were in a position to make a direct frontal assault on Port Moresby.

Port Moresby was being used for operating Catalinas, Hudsons and Mitchells, and on 4 May, P/O A. L. Norman was captain of Catalina *A24-18* of No 11 Squadron, RAAF, detailed for a reconnaissance of the Shortland Island-Tulagi area. While over the Coral Sea south of Bougainville, he reported being attacked. There was no further signal and Norman with eight other aircrew, failed to return.

Catalina *A24-12* with Flt Lt N. D. Fader was on a similar mission the following day and reported in position 08°00'S 154°23'E, probably two heavy cruisers and a tender. On the 6th another Catalina, *A24-20* flown by Sqn Ldr G. E. Hemsworth, reported two Japanese cruisers south-east of Misima Island. Hemsworth and crew failed to return and it is thought that they may have been shot down by an aircraft from the light carrier *Shoho*. The Japanese invasion force for Port Moresby had left Rabaul on 4 May escorted by four heavy cruisers and the *Shoho*. A strike force sailed southwards from Truk but east of the Solomons. It comprised two carriers, two heavy cruisers and six destroyers. The Allied forces included notably the two American carriers *Lexington* and *Yorktown*.

During actions which took place on 7 and 8 May, the Japanese carrier *Shoho* was sunk and the carrier *Shokaku* damaged. On the Allied side, the American carrier *Lexington* was sunk, and the carrier *Yorktown* damaged. The battle of the Coral Sea was unique in that opposing fleets did not see each other, successes and losses being the result of strikes by carrier-borne aircraft. It proved to be a strategic victory for the Allies as, when the enemy was thwarted in his object, he turned back; in this case from Port Moresby. Less immediately obvious was the loss to the enemy of many highly trained naval pilots with their aircraft on which much of his earlier successes had been based.

Raids by Australian Catalinas

Tulagi, which had served as a base for the RAAF, was occupied by the Japanese on 3 May at the time of the Battle of the Coral Sea. The Catalinas of Nos 11 and 20 Squadrons attacked Tulagi on 29 May with *A24-16, A24-25* and *A24-26* from 11 Squadron in addition to *A24-19* from 20 Squadron. They bombed the wharf and buildings including the former RAAF W/T station leaving large fires burning. Refuelling for the trip was at Belap Island, New Caledonia, using an auxiliary vessel. Three PBYs of the US Navy which had been detailed to take part, were unable to reach the target. The American tender USS *Curtiss* was then at Noumea.

A further raid followed on 1 June by both Australian squadrons when 500lb bombs and incendiaries were used against the southern end of Tulagi Island and Makambo Island causing severe damage to the wharf and installations. After refuelling at Havannah Harbour, Efate Island in the New Hebrides, they returned to Noumea.

On 26 June, *A24-17* captained by F/O R. M. Seymour was attacked by a US Navy Wildcat while about to land at Havannah Harbour. The fuel tanks and port aileron of the Catalina were damaged and a bullet just missed the head of the second pilot — Sgt J. B. C.

A24-305 'E' of No 3 OTU refuelling on Cairns river, October 1945. This PB2B-2 was sold to Asian Airlines in 1948.

Bramwell. It was a case of mistaken identity — the RAAF roundels had been confused with the Japanese 'meat balls'. Subsequently, the red circle of the RAAF markings was removed. Appropriately, *A24-17* of 11 Squadron was repaired by mechanics of the USS *Curtiss*.

The following night Sqn Ldr Atkinson in *A24-25* of 11 Squadron and *A24-27* flown by Flt Lt Higgins of 20 Squadron were raiding Lae and Salamaua continuously for four hours using 500lb bombs, 20lb fragmentation bombs and beer bottles, the latter providing a high pitched sound to disturb the enemy. A further modification in raid techniques was the use of bombs fuzed to detonate after six to twelve hours' delay. These were employed by three RAAF Catalinas during an attack on Lae on 30 June shared with American Mitchell aircraft operating from Port Moresby.

The Japanese landed troops in the Buna and Gona area on the northern coast of New Guinea on 22 July. The two Catalina squadrons responded with a series of harassing raids beginning with Flt Lt Higgins in *A24-27* and Sqn Ldr Chapman in *A24-14* attacking Gona beach on 25 July dropping fragmentation bombs and using machine-gun fire. These raids by the Australians were continued until the end of the month on the beach-heads but did not prevent the Japanese from moving inland to capture Kokoda on the 29th.

A list[5] dated 10 August 1942 of serviceable aircraft of the RAAF includes 52 Hudsons, 58 Kittyhawks but only four Catalinas out of a total strength of 215. The latter figure included three Catalinas which were unserviceable.

Milne Bay, Lae, Wau and the Bismarck Sea Battle

The Allies had gained a strategic victory in the Battle of the Coral Sea of 5-8 May 1942; and the turning point of the Pacific war was fought at Midway a month later (4-6 June). The Japanese now elected to fight two campaigns concurrently — those of Papua, New Guinea, and Guadalcanal. The Papua campaign was against Australian troops supported by American Air Forces and the RAAF; the Guadalcanal campaign by American Marines and troops supported by other American forces but with a small but significant contribution by the RNZAF and RAAF.

The Papuan campaign began in July 1942 with the Japanese landing troops on the northern coast of New Guinea; organised resistance by the enemy ended on 23 January 1943. On the night of 25 August 1942, Japanese troops landed in Milne Bay, Papua, but were countered by a greatly superior Allied force. There were some final shots from a Japanese cruiser and a destroyer which had entered the Bay on the night of 7 September as they withdrew with survivors from their depleted troops.

The enemy was still running the 'Tokyo Express' down 'the Slot' to Guadalcanal, however, and both Australian and New Zealand aircraft were giving support to American operations in the Solomons. Targets for Catalinas of Nos 11 and 20 Squadrons, RAAF, became Buka Island, Buin and Kahili on Bougainville but ranging as far north as Kavieng on New Ireland.

In November the Catalinas were using Bowen and Cairns in Australia as bases, and in the same month a regular operation or 'milk' run was initiated. This was reconnaissance of enemy shipping routes extending from New Britain to Lae and Finschhafen in New Guinea. It stemmed from the hold the enemy retained on Lae and Salamaua and with an anticipated thrust inland towards an airfield held by the Allies at Wau.

During one such 'milk run' on 6 January 1943, Flt Lt D. Vernon in *A24-1* with co-pilot P/O T. Harrison and navigator F/O W. G. Leslie, located an enemy convoy which was intended to reinforce and supply troops in the Lae-Salamaua area. Vernon first used fragmentation bombs against an enemy airfield at Gasmata and strafed grounded Zero fighters while a second Catalina captained by Sqn Ldr T. V. Stokes shadowed the convoy.

On returning to the convoy, which by then had been illuminated by American AAF aircraft, it was seen to comprise four transports escorted by a cruiser and four destroyers. Vernon attacked a transport vessel from 4,000ft with Leslie releasing four 250lb bombs. It was a near perfect attack with the second bomb on the stern, and the third amidships. There was a terrific explosion and the whole ship was enveloped in flames. It listed to port and further explosions followed. When a destroyer switched on a searchlight, Vernon

The rescue of the crew from *A24-100* of 42 Sqdn by *A24-59* of 43 Sqdn. *A24-100 RK-L* was hit by AA at Makassar and ditched on 23 October 1944.

flew down for his gunners to strafe the transport. The light went out and the destroyer changed course.

A sinking was verified in a reconnaissance by Beaufighters the following day. They sighted a whaler with six survivors and four empty lifeboats. The crew of Catalina *A24-1* of No 11 Squadron had sunk the passenger-cargo vessel *Nichiryu Maru* of 5,447 tons in position 6°30'S 149°E[6]. Vernon attacked the same convoy four days later and set fire to a merchant vessel east-south-east of Gasmata with a direct hit on the ship's forward hatch.

One of No 20 Squadron's more experienced pilots was Sqn Ldr Hodgkinson[7]. He, like many Australians then in the SW Pacific area, had served previously with RAF Coastal Command. On the night of 18 February he flew his 'own' aircraft *A24-10* on a bombing raid against Kahili on Bougainville Island, a trip of seventeen hours. The following night he led another raid with two other aircraft, *A24-25* flown by F/Lt Duigan and *A24-36* captained by Flt Lt N. D. Fader, while Hodgkinson was in *A24-1*.

Writing on the armament used, he gives:

'The standard bomb load was eight 250lb GP bombs fuzed nose and tail. "Grass cutter" extensions were fitted to the nose fuzes. This appendage consisted of a 3ft metal rod having a small disc fixed to the forward end. On contact with the ground, the bomb exploded some three feet above, thus spreading the blast and shrapnel in all directions. Hence "grass cutter". In addition to this load we carried twenty 20lb bombs plus twenty 25lb incendiaries. These were stowed inside the aircraft and fuzed and thrown out of the blisters by hand. There were also our own personal gifts to the Japs — beer bottles with razor blades inserted in the neck made a terrific noise and a supply of these helped to keep the enemy awake. To complete the load, crew armourers made their own devices. One of these consisted of a tennis ball attached to the pin of a Mills bomb, the idea being that when the tennis ball hit the ground, it would bounce and pull out the pin.

'Some raids were a case of drop your load and get out, others of nuisance value where one would stay in the vicinity of the target for some time dropping our load at intervals to

153

keep them awake. At first light the American bombers would go in low level to stir things up again. Bombing runs were carried out at about 4,000ft as it was difficult to coax the Cat with this load any higher.

'The return trip was a relatively easy operation and the aircraft became more civilised. Power was reduced to 1,700rpm and boost below 30inHg to gain maximum endurance. Navigation was a combination of astro, DR with occasional landfall when the weather was co-operative. Return to Cairns in bad weather was assisted by tuning the ADF onto the local radio station.'

The trip on 19 February was to Ballale Island immediately south of Bougainville. It was considered 'normal' except that much larger fires were started in the bombing raid; Vic Hodgkinson returned after a flight of just over sixteen hours. It was just one of a number by the Catalina squadrons in that month.

New Guinea and the Bismarck Sea Battle

Although by 22 January the Allies had gained effective control of Papua, there were still many Japanese troops in New Guinea and it was on 19 February that reports indicated that the enemy was about to reinforce Lae on the northern coast of New Guinea. About 300 Allied aircraft were available to counter such a move including Liberators, Bostons, B-17s, Beauforts, Beaufighters, Mitchells and Lightnings. Others such as Catalinas were intended for reconnaissance.

On 1 March a B-24 was airborne following a reported break in the weather. At 15:00hr the crew sighted fourteen ships escorted by Zero fighters. The convoy was steaming west, forty miles NW of Ubili, New Britain. This was the prelude to what came to be known as the Battle of the Bismarck Sea.

A24-10, captained by Vic Hodgkinson, was one of a number of aircraft sent out on further reconnaissance. His log for 1 March reads: 'Cairns-Milne Bay — search for 14MV, 4Drs, 3Crs North New Britain — not met frontal conditions — Milne Bay-Cairns'. The trip involved over 25 hours' flying. The Japanese convoy was again located on 2 March and eight merchant vessels escorted by five destroyers and a light cruiser were reported.

There were a series of attacks made by aircraft and during the night the enemy was shadowed by an Australian Catalina, *A24-14*, captained by Flt Lt Duigan in a flight of 15½ hours.

The Allies had already rehearsed a co-ordinated attack involving Australian Beauforts and Beaufighters together with American bombers and fighters. At this stage the Japanese convoy was off Huon Point and in range of Allied strike aircraft. Torpedoes were launched by the Beauforts followed half-an-hour later by Australian Beaufighters armed with four cannon in the nose plus six machine-guns in the wings. The Australians silenced the AA fire from the ships, making way for AAF bombers who must have learned the lesson of Midway and bombed from medium or low altitude. Reported losses of the Japanese are all of their eight transport vessels and four out of eight of their destroyers together with 20-30 aircraft.

Unlike other battles in the Pacific theatre, this had been fought by land-based aircraft. The success of the Allied planes may be attributed to the effective strafing by the RAAF Beaufighters countering AA fire from the enemy; followed by strafing and low level 'skip' bombing[8] by the AAF Mitchells. The Allies lost four aircraft due to enemy action — one B-17 and three Lightnings. Other factors contributing to the Allied success were: advanced intelligence or anticipation of enemy movements; effective reconnaissance; and close co-ordination and training of the squadrons.

The enemy had been able to land only 850 men and lost about 3,000. For General MacArthur it was the 'decisive aerial engagement' of the SW Pacific area war. For the Japanese it was their last attempted advance in New Guinea.

Elation following the Allied success against the Japanese convoy was dampened for the two Australian Catalina squadrons by the loss of Wg Cdr F. B. Chapman, DFC, together with his crew of eight on 8 March. His aircraft, *A24-22*, was last reported thirty miles SE of Gasmata. He was referred to as 'Chappie' and has been described as a 'charming bloke — one of the best . . . an excellent pilot'. On such occasions aircrew would look around, say little, and just get on with their job.

For Vic Hodgkinson this was to undertake a

search for the missing crew and as he recalls: 'We happened to be duty crew that day and at about 21:00hr I was detailed to search for our Commanding Officer, Sqn Ldr Chapman. He was on an anti-shipping reconnaissance patrol "milk run" in the area between north-east New Guinea and the south coast of New Britain, Solomon Sea. The patrol start point was 30 miles SE of Gasmata, New Britain, occupied by the Japs and covering the area to the west. It had been estimated from his last W/T signal that he had come down near the start point; the suspected cause being the one million candle power parachute flares which at that point would be set and armed. It is possible that the mechanism malfunctioned and ignited it inside the aircraft with little chance of survival for the crew. Such an incident occurred at a later date but the crew managed to land at night and run the aircraft ashore. A few escaped the Japs but most were shot.

'A24-10 was de-bombed and we departed Cairns at about midnight. En route we were diverted to Milne Bay, arriving at 05:00hr on the 9th. No doubt Command had second thoughts on exposing a vulnerable Catalina to the Japs thirty miles off Gasmata in broad daylight where they had Zero fighters. We would have been Cat's meat! Having refuelled, we spent the day awaiting instructions which arrived together with thirteen Commandos. We departed at 16:00hr complete with the Army and proceeded to the Trobiand Islands where the Commandos were taken ashore in dugout canoes to mop up seventeen Japs who had landed in invasion barges. No doubt they were survivors from the Bismarck Sea battle of 3 March.

'We arrived at the Trobriand Islands at 18:00hr. We searched the Gasmata area all night and our only sighting was a large surfaced Jap submarine. As we had no bombs, this being an ASR detail, we dropped flares until it submerged. Thirty miles off Gasmata and one hour after dawn, I decided to return to base. En route we were again diverted to Islet, one of the numerous small sand islands in this area, to investigate a Jap invasion barge reported ashore. There was no sign of life but the sea for miles around was full of dead Japs and some survivors on scattered wreckage. All from the Bismarck Sea battle. We alighted

at Milne Bay for fuel and debriefing at 09:30hr on the 10th, arriving Cairns 17:30hr.'

Sqn Ldr R. B. Burrage was another Australian who had earlier served with the RAF. On the night of the 24th he captained Catalina A24-17 on a rescue mission to Ea Ea on the north coast of New Britain. This was to pick up three American airmen from a B-26 who had been missing for ten months together with an Australian soldier. Necessary signals had been arranged in advance, and a touch-down was made while a diversionary bombing raid on nearby Ubili was in progress.

During the period 1 December 1942 to 31 March 1943, the two Australian Catalina squadrons, Nos 11 and 20, flew 20,152 hours and dropped 480 tons of bombs.

Mine-laying by RAAF Catalinas

Catalina operations in the north-western area were initiated following a survey of bases at Merauke on the south coast of Dutch New Guinea and Karumba and Groote Eylandt in the Gulf of Carpentaria on 9 April. Of particular significance was the start of mine-laying operations by No 11 Squadron on the night of 22 April 1943. Another important task was the supplying of coast-watchers who operated in enemy-held territories in New Ireland, New Britain and the Solomons. A Catalina flown by Flt Lt W. J. Clark of 11 Squadron was lost over Bougainville while on such a mission on

The crew of *RK-I*. of 42 Sqdn after being rescued in October 1944.

26 April. Coast-watchers could not only report enemy activity but assisted in recovering downed aircrew.

In the following months of 1943, Australian Catalinas were engaged in mine-laying, supply missions, 'milk runs' which were extended due to Japanese submarine activity, and raids on enemy bases. On 3 June, possibly twenty Japanese aircraft were destroyed during a raid on Babo in Northern New Guinea.

To forestall enemy aircraft attacking an Allied invasion force at Lae, Nos 11 and 20 Squadron Catalinas made a surprise raid on the Rabaul airfields of Lakunai and Vanakanau where 200 aircraft had been counted. They were led by Wg Cdr S. G. Stilling and Wg Cdr Green operating from Cairns but refuelling at Milne Bay. Another Catalina squadron was formed at Bowen on 1 May and became based at Karumba where, by 1 September it was operational. This squadron — No 43 — had a detachment at Bowen.

The Japanese had as much need for safe shipping routes to New Britain and other bases as did the Allies to Great Britain. President Roosevelt was aware of the success of US Navy submarines in attacking enemy shipping but submarines were vulnerable during mine-laying operations in shallow waters. Mine-laying by RAF aircraft off the German-controlled coastline had been seen to be successful relative to the effort and resources involved. RAAF Catalinas were given the task of mine-laying in addition to their other duties. With the torpedo racks available, they were able to carry either British or American mines and in fact used both types.

A Qantas certificate 'Secret Order of the Double Sunrise' dated 26/27 January 1945 and awarded to F/Sgt Robert Hicks. Certificates were awarded to those who completed a flight of greater than 24 hours.

On the night of 22 April, eight Catalinas from Nos 11 and 20 Squadrons laid mines in Silver Sound, New Ireland. Each aircraft carried two mines and operated from Cairns but were detailed to refuel at either Milne Bay or Port Moresby on return. Typically, those first on the scene were unscathed; those following such as Sqn Ldr Vernon of 11 Squadron, suffered AA fire and his aircraft was holed in the wing and a float.

Two nights later, Ysabel Passage, east of New Hanover, was mined, the purpose of such operations being to deny the Japanese safe anchorage south of Truk. In May, Seeadler Harbour, east of Manus in the Admiralty Islands, was mined, thus with the bombing of Rabaul, there were no safe harbours for the enemy south of Truk.

During July, on the nights of the 10th, 11th and 14th, the Catalinas, staging at Darwin, mined Babo in Maccleur Gulf, New Guinea, to disrupt a second Japanese supply route to Rabaul. This formed part of a strategic mining campaign against all harbours and routes in the Netherlands East Indies in range of RAAF bases.

Mines were laid in the channel south-west of Maccleur Gulf, near Geser Island on 29 July; Macassar in Celebes, and the straits between Madura and Surabaya in Java, were similarly treated in August. Both these areas were to be the target for a number of subsequent operations. On 25 August, four Catalinas from Nos 11 and 20 Squadrons flew to Darwin. They were A24-32, A24-40, A24-50 and A24-58 captained by Wg Cdr Green, Flt Lts Marsh, Miles and Bolitho. The American tender, USS *William B. Preston*, moored at Heron Haven was used for refuelling and Surabaya was mined on the nights of the 27th and 29th.

Of Catalinas lost in September, the first was A24-50 captained by F/O J. P. Oliver of 11 Squadron. It is thought that on the 2nd his aircraft crashed into the mountains of Nuhu Tjut Island, west of Dutch New Guinea. On the 30th Sqn Ldr S. G. Stilling captained an aircraft armed with torpedoes. This was A24-67 which was shot down over Pomelaa in Celebes after attacking a ship. He had with him as passenger Lt Cdr Carr, who was taken prisoner.

There was further mining in November with

Kendari in Celebes, Ceram, Waingapu in Sumba and Kavieng, New Ireland, all receiving treatment. During December, priority was given to bombing raids on Kavieng, but mining continued in January when five Catalinas flew to Kau Bay in Halmahera Island. Mines were sown despite five hours of daylight flying over enemy held territory. The captains were Flt Lts Davis, Lawrence, Foskett, Bolitho and Cowan.

A survey of Cygnet Bay, near Derby, Western Australia, was made on 23 January to check its suitability for Catalinas and a tender. It was to be an advanced staging post for mining Balikpapan in Borneo. Following the arrival of USS *William B. Preston* on the 19th at Cygnet Bay, sorties were undertaken on 22 and 25 February. It meant an operating radius of almost 1,000 miles.

General MacArthur, as part of his overall plan in a drive towards the Philippines, made landings at Aitape and Hollandia on the northern coast of New Guinea. By such means, he bypassed Wewak. This was the operation 'Reckless' which involved both American and Australian forces. Part of the Australian contribution was the laying of mines by Catalinas in the Woleai Atoll in the Caroline Islands. This was to deny its use by the Japanese fleet during the Hollandia landings, Woleai being a final stage on one sea route from Japan to Hollandia.

Eight aircraft of Nos 11 and 20 Squadrons flew from Cairns via Milne Bay to the Admiralty Islands where they arrived on 13/14 April. They moored in Lombrum Bay, Los Negros Island, adjacent to Manus. The Catalina crews were accommodated aboard the US Navy tenders *Tangier*, *San Pablo* and *Heron* in Seeadler Harbour. Mines were sown on the nights of the 15th, 17th and 18th at Woleai. During the raid on the 18/19th, No 20 Squadron lost two in the crew of Flt Lt E. C. Ham. They were Sgts N. C. Phillips and R. C. Ely who were killed when a shell exploded near a blister.

Joining the main convoy to Aitape on the 18th were 800 RAAF personnel; their acting SASO was Gp Capt C. D. Candy[*] who had previously commanded No 206 Squadron RAF and No 6 (C) OTU RAF, was on board the American destroyer *Nicholas*. No 43 Squadron, commanded by Wg Cdr C. F.

A24-10 over No 3 OTU Rathmines. This PBY survived service with Nos 11 and 20 Sqdns and was sold in 1947.

Thompson, was by this time based at Darwin with duties devoted to mine-laying.

During the Hollandia-Aitape operations, the three Catalina squadrons mined Woleai, Balikpapan; Manokwari, Sarong and Kaimana in Dutch New Guinea. The American tender USS *Childs* moored in Yampi Sound, Western Australia, became an advanced base for No 43 Squadron. On 21 April six Catalinas were airborne from Yampi Sound. When over Balikapan, *A24-53* captained by Flt Sgt D. G. Abbey was shot down in flames. *A24-35* flown by Flt Lt R. H. S. Gray was severely damaged by shrapnel. Both Gray and his co-pilot were wounded but they managed to bring the aircraft back to base where it was beached. Further mining was undertaken at Balikpapan on the 24th and 27th. The Japanese destroyer *Amagiri*[*] was sunk due to a mine on the 23rd and the harbour was closed from 20 until 29 April.

On 17 and 27 May Allied landings were made on Wakde and Biak islands off New Guinea, and to give indirect support to the operations, there was further mining of Balikpapan, Kaimana and Surabaya by the Australians. One of the navigators with 43 Squadron who was on the trip to Balikpapan on 27 April was Tom Trebilco. He was airborne at 15:10hr in *A24-75* which was captained by Flt Lt David Joyce. They flew at 1,000ft over the Indian ocean which, as Trebilco recalls, 'was as usual calm and peaceful'. En route for Balikpapan a slow climb was made to clear the first islands at 9,000ft and with an awareness of Java's Mount Mahameru of 12,000ft. The Catalina was painted black, the exhausts were muffled and no lights were used, with the crew conscious of danger from enemy fighters and radar-controlled AA. They enjoyed a meal of fish cooked in the aircraft, and twenty minutes before ETA at Balikpapan, Trebilco moved forward from the navigation compartment to the nose, while the pilot began a descent to sea level. At the required altitude for release, the fuzes of the two 1,000lb mines were set, and in a precise bombing run, the mines were dropped, their momentum being reduced by parachutes. There was little enemy opposition and the Catalina climbed to 6,000ft on a southerly course returning to base after a flight covering 2,000 miles in about eighteen hours.

There had been intelligence reports of a Japanese convoy comprising five merchant vessels and two warships anchoring in Vesuvius Bay, Sula, in the Celebes group. Three Catalinas of 43 Squadron were ordered on a strike from Darwin. This was on the night of 4 May. The first on the scene was *A24-10* captained by Flt Lt R. Miller and the Catalina was subjected to accurate AA fire. Miller was able to release his bombs but reported near misses.

Following Miller, was Flt Lt Joyce in *A24-56* who had Tom Trebilco as navigator. Of this trip, Trebilco recalls that it was 700 miles to the target and with few landmarks. For his navigation, he opted for astro rather than dead reckoning as the latter would have required dropping flame floats to check drift, and the floats might well betray their presence. By the time Joyce arrived over the harbour, the enemy ships had slipped anchor and were under way. He selected one for attack from 7,000ft; Trebilco, now as bomb-aimer, saw the ship only as a dark shape ahead of a phosphorescent wake. At the instant the bombs were released, the vessel made a sharp turn, and the bombs exploded where the ship might have been. The ship had responded with AA fire and a shell exploded just ahead of the Catalina, and the gunners in the blisters reported not only AA fire aft, but also the presence of two enemy fighters. The third Catalina from 43 Squadron did not reach Vesuvius Bay, and attacked an alternative target.

No 42 Squadron was formed on 1 June at Darwin and Wg Cdr J. P. Costello, who had served previously with Nos 10 and 20 Squadrons, became their Commanding Officer. On 11 July the squadron became based at Melville Bay. With 42 Squadron given mine-laying as its main task, extending to Celebes and Borneo, No 11 Squadron was re-deployed at Rathmines on anti-submarine patrols.

Macassar in Celebes became one of 42 Squadron's targets and on the night of 11 October four of their Catalinas were over that area. They experienced AA fire but it proved ineffective. It was very different the following night. Four Catalinas were again deployed and the first two were able to release their mines unscathed. The third, *A24-96*, was hit by cannon fire as a result of going close inshore. The fourth Catalina, *A24-102*, was captained by Flt Lt Lindsay Oats. After making an accurate run and releasing his mines, he found himself over a Japanese destroyer. AA fire from the warship was accurate and removed much of the Catalina's tailplane. The aircraft became very unstable and the crew had to remain in fixed positions to avoid a constant dive or climb. For Lindsay Oats, this was one of his two worst trips.

On 14 October two aircraft of 42 Squadron were again over Macassar. They were *A24-93* flown by Sqn Ldr K. W. Grant and *A24-90* captained by Flt Lt C. A. Williams. Grant's crew, after their mines had been released, noticed first a short burst from an AA gun and then a blazing object in the water. This was the demise of *A24-90* which failed to return to base. Williams was lost together with a crew of eight.

In a further mine-laying operation over Macassar on the 23rd, one of the four Catalinas, *A24-100* captained by F/O C. D. Hull, was hit by AA in the starboard engine causing an oil leak and then complete failure. About an hour later, the port engine failed and an open sea landing was made. His position had been received, however, and the following day F/O A. A. Etienne of 43 Squadron in *A24-59* touched down near *A24-100* and the crew were rescued south-west of Celebes.

In November, 43 Squadron had a detachment at Morotai, operating from the US Navy tender USS *Tangier*. The Australians lived aboard with their aircraft moored nearby. On Thanksgiving Day, the Americans treated the RAAF crews to a celebration dinner which included roast turkey, cranberry sauce, and the table was set with silver cutlery — very different from Catalina cuisine. Refuelling by USS *Tangier* enabled the RAAF Catalinas to extend their range to Tarakan off the coast of Borneo in addition to Balikpapan. It was mining of the latter which resulted in the Japanese ships *Seito Maru* and *Kokko Maru* being sunk at the end of October[11].

A flight engineer, Bill Webb, who joined 42 Squadron about this time, gives the following account: 'There were nine members of our crew. These included the Captain, 2nd pilot, two flight engineers, armourer and rigger. It was one of the few crews of which all members were single. We were posted to 42 Squadron at Melville Bay.

'On 22 December at 08:30hr we were airborne in *A24-97* and at Darwin four hours later, we landed and were billeted. On the 23rd we were briefed following the ground staff's refuelling and arming the Catalina with mines, etc. We were told our destination only after becoming airborne, following the opening of a sealed envelope by the captain.

'Engineers had a control panel set up in between the main plane and the hull in the superstructure. We could see out of small windows on each side of the superstructure and our job when we were airborne was to keep an eye on the engines and complete the engineer's log every twenty minutes at which time he reported to the captain, the fuel quantity left, our rate of consumption of fuel and subsequent estimated safe flying time.

'Getting the old ship airborne was quite a business. With 1,160 Imperial gallons of fuel, over 4,000lb of mines and the crew, etc, we were well overloaded. The twin row Wasp engines were stretched at 2,700revs with 48inHg boost. The pilot had to porpoise the ship back and forth to break the suction underneath and get up onto the front step. We would often crash back onto the water, sometimes up to nine times and often travel miles before the airspeed would be sufficient for us to remain airborne.

'The cylinder head temperatures would get dangerously close to the maximum permissible, ie, 260°F, before we were at cruising altitude at which time we would drop revs and boost, etc. It was a relief to see the fuel flow meters slow down as we knew we could barely carry enough fuel to get us to the target and back.

'This was our first trip and we were heading for Macassar in the Celebes to plant our mines. We had heard tales of balloons with wire ropes attached and many other discouraging things set up to snare us.

'The engineers took two hourly shifts at the control panel and the one not rostered at the panel was responsible for the 0.303 Browning in the tunnel. The other gunners had a 0.5 Browning at each blister and there was another Browning in the nose.

'Ocean was all we could see for hours after leaving Darwin. The Cat was so slow, we spent a lot of time watching for any enemy that might interfere with our sneaky little plan. Gradually it got dark, and if there was no moon or there was bad weather, it really was dark. We would be praying for good weather over the target area and that when we descended to low altitude, we would be in the correct place and not about to run into

Black Cat *RK-H, A24-102* which was received by No 42 Sqdn RAAF in August 1944. It later served with No 114 Air-Sea-Rescue Flight.

something. As we were often a lone aircraft on these missions, it was not known what happened to Cats that didn't return. We were fairly well equipped should we come down in one piece. We each had a jungle knife strapped to our left foreleg, a Smith and Wesson 0.38 revolver on our belt and rations for a limited period. We also had between us one Thompson sub-machine-gun and a 0.303 rifle plus ammunition. The cheerful briefing officers would tell us that the Japs would shoot us rather than take us prisoner should we come down there.

'A red light glowing "Auto Rich" would come on in the engineer's panel and I would know that we were about to descend to the target area. The rich mixture took some of the glow out of the two blazing exhausts and helped to hide us a little longer. Also it was necessary in case we suddenly needed full power to get out of an awkward situation.

'So I would push the two big levers from Auto Lean to Auto Rich and listen on the intercom to the captain and navigator discussing the approach, ie, the necessary direction and height to come upon the point at which we were to set speed and make countdown for the drop. Chas, the navigator, at this point was down at the bomb aimer's window in the front of the plane; the captain always took the controls over the target and the 2nd pilot had his hand on the bomb release buttons.

'Finally, when we reached the correct position, ie, the correct point, in the correct

A24-112 a PBY-5A with No 112 Flight RAAF, at Learmouth, September 1945. It served with the ASR flight until taken by No 11 Sqdn in 1949.

direction at the correct speed; w "45,44,43,42 seconds, etc. Go one straightway, "20,19,18, etc. Go two mines were gone, dropped exactly wh should have been; the old ship se heave a sigh of relief with the los weight. With lots less fuel as well, w revs and boost and navigated out of The Nips weren't kind enough to turi lights to help us see our way in and ou was a sudden scream on the intercon Ralph, Turn!" — It was Chas from tl aimer's position. "I can see it, I can Ralph replied.

'I could barely see trees and land gc my little engineer's window, then a lit the mast of a ship. I was ever hopi Ralph really could see much bett where he was in the ship. The keen ey gunners in the blisters, the captain pilot and others were searching for ai sition. It seemed the rumour about t balloons was either not true or we ha them.

'At about 2am, the two Wasp engii still roaring on all 28 cylinders and S Armourer/Air Gunner, was down at plate in the engineer's compartment b panel where the engineer sat. He hanc me a cup of tomato soup. After all th still think tomato soup has never t good.

'From then on assuming that the Ni alone, all that remained was to get ' Darwin with the fuel we had left. ' turns at watch and turns at the old "b screen" which consisted of a screen w going out from either side of a centre was necessary to be able to tell from distance and shape, how far away th was and whether it was land or aircraft, etc.

'When daylight came, we were sti Sumba and had missed our turn down the Sumba Strait. So we were almost the waves along the top of the islands detection by enemy radar. Finally w south and with very little fuel left, th were running at very low revs at 1 with lean mixtures as we were hoping least close enough to Australia to bre silence.

'Eventually, at about 10:00hr,

hours after take-off, we sighted land. Back on the water we checked our fuel. The float type petrol gauges were not very accurate at small quantities, particularly when the chord angle kept altering as much as it did when the flying boat was rocking on the water, but we certainly had very little fuel left in the tanks. At about 11:00hr we headed for a shower, a feed and a sleep which I thought should last forever.'

Bill Webb and his crew survived seventeen mine-laying operations in addition to many other trips.

As part of General MacArthur's Philippines campaign, landings on Mindoro were scheduled for 15 December. In support of this campaign, all four of the Australian Catalina squadrons, Nos 11, 20, 42 and 43 were required to lay sixty mines in Manila harbour during one night. 11 Squadron provided six aircraft which were brought foward from Rathmines via Darwin and Melville Bay and Woendi Island near Biak to Leyte from where they would operate on the 14th.

Nos 20 and 42 Squadrons each provided six aircraft, and 43 Squadron, seven. Included in the latter was *A24-102* captained by Lindsay Oats for whom this proved his second worst trip. Although briefed that the safe height in the event of a pre-detonation of mines was 1,200ft, their runs were made at 200ft or 400ft. Strong Japanese air and ground defences necessitated some support for vulnerable Catalinas, and American B-24s undertook diversionary raids while another Catalina dropped 'window' to confuse radar defence systems.

On 14 December the Catalinas were airborne at two minute intervals from Jinamoc Island. The first to be airborne was Flt Lt H. C. Roberts in *A24-64* of 43 Squadron. He failed to return, due it was believed, to him flying into a mountain, a fate almost shared by two other aircraft. Because operations at Leyte would not permit night landings, the Catalinas circled Samar until dawn. This precaution resulted from the need to avoid shipping in San Pedro bay during darkness. For the No 11 Squadron Catalinas, the operation involved a record flight on return of about 9,000 miles.

For one of No 20 Squadron's pilots, Frank Parsons, a mine-laying trip proved to be his

The PB2B-1, *A24-205* coded RB, of No 20 Sqdn at Darwin, 30 January 1945. It crashed on take-off 9 August.

first operational sortie. This was on 21 December as a second pilot to the CO Wg Cdr Wearne. He recorded his experiences in a letter at the time: 'We left Darwin at 8am on 21 December and flew to West Bay down the coast in Western Australia arriving there at 11:30am. Here we had lunch, refuelled and took off at 3pm. It was a very long run to take off — 90 seconds. Of course we had a heavy load, 1,460 gallons of fuel and two large mines. It was now ten hours to the target. There is little to say about the trip up, it was very quiet except for our passing through a couple of violent storms and within about ten miles of Soembawa, a Japanese occupied island, but saw nothing. I guess I said all the prayers I could think of on the way up!

'Being my first trip and not knowing what to expect, I was rather apprehensive. We reached the target at 1am and on the way in saw one burst of AA which appeared to be from an Oerlikon gun. However, it was a long way from us. We came on datum, did our mining successfully, and as we came away three or four searchlights shot up into the blackness, the long fingers of light waving about trying to catch us.

'These too, did not come near us. Believe me I was doing a bit of quiet thinking whilst over the target! Set course for home immediately — I had a couple of hours sleep then took over from the skipper at dawn. So as you see it was a quite uneventful trip — but I didn't mind! We were back in Darwin at our base at 12:30 on Friday this morning.' The

161

A Catalina cartoon which was presented to Lindsay Oats of 42 Sqdn RAAF after his aircraft became stranded on a sand-bank.

sortie had been to Surabaya harbour, Java and the same target prevailed for Parsons' second and third trips.

His third mission was on the night of 11 January and, as he recorded the following afternoon: 'We went up passing over Savu Island where many native villages and surrounding cultivations were seen, then through the passage between Soembawa and Flores Islands, then west to the southern end of Surabaya town.

'However, last night's story wasn't quite the same. We left yesterday morning at 8am same scheme as usual — from Darwin to West Bay-Surabaya-West Bay-Darwin. Took off from West Bay at 3pm after having lunch there, for Surabaya.

'This time we went up across the narrow neck of land in the centre of Soembawa — here passing a large volcano. Thence to Madura along its northern coast and into Surabaya harbour. We found ourselves running right into the town before we realised it, so we swung sharply away. Searchlights by this time were up but they didn't bother us overmuch. We found our datum and commenced our mining run. About halfway along it the searchlights came on again, four of them swinging to and fro across the sky probing for us. Once I thought they had us but just as I felt sure the beam was going to swing right into us — it was switched off!

'At the same time a ship loomed up just on our starboard and threw a bit of AA up at us, but he too missed — thank goodness. So this was my baptism of fire. I found no real feeling

of fright — there was no time to, but I did feel pretty peculiar! We got our mines away OK. The trip back was uneventful and we landed at Darwin 12:15 today.'

In the following weeks, Frank Parsons was on a few strikes in addition to a further mine-laying operation. During one trip his crew ran into a tropical cyclone and were 'tossed about like a cork in a rough sea' for 2½ hours. On another mission, the Catalina suffered AA fire in the wing — just missing the fuel tank.

One of the tasks given to the Catalina crews was to supply outposts and that highly respected fraternity — the coast watchers. Frank Parsons enjoyed such a trip on 16 February. His contemporary account reads thus: 'Today we were detailed to take supplies to one of the outposts on Seroe Island near Timor and also to bring back a very sick man. It was only a 3½ hour trip and on arriving we found it was a volcanic island with smoke coming from a still active volcano rising straight out of the sea. It was only three miles across. We quickly found the white village church we'd been told to look out for and after one circuit of the island, saw the Dutch flag flying which gave us the OK to land.

'As we flew around we could see groves and groves of banana trees and huge terrace gardens on the sheer slopes of the island. There were four villages and these could be seen plainly on the few flat places — typical bamboo and grass huts around a central square. We landed in beautifully calm water on the eastern side of the island and anchored in about 18ft of the clearest water I've ever seen. One could see the bottom perfectly in every detail of rock and gorgeous coral.

'As soon as we had anchored there were three native canoes alongside laden with natives and in one of them a Sergeant who turned out to be a chap I had known well at Nowra — Alan Danelly. He is in charge of the RAAF party on the island. We were told later that when the Cats came in it was declared a holiday for all the villages and so there was a great crowd of natives to welcome us on the beach, the women in multi-coloured skirts, red, blue, green and yellow, pink and so on, and literally dozens of naked children running everywhere — the men are a fine strong type. Their colour is really only "dusky" as they are only quarter castes and so have comparatively fair skins.

'*M*' of 42 Sqdn RAAF at the moorings, Cairns in July 1944. The front turret is armed with two machine guns.

'We soon unloaded and went ashore in canoes. Here the doctor whom we had brought with us to tend the sick chap held an impromptu sick parade; mothers brought their babies and both men and women came with all sorts of complaints and diseases, but there was little the doc could do really. Actually the people were pretty healthy altogether.

'Don then suggested we go up to the "Kapola campon" — the village, and have a drink with the native chief. Gosh, what a climb! We went up about 1,200ft in 5/8th mile and were thoroughly knocked out by the time we reached the top. The chief showed us to his house and seated us at tables on the verandah. He was very thrilled to have us and smiled the whole time. He was an old man about 75 with white hair and white moustache. He was wearing a white shirt, and trousers so looked quite distinguished.

'A fine looking chap who was the village teacher served us first with glasses of water and then smaller glasses of "jungle juice" — and boy, was it potent! It really tasted like a combination of whiskey and champagne. What really amazed me were the beautiful etched glasses we used which were made by the islanders themselves. There is some substance obtainable near the mouth of the volcano which resembles glass and they grind and polish it into tumblers. I took a couple of snaps of the chief and the teacher with the boys of our crew and then it was time to go.

'Back down the mountain side to the white beach, we left laden with bananas, mangoes, coconuts, cucumbers and so on. It was a typical island paradise — complete with pretty native girls, blue water, waving coconut palms, coral and as I said, even to a smoking volcano. I won't forget my visit to Seroe for many years.'

General MacArthur's forces had landed without opposition in December 1944 on Mindoro Island, and in January 1945, four divisions were landed north of Manila. American aircraft carriers were operating in the South China Sea and in January, raids were being made on Saigon and Hong Kong. The Japanese continued to attempt maintaining supply lines from the East Indies despite severe losses due to submarine and aircraft attacks. Operations by the Australian Catalinas reflect this situation. Mines were laid near Formosa, the Pescadores, Amoy, Hainan Strait and Hong Kong.

At Jinamoc in the Philippines, a detachment was provided by Nos 20 and 43 Squadrons beginning in February. A refuelling stop was arranged in the Lingayen Gulf using the tender USS *Orca* and operations began on 3 March with the mining of Yulinkan Bay, Hainan Island.

The operational log for *A24-97* captained by Flt Lt Bruce of 42 Squadron shows a series of mine-laying sorties taking off from Melville Bay, touching down at Darwin and West Bay for mine-laying at Surabaya, Java and Laut Strait, Borneo. Flt Lt Bruce was on such sorties throughout January and February with an overall flight time of about 24 hours for each operation.

During the first half of 1945, mines were laid near ports along the China coast at Macao, Hong Kong, Swatow, Amoy, with 169 mines sown in March and 193 in April. There were other specific targets such as Malasoro Bay in Celebes, and Laut Strait, Borneo. For the latter, *A24-97* of 42 Squadron operated from Darwin but touched down at West Bay. *A24-88* of 42 Squadron flew via West Bay on the outward trip but returned via Sumbawa and Timor back to Darwin.

A24-102, also of 42 Squadron, had a round trip of almost 20 hours from West Bay to lay mines at Surabaya on 7 February. The same aircraft captained by Lindsay Oats but operating from Leyte, flew via the Lingayen Gulf to lay four 1,000lb mines from 300ft at Takao. Oats' longest trip was from Leyte to Swatow on 17 March, for which he made a refuelling stop in the Lingayen Gulf. He found Swatow shrouded in thick fog and returned with his 4,000lb load of mines to Leyte after a flying time of 24½ hours.

Single Catalinas were involved in mine-laying in the Banka Strait east of Sumatra in June and August. Thus Flt Lt Bruce in *A24-97* sortied from Labuan in north-west Borneo on 23 June and again on the 29th, returning via Jinamoc and Moratai to Melville Bay on 3 July. 132 mines were laid in June followed by 117 in July. On 29 May two Catalinas were mining the approaches to Swatow. *A24-309* captained by Granger was holed in the port mainplane and suffered structural damage due to the blast from their last mine which fell in shallow water.

Mine-laying was suspended by 10 July 1945.

According to George Odgers[12], the RAAF claimed 23 ships sunk and 27 damaged, but both he and John Robertson[13] give a figure of nine ships being sunk by RAAF-sown mines. Against these figures is the loss of eleven Catalinas in laying 2,500 mines during the period April 1943 — August 1945.

The RAF historian, Denis Richards in *The Fight Avails* (page 99), gives the following figures for RAF mine-laying: April 1940-March 1943 16,000 mines sown for the loss of 329 aircraft with 369 ships sunk totalling 361,821 tons, set against 648 aircraft lost in shipping strikes sinking 107 vessels totalling 155,076 tons.

For the Australian Catalina crews, the worst enemy, as in other theatres, must have been the weather. With a slow, ponderous and overloaded aircraft covering overall up to 9,000 miles for one operation, their achievements were remarkable. The bald statements made in RAAF official records indicate clearly the RAAF aircrew attitude in accepting the need for long trips, precise navigation, hostile weather and terrain but coolly observing the enemy's reaction, returning with limited fuel and perhaps a seriously disabled aircraft.

Most of the mine-laying in the Pacific areas was undertaken by the heavy long range bombers, B-29s of the AAF. Three types of mine are referred to by Craven & Cate; acoustic, magnetic and 'unsweepable'. The mines were to be dropped using radar (Type AN/APQ/13) and there were static lines for parachute release. A figure quoted for two nights in March 1945 is 1,070 tons of mines. The Allied anti-shipping effort resulted in the Japanese initiating the closure of their convoy routes by December 1943, and by September 1944 abandoning regular contact with its south and South Pacific bases. With the capture of Iwo Jima by the Allies, Japanese traffic southwards was stopped and Japanese convoy routes to Formosa and Singapore were lost.

By March 1945, 35 out of 47 Japanese convoy routes were closed. The Shimonoseki Strait near their homeland was constantly being mined and no major warship passed through after 27 March. By 27 April, 18 ships of 30,917 tons were sunk or damaged by mines in Shimonoseki Strait. By May 1945, it was estimated that on average 80 Japanese ships were tied up daily due to mining. In addition,

Black Cat squadron No 20 RAAF which was formed in August 1941 and disbanded in February 1946.

349 ships with 20,000 men were assigned for mine-sweeping.

The US Strategic Bombing Survey[14] gives 8,900,000 tons of Japanese shipping being sunk by all causes with 54.7 per cent by submarines, 16.3 per cent by carrier aircraft, 10.2 per cent by AAF aircraft and 9.3 per cent by mines. Navy and Marine aircraft land-based aircraft sank 4.3 per cent, less than one per cent were sunk by surface ships' gunfire, and marine accidents accounted for 4 per cent.

Captain Roskill[15] in his final volume states Allied submarines as having been the 'most successful blockade instrument' but gives the air-laid mine as the most successful weapon in sealing off the Japanese mainland.

No direct comparison should be made of the RAAF Catalina results and the AAF B-29s. The Australians were operating relatively few Catalinas which were still basically 'patrol planes' of a pre-war era; the B-29s were then very recent long-range bombers. The Catalinas were operating from 'scratch' bases and with the aid of 7th Fleet seaplane tenders. In the Pacific theatre they pointed the way and with success.

Johnson & Katcher[16] credit the RAAF with laying 2,498 mines on target for the loss of eleven aircraft, and give 1,128 successful sorties out of 1,215 aircraft which were air-borne. They comment that the Catalinas were suited where a few mines needed to be laid accurately over many wide-spread targets. Out of a total of 108 targets for all types of aircraft, the RAAF covered 49 in conjunction

RB-L of No 20 Sqdn airborne at Cairns, January 1944.

165

with four of the 5th Army Air Force aircraft. The overall percentage losses for all types of aircraft was 1.16 per cent for 4,760 airborne.

With the cessation of hostilities, the Catalinas squadrons undertook surveillance, transport of service personnel and mercy missions. No 42 Squadron was disbanded at Melville Bay on 30 November, and 43 Squadron on 11 March 1946. No 11 Squadron was disbanded at Rathmines on 15 February 1946 but at the same base, a Search and Rescue wing was formed on 1 October 1947 with personnel from Nos 112 and 114 Air-Sea-Rescue flights from Port Moresby. The unit was designated No 11 Squadron (GR) on 1 July 1948.

1 The official Australian list gives *A24-1* with RAF serial No *AH534;* the Pacific Islands Aviation Society give *A24-1* c/n 40 Reg *VH-AFA*, but also a PBY-4 c/n 27 Reg *VH-AFB* with RAF serial No *AH534*.

2 Gp Capt Sir Richard Kirkland, CBE, DFC, RAAF (Ret) adopted his stepfather's name 'Kirkland', and 'Richard' from 'Dick' as the RAAF knew him.
3 See the author's *Seek and Strike* p189.
4 WSC, Vol IV, pp121-2.
5 D. Gillison, p575.
6 *Japanese Shipping Losses* (1947) credits the AAF.
7 Captain V. A. Hodgkinson, DFC, MRAeS, Nos 10 & 20 Squadrons, RAAF.
8 SWR, Vol II, p422 states it was possible due to five-second delay fuzes.
9 Air Vice-Marshal C. D. Candy, CB, CBE, RAAF, + 4.3.85 (See also the author's *Seek and Strike*).
10 *Amagiri* (1,950 tons) sunk 02°10'S 116°45'E 23.4.44 credited to AAF mine.
11 *Seito Maru*, 2,219 tons, sunk by RAAF mine 26.10.44, 03°14'S 116°13'E. *Kokko Maru*, 2,863 tons, sunk by RAAF mine 29.10.44, 01°17'S 116°48'E.
12 JO, p372.
13 JR, p215.
14 C&C, Vol V, pp662-675.
15 SWR, Vol III Pt 2, pp231-2.
16 *Mines Against Japan*, Ellis A. Johnson & David A. Katcher, pp25 & 35.

Chapter 18
Royal New Zealand Air Force
Rescue Operations

Pacific prelude

Following much of the destruction of the American fleet at Pearl Harbor, the capitulation of the British at Singapore, and the surrender of the Dutch in Java; New Zealand became part of the Allies' Pacific Zone, while Australia was incorporated into the South-West Pacific area under the command of General MacArthur. Included with Australia in the SW Pacific were the Northern Solomons, New Britain, New Guinea, The Netherlands East Indies, east of Sumatra; Borneo and the Philippines. The Pacific Area commanded by Admiral Nimitz, was subdivided into North, Central and South commands.

At the time of Pearl Harbor, New Zealand had no Catalinas, but her first line aircraft, headed by 36 Hudsons, included two Singapore flying boats. In December 1941, the RNZAF had 10,500 personnel in New Zealand and 450 in Fiji. During the first two years of the war most of the New Zealand Air Force personnel were with the RAF and the Fleet Air Arm squadrons away from the Pacific area. It was not until April 1943 that the RNZAF received the first of its Catalinas. They ultimately took delivery of 22 PBY-5s (*NZ4001-NZ4022*) and 34 Canadian Boeing PB2B-1s (*NZ4023-NZ4056*).

These Catalinas were ferried from North America to Fiji, with the first arriving at Lauthala Bay on 3 April 1943 under the command of an American Naval officer. By 21 May, seven Catalinas had arrived at Lauthala Bay, and eleven aircraft were on the strength by 30 June, a peak being reached on 31 December 1944 of 52 Catalinas. The PBY-5s were allocated to No 6 Squadron; the PB2B-1s to No 5 Squadron and No 3 OTU.

The role of the Catalinas in New Zealand service was maritime reconnaissance, anti-submarine patrols and air-sea-rescue. The

South Pacific area covered by the RNZAF was about 6,000,000 square miles. The service for which their Catalinas are best remembered is in air-sea-rescue or 'Dumbo' mercy missions.

No 5 (Flying Boat) Squadron of the RNZAF was formed in Fiji in November 1941. The squadron received its first two aircraft — outdated Short Singapores — on the 18th. These were flown down from Seletar via Java, Northern Australia, New Guinea, the Solomons and the New Hebrides. Two more Singapores arrived in December and in January 1942, they were operating from Suva Bay on anti-submarine and shipping escort duties. By 20 February, one of these Singapores had been lost by running onto a reef. In November 1942, when the squadron was still equipped with Singapores and the obsolescent Vincents, No 5 Squadron was disbanded.

Writing on the role of the Singapore flying boats with No 5 Squadron, New Zealander Don Martin recalls: 'The boats were to provide New Zealand's only defence of the South Pacific Ocean and provide communication between the islands in the South Pacific'.

Don Martin was one of those to convert to Catalinas with No 3 OTU at Lauthala Bay, Fiji. This unit was formed in February 1944 and served to train crews on Catalinas for both No 5 and No 6 Squadrons of the RNZAF. Initially No 3 OTU used PBY-5s but later received PB2B-1s. No 5 Squadron was re-formed in Fiji in July 1944 based at Lauthala Bay. It served as a transport unit to Tonga, Samoa and the Gilbert and Ellice Islands.

In October 1944, No 5 Squadron moved to Segond Channel, Espiritu Santo, in the New Hebrides from where it was to operate largely on anti-submarine patrols and shipping escorts. The unit was commanded by an ex-RAF officer, Wg Cdr Jack W. H. Bray. No 5

Squadron remained based at Espiritu Santo until October 1945, but post-war was re-formed and became stationed in Fiji. After No 5 had been disbanded in November 1942, its aircrew were absorbed into a new unit which was subsequently designated No 6 (Flying Boat) Squadron.

In April 1943, seven pilots, three wireless operator-air gunners and four flight engineers were attached to the Pacific Ferry for Catalina training as a prelude to ferrying aircraft from San Diego to Lauthala Bay in Fiji. No 6 Squadron was officially formed there on 25 May 1943 following the arrival of the first seven Catalinas. Wg Cdr G. C. Stead, DFC, an ex-RAF officer, became CO with, as Flight Commanders, Sqn Ldrs R. B. L. MacGregor and A. V. Jury. The squadron's establishment was fourteen pilots, six navigators, fifteen Wop/AGs, five Air Gunners and 111 ground staff. With Sqn Ldr MacGregor, some of the aircrew had been attached to the American tender USS *Curtiss* then located in Segond Channel. The attachment served to acquaint the New Zealanders with American methods of operating PBYs.

The first 'Dumbo' mission of the new unit was flown by Sqn Ldr MacGregor on 2 May in *NZ4001*. He made an open sea landing to pick up nine survivors of the American ship *Van-derbilt* which had been torpedoed. MacGregor was subsequently awarded the AFC. On 5 June MacGregor, with his crew, was posted missing. This followed extensive searches by a number of aircraft over three days. The only trace of the lost Catalina and crew was some personal gear located by the coastguard at Kadavu.

By 1 August, No 6 Squadron was considered fully operational and in the following days arrangements were made for a detachment to Tonga where the crews were accommodated by the US Navy. At Tonga, 'hunter-killer' tactics against submarines were exercised. During a night take-off on 23 September, Sqn Ldr L. H. 'Pop' Higgins was killed together with a crew of three. This was in Catalina *NZ4002* which reached a height of 200ft before crashing into the sea and catching fire.

In October 1943, the squadron moved from Fiji to Espiritu Santo in the New Hebrides, with the main body leaving Lauthala Bay on 1

October, and with most flown in seven Cata-linas, but others by C-47s. The following day it was announced that F/O G. E. Gudsell[1] had been awarded the US Air Medal in recognition of his duties undertaken while flying Hudsons of No 3 Squadron, RNZAF, from Guadalcanal.

While based at Espiritu Santo in the New Hebrides, No 6 Squadron undertook a series of patrols, searches, and gave cover for sorties by other aircraft, in addition to some 'Dumbo' missions. On 11 November, F/O McGrane, captain of Catalina *NZ4021*, acted as anti-submarine escort to an American transport the *San Juan* which had been damaged by an enemy submarine. Because conditions preclu-ded McGrane making an open sea landing, his aircraft served to guide rescue ships to the area which extended over twenty miles. Further cover was given by aircraft of Nos 4 and 6 Squadrons, and over a period of two days, 1,180 men were rescued.

Towards the end of November, the No 6 Squadron detachment at Tonga was with-drawn to Espiritu Santo. A further move was decided for the unit, and following an inspec-tion by the CO, Wg Cdr Scott, the squadron transferred to Halavo Bay, Florida Island, in the Solomons group. Ground crews left by surface vessel and others moved in a series of transit flights which were completed by Christmas Eve. Florida Island, north of Guadalcanal, was to be the squadron's base for the next two years.

One of the ground staff — an engineer, Jack Wakeford who was with the squadron during that period, recalls: 'Life in the Solomons was quite pleasant; although it was hot, the sea breezes tempered the conditions and boating, swimming and fishing were common. There was malaria in the area but with stringent medical control, Atabrine, mosquito netting and clothing regulations meant that very few cases were reported.

'The United States Navy had previously occupied our base and we inherited their amenities such as food supplies, refrigeration and entertainment (movies and concert par-ties). We were only two days' flight from New Zealand so there was a regular mail service. For flying personnel there was four weeks' leave every six months so nobody was away from home very long.

168

No 6 (Flying Boat) Squadron RNZAF at Halavo Bay, Florida Island, Solomons in 1944.

'The Catalinas were able to take heavy loads and when men were being ferried home, we took 25 troops and their equipment, plus other freight and there always seemed to be room for another one. Owing to the abundance of spare parts there was no "cannibalization" of aircraft and the rate of serviceability was high.'

While taking off on 12 January, Catalina *NZ4021* flown by Wg Cdr Scott, had the hull torn open. The hull was repaired by the crew in the air sufficiently well for an emergency landing to be attempted near the USS *Chandeleur*. This ship hoisted the Catalina aboard for permanent repairs.

F/O W. B. 'Bill' Mackley, DFC, was captain of one of two Catalinas on a search for a missing B-24 on 26 January. There was a crew of eleven in his aircraft *NZ4013*, but when south-east of Ontong, Java, he sighted three rafts and made an open sea landing to pick up ten survivors from the B-24.

During February 1944, No 6 Squadron undertook a series of successful 'Dumbo' missions involving open sea landings. On the 4th F/O Beauchamp in *NZ4017*, while on a routine patrol south of Nauru, sighted four dinghies. He touched down to pick up five survivors from a ditched B-24. On the 11th F/O Hendry picked up six survivors from a B-25 which had been hit by AA fire while on a raid over Vanukanau. They had ditched forty miles west of Buka.

Two of No 6 Squadron's Catalinas, *NZ4014* and *NZ4020*, had been detached to form a flight in the Treasury Islands on the 9th based on the small American seaplane tender USS *Coos Bay* (AVP-25). One of these aircraft, captained by Flt Lt McGrane, rescued a ditched P-39 fighter pilot on the 13th southeast of Cape St George. On the 18th, the same Catalina *NZ4020*, but flown by F/O Hitchcock, located a dinghy with three occupants just north of Buka. They were Americans from a B-25 which had ditched after being hit by AA. One of the occupants was dead. Both Hendry and Hitchcock made two more rescues from the open sea on the 21st and 22nd respectively, with two F4U American pilots picked up off Torokina, and two survivors from a ditched SBD west of Buka passage.

Although in the early months of 1944, No 6 Squadron made sightings of enemy submarines, no attacks are recorded in the unit's 'Brief History'. This was perhaps due to lack of cloud cover, and perhaps also, that the squadron's role was seen as air-sea-rescue when by March it had gained a reputation for its 'Brief History'. Operations in the following months continued to include many 'Dumbos' together with escort duties and searches for submarines.

On 26 September, following the report of a C-47 transport failing to return, two Catalinas were detailed for a search. The missing aircraft was located on Bellona Island and three days later another Catalina took a salvage crew to the scene. While the Catalina was at anchor, a torpedo-bomber aircraft from Treasury Island ditched nearby. Seven personnel were rescued by the Catalina from the ditched aircraft.

While operating from Espiritu Santo on 11 October, W/O Donaldson in Catalina *NZ4013* was detailed to search for survivors from a J2F which was reported missing west of the island. The J2F crew was located and the Catalina landed in a heavy sea for the rescue.

Catalina *NZ4018 XX-U* of No 6 Sqdn RNZAF.

Two survivors were picked up, but in an attempted take-off, due to the rough sea conditions, the aircraft water-looped and a float was damaged. It proved impossible to brace the float effectively and subsequently the Catalina was taken in tow but suffered a pounding in the heavy seas and broke away from the tow line before turning over and sinking. The Catalina crew were rescued by the tow boat.

Five days later F/O Sheehan, the captain of Catalina *NZ4010*, made an open sea landing near the American ship *Maco Victory*. A sick seaman was picked up and taken to hospital in Tulagi.

In December, due to lack of rain, water rationing was imposed on No 6 Squadron with all personnel limited to half-a-bucket per day. The unit was inspected by the AOC, Sir Robert Clark-Hall, on the 27th. The following day the AOC was flown by Catalina to visit units Nos 53 and 58. These were isolated radar units and it was one of the squadron's duties to supply them by air. 53 was at Cape Askolabe, Malaita, while No 58 was based at West Cape, Guadalcanal.

A Catalina was airborne on 5 January to deliver mail to the Stewart Islands, but en route was to look out for a missing B-24. On landing in the Stewart Islands, a native boy was picked up who was suffering from gangrene in a leg. He was flown to Tulagi and in the hospital the medical officer found it necessary to borrow a hacksaw from the engineering section to undertake an amputation. He was too late, however, to save the boy.

Three days later, No 6 Squadron's marine officer left with his crew for Selwyn Bay, Ugi Island, which is south of Florida Island in the Solomons group. En route in their surface

vessel, a launch was encountered in a helpless condition. On board were American officers and nurses. After giving some assistance to the Americans, the New Zealanders took the launch in tow to Koli Point.

Twelve personnel were killed on the 27th. This was with Catalina *NZ4022* which was on a test flight from Lauthala Bay but crashed near Mbeqa Island. There were six survivors, albeit injured from the crash.

On 24 April No 6 Squadron held an informal farewell party for 41 Americans who were due to return to the USA. This close liaison and regard for the other services operating in the Pacific areas is confirmed over forty years later by an ex No 6 Squadron Catalina captain, Don Martin, who recalls: '. . . the American Black Cat squadrons with whom we combined on some operations in the Solomons and with whom we socialised on a few occasions. The Americans in addition to saving us from Japanese occupation, were very kind to us.' (It was Don Martin's wish that I put him in touch with US Cat men with whom I'd been in contact.)

In the following months, the squadron continued to fly 'Dumbo' missions and in particular, to provide air-sea-rescue cover for the many air strikes by bomber and fighter aircraft made against Rabaul and Kavieng. On 12 June the unit was honoured by an official visit by His Excellency The Governor-General of New Zealand, and C-in-C, Marshal of the RAF Sir Cyril Newall. Sir Cyril had served with the RAF as Chief of Air Staff from 1937 until 1940.

On 9 August F/O Regan successfully completed the squadron's 79th air-sea-rescue mission. In this he touched down in rough conditions off the Kakanga river to pick up a ditched F4U pilot who was flown back to base. On 15 August the squadron was informed of Japan's unconditional surrender. A Thanksgiving service was held, and in the evening an impromptu show was organised.

The last wartime operation by No 6 Squadron was flown by Wg Cdr Smith and F/O Regan to drop leaflets over Nauru and Ocean Islands on 8 September. They landed at Tarawa and returned to base on the 9th. No 6 (Flying Boat) Squadron ceased to be operational from that day. It was re-formed at Hobsonville in May 1952 and by March 1953 was undertaking conversion to Sunderland flying boats. In December 1953, Catalinas of the squadron escorted the liner *Gothic* which was taking HM the Queen into Auckland.

An officer from No 6 — Sqn Ldr R. K. Walker, AFC, was posted to Lauthala Bay in 1954 to become CO of No 5 Squadron. The last flight of 6 Squadron was in June 1957 to Lauthala Bay, Fiji. It was disbanded the following month. One of No 6 Squadron's more distinguished navigators was Sir Edmund Hilary who gives some account of his Catalina experiences in the South Pacific in his autobiography[3].

RNZAF and the Pacific Ferry

Warrant Officer R. M. Cowern was a New Zealand navigator who served with No 6 Squadron before undertaking a series of ferry flights with No 2 Pacific Ferry. His training extended from September 1942 until April 1943 and he was posted to No 6 Squadron in the following July. While with the squadron he was not confined to a specific aircraft or crew but flew as navigator to many of the unit's Catalina captains but notably F/Lt Francis. By the end of March 1944 he had completed just short of 600 hours' flying and in April was posted to the Pacific Ferry. Cowern was then flown as passenger in a series of stages and

using various types of aircraft from Guadalcanal to San Diego taking about three weeks.

One of a number of ferry trips which Cowern undertook was to collect *NZ4037*[4] from San Diego. The Catalina was captained by Flt Lt Francis who had as other crew members F/O Sill, F/O McConnell, and Flt Sgts Peryman and Gardiner.

Catalina *NZ4037* was airborne just after midnight on 17 June with course set for Hawaii, flying at 117kt at 4,500ft but later climbing to 8,500ft. Initially Cowern, in his navigation, used bearings and fixed his positions by dead reckoning, but after four hours' flying began fixing his position every hour by means of star shots. The aircraft touched down at Kaneohe after a flight of 18hr 10min. This was the longest leg of the ferry trip and with twelve hours out of the eighteen flown at night.

The second leg of the ferrying was to Palmyra Island with Flt Lt Francis continuing as captain of *NZ4037* which was airborne from Kaneohe on the 19th. They were flying almost due south at about 120kt air speed and at 2,000ft. Cowern's navigation was now aided by a series of sun shots and some loop bearings. They touched down at Palmyra Island after 7hr 40min; Palmyra Island was an alternative route from Kaneohe, some aircraft in the Pacific ferry flew direct from Kaneohe

KN-D *NZ4049* Bu.No. 73113 of No 5 Sqdn RNZAF with its post-war code of 'KN'.

to Canton Island, a distance of 1,650 miles.

En route from Palmyra Island to Canton Island, navigation was similar to that of the previous leg, but with additional bearings using the radio loop aerial. The final leg on 21 June followed the regular route from Canton Island to Lauthala Bay, Viti Levu, in the Fiji Islands where *NZ4037* was waterborne after a flight of 8½ hr. The overall flying time for the ferry from San Diego to Fiji was 40hr 40min.

W/O Cowern, who had already completed a number of ferry flights in earlier months, flew at least once more on this route when Catalina *NZ4047* was delivered to Fiji on 14 September. The total distance from USA to Fiji by such routes was about 5,000 miles. The New Zealanders were to receive a total of 56 Catalinas, 34 PB2B-1s and 22 PBY-5s.

New Zealanders in West Africa

By May 1943 the Battle of the Atlantic had turned in favour of the Allies and the north-western approaches to the United Kingdom were no longer a happy hunting ground for U-boats. Admiral Dönitz began deploying his U-boats in ostensibly less vulnerable areas. There were convoys being routed from the United Kingdom down to the Cape of Good Hope but by 1943, however, much of the West African coastline was being covered by land-based aircraft.

A squadron of the RNZAF had begun forming at Stranraer in Scotland at the end of March 1943. It was commanded by Wg Cdr D.

Sunderland flying boats of the RNZAF with *NZ4116* a Mark V in the foreground. Sunderlands were operated by both Nos 5 and 6 Sqdns of the RNZAF from 1945 until 1967.

W. Baird who had joined the RAF in 1931 but had in 1940-41 served with the New Zealanders in Fiji. Initially, the squadron had only three crews, but others were to follow including Flt Lt P. R. Godby whose earlier service had been with RAF Ansons on 48 Squadron. Godby was one of the new 490 Squadron's first Flight Commanders.

A Catalina captain with 490 was Keith Patience, who after operational training at No 4 (Coastal) OTU of the RAF, gained more Catalina experience as second pilot with the Canadian squadron, No 422. No 490 Squadron of the RNZAF was now to become one of a number of Allied squadrons which served to protect the convoy route along the African coastline from Gibraltar to the Cape.

The squadron's CO, Wg Cdr Baird, and F/O Patience were two of the first to fly out to their West African base at Jui. Patience was airborne from Stranraer on 15 June 1943 in Catalina *FP242*, an aircraft which had previously seen service with Nos 210 and 190 Squadrons. The transit trip was via Mount Batten, Gibraltar and Bathurst before arriving at Jui on 22 June.

Patience's first operational sortie with 490 Squadron was two days later, a trip of just less than thirteen hours to provide escort to convoy OSS49. Thereafter, his duties were to include coastal reconnaissance, searches for U-boats and air-sea-rescue in addition to further convoy escorts.

'Jui', meaning the 'swamp of death', was justly named. The Catalinas were moored in an estuary with the base constructed on low land surrounded by mangrove swamps with very high humidity. Hills effectively cut off sea breezes which might otherwise have alleviated the atmosphere. A feature at that time was the number of ships where were routed individually and for which escort needed to be provided. There was one particularly notable air-sea-rescue operation in which 490 Squadron played a part. This followed a merchant vessel *Fernhill* which was torpedoed about 400 miles off Freetown on 6 August. F/O R. M. Grant was one of those airborne on a rescue mission. He located two lifeboats and three rafts within five minutes of reaching the reported position.

His crew, in addition to dropping a radio transmitter to the *Fernhill*'s survivors, released also a pack of some of their own

A Short Singapore flying boat. No 5 Sqdn RNZAF was equipped with these from November 1941 to November 1942.

clothing plus emergency rations. A second Catalina from 490 Squadron captained by F/O N. A. Ward led another merchant vessel to the survivors from *Fernhill* who were picked up. A third Catalina then acted as escort to the rescue ship.

While acting as second pilot on 11 August, Ward attacked a U-boat. His depth charges were seen to fall astern of the submarine. The bows of the vessel rose out of the water, and the U-boat then began turning in circles, indicating that its steering may have been damaged. After exchanging some fire with the Catalina, the U-boat submerged.

On 23 October 1943, Catalina *FP242* was one of those airborne to search for survivors of the ship *Lithiopa* which had apparently been torpedoed. In November escorts were flown for more, individually routed ships *Cilicia* and the M/V *Canada*; in December there were the *Dunottar Castle*, *Esso Norfolk* and the M/V *New Northland* to be covered.

The log of Keith Patience for early 1944 shows escorts for convoys but no more individually routed ships. In January, Wg Cdr B. S. Nicholl succeeded Baird as CO of 490 Squadron. By 19 May Keith Patience had completed his tour of operations having flown more than the requisite 800 hours with an overall total of 1,400 hours. He returned to the United Kingdom in Catalina *FP242* taking three passengers in addition to his crew.

Later in 1944, 490 Squadron was operating Sunderlands such as *EJ169* in which earlier that year I had flown on an air test at Wig Bay. At that time there was a batch of Sunderlands in the ML series including *ML869* which was flown by F/Lt 'Happy' Adams from Wig Bay to Oban. From there it must have found its way to 490 Squadron in West Africa. The squadron continued operating with Sunderlands well into 1945. Sunderland *EJ165* was appropriately returned to Wig Bay on 22 June by Flt Lt Wright, with navigator P/O P. D. Lee.

1 See the author's 'Seek and Strike'.
2 *No 6 Flying Boat Squadron RNZAF Brief History*, by F/O G. A. Wrathall, 1966.
3 *Nothing Venture Nothing Win*, Hodder & Stoughton, 1975.
4 PB2B-1 Bu Aer No *73047*, Manufacturer's No 28136.

Chapter 19
AAFUS Emergency Rescue Operations

North Sea rescue missions

The British Air Ministry had agreed in September 1942 to provide air-sea-rescue cover for the American 8th Army Air Force aircraft which were operating from Britain. It became apparent, however, that losses of American aircrew were greater than for RAF crews due to their differences in procedure in emergency, their equipment, and their reluctance to follow an organised ditching procedure in preference to baling out. Following some training, the 8th AAF eventually took part in ASR operations and in 1943, the 65th Fighter Wing began operating a rescue control station which was initially at Hornchurch, Essex.

On 9 May 1944, a unit equipped with P-47s and designated Detachment B, Flight Section HQ 65th Fighter Wing, became operational. They were controlled from Saffron Walden but operated from Boxted, Essex. In January 1945 the unit was re-designated the 5th Emergency Rescue Squadron and by 1 February its strength was ten officers with 65 enlisted men. By 28 February these numbers had increased to 75 and 298 respectively. They became equipped with Catalina amphibian OA-10As in addition to the P-47s and were to receive also B-17s adapted to carry an airborne lifeboat.

In addition to basic ground training for newly arrived crews, wireless operators were required to take seven hours of coded messages per week; navigators were instructed to use 'Gee', a specialised form of radar which could be used over the North Sea. The pilots of the Catalina amphibians gained experience in water landings.

While on an operational training flight on 3 February, OA-10A 'Teamwork 73' captained by 2nd Lt Donald E. Combs, received a radio message to search for two dinghies. Later, at 17:05hr, Combs received another message from a lead plane that the Dutch coast was in sight and directing him to head west. He was then signalled visually by a Wellington which had appeared and which then headed north to circle an area where three dinghies were sighted. Two were tied together and occupied, a third was some distance away. There were eight men in the two dinghies and their position was marked with flares.

After attempting a 'normal' landing and suffering a severe bounce, Combs made a fully stalled touch-down. After two or three attempts to make a safe approach to the dinghies due to wind, tide and swell, they were reached and a rope was thrown from a blister. It was caught, and all survivors were recovered. The swell was estimated at 8-10ft and during take-off the port float was damaged and the bomb aimer's window was broken. They became airborne, however, and after crossing the coast at 2,000ft, landed at base.

On 23 February there was heavy rain, low visibility and height of cloud base 400ft but three of 5th ER Squadron's aircraft were sent to Manston. While there, a report of a dinghy with three survivors off Cromer was received. They were over Clacton at 15:40hr and at 18:15hr, 2nd Lt Peter Vorinski sighted the dinghy. Smoke floats and two dinghies were dropped, and one of the aircraft, Catalina 'B', touched down where a man in a Mae West with a half-submerged dinghy was thought to be. Finding nothing, the Catalina then taxied to the dinghy and three men were picked up and returned to base. This OA-1-A 'Teamwork B', was captained by 2nd Lt John B. Lapanas.

During the month of February, 5th ER Squadron was involved in the rescue of 29

A simulated air-sea-rescue by a USAF *OA-10* in 1945.

men; of these, six were dead. The Squadron's actual pick ups are in the two foregoing accounts.

When a fighter pilot reported engine trouble on 12 March, control gave his position as 52°30'N 02°38'E for baling out. 2nd Lt John V. Lapenas was airborne in Catalina 'Teamwork 75' at 09:05hr and at 12:53hr was warned of the emergency. About half-an-hour later he sighted two more aircraft from the squadron circling a dinghy. Within eighteen minutes, Lapenas had touched down, rescued the pilot in the dinghy and was airborne again.

Distressed enemy aircrew were given no less consideration. Two days later 1st Lt William C. Thatcher in 'Teamwork 74' was ordered to position 52°24'N 03°50'E to join a fighter which had sighted a life raft. He made three attempts before reaching the raft, but was on the water for only fifteen minutes. The survivor in the dinghy proved to be a German who, on being taken aboard the Catalina, was undressed, dried and put into a sleeping bag. The Catalina returned safely to base escorted by four P-47s.

On 21 March, the enemy did not display the same magnanimity. 1st Lt John A. Carroll flying Catalina 'Teamwork 70', was ordered to position 04°29'E 52°20'N which is just off the Dutch coast near Ijmuiden, a hazardous area

at that time for any aircraft, most of all for a ponderous, lightly armed Catalina, albeit with four P-51s as top cover.

Lt Carroll, despite the danger, patrolled a mile off shore. He was directed by a Spitfire to a point northwards at position 52°27'N 04°32'E and sighted a raft. He dropped some floats and began his approach. Immediately he was subjected to 20mm cannon fire. On sighting an empty dinghy, he circled the area and located a man in an individual 'K' type dinghy. He flew straight towards the shore, made a steep 180° turn and then landed in the open sea. All this time 20mm fire from the shore was following him. While taxying to the dinghy, shore batteries opened up in earnest, and were bracketing both the dinghy and the Catalina. He tried to taxy fast on different headings but was prevented by the rough sea. Carroll now felt that he would be endangering both the ditched pilot and his own crew. While taking off, the shore batteries' fire was increasing, with both 20mm and 40mm calibre. By now one engine was running roughly, a propeller had been damaged and there was other damage to the aircraft. He must have been in range of the enemy shore batteries for almost two hours.

About the same time, another Catalina, 'Teamwork 72' captained by 2nd Lt Donald E.

175

An OA-10A-VI serial No *433924* of the USAF.

Combs, was on what was initially a futile search until directed to look for a downed Walrus aircraft. It was located, he touched down and picked up the crew of three. But in attempting to take off again, the Catalina was damaged and he was aware that they were drifting towards the enemy coast. Combs taxied for two hours and anchored. The Walrus crew were transferred to another craft, and then Catalina 'Teamwork 72' was able to take off again with just its own four-man crew.

Two days later, six RAF aircrew were fortunate in being rescued by a 5th ER Squadron Catalina as they were found about seventy miles west of their reported position. They were picked up by 1st Lt William Thatcher who, to judge from his terse report, must have considered the mission routine.

Catalina 'Teamwork 71' was airborne from Halesworth, Suffolk, at 12:20hr on 30 March and, while on patrol just over an hour later, was warned of a B-24 'V' which was heading west with three engines out at 16,000ft and losing height at 800ft/min. 2nd Lt Donald E. Hicks, the Catalina's captain, sighted the B-24 at 13:35hr when it was down to 6,000ft. It was followed down until the B-24 ditched in position 53°27'N 03°46'E and broke in half. The Catalina crew saw a number of men with Mae Wests, and Lt Hicks landed despite swells of 10-12ft.

There was much debris to avoid and the high seas made visibility so difficult that the co-pilot, Lt Harrington, stood in his seat to direct Hicks by intercom. A strong wind and the high seas made it necessary to use full engine power and water was shipped through the turret and the pilot's hatch. The engines were cut allowing the Catalina to drift down wind, when the engines were again used in an attempt to taxy up to the survivors. This procedure was followed four times. The only way of reaching the men was by throwing lines to them. Again due to the very high seas, not all of the survivors could be seen, but two managed to grab the lines which were thrown and they were hauled aboard.

Nearly two hours later, and after dumping 400gal of fuel, Hicks attempted to take off. Due to the quantity of water which had been shipped, the Catalina was nose heavy and could not be brought onto the step. With the seas striking the propellers, engine revs could not be taken above 2,100rpm, and the engines cut a number of times. By now, the hull of the Catalina was leaking and an emergency transmission was made. When a formation of B-24s was sighted, flares were released, and one of the B-24s circled the Catalina which was now itself in distress.

During the day, a number of aircraft circled the area, including two more Catalinas, but they were warned by Aldis lamp not to attempt a landing. Of the two B-24 survivors, one was found to have suffered internal injuries and was given a morphine injection to relieve the pain. Both were made warm and put into bunks. Due to the bilge pump failing through lack of grease, it was necessary to continue baling by hand. Non-essential equipment had already been jettisoned prior to the attempted take-off, and now emergency gear was made ready for a possible abandonment. A Catalina and a Warwick continued to circle them until after dark when magnesium flares were dropped.

At 21:00hr a launch 'Seagull 33', was sighted and lines were taken. The two pilots were the last to leave Catalina which by then had 2½ ft of water aboard due to the baling having ceased. The launch could make only two knots in an attempted tow of the aircraft, and due to its sinking condition and proximity to the enemy, it was abandoned.

Donald Hicks made a number of pertinent recommendations: 1. For large capacity bilge pumps, feeling that so equipped, a take-off might have been achieved; 2. For ropes more suited to use as life lines; 3. That rafts be kept in the blister section, due to the time taken to remove them (ten minutes) from the living

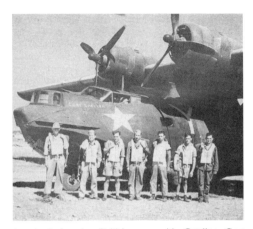

A mixed American/British crew with Catalina *Goat Smeller* which flew on rescue missions with the 12th AAF in the Mediterranean and Adriatic areas.

compartment; and 4. That a launch be warned when a Catalina was about to touch down in open sea.

Also on 30 March another of the squadron's Catalinas, captained by Lt Lapenas, touched down in open sea to pick up a man sighted in a dinghy. Heavy seas prevented a take-off, and the crew used their dinghies. The RAF dropped lifeboats, some breaking up. Ultimately the Catalina crew boarded one. Then German fighters approached and strafed the lifeboat. The Americans again took to their dinghies.

Figures given for distressed crews of the 8th Army Air Force are 28 per cent recovered in 1943; 43 per cent for bomber crews and 38 per cent for fighter pilots in 1944; but by September 1944, 90 per cent of AAF crews in the European theatre who had ditched were being saved[1].

By the end of March 1945, a rescue procedure which had been pioneered by Hudsons of 279 Squadron, RAF, was being applied by the 5th ER Squadron, AAF. Thus on 31 March, 1st Lt E. H. Newkirk, captain of a B-17 'Teamwork 88', released an airborne lifeboat in position 53°52′N 06°57′E. The position may be out, but could well have been off the notorious Den Helder area. The ditched crew boarded the lifeboat and were later seen heading west at 5kt. By such means, risking the crew of a Catalina together with their aircraft in danger areas was avoided.

Air-sea-rescue operations in the Mediterranean area

Air-sea-rescue operations in the western Mediterranean were initiated by the British. In February 1943, No 283 Squadron of the RAF was forming and later operated Walruses and Warwicks. The American 12th Army Air Force required its own rescue unit to augment the British ASR service and a small detachment was formed. Pilots were obtained from Pensacola and Jacksonville together with five old Catalinas which had been used for training. These PBY-5As were flown out by Air Transport Command pilots leaving the USA in June 1943 for Malta via South America and West Africa. Three arrived on schedule but one was damaged at Puerto Rico and another force-landed at Rio de Oro, in the Spanish Sahara, and was impounded with the crew interned.

Although assigned to the 12th AAF, the three American Catalinas came under 242 Group, RAF control, and on occasions had mixed American/RAF crews. Due to lack of maintenance facilities on Malta for Catalinas, they were transferred to Bizerta, Tunisia. Even then there were some difficulties and the aid of the USN Air Station at Port Lyautey was obtained in supplying spare parts, etc. Open sea landings by pilots lacking experience in such operations made it necessary to ground planes to replace plates, rivets and perspex which were damaged in such rescues.

OA-10 *42-10924* of the 12th AAF being taxied on one float by Lt Robert Smith after a rescue operation on 18 August 1943 which involved 1 hour 18 minutes flying but 18 hours 20 minutes on the sea with one float.

Their first rescue mission was on 17 July 1943 when the pilot of an RAF Hurricane fighter was picked up after having been adrift in a dinghy for eight days. On 30 July, one of the Catalinas picked up five aircrew from a dinghy following the ditching of a B-26. A heavy landing by the amphibian required eight hours work by the Catalina crew before it could take off again.

An Allied bombing shuttle service was organised by the Allies with aircraft such as the B-17 Flying Fortress taking off from England, making their bombing attack and then landing on the newly captured airfields in North Africa. From North Africa they were re-armed and then returned to Britain after bombing another target.

Three[2] of these B-17s ditched in the Mediterranean on 18 August due to lack of fuel, but a fix had been obtained on one of the aircraft. A Catalina, No *42-10924* flown by Lt Robert Smith with Charles 'Chuck' Zoet as co-pilot, was directed to the area escorted by ten P-38s. Two dinghies were sighted, occupied by ten survivors from a B-17; Smith, in the Catalina, made an open sea landing but in so doing, the starboard float was torn off.

Chuck Zoet promptly moved out onto the port wing to prevent the starboard wing from going under the water and capsizing the aircraft, his weight providing opposite torque. Another crewman then took his place while Zoet directed the pick-up of the survivors. The loss of a float precluded any take-off by the Catalina, and it was taxied towards the North African shore. Meanwhile an RAF Spitfire directed them to ten more survivors from a second B-17.

At 16:00hr, seven hours after the initial touch-down, and with an additional twenty aircrew on board, an RAF ASR launch came alongside and relieved the Catalina of the survivors from the B-17s. A second RAF launch now appeared and took the Catalina in tow, returning back to base at 03:00hr the following morning. The mission had involved 1hr 18min flying, but 18hr 20min at sea with one float. The positions of the two rescues — 39°07'N 07°41'E and 37°51'N 07°32'E — are in the area south-west of Sardinia.

Two aircraft were lost in rescue missions due to enemy action and on 13 December the flight returned to America. There it formed a nucleus for a newly established ER school at Keesler Field, Mississippi, for the Army Air Force to train its own units. The 1st Emergency Rescue Squadron arrived at Casablanca on 12 March 1944 commanded by Lt Col Littleton J. Pardue. It was organised into three operational flights A, B, and C, together with an HQ flight. On 1 April, a move was begun to Ajaccio, Corsica, and in May, A and B flights transferred to Grottaglie and Foggia in Italy to cover Allied bombing flights across the Adriatic Sea. For the invasion of southern France, A Flight returned to Corsica while B Flight remained in Italy to cover diversionary operations.

A Wellington, *LN280* of 104 Squadron, ex-Foggia, ditched off Corsica about midnight on 16 April. Five of the crew were lost, but an RAAF officer, Flt Lt W. C. Gilleland, was thrown clear. For the next sixteen hours he drifted 48 miles in a dinghy before being rescued by Capt M. A. Gray of the 1st ERS on 17/18 April.

Another Wellington was airborne from Foggia at 23:30hr on 12 May. After leaving Elba at 03:00hr on the 13th, it was attacked by a Junkers Ju 88. The Wellington's instrument panel was damaged and its tail unit destroyed, the port wing and fuselage were hit, and the bomb doors were torn off. At 10,000ft it went into a spin and crashed into the sea ten minutes later. Two of its crew managed to come to the surface — F/O Peter E. Gooch and a Canadian, F/O Fred E. Sturmy, who was commissioned in the RAF. Their dinghy had drifted away but Sturmy swam out and recovered it. Five hours later, the dinghy with the two survivors was sighted by a B-25.

For the rescue, Lt Col Pardue was airborne in Catalina *858* from Ajaccio. He had no fighter cover but requested a B-25 while making an open-sea landing. This was about fifteen miles south of Elba in position 41°57'N 11°11'E. After picking up Gooch and Sturmy, the Catalina had an escort of two P-39s for the return to base.

On 2 July, B-17 No *232103* of 419 Squadron, 301st Bomb Group, was one of five airborne from Foggia to bomb a bridge at Szolnok in Hungary. During the raid it was hit by AA but not dangerously. On the return flight, however, when twenty miles from the Yugoslav coast, it was hit again but by heavy flak which damaged both fuselage and the port wing. One of the crew, a gunner, was wounded in the leg. While still over the Adriatic, there was smoke from an engine and the wing became red hot.

It proved necessary to ditch, and this was in position 42°50′N 16°50′E where the B-17 remained afloat for only 1½ minutes. It was time enough, however, for most of the crew to escape through the radio hatch, but the engineer — T/Sgt N. Benninger — was drowned. The area was circled by other B-17s and two P-38s. Two hours after the ditching, Catalina *958* flown by Lt Milburn and Capt Ruckman, touched down in a choppy sea. 600gal of fuel were jettisoned before the Catalina was taxied to the dinghy which by then was west of Dubrovnik in position 42°31′N 17°41′E.

Rescues in the following month included one who had made a second ditching in three weeks. He was a Hurricane fighter pilot, Flt Lt Arnold E. Walker. While strafing a German schooner, his aircraft's oil tank was hit by AA and he baled out from 4,500ft while 25 miles south-west of Galiola Island. It took him twelve hours to reach the edge of a beachless island where he was marooned for 5½ days. A Catalina of the 1st ERS, No *959*, landed ten miles north-west of Ancona at Falcanara Field where bearings were given and a fighter escort of twelve P-38s was arranged. The Catalina, with three British passengers on board, made a flight of 85 miles across the Adriatic Sea to the Gulf of Quarnaro which was then described as the 'Nazi Lion's Mouth'. It touched down on a calm sea at 17:05hr, recovered Flt Lt Walker and was airborne again in eight minutes, returning safely to base at 20:00hr on 8 August.

In addition to rescues of many Allied aircrew, the 1st ERS of the American AAF was no less prepared to undertake mercy missions for the enemy and there are a number listed in the records. Thus, for example, on 8 June 1944, one of their Catalinas picked up aircrew from a Junkers Ju 88, two wounded and one dead German at position 39°28′N 18°25′E which is about twenty miles off Cape San Maria di Leuca near the Gulf of Taranto.

On 1 January 1945, instructions were received for two flights from No 1 ER Squadron to go to India. By the 8th they had departed except for four B-17s which left on 1 March. In India, these flights formed No 7 ER Squadron.

The pick-up of B-17 crews south-west of Sardinia with the *OA-10* 2nd pilot — 'Chuck' Zoet on the wing directing operations, another crew member is on the port wing to apply torque.

US Army Air Force rescues in the Pacific Areas

Unlike the North Sea and Mediterranean areas, the American AAF in the Pacific theatre was unable to depend on an efficient RAF air-sea-rescue organisation. The first recorded effort towards AAF involvement in rescue missions was by Maj John H. Small, Jr, who, after arriving in New Guinea, began directing air searches for missing aircrew in July 1943. He received four Catalinas in August and his service was to rescue 455 ditched aircrew by the end of April 1944.

It was in August of 1943 that the American Joint Administrative Committee had been instructed by the Chiefs of Staff to study the question of air-sea-rescue, and the AAF made plans for seven ASR squadrons to be equipped with Catalinas[1] but meanwhile, many rescues in the Pacific areas were continuing to be undertaken by the USN, RAAF and RNZAF.

While on a flight from Guadalcanal to Espiritu Santo on 27 January 1943, the Commander of the 13th Air Force — General N. F. Twining — was one of fifteen who ditched in a B-17 off the New Hebrides in the Coral Sea. He, with his companions, was picked up by a US Navy Catalina commanded by Lt Robert Feddern six days later.

179

The 2nd Emergency Rescue Squadron had been formed at Hamilton Field, California, in December 1943 and after training at Keesler Field, began to move to the 5th Air Force area in July 1944 to operate from Biak Island off New Guinea.

It appears very likely that a 'Hudson' friend[4] of mine may have been the first to be rescued by an AAF Catalina in the Pacific area, as in the following account: On 26 July 1944 some B-24 USAF aircraft were ordered to bomb the Japanese held airstrip and buildings at Ransiki in the western part of Dutch New Guinea. Photographs taken earlier of the target area had shown only three AA gun emplacements at each end of the airstrip, and weather forecasts were good for the morning.

Over the target area, Bill Amos had just released bombs from the B-24 which he was commanding, when he was aware of two direct AA hits to his aircraft. He peeled off immediately away from the rest of the formation. One engine was on fire, another was rapidly losing oil and racing. He headed east and checked on his crew. The co-pilot, Bill Rush, was slightly injured. The bomb-aimer however, Jim Bishop, had been severely wounded in the abdomen, and others in the crew bandaged his wounds and administered morphine.

Height was now being lost on the two remaining engines which were overheating, and with their airspeed then at 100kt, the nearest friendly base was Wakde Island, two hours away. On the radio guard frequency, signals were blocked by some Naval transmissions and Amos gave orders for ditching procedure to be followed. On ditching, a dinghy was released and inflated. The bomb-aimer had been given two life jackets for support but he was unconscious and needed another man to support his head. When the aircraft sank, four rear gunners went down with it; they had given all their attention to Jim Bishop. An emergency radio was found floating and was operated by now, some of the six survivors.

With a sheet, rain water was collected during a passing squall, and with an improvised drogue, some small purple fish were caught and eaten. During the night, it became apparent that Jim Bishop had died, and there was a reluctant but unanimous decision made

and acted upon, with one of the crew speaking the first three lines of the 23rd Psalm.

The remaining five were now surrounded by mist over the sea and their dinghy which was in sighting distance of Geelvink Bay, a Japanese naval base. Engines were heard and they wondered. At daybreak they saw the coast only a mile away with enemy lorries moving. During a ran squall, a B-25 broke cloud but seemed unaware of the dinghy and its occupants.

In the early afternoon a Catalina was seen heading their way, and when at a quarter-of-a-mile distant, one of the ditched crew jumped up and waved madly although by then waves were running at 3-4ft high. Typically, as the Catalina touched down it disappeared! It was then seen again only 100ft away; the engines were cut, and the dinghy was paddled to a blister, where the cry was heard: 'Hey, you guys wanna ride?'

After the engines were re-started, a gunner sank the dinghy with a spray of bullets. Bill Amos was invited forward to take-off, where the captain grabbed his arm and gestured him to behind the pilot's seat. As Amos recalls: 'For one accustomed to hard runways it was a hairy exhibition of a new way to kill yourself. The throttles were eased forward and the plane began accelerating in a wallowing, erratic path through the water. This kept increasing, and at 40kt started smashing through each three foot wave with a series of gigantic thuds. The speed increased and the plane-to-wave impacts changed to a succession of shuddering crashes as each wave, now a solid obstacle, tried to destroy this foreign thing that refused to conform to wind and water motion.

'Now a solid curtain of water flowed down each side and forward window making visibility out of the cockpit impossible. Unconcerned, the pilot continued manoeuvring. A shaft of water erupted out of the floor and the navigator reported that the drift meter housing had been torn away, the pilot nodded. The impacts diminished and the captain yelled that he wondered if they'd ever get onto the step.'

Amos looked at the pilot who was now sweating heavily and it occurred to him that perhaps he should have been more concerned about that stage in his rescue[5].

This pick-up proved to be one of the first made by the Army Air Corps crews, this particular crew having arrived in New Guinea only three days earlier, and it was their first rescue mission. In six sweeps round the enemy coastline, this Catalina had been shot at by the Japanese. Despite shortage of fuel, the captain — John Denison — had made a last search southwards and in a final run, sighted the dinghy. On land near the dinghy, it was reported that about sixty Japanese soldiers had been cut off from supplies and had resorted to cannibalism.

The record of the 2nd Emergency Rescue Squadron gives this as their first operational mission. Lt Denison had searched the reported area for seven hours before sighting the dinghy two miles away. He picked up the survivors at 10:00hr after Bill Amos and his crew had been in the dinghy for thirty hours.

In this year of writing — 1986 — Bill Amos resides in Albuquerque, happily growing peaches and melons. Another ex-AAF pilot — John Crawford in New Jersey — tells me he has located two of the Catalina rescue crew.

Two days after the rescue of Bill Amos, No 2 ER Squadron was ordered to evacuate wounded men from within enemy-held territory in Dutch New Guinea, near Lake Rombebai. For this operation, Captain E. Wientjes

touched down on the lake and taxied within 100yd of the shore. A dinghy was launched and ten Allied soldiers were picked up together with a Japanese prisoner. That morning the Allied soldiers had overpowered a guard and had then been attacked by about fifty of the enemy. Fifteen of the enemy were accounted for, but seven of the Allies had suffered wounds from Japanese sabres, knives and bayonets.

After attention by a medical officer, the soldiers were taken by dinghy to the Catalina. The amphibian was taxied into deep water, seaweed was removed from the landing gear, heavy equipment was jettisoned together with 500gal of fuel, and after three attempts at take-off, they were airborne. This was in sight of the enemy on the shore a thousand yards away, but no shots were exchanged. The survivors were taken to Owi Island before transfer to the 92nd General Hospital. They stated: 'We prayed for daylight and a PBY, and if heaven looks anything like a PBY we are going to change our ways'.

The following month Captain Wientjes evacuated eleven men from Warsaw Bay, Biak Island. One was wounded, the other ten had typhus and were taken to Owi Island.

An OA-10B of the 1st Rescue Sqdn, USAF. The OA-10B was the US Army's equivalent of the USN's PBY-6A, and shows the characteristic high fin.

On 9 September, 1st Lt James F. Scott while on patrol was ordered to position 01°00′S 127°45′E off Tifore Island between Celebes and Halmaheras. He sighted a crew of five from a B-25, with four of the five supporting the other man due to his life jacket having been punctured by enemy fire. Their dinghy had gone down with the B-25. Lt Scott landed in open sea with four-foot swells and picked up the survivors.

1st Lt George A. Barnes was airborne from Middleburg Island at 03:45hr on the 30th to cover a B-24 strike on Balikpapan. After flying through storms for over six hours he reached orbit point in the Gulf of Toronaldo, Celebes. While still circling three hours later, he saw a B-24 losing height with an engine on fire. Its crew baled out and Lt Barnes touched down half-a-mile from the first two who were sharing a one-man dinghy. After recovering them he taxied two miles and picked up the entire crew of ten despite heavy swells which were increasing. Because of the load, guns, ammunition and 150gal of fuel were jettisoned. After four attempts the Catalina was finally airborne. Barnes had been down on open sea for almost 1½ hours, most of the time spent in trying to take off. On returning to base, an air-raid was on, and the Catalina had to circle twenty miles away before touching down again after a mission of over seventeen hours.

During October, some members of the RAAF were rescued by the 2nd ER Squadron. They were F/O Downing on 2 October who was returned to his base at Noemfoor, and F/Os R. H. Falker and Donald E. Andrew on the 7th and 12th respectively.

1st Lt Kenneth N. Hunter of the 2nd ER Squadron was airborne from Middleburg Island at 13:55hr on the 7th having been briefed to search the area of 01°58′S 130°E. On reaching that position a dinghy was seen heading towards the Catalina. Its occupant was F/O Falkner who, during a raid on the 4th, had his engines shot out. After ditching he had existed on boiled crabs and coconuts.

While searching the south-east coast of Misool Island on the 12th, 1st Lt Harry H. Pennington became aware of a mirror signal two miles east of Kafnikolep river, west of Ceram. On circling the area, he sighted a white man with a group of natives. Lt Pennington landed his Catalina and the natives

brought out F/O Donald E. Andrew, RAAF. His squadron, No 75, had been operating Kittyhawks. F/O Andrew had baled out on the 9th due to fuel shortage after being lost in a storm, and during his descent his parachute caught in a tree and he fractured his wrist. He was returned to Sansapor.

On 22 November, Lt Strader was in one of a pair of P-38s which were shot down while raiding Macassar. He went down about 40ft in the water before he could extricate himself from the aircraft. Back on the surface, he partly inflated his Mae West and turned his dinghy with its blue side uppermost and hid from a series of searches by Japanese surface craft, at one time being almost run down by them.

The following day when he heard aircraft, he reversed his dinghy and flashed with a mirror. The aircraft were a Catalina commanded by Lt John R. Dickinson and an escort of P-38s. Strader was then seven miles west of Macassar but the Catalina touched down with Dickinson keeping the engines running due to a close enemy. Jammed gear kept him on the water for twenty minutes but Strader was picked up and the PBY returned to Middleburg after a mission of just under eighteen hours and with 40gal of fuel remaining. The escorts which had to return earlier had been in the air for 10½ hours.

On 19 December a Catalina of the 2nd ER Squadron commanded by 1st Lt N. Hunter, rendezvoused at position 05°11′N 120°38′E with a fighter escort en route to Languyan Point to pick up four survivors. At Languyan Point friendly natives were sighted, and on touching down the Catalina crew was informed that the survivors were half-a-mile up river with guerrilla Col Suares.

The four survivors were from a B-24 which had been attacked by twenty Japanese fighters on 1 November, setting the aircraft on fire. The crew baled out but two were shot and killed by the fighters as they parachuted down. Others were lost later. The four who were recovered, led by Lt John W. Emig, had been in a dinghy but without paddles and had drifted south. They were all wounded and they bathed their wounds in the sea. During the day they covered themselves with a blue sheet to prevent detection by the enemy. By the fourth day their water was gone and they were left with peanuts and pemican. On the ninth day it rained and they collected as much as possible. Fish and birds caught by hand were eaten raw with no meat wasted, but from the 19th to the 29th day they were without food.

On the 29th day, a Navy plane dropped food from which some chocolate and milk tablets were recovered. On the 33rd day land was sighted and they found some dried coconuts. In 33 days they had drifted 600 miles. It was on Sibuti Island that they were found by friendly natives.

In December, two rough sea landings were made in mercy missions. The first of these was on the 22nd when 1st Lt Harold W. Strub picked up eight survivors from Caranga Point, Mindanao. To take off, 550gal of fuel were jettisoned. Despite damage to the hull both on landing and take-off, the Catalina, 'Playmate 42', returned to Morotai.

On 28/29 December 1st Lt Robert L. Rohlfing, while airborne to cover a strike on

Tarakan, was ordered to position 06°10'N 122°45'E for reported survivors off Natanel Point, Basilan Island. While searching the area, flares and mirror flashes were sighted. Rohlfing landed in a rough sea to pick up five survivors from an 822 Squadron raid on Zamboanga, Mindanao. In ditching, the rear gunner from their B-25 was lost.

The year 1945 began for the 2nd ER Squadron with the pick up of two B-25 crews within sight of the enemy. The B-25s, *J135* and *J920* of the 405th Bomb Squadron flown by Lts Smith and Gunn, had ditched fifteen miles north-west of Tarakan, Borneo, on 30 December. Capt Wientjes in 'Playmate 42' was airborne from Morotai at 02:55hr on 1 January. After flying for seven hours, mirror flashes were seen on the shore. The Catalina touched down five minutes later and some survivors swam out pushing a dinghy with an injured man on board. Twelve men were picked up and within thirty minutes of

A citation to the 2nd Emergency Rescue Sqdn presented to them by the 347th Fighter Group, AAF after a series of rescues in the South Pacific area.

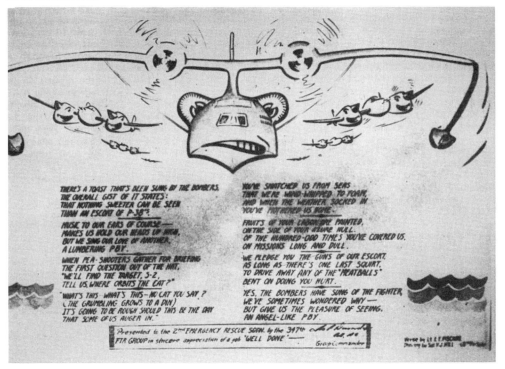

touching down, the Catalina was airborne again, and just in time, as a Japanese patrol boat was heading for that area.

The two ditched crews, after escaping from their B-25s, had met up at position 03°30'N 117°25'E but swampy conditions meant them remaining in their dinghies much of the time. At one stage, an enemy search party had been avoided by deflating the dinghies and by the men standing in water with only their faces exposed.

1st Lt Scott was airborne at 06:50hr on 5 January to give strike cover. While on patrol he was advised of two B-25s having or about to ditch. One of these was off Tifore Island, the other off Menado, Celebes. It was over five hours when he touched down in a very rough sea off Menado. While picking up six survivors, the Japanese shore batteries opened up. Although rounds were falling 15ft from the wing, the Catalina was airborne again within ten minutes but still under fire.

Scott touched down again at position 01°00'N 125°40'E where the second B-25 crew was recovered. The Catalina was now heavily loaded and it was necessary to jettison 500lb of equipment. After a long run, the aircraft was airborne again later to land at Mar, Sanapo, on the Vogelkop Peninsula.

By the middle of February, the squadron had rescued 274 survivors with eleven Catalina crews operating. In over half of these rescues, the crews were subjected to enemy attacks. In addition to the rescues, 56 personnel had been evacuated. The areas covered were New Guinea; Halmaheras, Celebes; Palau, Borneo and the Philippines, and operating from bases at Nadzah, Hollandia, Biak, Middleburg and Morotai.

The Americans had set an invasion date of 10th March for Zamboanga, Mindanao. This was to provide a base for an advance on Borneo and flights to the South China Sea. On 4 March, the 2nd ER Squadron covered a B-25 strike on Zamboanga. 1st Lt Frank Rauschkolb was airborne from Morotai at 05:15hr in 'Playmate 42' and was directed to a ditched B-25 crew a mile off shore. When about to touch down near their dinghy, several Japanese barges opened fire. He called up more B-25s to cover him. He was subjected nonetheless to machine-gun and mortar fire as he taxied to the survivors' dinghy to pick up five

men. Rauschkolb then taxied to another downed crew picking up another six. One engine cut for fifteen minutes due to overheating. There was then further taxying out through a coral reef to the open sea and because it was too rough for take-off, an additional fifteen miles of taxying was necessary to just off Malanipa Island to rescue a third crew.

The Catalina was now overloaded with 25 men on board and was leaking badly. 400gal of fuel were jettisoned. It was airborne again at 11:40hr and reached Morotai at 16:15hr. All three B-25s of the rescued crews had been shot down by accurate and intensive flak over Zamboanga but had lost only one man out of eighteen.

During the following months of April, May, June and July, the squadron was engaged in a series of searches, evacuations and emergency rescue cover for strikes against the enemy on Borneo and Celebes. By July, in addition to the customary fighter escort for hostile areas, airborne lifeboats carried by B-17s were being used. In addition to the obvious disadvantage of survivors perhaps being in no fit condition to operate the gear in a lifeboat, overheating of the engines of the airborne lifeboat is recorded.

What 'comes through' in the reports of the 2nd Emergency Rescue Squadron of the AAF is their persistence in search and rescue operations; never giving up so long as the possibility of a pick-up remained. They quite frequently touched down in rough seas with heavy swells and risked at the same time, fire from a merciless enemy. The 2nd ER Squadron received an exceptional tribute in the form of an illuminated address[6] from the 347th Fighter Group in the South-West Pacific theatre.

On 4 August, C Flight of 2nd ERS moved from Morotai to Clark Field to cover rescue operations for the area of China and north of Okinawa and Luzon. Their last strike cover mission was on the 13th under the command of Captain Scott. During the period of operations in the South Pacific the squadron record includes reference to living conditions with pyramid tents and on occasions without flooring which in flat jungle areas and heavy rain presented problems.

Camp hygiene was strictly controlled and

malaria and dengue fevers were exceptions rather than the rule. Common ailments were fungus skin disorders and gastric and respiratory troubles. The latter were found to prevail notably after a dry spell followed by very wet conditions. The best treatment for the skin complaints was sea bathing and such disorders were found to decline in areas such as Zamboanga and Palawan where they camped on sandy beaches with coconut palms. Prophylactic treatment was given against typhoid, tetanus, typhus, cholera and malaria. Reference is made to a gnat whose bites caused large blisters with inflammation, which were treated with 10 per cent silver nitrate solution after removal of the skin.

The 6th ER Squadron arrived in April 1945 and in July one section of this squadron operated from Okinawa, the other section from Ie Shima. Following a request for ASR support for B-29s operating from the Marianas, the 4th ER Squadron with Catalinas was deployed; their first flight arriving on 23 March, and in April, three of the twelve aircraft which had arrived moved to Peleliu.

In the latter stages of the war against Japan, heavily armed B-29s were equipped with rescue material. Rescue services were so arranged that any part of the routes to Japan could be reached by air in thirty minutes or by surface or submarine vessel within three hours. But by 14 August 1945 PBYs still formed part of the ASR service.

From a summary of 20th Air Force operations giving ASR statistics for the period November 1944 to July 1945[7], of 1,310 aircrew who ditched, crashed or parachuted, 654 were rescued, with the percentage varying between 13 per cent for January 1945 and 80 per cent in May 1945.

Post-war movements of the AAF rescue squadrons

By the end of the war in the Pacific, rescue squadrons Nos 2, 3, 4, 6 and 7 were still active. The 1st ER Squadron returned from the Mediterranean to America in 1946 and was disbanded in March, but in September was reformed to become the 1st Rescue Squadron in the Caribbean.

HQ of the 2nd Squadron moved from Morotai to Luzon in September 1945. In

Awards being presented to members of the 2nd ER Sqdn AAF on Morotai Island in 1944.

March 1947 it was deployed at Okinawa where the 2nd Squadron absorbed the 6th Squadron's personnel and equipment.

The 3rd ER Squadron with the 5th Air Force moved in August 1945 to Japan but had one detachment in Korea. The 4th was deployed in North Guam; the 7th had been effectively disbanded in January 1946 but was officially inactivated on 15 May at Hawaii.

The 5th Squadron, which had served in England with the 8th AAF, had returned to the USA in 1945. This squadron was involved with training personnel for other units in 1946 following the formation of an Air Rescue service with HQ at Morrison Field, Florida. Two other squadrons had their headquarters at Andrews Field, Maryland, and at Hamilton Field, California. Both squadrons had detachments with five of these ostensibly covering the whole area of USA. Although largely equipped with C-47s, they had also some lifeboat-carrying SB-17s and twelve OA-10As Catalina amphibians as well as seventeen helicopters.

1   Figures from *A History of the Air Rescue Service*, Ed J. L. Vandergift. Jr. Rollins Press Inc, Fl, 1959, p10.
2   Possibly three from operation 'Juggler', the bombing of aircraft works at Regensburg by 140 aircraft from 4th Bombardment Wing, 8th AAF.
3   C & C, Vol VII, p480.
4   Lt Col William Amos, USAF (Ret). See also the author's *Seek and Strike*.
5   Rescue aircraft: OA-10A *44-33876* Lt John S. Denison, Lt Eric Lakes. Lt Peter Naylor. T/Sgt John Cunningham, Sgt Raymond Bean, Sgt George Bock and Sgt Franklin Besse. Position: 135°E 1°30'S.
6   Ibid page 458.
7   C & C. Vol V, p606.

Chapter 20
Other Services

United States Coast Guard

Following the loss of the liner *Titanic* in 1912, international ice patrols were instigated and the United States Coast Guard service stemmed from such work. In addition to many light patrol craft operated by the service in World War 2, a squadron was formed equipped with Catalina amphibians.

The earliest reference to the flying arm of the USCG service given in the official *United States Naval Aviation 1910-1970* is in March 1916 when two officers were assigned to Pensacola for flight instruction following agreement between the US Treasury and the US Navy. In April 1917 the USCG was transferred from the Treasury to operate as part of the Navy. A similar arrangement occurred in World War 2 when the Service was transferred on 1 November 1941 to operate under Naval control.

The Greenland government requested American protection from the Nazis on 3 May 1940 and a USCG vessel landed a representative at Ivigut west of Cape Desolation in the same month. Greenland, as also Iceland, lay adjacent to the great circle route from North America to the British Isles, and bases there could serve for or against the Allies. On 9 April 1941 agreement was reached with the Danish government for America to undertake the defence of Greenland, and in October, an officer of the USCG — Cdr Edward H. Smith — was appointed overall commander.

Squadron VP-6, USCG, was commissioned at Argentia, Newfoundland, on 5 October 1943 and was commanded by Cdr D. B. MacDiarmid, USCG. Its duties were to take over the rescue operations then being covered by US Navy aircraft in Greenland and Labrador of Squadron VB-126. The squadron's two main bases were to be Argentia, Newfoundland, and Narsarssuak, Greenland. With Narsarssuak located approximately 775 miles

from Goose Bay, Labrador and Iceland, it became the major Greenland base for the US Navy and the US Army. Narsarssuak was given the Army code 'Bluie West 1' (BW1), all of the eight Greenland stations being 'Bluies'.

Initially squadron VP-6 was assigned ten PBY-5As, nine operational and one spare. They began operations, however, with six aircraft. Their duties became not unlike that for some RAF Coastal Command squadrons as they were required to undertake anti-submarine patrols, convoy escorts, air-sea-rescue missions, ice patrol and surveys, and some transport trips. When more aircraft became available, two Catalinas were detached to Reykjavik, and two more to Frobisher Bay. All major overhauls of aircraft were undertaken at Argentia. This was on rotation, and must have been a welcome change for the crews.

Conditions at Bluie West 1 were described as being with a single concrete runway sloping down from a mountain at one end towards Narsarssuak fjord and bounded on each side by 4,000ft mountains. These geographical conditions meant that all take-offs must be downhill towards the fjord and all landings uphill in the direction of the mountain irrespective of surface winds which were seldom less than 25kt. For recreation at BW1, VP-6 personnel had films, bowling, ski-ing and shooting.

One of the squadron's exceptional rescue missions was by Lt Cdr J. D. McCubbin in February 1944. While on a routine ice patrol he sighted a red flare. It proved to be a distress signal from the British trawler HMS *Strathella* which had been adrift for five weeks. The coast guard cutter *Modoc* was signalled to the area.

By May 1944, VP-6 had twelve Catalinas with three at Argentia, two in Northern Canada, two at Reykjavik and five at BW1.

Cdr W. I. Swanston relieved the CO, Cdr MacDiarmid, as Commanding Officer. An experienced pilot — Robert Gregory — also joined the squadron in May. Although he had many hundreds of hours flying, he was given additional training at the Coast Guard Air Station, Elizabeth City, North Carolina, undergoing for example, a number of training flights in PBY *46575*. He flew to Argentia the same month and describes the airfield as having fine facilities, and where the mail plane would bring in the Boston newspaper the same day as printed, weather permitting.

Gregory had a number of trips to Goose Bay where landings were described as frightening with snow under the wings on the runway. His trips during July included one to Bluie East 2 on Angmagsalik Island, delivering mail and supplies; and anti-submarine patrols off Prince Christian Sound. On the 27th he made a seven-hour search for a missing C-54 aircraft.

From December 1944 to April 1945 Gregory completed a series of ice patrols including one on 4 April to determine the extent of the ice to the south-east. His final trip was on 19 April, a ten-hour flight from Argentia to Floyd Bennett Field, New York, with two other pilots and twelve passengers.

The surrender of Germany in May 1945 removed the need for anti-U-boat searches, but other duties such as ice patrols and search and rescue continued. On the 30th Commander Swanston was relieved by Cdr L. E. Seeger, USCG.

In August VPB-6, as by now it had been redesignated, transferred from Bluie West 1, Greenland, to Argentia, Newfoundland. It was disestablished as a USN squadron in January 1946.

PBY-5 Bu.No. 2290, the second PBY-5 to be produced. It was allocated to the US Coast Guard service.

Catalinas Operated by the Free French

A Free French unit equipped with Catalinas — Squadron 6F — was assigned to the US Navy in November 1943. Before the end of 1943, the twelve PBY-5As forming 6e Flottille d'Exploration became known as VFP-1 (French Patrol Squadron No 1) and was attached to Fleet Air Wing 15 of the US Navy with headquarters at Port Lyautey in French Morocco.

VFP-1 was posted to Agadir, a naval air station where a USN squadron VB-132 equipped with PV-1 Venturas was already engaged in convoy escorts and general Coastal Command work. VFP-1 was immediately operational on convoy escorts, meteorological flights over and around Madeira, and daily surveillance of the Canary Islands where it was suspected U-boats were gaining assistance. No U-boats were sighted by the Free French Catalinas.

On 19 July 1944, the squadron joined l'Escadrille 4S at 2 Aspretto, Corsica, under the command of L. V. de Levis de Mirepoix and a detachment covered the landings in Corsica forming part of the build-up to 2,000 Allies in Corsica and Sardinia as prelude to operation 'Anvil' or 'Dragoon'.

On 15 August under operation 'Anvil', landings were made by the Allies in southern France between Cannes and Hyères. The French Catalinas served in supporting the landings at St Tropez, notably searching for mines. During these operations the squadron undertook 48 missions but lost one aircraft in the Bay of St Tropez. Their Chef de bord was L. V. Lemeur. During that period 6F had aircraft operating from Naples, Ajaccio and Ramatuelle. In October 1944, 6F left its Aspretto base for Morocco.

According to Jean-Jacques Loité, a pilot who had served with this first Free French Catalina squadron, it had been General de Gaulle's wish to have his men present in all theatres of war. As part of the policy he wanted a Coastal Command squadron to serve with the US Navy in the Pacific but the squadron was diverted to the Mediterranean area. The Free French Navy recalled its personnel serving with the Air Force and sent them to Jacksonville or Pensacola in USA for conversion courses. Jean-Jacques Loité was one of many Allied pilots, including some serving not only with the USN but also the RAF and FAA, who trained at Pensacola, an establishment remembered with pride and respect.

As the land war in Europe intensified, U-boat activity moved northwards from the Mediterranean. The American squadron VB-132 was disbanded and its PV-1 Venturas were transferred to VFP-1. In turn, five Catalinas of VFP-1 were modified and used as transport aircraft for VIPs, also to fly ammunition and supplies to a French dive-bomber squadron based at Cognac and engaged in dislodging German pockets at St Nazaire and along the Atlantic coast.

Loité applied for a posting to the United Kingdom and in February 1945 left the squadron which was still based at Agadir. As most personnel serving with VFP-1 were not regular Navy types, but reserve volunteers, they were released from the service between June and September 1945. Some chose to stay and were eventually sent to Indo-China.

The French squadron 8FE (la 8ᵉ Flottille d'Exploration), was formed on 29th April 1944 and was equipped with amphibian Catalinas (PBY-5As). In August fourteen of these Catalinas were deployed at Agadir in North Africa. They later re-grouped at Port Lyautey and took part in operations of Coastal Command. The squadron was given the American designation of French Patrol squadron No 2.

During the period of Allied landings in Provence, 8FE with three aircraft at Cuers, was detailed for reconnaissance of the Mediterranean and participated in the re-conquest

Catalina *F.31* showing the Cross of Lorraine, the insignia of the Free French whose Catalinas were involved with the Allied landings in Corsica, Sardinia and Southern France.

of France. On the fuselage of their Catalinas they had a wolf's head insignia said to have originated from General Chassin of l'Armée de l'Air who had commanded the squadron in 1926.

In December 1944, some seventeen Catalinas were based at Agadir of which five were detached at Cuers. In January 1945, 8FE was deployed in the West African theatre of operations for convoy escort duties to counter German U-boat activities. On 11 September the 'Force Navale d'Extrême-Orient' was formed and entailed the re-organisation of l'Aéronautique Navale. This resulted in the formation of 'Group Aéronaval d'Indochine' and on 26 September, four Catalinas left Agadir by air for Indo-China. They arrived at Tan Son Nhut on 10 October and represented for a time, French aviation in Indo-China in maintaining reconnaissance and observation of ground attacks for the benefit of the expeditionary forces.

Squadron 8FE assumed the designation '8F' on 5 December following the entry into the service of five Spitfires of l'Armée de l'Air. The Catalinas continued to be the main military aircraft covering the expeditionary army. They remained further, the main aircraft capable of intervening in the remote areas — plateau Moi, South Annam, and High Laos. During the retaking of Haiphong, three Catalinas used the waters near the Gao Tao Islands; Force Z ensured the landing of General Leclerc's forces and they were free of detection from the air.

Very quickly, Squadron 8F was able to operate over the skies of Indo-China, Siam, Tonkin, Laos, Annam, Cambodia, Cochin-China, Tonle-Sap, Mekong, Fleuve-Rouge and Baie d'Along. They served all, with transport of troops, equipment and medical supplies. They participated in maritime blockade, revictualling encircled areas, surveillance missions, transport of VIPs, liaisons, reconnaissance, etc. In May 1946, the 'grands oiseaux blancs' wanted to re-form in the Mother country, and it was with No 6 that operations were undertaken.

In 1947, 8F from its base at Cat-Lai, maintained maritime surveillance and participated in the operations 'Léa', 'Catherine', and 'Dédale', meriting awards for such work. The French High Commission in Indo-China gave

A PBY-5A *Papoose No. 852* of the Royal Danish Air Force which was in Danish service from June 1947 until December 1960.

testimony to their gratitude for the results achieved by No 8 Squadron 'Tetes de Loup Noir'; 2,000 hours flying on war missions, the transportation of 3,000 passengers and thirty tons of freight. 200 personnel were evacuated without reckoning with the clearing and control of la plaine des Joncs, Bassac and Bas Mékong.

On 2 April 1948 there was reorganisation by the Command of l'Aéronautique Navale in Indo-China which changed deployment of 8F with three Catalinas to Hai-Phong, Nha Trang and Saigon; two others were destined for operations over Tonkin and Cochin-China. In the last quarter of 1949, there was a change in 8F's activities and the need for their four machines at Cuers was reviewed.

At the end of 1950 ten Privateer PB-4Y aircraft were provided to equip 8F, and their Catalinas were transferred to Squadron 8S. The resulting deployment was one Catalina and ten Privateers at Tan Son Nhut; one or two Catalinas at Haiphong, and one or two Catalinas at Tourane. 8F was disbanded on 26 May 1953 and was replaced by Squadron 28F which retained their aircraft.

Catalinas in Danish service

In January 1946 the Danish 'Mariners Flyvevasen' (Naval Air Arm), was scheduled to continue with photo-survey work in Greenland. Being amphibians with long-range capability, PBY-5As were considered suitable. An aircraft purchasing commission was sent to the USA and Canada and six ex-RCAF Catalinas were purchased at $15,000 each, although four times that amount was required for a major overhaul with the de Havilland Company in Canada. They were given the numbers *FM51-FM56*, FM standing for 'flying boat monoplane'. Two of the aircraft were ferried to Jacksonville Naval Air Base, Florida, and it was there that the training of three Danish crews was completed by the US Navy in May 1947.

Following the completion of a third aircraft, three Catalinas arrived at the Danish Naval Air station in Copenhagen on 6 June after a ferry flight time of 34 hours made via Gander, Meeks Field, Iceland and Alborg.

Within the Naval Air Service, a Catalina group had been formed on 10 February 1947, and in the summer of that year, Catalinas were serving in Greenland. One was used to support the Pearyland expedition and operated from Young Sound on the east coast, while a second aircraft was on photo-survey work from Bluie West 1. Although this became the main task of the Catalinas, they were also used for routine transport, patrols and air-sea-rescue missions.

189

Aircraft were used to support further Danish expeditions with *852* (*FM52*) going to Luanda, Angola, in December 1950, and *851* (*FM51*) to Mombasa in March 1951. Bases for the Catalinas in Denmark were changed from the Copenhagen seaplane base to Kastrup airport and later in April 1956 to Vaerløse.

In November 1956 eight PBY-6As were acquired from the US Navy. The aircraft were ferried from store at Litchfield Park to New Orleans for modifications such as the removal of the front turret and major overhaul. These aircraft were intended as replacements for the PBY-5s and could be distinguished from them by a modified nose section and a higher tail plane. Delivery was taken between April 1957 and February 1958.

Changes occurred also in the Danish operating units. The Catalina group which was initially based at a naval air station was transformed into 1LF, which together with 2LF, amalgamated to form Squadron No 721 when the Royal Danish Air Force was formed in 1951. No 721 Squadron remained at Copenhagen until December 1952 and then transferred to Kastrup before making another move to the air base at Vaerløse in April 1956. A second squadron — No 722, which also operated Catalinas — was based at Vaerløse, but had permanent detachments in Jutland and Bluie West 1 in Greenland.

In 1963, three Danish Catalinas were lost in Greenland. *L865* crashed into the mountains at Cape Desolation on 10 August and all twelve on board, crew and passengers were killed. On 24 October, *L862* and *L864* were lost in a hangar fire at Bluie West 1.

PBY-6A *L867*, made a forced landing WSW of Upernavik on 3 May 1964. This was due to engine trouble and occurred in open sea. All on board were rescued by a USAF Albatross from Sandestrom. On 11 December 1969, *L853* crashed in the Kattegat north of Sealand. The co-pilot was killed but the rest of the crew and passengers were saved.

When 722 Squadron converted to Sikorsky S-61 helicopters, the remaining Catalinas were returned to 721 Squadron. Near the end of their service life, three Danish Catalinas undertook a long formation flight round Denmark in 1970; they were *L861*, *L863* and *L868*. In 1972, two of these aircraft, *L868* and *L863* but registered as *N15KL* and *N16KL*, flew to the USA; *N15KL* to the Larkin Aircraft Corporation, Watsonville, California, on 9 June followed by *N16KL* on 13 July.

When with the Confederate Air Force on 18 August 1975, *N15KL* had an engine failure just after take-off. While making an emergency landing, a section of the structure near the wing, broke up and crashed through the cockpit. Three were killed, two were rescued.

PBY-6A No *863* of the Royal Danish Air Force. It was off charge in November 1970 and sold with the registration *N16KL*.

There is a gap in the record of the Danish Catalina PBY-6A *L866* when it served with the US Navy. Copies of record cards give the Bureau No *63993* and the delivery date to the USN as 4 May 1945. It then served with Squadrons VPB-100 and VPB-71 up until October 1946. The aircraft may have been assigned to Fighter Squadron No 212 in February 1953, and certainly in March 1953 was stored at Litchfield Park, Arizona, until 1956 only to be stricken from the USN inventory on 23 November.

Seven years later in a test flight with the Royal Danish Air Force, when flying at 6,000ft a noise like an explosion was heard by the crew. Power had been cut and they were in a right-hand turn. It was discovered later that ten square metres of the starboard wing were missing.

L866 made the final Catalina flight for the RDAF in May 1974 and on the 30th was transferred to RAF Colerne. In May 1984 I saw this same machine at my last wartime station — RAF Cosford. It was with Danish markings and complete with APU, bunks and ashtrays. However, as with the Lockheed Hudson at Hendon Museum, it was stripped of armament, radio and radar.

Catalinas of the Swedish Air Force

In the 1940s a delegation from the Swedish Air Force was sent to the American Coast Guard service to observe their air-sea-rescue activities. Subsequently the Swedish authorities purchased three Catalinas which were Convair PBY-5As and in Sweden were designated Tp47s, the 'Tp' representing a transport role. Modifications undertaken included the removal of all weapons and armament and replacement of the forward turret by a radome. The latter operated in conjunction with a radar station (AN/APS-3) which was installed. Six stretchers were provided in the fuselage and two chairs were located to the rear of the cockpit on the port side. The latter were intended for a doctor and a nurse.

The aircrew normally comprised two pilots, a navigator, a signaller and an aircraft mechanic/flight engineer. In addition, for arduous reconnaissance missions, two observers were positioned at the blisters. Specialised navigation equipment included a radar system with the Swedish designation 'PN-54', the 'PN' representing 'navigation radar' but included a landing facility.

The maximum take-off weight of the Swedish modified Catalinas was 15,400kg (33,957lb)

Tp47 a PBY-5A of the Swedish Air Force at Malmen, Linköping.

giving a maximum estimated duration of nineteen hours although routine missions had the fuel load adjusted for ten hours. Under calm conditions take-off from the sea required 1,800m (1,970yd) for the aircraft to become airborne, but for take-offs from small lakes the jet-assisted method using rockets, one each to port and starboard was used.

A special unit of the Swedish Air Force was 'Flygräddingsdivisionen' abbreviated to FRAD. Its main role was air-sea-rescue and was organised in the manner of a squadron but formed part of F-2 of the Swedish Air Force based at Roslagens flykar, a sea station at Hägernäs, ten miles north of Stockholm. FRAD, the rescue unit, was required to operate over the whole of Sweden and undertake various other duties in addition to standby cover for other aircrews who might baleout. Transport missions were for people, food and equipment. An important role was taking kidney patients to Lund, Scania, in Southern Sweden to a hospital which for a time had the only available kidney unit.

In winter, ice-reconnaissance missions were made for shipping and during one winter, bales of hay were parachuted to sheep located on Farön, an island in the Baltic Sea, the name 'Farön' appropriately meaning 'the island of sheep'.

The three Catalinas with the Swedish Air Force were in service for nineteen years covering the period 1947-66. One of the three was shot down by two Russian MiG-15 fighters in June 1952 during a search for survivors of a missing DC3 over the Baltic Sea. The Catalina crew was rescued by a German ship. One of the pilots had received a serious wound in an arm as a result of the Russian attack. It is thought that the DC3 survivors may have finished up in Siberia.

Of the nineteen years in service, thirteen proved most active, and in that time the Catalina crews completed a total of 6,000 missions. Of these, 4,500 were connected with Air Force routine operations and training programmes. 150 ice-reconnaissance trips were made and about 110 transfers were achieved of sick people from rural areas of Sweden to the kidney unit at Lund. During summer, the Catalinas were normally based at Hägernäs, and in winter at Stockholm/Broma or at Barkarby, a SAF air station, where F-8 Wing was based.

Catalina No 89 of the Swedish Air Force at the summer base — Hägernäs 10 miles north of Stockholm. Catalinas in Sweden were flown on mercy missions.

An amphibian of the Indonesian Air Force; a number of PBY-5As were received from the Dutch (Netherlands Militaire Luchvaart), following Indonesian independence.

Catalinas over Chile

Chile received ten Catalinas, three PBY-5 flying boats from the US Navy and seven OA-10A amphibians from the US Air Force. The three PBY-5s were received on 23 June 1943, one of them being under the command of Commandante Felipe Araya who took delivery at Pensacola. One of the OA-10As also arrived on 23 June; this was aircraft *7295* which was given the Chilean number (ITOF)404.

On 28 June 1948, three more OA-10As arrived and were given the numbers *560, 561* and *562*. The first of these, *560*, but with an earlier number *405*, was named 'Manutara' and on 19 January 1951 it was piloted by the then Gp Capt Roberto Parrague Singer on a direct flight from La Serena to Easter Island, a distance of 2,047 miles and a record for his country. At Easter Island he touched down on an improvised airstrip at Mataveri. A civil air service was formed by Roberto Parrague known as 'Aeroservicios Parrague'. He returned to Easter Island with one of the aircraft he had purchased in 1959 thus beginning a regular service which was maintained for three years. On 15 June 1961 Catalina 'Manutara' crashed in Lake Penuelas and all in the crew were killed.

Between 27 August and 12 September 1965, General Parrague undertook a flight between Tahiti and Chile in an amphibian PBY-6A named 'Manutara II' taking about 76 hours to cover, 16,000km (9,942 miles). This aircraft was given the registration *CC-CNP65* and was to be based at Los Cerrillos.

The OA-10A No *406* which was named 'Skua' undertook a flight from Los Cerrillos to Santiago and Punta Arenas as the first phase of a visit to the Antarctic. It was piloted by Sqn Ldr Humberto Tenorio. This began on 25 December 1955, but while flying from Punta Arenas to the air base on the Isle of Decepcion on the 28th there was the risk of fire and on the 29th, *406* returned to Punta Arenas. *406* was to remain in service until January 1963.

Indonesia and Catalinas

During the post-war period leading up to the independence of Indonesia from the Netherlands, two Catalina PBY-5A amphibians were used by the Indonesians to penetrate the Dutch blockade. The aircraft had the registration numbers *RI-005* and *RI-006* and were based at Campur Darat Lake, Tulungagung, East Java and at Singkarak Lake, West Sumatra. They were flown overseas to obtain weapons and other supplies.

PK-CTA 'Alor' c/n 9796; an ex-military PBY-5A which became a thirteen passenger aircraft with KLM but was transferred with others to Garuda Indonesian Airways. 'Alor' crashed at Poso, Celebes on 8 March 1948.

RI-005 was sunk in the Batanghari river in Jambi Province on 29 December 1948 as the result of an accident. *RI-006* was damaged at Maguwo Air Force Base, Yogyakarta, during a Dutch air strike on 19 December 1949.

The Republic of Indonesia gained recognition of its independence by the Dutch on 27 December 1949 and on 27 June 1950 there was a transfer of authority of a Militaire Luchvaart base from the Dutch to the Indonesians.

Subsequently, some PBY-5As were received from the Militaire Luchvaart. They became attached to No 5 Squadron under a composite Group Command and were located at Bugis Air Base, Malang. From there, operational missions included maritime patrols, air-sea-rescues, reconnaissance and transport.

KLM have provided the following information concerning Catalinas which they operated in Indonesia: they received ex-military PBY-5A amphibians, four of which served as thirteen-passenger aircraft from 1947 onwards. They were to become the property of the Indonesian government but were in use by KLM Interinsular Services from 1948 to 1950.

After Indonesia's independence, the aircraft were transferred to Garuda Indonesian Airways. Their maximum take-off weight was 13,393kg (29,531lb) and maximum load, 1,700kg (3,748lb). These Catalinas included aircraft 'Alor' with the registration *PK-CTA* (c/n *9796*) which crashed at Poso, Celebes, on 8 March 1948. Three others which served with KLM from 1949 onwards were Model 28-5As; they were fitted with large square windows and carried eighteen passengers. On 1 January 1950 they went to Garuda.

Appendix A
Technical data

Model	Engine	hp	Length	Height	Weights (lb) Empty	Gross	Max	Speeds (mph) Max	cruise	ldg	Ceiling	Climb	Range (miles)
XP3Y-1	P&W R1830-58	825	63'6"	18'6"	12,512	19,793	24,803	169		58	18,600'	1200'/m	4270
XPBY-1	P&W R1830-64	850	63'6"	18'6"	13,000	20,226	25,236	184		58	24,000'	1087	4010
PBY-1	P&W R1830-64	900	63'6"	18'6"	14,576	20,671	28,447	183		67	23,600	840	4042
PBY-2	P&W R1830-64	900	63'6"	18'6"	14,668	22,490	28,640	178	103	68	21,100	860	2131(p)
PBY-3	P&W R1830-66	1050	63'6"	18'6"	14,767	22,713	28,863	191	114	67	24,400	930	4170
PBY-4	P&W R1830-72	1050	63'6"	18'6"	16,837	24,813	32,011	197	115	71	24,100	870	4430
PBY-5(e	P&W R1830-82	1200	63'10"	18'11"	17,400	26,200	33,389	200		72	21,600	990	1895
PBY-5(l	P&W R1830-92	1200	63'10"	18'11"	17,526	31,813	34,000	195	110	75	18,100	660	2860(p)
PBY-5A	P&W R1830-92	1200	63'10"	20'2"	20,910	33,975	35,300	175	117	78	14,700	518	2545(p)
PBN-1	P&W R1830-92	1200	64'8"	21'3"	19,288	36,353	38,000	186	111	78	15,100	518	3700
PBY-6A	P&W R1830-92	1200	63'11"	22'4"	21,480	34,500	36,400	178	107	79	16,200	630	1535(p)
PB2B-1	P&W R1830-92	1200	64'8"	20'2"		33,133		187			15,800	660	2690(p)
PB2B-2	P&W R1830-92	1200	64'8"	20'2"		37,000		165	117		14,100		2485
Canso-A	P&W R1830-92	1200	63'10"	20'2"	20,900	33,970	35,300	179	117	78	15,000		2545(p)

Wingspan: 104ft but PBN-1 & PB2B-2 both 104ft 3in. Fuel capacity: 1,750 US gal (with non-self-sealing tanks) excluding PBN.

Appendix B
RAF Catalina deliveries

Mark	Type	Quantity	Serial	Received
I	PBY-4	1	P9630	July 1939
I	PBY-5	28	W8405-W8434	March 41-July 41
I	PBY-5	15	Z2134-Z2153	June 41-Nov 41
I	PBY-5	39	AH530-AH569	March 41-July 41
I	PBY-5	9	AJ154-AJ162	Nov 41-Jan 42
II	PBY-5	7	AM264-AM270	Jan 41-Apr 41
IB	PBY-5B	170	FP100-FP324	July 42-Feb 43
III	PBY-5A	12	FP525-FP536	Apr 42-May 42
—	Canso	2	FT998-FT999	June 1945
IVA	PBY-5B	11	JV925-JV935	Sept 43-Nov 43
IVA	PBY-5B	51	JX200-JX269	May 43-
IVB	PB2B-1	211	JX270-JX635	Jan 45
—	Model 28	1	SM706	Oct 1940
IIA	PBY-5	21	VA703-VA732	Feb 42-May 42
—	GST	1	HX850	Impressed Nov 41

Appendix C
RAF Catalinas — individual aircraft

Serial	Units	Remarks
P9630	MAEE-228-240-MAEE-210-MAEE	Trials a/c; crashed Dumbarton, 10.2.40.
W8405	240-205-240	SOC 28.2.46.
W8406	4 OTU-210-202-205	SOC 31.12.44.
W8407	202	Crashed at Gibraltar, 7.6.41.
W8408	4 OTU-131 OTU	Crashed after take-off, 8.11.43.
W8409	202-205	FTR 12.1.42.
W8410	202-4 OTU-131 OTU	To 4889M 10.44.
W8411	205	FTR 21.9.41 from Chagos Archipelago.
W8412	202-413	SOC 29.12.44.
W8413	205	Caught fire 9.1.42, Seletar.
W8414	210-131 OTU	Crashed 26.5.42, Castle Archdale.
W8415	210-202-413-202-209	SOC 28.9.44.
W8416	209-210-202-210	FTR 11.11.42 off Morocco.
W8417	205	FTR 7.12.41.
W8418	210-202-210-240	Crashed 23.12.41 Pembroke Dock.
W8419	119/413	DBR 15.12.41.
W8420	210-202-210-131 OTU	SOC 10.44.
W8421	202-413	FTR 8.4.42.
W8422	413	Sank 10.11.41.
W8423	205	FTR 7.12.41.
W8424	202-413-210-330-210-1477F-333-131 OTU	SOC 6.11.44.
W8425	202	Crashed at Gibraltar, 11.8.41.
W8426	205	Crashed 23.7.41 NE of Port Victoria.
W8427	240-413-209	SOC 1.4.44.
W8428	413-209-265	Crashed 1.8.44, Kisumu.
W8429	205	Damaged in action 17.1.42.
W8430	RCAF-45 Group	Crashed 7.10.44, Bermuda.
W8433	205	Lost in evacuation 2.42.
W8434	413	Hit mast Sullom Voe, 2.1.42.
Z2135	240-413-205-240	SOC 28.2.46.
Z2141	413	Sank 10.11.41.
Z2142	209	SOC 28.9.44.
Z2143	240-4 OTU-131 OTU	SOC 15.9.44.
Z2144	205	Shot down 5.4.42 by Jap carrier a/c.
Z2145	4 OTU-210-202-210-4 OTU	Sank 16.5.43, Alness.
Z2146	240	SOC 18.12.44.
Z2147	202-4 OTU-131 OTU-302 FTU-131 OTU	Crashed 9.1.44, Killadeas.
Z2148	240	Hit high ground 19.1.42, Sullom Voe.
Z2149	MAEE-413-209-413-202-413	SOC 5.10.44.
Z2150	210-4 OTU	Hit by AH562 1.3.43. in gale, Alness.
Z2151	413-205	Damaged 19.1.32 — abandoned.
Z2152	MAEE-302 FTU-131 OTU	Crashed 20.8.44, Killadeas.
Z2153	240	Crashed 3.12.41, Lough Erne.
AH530	209	Hit drifter 14.12.41, Pembroke Dock.
AH531	210-4 OTU	Sank in gale 5.9.42, Invergordon.
AH532	210	FTR 20.4.41.
AH533	210	Hit hill 15.7.41, Jura.
AH535	210	FTR 17.5.42.
AH536	240	Sank 7.5.41, Lough Erne.
AH537	202	FTR 5.6.41 en route Gibraltar.
AH538	202-131 OTU-202-131 OTU	SOC 26.9.45.
AH539	210-131 OTU	Damaged 9.1.45, Oban, & SOC.
AH540	205	FTR 30.12.41.
AH541	4 OTU-131 OTU	Crashed 17.4.44, Lough Erne.
AH542	209-413-209-210-202-210-4 OTU-302 FTU	SOC 8.43.
AH543	209-210-209	Ditched 13.10.42 5m NE Lourenco Marques.
AH544	209-202-4 OTU-302 FTU-131 OTU-302 FTU	SOC 15.9.44.
AH545	209-210-119	Sighted Bismarck 26.5.41; FTR 15.7.42.
AH546	240-205	SOC 31.7.44.
AH547	210	Crashed 11.1.42 on take-off at Oban.
AH548	240-209-265	Damaged 1.11.44, Victoria Harbour, Seychelles.
AH549	240-209-240-413	SOC 31.12.44.

196

Serial	Units	Remarks
AH550	210-413-212	SOC 5.7.45.
AH551	210-413-210-202-210-4 OTU-131	Spun into hill 16.10.43, Fermanagh.
AH552	209	For airframe instruction 27.8.41.
AH553	209-240-205	SOC 30.11.43.
AH554	202	Destroyed in air raid 7.5.41, Greenock.
AH555	202	Destroyed in air raid 7.5.41, Greenock.
AH556	413	Crashed 23.8.41 on take-off, Loch Ryan.
AH557	209	Damaged 1.7.41, Afiordur, Iceland.
AH558	209	Crashed 22.2.42 on take-off, Pembroke Dock.
AH559	4 OTU-210	Crashed 4.11.42 on take-off, Gibraltar.
AH560	OADF	Ditched 23.5.41 off Portugal.
AH561	119-413	FTR 25.6.42.
AH562	202-4 OTU-202-210-4 OTU	Sank 1.3.43, Alness.
AH563	240	To BOAC 22.6.41 as *G-AGDA*.
AH564	MAEE-Saro-MAEE-131 OTU	Sold 10.3.47 as scrap.
AH565	209	Wrecked in gale 22.9.41, Akranes, Iceland.
AH566	413	FTR 19.10.41 from Tromso.
AH567	209-240-413	Ran ashore on take-off 19.5.44, Koggala.
AH568	4 OTU	Sank in gale 7.4.43, Alness.
AH569	413-209-413	For spares 15.12.41.
AJ154	202-205	Lost in Far East 2.42.
AJ155	413-205-202-413	Shot down 4.4.42 by Jap. carrier a/c, Bay of Bengal.
AJ156	413-202-240-209-205	Crashed on take-off 18.12.42, Pamanzi.
AJ157	202	Flew into hill 21.1.42, 3m NE Carnero Point, Spain.
AJ158	413-202-413-202	Attacked by French fighters 18.5.42; ditched off Oran.
AJ159	202-4 OTU-131 OTU	SOC 28.8.45.
AJ160	209-202-205	Crashed on take-off 1.2.44, Kelai, Ceylon.
AJ161	202-205	Damaged beyond repair 15.1.43.
AJ162	240-202	FTR 11.9.42.
AM258	—	See *SM706*.
AM264	MAEE-240-4 OTU	To 3435M 11.42.
AM265	240	Crashed 21.3.41, Kinlough, Eire.
AM266	240-MAEE-4 OTU-131 OTU	Damaged 3.3.44, Killadeas.
AM267	240-4 OTU-131 OTU	SOC Oct. 44.
AM268	240-4 OTU	SOC 15.5.43.
AM269	240-4 OTU	Crashed on take-off 15.8.42, Stranraer.
AM270	240-4 OTU-131 OTU-4 OTU-131 OTU	SOC 15.9.44.
FP100	302 FTU	Ran ashore in gale 29.12.42, Stranraer.
FP101	210-202-210-131 OTU	Hit ground 7.8.43, Lough Erne.
FP102	210-190-302 FTU	SOC 28.12.44.
FP103	422	Crashed 8.9.42, Whalsey, Shetlands.
FP104	210-204-210-302 FTU-265-209	SOC 22.8.44.
FP105	422-131 OTU	SOC 7.11.44.
FP106	422-131 OTU	SOC 30.12.45.
FP107	210-202-302 FTU-209	SOC 27.7.44.
FP108	302 FTU-490	SOC 26.10.44.
FP109	210-190-302-FTU	Hit by drifting destroyer 27.12.43, Gibraltar.
FP110	119-202-131 OTU	Crashed 24.5.43, Lough Erne.
FP111	202-302 FTU-202-259	SOC 29.8.46.
FP112	210-190-302 FTU-490	Crashed 18.11.43 off Jui, Sierra Leone.
FP113	210-190-302 FTU-209	SOC 29.8.46.
FP114	202-190-302 FTU-202	Lost 3.8.43 en route to Gibraltar.
FP115	210-190-210-302 FTU-209-F.Ft.	Crashed 8.7.45, Kisumu.
FP116	OADU	Crashed 13.3.43 on landing at Bermuda.
FP117	202-302 FTU-191	Crashed 3.10.43 on take-off, Korangi Creek.
FP118	202-302 FTU-490-262	SOC 12.7.46.
FP119	202	Lost 25.9.42.
FP120	40TU-131 OTU	FTR 3.11.43.
FP121	202-210-1477 Flt-333	Damaged B.R. 17.5.44. 'Jøssing'.
FP122	202-302 FTU-202-302 FTU	Crashed 11.11.43 on landing at Bathurst.
FP123	202-302 FTU-270	Crashed 31.1.44 on take-off at Apapa.
FP124	210-202	FTR 3.11.42.
FP125	210-190-302 FTU-190	Crashed 4.9.43 on landing at Sullom Voe.
FP126	302 FTU-259	SOC 29.3.45.
FP127	—	Foundered 20.12.42, Irish Sea.
FP129	302 FTU-262	SOC 12.7.46.
FP131	210-302 FTU-205	Damaged B.R. 4.7.44 having run onto rocks, Koggala.
FP133	302 FTU-259-191-209	SOC 29.8.46.
FP134	131 OTU-302 FTU-628	SOC 26.10.44.
FP135	—	Lost 18.12.42 on delivery flight.
FP136	302 FTU-259	Crashed 21.11.43 on take-off, Aden.
FP138	—	Lost 7.4.43 off French coast, ex-Bermuda.

197

Serial	Units	Remarks
FP151	—	Lost 12.1.43 on delivery flight.
FP152	212-131 OTU-302 FTU-212-270-628-240	SOC 30.8.45.
FP153	202	Shot down by Allied convoy 20.11.42.
FP154	212-210	Crashed 22.3.43 off Sagres, Portugal.
FP155	210	FTR 10.7.43.
FP159	MAEE-302 FTU-413-262	SOC 12.7.46.
FP160	212-302 FTU-212-270	Lost 4.3.44, Redhills Lake, China Bay.
FP161	212-270	Lost 4.3.44, Redhills Lane, China Bay.
FP162	212-302 FTU-212	SOC 31.8.44.
FP163	212-302 FTU-212	SOC 28.2.46.
FP164	202	To 3634M 1.43.
FP165	212-302 FTU-212-240	SOC 31.5.45.
FP171	212-302 FTU-265	Crashed 8.4.43 on take-off from Gibraltar.
FP172	202-302 FTU-490	SOC 1.5.46.
FP173	212-302 FTU-270	Crashed 10.2.43 on take-off Bunce River, S. Leone.
FP174	210-302 FTU-262	SOC 12.7.46.
FP175	212-302 FTU-212	Crashed 6.6.43 on landing 30m SSW Masirah.
FP180	202-210-202-302 FTU-191-628	Crashed 4.10.44 on special operation.
FP181	202-190-2302 FTU-202-131 OTU	SOC 7.11.44.
FP182	212-202-190-302 FTU-240	SOC 28.2.46.
FP183	210-190-210-333	'Vingtor II' SOC 23.12.44.
FP184	131 OTU	Flew into hill 30.12.42, 3m SE Ballantrae.
FP185	210-302 FTU-262	SOC 12.7.46.
FP191	131 OTU-302 FTU-628	Crashed 16.5.44 on landing, Redhills Lake.
FP192	302 FTU-270-265	Caught fire 18.2.45, Dar-es-Salaam moorings.
FP193	4 OTU-131 OTU	Hit water 9.1.44 in dive, Lough Erne.
FP194	212-302 FTU-131 OTU	Crashed 10.5.43 on landing, Killadeas.
FP195	4 OTU-131 OTU	SOC 12.1.45.
FP201	302 FTU-212	SOC 26.10.44.
FP202	302 FTU-212	SOC 26.10.44.
FP203	4 OTU-131 OTU	Undershot 16.8.44, Killadeas.
FP204	302 FTU-209	SOC 29.8.46.
FP205	4 OTU-131 OTU	SOC 12.1.45.
FP209	—	Crashed 12.11.42 off Nova Scotia.
FP211	4 OTU-131 OTU	Sold as scrap 10.3.47.
FP212	202-131 OTU	SOC 26.10.44.
FP213	202-302 FTU-210-202-302 FTU-131 OTU	SOC 4.2.45.
FP214	202	Struck high ground 9.6.43, Algeciras.
FP215	210-190-302 FTU-240	SOC 19.10.44.
FP221	—	To BOAC 27.10.42 as G-AGFL.
FP222	202-190-210-302 FTU-333	'Ulabrand'. To No.1 Radio School, Greenock 1.1.45
FP223	202-302 FTU-202-205	SOC 26.4.4.5.
FP224	302 FTU-270	Ditched 27.4.43 off Liberia when engine caught fire.
FP225	302 FTU-270-240-628	SOC 28.2.46.
FP226	302 FTU-262	To SAAF 15.2.45.
FP227	131 OTU-209-265	SOC 31.5.45.
FP228	202	Sank 29.12.42 after collision with W6004.
FP229	302 FTU-270-205	SOC 28.9.44.
FP230	202-302 FTU-191	Unknown.
FP231	302 FTU-212	Hit houses 27.6.44 on take-off, Trombay.
FP232	210	FTR 13.6.43.
FP233	202-302 FTU-240	SOC 31.5.45.
FP234	302 FTU-212-240	SOC 29.3.45.
FP235	302 FTU-259	SOC 29.8.46.
FP236	302 FTU-270	SOC 24.3.44.
FP237	210-212	Hit 27.12.43 by destroyer in Gibraltar.
FP238	131 OTU	SOC 28.11.44.
FP239	131 OTU	Struck hill 30.12.42, 1m NW of Omagh.
FP240	131 OTU	FTR 22.11.43.
FP241	202-302 FTU-202-302 FTU-205	SOC 5.10.44.
FP242	210-190-302 FTU-490	SOC 25.4.45.
FP243	131 OTU	SOC 30.12.45.
FP244	—	To BOAC as G-AGFM 27.10.42.
FP245	131 OTU	SOC 12.1.45.
FP246	302 FTU-212	Collided with boat 14.4.4(?), Korangi Creek.
FP247	302 FTU-259-209	Crashed 15.3.45 on take-off, Seychelles.
FP248	302 FTU-270	Crashed 13.3.43 on take-off, Bunce River.
FP249	210-202-131 OTU	Sold as scrap 10.3.47.
FP250	302 FTU	Sank in gale, 6.2.43, Greenock.
FP251	302 FTU-262	SOC 12.7.46.
FP252	210-302 FTU-FE	Unknown.

Serial	Units	Remarks
FP253	302 FTU-270-262-212	SOC 19.7.45.
FP254	210-302 FTU-262	SOC 12.7.46.
FP255	MAEE-202-302 FTU-265-205	Ditched 11.6.43 in Indian Ocean.
FP256	302 FTU-259	SOC 30.11.44.
FP257	302 FTU-262	To SAAF 15.2.45.
FP258	302 FTU-490	Sold as scrap 10.3.47.
FP259	302 FTU-210-202-131 OTU	SOC 12.1.45.
FP260	MAEE-302 FTU-260-265(?)-259	SOC 29.8.46.
FP261	302 FTU-	To East Africa; SOC 29.8.46.
FP262	210-302 FTU	To East Africa; SOC 29.8.46.
FP263	302 FTU-265	SOC 29.8.46.
FP264	210	Sank 30.5.43, Hamworthy, after flak damage.
FP265	302 FTU-262	Crashed 25.6.43 on take-off, St Lucia.
FP266	—	Lost 25.12.42 on delivery flight.
FP267	190-210-302 FTU-259	SOC 29.8.46.
FP268	202-302 FTU-	To East Africa, SOC 29.8.46.
FP269	190	Struck hill 23.4.43 on Faroe Islands.
FP270	302 FTU-262	To SAAF 15.2.45.
FP271	210	Ditched 17.4.43, 7m W of Finisterre.
FP272	202-302 FTU-265	SOC 29.8.46.
FP273	302 FTU-209-259	SOC 16.8.45.
FP274	302 FTU-262	SOC 12.7.46.
FP275	302 FTU-205-259	Crashed 7.6.43 on approach at St Lucia.
FP276	302 FTU-205	SOC 18.12.44.
FP277	210-202-302 FTU-265	SOC 27.6.46.
FP278	302 FTU-490	Sold as scrap 10.3.47.
FP279	302 FTU-262	SOC 12.7.46.
FP280	202-190	Ditched 12.10.43 off Shetlands.
FP281	302 FTU-259-209	SOC 29.8.46.
FP282	302 FTU-413	SOC 5.10.44.
FP283	302 FTU-259	SOC 29.3.45.
FP284	302 FTU-212-262	SOC 30.11.44.
FP285	302 FTU-202-302 FTU-202-190-302 FTU-209-259	SOC 25.7.46.
FP286	210	Interned 31.3.43 Santa Rita, Portugal.
FP287	210	Crashed 28.4.43 on overshoot, Hamworthy.
FP288	302 FTU-262	SOC 12.7.46.
FP289	302 FTU-209	Ran aground 12.5.43 Tombeau Bay, Mauritius.
FP293	302 FTU-191	SOC 28.12.44.
FP299	USN-302 FTU-490	Gale damage 17.11.44 at Scar Point, Wig Bay.
FP300	302 FTU-191-265	SOC 29.8.46.
FP301	302 FTU-205	SOC 12.10.44.
FP302	302 FTU-209	Hit sea 20.8.43, Mombasa.
FP303	302 FTU-191	SOC 31.8.44.
FP304	302 FTU-270-240	SOC 28.2.46.
FP305	302 FTU-265	Ditched 12.12.43, Bandar Kassim.
FP306	302 FTU-413	SOC 26.4.45.
FP307	302 FTU-191-262	SOC 12.7.46.
FP308	202-190-210-302 FTU-209-CFF	SOC 29.8.46.
FP309	—	Lost 7.2.43 on delivery flight.
FP310	302 FTU-191-265-259	SOC 29.8.46.
FP311	210-190-302 FTU-265	SOC 29.8.46.
FP312	190	Damaged beyond repair 2.1.44.
FP313	302 FTU-191-265	SOC 29.8.46.
FP314	1477 Flt-333	'Viking'. SOC 20.12.44.
FP315	302 FTU-191-262	SOC 26.10.44.
FP316	202	Sank 15.6.43 Gibraltar, after damage on take-off.
FP317	202-302 FTU-202	Crashed 19.10.43 Gibraltar, during approach.
FP318	202-210-302 FTU-209	SOC 29.8.46.
FP319	302 FTU-191	SOC 5.10.44.
FP320	302 FTU-191	Collided with *JX332*, Korangi Creek 29.7.44.
FP321	4 FPP	Damaged 22.4.43 beyond repair.
FP322	202-302 FTU-262	SOC 12.7.46.
FP323	302 FTU-413-265	SOC 19.7.45.
FP324	190-302 FTU-490	SOC 26.10.44.
FP525	330	*GS-Z*. Shot down by U-boat 21.9.42.
FP526	330-4 OTU-131 OTU-MAEE	SOC 24.1.45.
FP527	330-131 OTU	SOC 1.8.44.
FP528	119-330-131 OTU	SOC 3.8.44.
FP529	119-330-119-330-131 OTU	SOC 1.8.44.
FP530	45 Group	To USA 13.12.45.
FP531	330-4 OTU-131 OTU-302 FTU	SOC 3.8.44.

Serial	Units	Remarks
FP532	45 Group	To USA 13.12.45.
FP533	119-330-4 OTU-131 OTU	SOC 3.8.44.
FP534	MAEE-330-VP72	To US Navy.
FP535	330	FTR 5.11.42.
FP536	210-330-131 OTU-302 FTU-131 OTU	SOC 3.8.44.
FT998	45 Group	SOC 30.5.46.
FT999	45 Group	SOC 8.11.45.
HK850	—	Broke adrift 23.2.43, Aboukir.
JV925	131 OTU	SOC 26.3.47.
JV926	202	SOC 26.3.47.
JV927	—	Returned to USA 29.7.47.
JV928	210	FTR 18.7.44.
JV929	210	Damaged 19.7.44 beyond repair.
JV930	210	SOC 26.3.47.
JV931	210	SOC 26.3.47.
JV932	202	SOC 26.3.47.
JV933	333	Sold as scrap 10.3.47.
JV934	131 OTU	SOC 26.3.47.
JV935	131 OTU	SOC 26.3.47.
JV200	202-131 OTU	SOC 26.3.47.
JX201	202	Hit hill 18.8.44 Carnero Point, Gibraltar.
JX202	MAEE-190-210-202	SOC 26.3.47.
JX203	190-210	Crashed 11.1.45 on take-off, Sullom Voe.
JX204	202-210-202	SOC 26.3.47.
JX205	302 FTU-202-321	SOC 26.3.47.
JX208	202	Struck a hill 19.12.44 Castlegregory, Tralee.
JX210	190-210	Dived into ground 25.3.44, Sullom Voe.
JX214	202	SOC 26.3.47.
JX215	MAEE	Sold as scrap 10.3.47.
JX216	4 OTU-131 OTU	SOC 14.6.45.
JX218	4 OTU-131 OTU	SOC 6.11.47.
JX220	202-131 OTU	SOC 6.11.47.
JX221	202	SOC 26.3.47.
JX222	MAEE-190-210-202	Sold 19.4.47.
JX223	190-210-202	SOC 26.3.47.
JX224	MAEE-190-210-202-333	Crashed 1½m SW Oakington, 14.8.45. 'Vingtor IV'
JX225	202	Crashed 7.8.44 on landing at Gibraltar.
JX226	202-131 OTU	SOC 10.3.47.
JX227	202	SOC 10.3.47.
JX229	202	SOC 31.5.46.
JX240	231	SOC 30.8.45.
JX241	131 OTU	Sold as scrap 10.3.47.
JX242	MAEE-202	Crashed 20.11.44 Church Hall, Fermanagh.
JX243	190-210	SOC 26.3.47.
JX244	202	SOC 26.3.47.
JX245	—	Sold as scrap 10.3.47.
JX246	190-210	SOC 26.3.47.
JX247	210	Sold as scrap 10.3.47.
JX248	131 OTU	Sold as scrap 10.3.47.
JX249	210	SOC 26.3.47.
JX250	202	SOC 26.3.47.
JX251	131 OTU	Sold as scrap 10.3.47.
JX252	131 OTU	Crashed 26.11.44 1m S Fly Lodge, Lough Erne.
JX253	210	Sold as scrap 10.3.47.
JX254	210	SOC 26.3.47.
JX255	210-202-131 OTU-202	SOC 26.3.47.
JX256	202-259-202	SOC 26.3.47.
JX257	210	FTR 3.4.45.
JX258	202	Struck high ground 15.6.44 Melilla, Morocco.
JX259	210	Ditched 12.1.45 10m N of Durness.
JX260	202-210-202	SOC 26.3.47.
JX261	302 FTU-202	Sold 28.6.47.
JX262	210	SOC 26.3.47.
JX263	210	SOC 26.3.47.
JX264	210	SOC 10.3.47.
JX265	333	'Vingtor III'. SOC 14.6.45.
JX266	210	Flew into sea 16.11.44 off Orkneys.
JX267	190-210-202	To USA 6.8.47.
JX268	210	Sold as scrap 10.3.47.
JX269	302 FTU-202	SOC 26.3.47.
JX270	302 FTU-191	SOC 28.6.45.

Serial	Units	Remarks
JX271	302 FTU-212	SOC 21.6.45.
JX272	302 FTU-321	SOC 21.6.45.
JX273	302 FTU	Struck hill 12.5.44 Vatersay, Argyll.
JX274	131 OTU	SOC 26.3.47.
JX276	302 FTU-413	To Netherlands 25.7.46.
JX277	—	SOC 29.12.43.
JX278	302 FTU-240	SOC 12.7.45.
JX279	302 FTU-205	SOC 28.6.45.
JX280	302 FTU	To Far East; SOC 28.2.46.
JX281	302 FTU-413	Crashed 19.5.44 on take-off at Koggala.
JX282	302 FTU	To Far East; SOC 27.12.45.
JX283	—	SOC 18.9.45.
JX284	302 FTU-262	To SAAF 15.2.45.
JX285	302 FTU-205	To Far East.
JX286	CODU-302 FTU-205	Sold as scrap 10.3.47.
JX287	—	To BOAC 16.3.44 as *G-AGKS*.
JX288	302 FTU-321	To Netherlands 25.7.46.
JX289	302 FTU-413	To Netherlands 25.7.46.
JX290	302 FTU-205	SOC 27.12.41.
JX291	302 FTU	Crashed 15.4.44 on landing at Oban.
JX292	302 FTU-240	SOC 16.8.45.
JX293	302 FTU	To Far East; SOC 26.4.45.
JX294	302 FTU-321	SOC 31.5.45.
JX295	—	Sold as scrap 10.3.47.
JX296	302 FTU-191	SOC 28.6.45.
JX297	—	Sold as scrap 10.3.47.
JX298	302 FTU-628-240	To Netherlands 25.7.46.
JX299	302 FTU	To Far East; SOC 27.12.45.
JX300	302 FTU-212	Wrecked 26.10.44 in gale at Redhills Lake.
JX301	302 FTU	To Far East. SOC 12.7.45.
JX302	131 OTU	SOC 26.3.47.
JX303	302 FTU-240	SOC 29.11.45.
JX304	—	Sold as scrap 10.3.47.
JX305	131 OTU	SOC 26.3.47.
JX306	302 FTU	To Far East; SOC 21.6.45.
JX307	302 FTU-240	SOC 12.7.45.
JX308	302 FTU-212	SOC 29.11.45.
JX309	131 OTU	SOC 26.3.47.
JX310	302 FTU-191	SOC 12.7.45.
JX311	302 FTU-240	SOC 28.6.45.
JX312	240	SOC 26.4.45.
JX313	302 FTU-321	SOC 21.6.45.
JX314	302 FTU-212	Sank 25.10.44 in gale at Redhills Lake.
JX315	302 FTU-321	SOC.
JX316	302 FTU-205	SOC 9.8.45.
JX317	302 FTU-240	SOC 27.12.45.
JX318	302 FTU	To Far East; SOC 28.6.45.
JX319	262-191(?)	To SAAF 15.2.45.
JX320	302 FTU	To Far East; SOC 28.2.46.
JX321	302 FTU	To Far East; SOC 31.5.45.
JX322	302 FTU	To Far East; SOC 7.5.47.
JX323	—	Sold as scrap 10.3.47.
JX324	302 FTU-212	SOC 29.11.45.
JX325	302 FTU-212	SOC 21.6.45.
JX236	302 FTU-240	SOC 26.4.45.
JX327	302 FTU	To Far East; SOC 26.8.44.
JX328	191	Wrecked 26.10.44 in gale at Redhills Lake.
JX329	—	Sold as scrap 10.3.47.
JX330	302 FTU	To Far East; SOC 26.7.45.
JX331	302 FTU-205	SOC 26.7.45.
JX332	302 FTU-191	SOC 29.11.45.
JX333	302 FTU-413	SOC 27.12.45.
JX334	628-240	SOC 16.8.45.
JX335	302 FTU-212	SOC.
JX336	302 FTU-205	SOC 28.6.45.
JX337	302 FTU	To SAAF 1.10.45.
JX338	302 FTU	To Far East; FTR 31.10.44.
JX339	302 FTU-413-212	SOC 16.8.45.
JX340	131 OTU	SOC 26.3.47.
JX341	302 FTU-212-240	Damaged hull 31.7.45 at Pegu, Burma, & SOC.
JX342	302 FTU-212	SOC 27.12.45.

Serial	Units	Remarks
JX343	302 FTU-191	SOC 5.7.45.
JX344	302 FTU	To Far East; SOC 23.8.45.
JX345	—	Sold as scrap 10.3.47.
JX346	302 FTU-191-205(?)	SOC 9.8.45.
JX347	302 FTU-191-262-628	SOC 29.11.45.
JX348	302 FTU-262	To SAAF 1.10.45.
JX349	302 FTU	To Far East; SOC 29.11.45.
JX350	302 FTU-191	SOC 9.8.45.
JX351	302 FTU	To Far East; SOC 26.7.45.
JX352	302 FTU-205	SOC 29.11.45.
JX353	302 FTU-262	To SAAF 15.2.45.
JX354	302 FTU-321	To Netherlands 25.7.46.
JX355	302 FTU-191	SOC 9.8.45.
JX356	333	To Norway 21.12.45.
JX357	302 FTU	To Far East; SOC 9.8.45.
JX358	302 FTU	To Far East; SOC 16.8.45.
JX359	302 FTU-191	To Netherlands 25.7.46.
JX360	302 FTU	To Far East; SOC 26.7.45.
JX361	—	Sold as scrap 10.3.47.
JX362	302 FTU-262	To SAAF 15.2.45.
JX363	—	Sold as scrap 10.3.47.
JX364	—	Sold as scrap 10.3.47.
JX365	302 FTU-321-205	SOC 29.11.45.
JX366	302 FTU-212	SOC 29.11.45.
JX367	302 FTU-262	Crashed 1.45 Umsingazi Lake, Natal.
JX368	—	Sold as scrap 10.3.47.
JX369	302 FTU-191	Wrecked 26.10.44 in gale, Redhills Lake.
JX370	302 FTU	Sold as scrap 10.3.47.
JX371	302 FTU	Sold as scrap 10.3.47.
JX372	—	To Norway 27.2.46.
JX373	302 FTU	Sold as scrap 10.3.47.
JX374	302 FTU-191	SOC 16.8.45.
JX375	302 FTU-191	SOC 16.8.45.
JX376	302 FTU-205	SOC 29.11.45.
JX377	302 FTU	Sold as scrap 10.3.47.
JX378	333	To Norway 28.4.47.
JX379	131 OTU	SOC 26.3.47.
JX380	131 OTU	Sold as scrap 10.3.47.
JX381	—	To Norway 10.5.47.
JX382	302 FTU-333	'Ulabrand II'? Sold as scrap 10.3.47.
JX383	131 OTU	SOC 26.3.47.
JX384	—	Sold as scrap 10.3.47.
JX385	131 OTU	SOC 26.3.47.
JX386	MAEE-302 FTU	Sold as scrap 10.3.47.
JX387	302 FTU	Sold as scrap 10.3.47.
JX388	—	Sold as scrap 10.3.47.
JX389	131 OTU	SOC 26.3.47.
JX390	—	Sold as scrap 10.3.47.
JX391	—	Sold as scrap 10.3.47.
JX392	302 FTU-MAEE	SOC 26.3.47.
JX393	—	SOC 10.3.47.
JX394	302 FTU	To Norway 21.12.45.
JX395	302 FTU-333	To Norway 17.2.46. Sold for K25,000(?).
JX396	302 FTU	Sold as scrap 10.3.47.
JX397	302 FTU	Sold as scrap 10.3.47.
JX398	333	To Norway 4.2.46.
JX399	MAEE	Sold as scrap 10.3.47.
JX400	302 FTU-333	To Norway 6.2.46.
JX401	302 FTU	Sold as scrap 10.3.37.
JX402	302 FTU-CFF	To Far East; SOC 26.9.46.
JX403	—	Sold as scrap 10.3.47.
JX404	—	Sold as scrap 10.3.47.
JX405	—	Sold as scrap 10.3.47.
JX406	—	Sold as scrap 10.3.47.
JX407	—	Sold as scrap 10.3.47.
JX408	—	Sold as scrap 10.3.47.
JX409	MAEE	Sold as scrap 10.3.47.
JX410	302 FTU -333	To Norway 4.2.46.
JX411	333	To Norway 6.2.46.
JX412	333	To Norway 21.12.45.
JX413	302 FTU	To Far East; SOC 27.12.45.

Serial	Units	Remarks
JX414	—	SOC 10.3.47.
JX415	—	SOC 10.3.47.
JX416	—	SOC 10.3.47.
JX417	—	SOC 10.3.47.
JX418	—	SOC 10.3.47.
JX419	302 FTU	To Norway 1.4.47.
JX420	—	Sold as scrap 10.3.47.
JX421	131 OTU	SOC 26.3.47.
JX422	131 OTU	SOC 25.10.45.
JX423	302 FTU	Lost 13.1.45 en route to Gibraltar.
JX424	131 OTU	SOC 26.3.47.
JX425	131 OTU	SOC 26.3.47.
JX426	302 FTU	To Far East; SOC 29.11.45.
JX427	131 OTU	SOC 26.3.47.
JX428	302 FTU	To Far East; SOC 29.11.45.
JX429	302 FTU-205	SOC 29.11.45.
JX430	302 FTU-205	SOC 29.11.45.
JX431	302 FTU-205	SOC 29.11.45.
JX432	302 FTU-205	SOC 29.11.45.
JX433	302 FTU	To Far East; SOC 26.9.46.
JX434	302 FTU	To Far East; SOC 29.11.45.
JX435	302 FTU-240	Crashed 27.6.45 on landing Cocos Islands.
JX436	302 FTU-205	SOC 27.12.45.
JX437	302 FTU-205	SOC 27.12.45.
JX570	202	SOC 26.3.47.
JX573	4 OTU-131 OTU-333	'Vingtor V'. Sold as scrap 10.3.47.
JX574	190-210	FTR 9.6.44.
JX575	—	To BOAC 13.7.43 as G-AGID.
JX576	190-210-4 OTU-131 OTU	Wrecked on rocks 20.7.44, Killadeas.
JX577	—	To BOAC 13.7.43 as G-AGIE.
JX578	131 OTU	SOC 6.11.47.
JX581	210	Struck rocks 5.5.44 on overshoot, Sullom Voe.
JX582	333	'Viking II'. To Norway 21.11.45.
JX583	202-210-333-210	SOC 6.11.47.
JX584	4 OTU-131 OTU	SOC 26.3.47.
JX585	202	Hit obstruction 30.5.44 Gibraltar and beached.
JX586	302 FTU-205	SOC 29.11.45.
JX587	302 FTU-205	SOC 29.11.45.
JX588	302 FTU	To Far East; SOC 29.11.45.
JX589	—	Sold as scrap 10.3.47.
JX590	333	To Norway 15.5.47.
JX591	302 FTU-205	SOC 30.5.46.
JX592	302 FTU-	To Far East; SOC 27.12.45.
JX593	302 FTU-205	FTR 27.5.45 from Bay of Bengal.
JX594	302 FTU-205	SOC 27.12.45.
JX595	302 FTU-205	SOC 28.2.46.
JX596	302 FTU	Crashed 12.4.45 on take-off at Oban.
JX597	302 FTU	To Far East; SOC 29.11.45.
JX598	302 FTU	To Far East; SOC 27.12.45.
JX599	302 FTU	To Far East; SOC 27.12.45.
JX600	302 FTU	To Far East; SOC 27.12.45.
JX601	302 FTU	To Far East; SOC 29.11.45.
JX602	302 FTU	To Far East; SOC 28.2.46.
JX603	—	Nose caved in 14.12.44 taxying at Wig Bay.
JX604	210-ASWDU	Sold as scrap 10.3.47.
JX605	302 FTU-240	To Far East; SOC 26.9.46.
JX606	—	Sold as scrap 10.3.47.
JX607	302 FTU	To Far East; SOC 27.12.45.
JX608	302 FTU	Struck high ground 6.3.45 Sedjenane, Tunisia.
JX609	302 FTU	To Far East; SOC 29.11.45.
JX610	302 FTU	To Far East; SOC 27.12.45.
JX628	45 Group	Returned to USA 22.2.45.
JX629	45 Group	Returned to USA 22.2.45.
JX630	—	Unknown.
JX632	MAEE	Unknown.
JX634	45 Group	Hit buoy 27.2.45 at Wig Bay.
JX635	45 Group	Returned to USA.
SM706	209	Ex NC777 & AM259; to BOAC 10.12.40 as G-AGBJ.
VA703	209	Wrecked 14.7.43 in gale at Madagascar.
VA712	45 Group	Returned to USA.
VA713	209	Crashed 8.9.42 on take-off at Pamanzi.

Serial	Units	Remarks
VA714	240	SOC 31.8.44.
VA715	209-210(?)	SOC 4.8.44.
VA716	240-212-240	Crashed 25.7.44 on landing at Redhills Lake.
VA717	240	SOC 12.10.44.
VA718	240	Driven ashore 16.9.44 in gale at Diego Suarez.
VA719	—	Lost before delivery.
VA720	240-204-240	SOC 11.12.44.
VA721	—	Ditched near Malin Head 6.3.42 and foundered.
VA722	210-4 OTU-131 OTU	SOC 17.8.44.
VA723	240	SOC 20.9.45.
VA724	—	Lost before delivery.
VA725	MAEE-210	FTR 3.7.43.
VA726	240	Crashed 20.10.42 6m from Redhills Lake.
VA727	209	Sank 2.9.42 Mombasa when DC exploded.
VA728	210-4 OTU-302 FTU-4 OTU-302 FTU	Crashed 4.11.43 Oban on landing.
VA729	240-210	FTR 13.6.43.
VA731	240-131 OTU	SOC 11.9.44.
VA732	240	Damaged 16.8.44 by Allied ship's AA, beached.

Note: FTR = Failed to Return.
SOC = Struck Off Charge.
Numbers under 'units' are of squadrons unless stated otherwise.

Appendix D
RAAF Catalinas

RAAF No A24-	Type	US No (cn)	RAF No	Rec'd	Abbreviated history
1	PBY-4		AH534*	2.2.41.	STF 5.2.41. 11 Sqdn 19.3.42. 20 Sqdn 14.8.4. 11 Sqdn 13.12.41. 3 OTU 4.4.43. Crashed Darwin 30.8.45. Conversion 18.10.45.
2	PBY-4	57	—	27.2.41.	STF 12.3.41. 11 Sqdn 13.5.41. 20 Sqdn 14.8.41. STF 8.6.42. 11 Sqdn 30.8.42. 3 OTU 14.4.43. Sold to J. Botterill & J. W. Fravey 8.12.47.
3	PBY-4	78	—	12.3.41.	11 Sqdn 30.5.41. 20 Sqdn 14.5.41. STF 8.1.42. 11 Sqdn 19.1.42. Lost by enemy action 1.3.42.
4	PBY-4	113	—	12.4.41.	11 Sqdn 22.6.41. 20 Sqdn 14.8.41. STF 31.1.42. 20 Sqdn 9.7.42. 3 OTU 15.9.43. Sold to Kingsford Smith Aviation Service 30.10.46.
5	PBY-4	164	—	17.6.41.	11 Sqdn 27.7.41. 20 Sqdn 14.8.41. Damaged by E/A Rabaul 3.2.42. 11 Sqdn 12.4.42. Destroyed at Port Moresby moorings by E/A 25.4.42.
6	PBY-4	189	—	5.7.41.	11 Sqdn 7.8.41. 20 Sqdn 14.8.41. STF 6.9.41. 11 Sqdn 17.1.42. Lost by enemy action 1.3.42.
7	PBY-4	218	—	21.7.41.	20 Sqdn 8.9.41. 11 Sqdn 11.9.41. FTR (?). Struck submerged object 23.1.42, Watom Island; Write off.
8	PBY-4	250	—	16.5.41.	20 Sqdn 11.9.41. FTR (?).
9	PBY-4	259	—	26.5.41.	11 Sqdn 4.10.41. FTR 21.1.42 Salamaua.
10	PBY-4	270	—	9.9.41.	11 Sqdn 20.10.41. 20 Sqdn 9.7.42. 3 OTU 6.4.43. Sold 8.12.47.
11	PBY-4	279	—	9.9.41.	11 Sqdn 26.10.41. Crashed Kavieng 15.1.42.
12	PBY-4	299	—	19.9.41.	11 Sqdn 29.10.41. 20 Sqdn 18.3.42. 11 Sqdn 4.5.42. 20 Sqdn 18.7.42. Destroyed in storm, Rathmines 15.9.42.
13	PBY-4	307	—	19.9.41.	11 Sqdn 16.11.41. FTR Rabaul 25.2.42.
14	PBY-4	313	—	7.10.41.	20 Sqdn 1.12.41. 11 Sqdn 7.4.42. 3 OTU 14.6.44. Sold to Kingsford-Smith Aviation Service 3.10.46
15	PBY-4	322	—	7.10.41.	11 Sqdn 8.12.41. Crashed into hill Port Moresby 8.12.41. Conversion 9.1.42.
16	PBY-4	332	—	7.10.41.	11 Sqdn 6.12.41. 20 Sqdn 11.3.42. 11 Sqdn 21.5.42. 20 Sqdn 22.8.42. 3 OTU 21.2.43. Water looped Rathmines 10.4.43. Conversion 15.6.43.
17	PBY-4	342.	—	22.10.41.	STF 25.10.41. 20 Sqdn 3.1.42. 11 Sqdn 9.7.42. 3 OTU 29.3.43. Conversion 4.12.45.
18	PBY-4	350	—	23.10.41.	11 Sqdn 30.1.42. 20 Sqdn 3.4.42. FTR Coral Sea 4.5.42.
19	PBY-4	9734 (RCAF)	—	10.3.42.	20 Sqdn 6.4.42. E/A damage Tulagi 30.4.42. 3 OTU 7.12.42. Sold to Kingsford-Smith Aviation Service 3.10.46.

RAAF No A24-	Type	US No (cn)	RAF No	Rec'd	Abbreviated history
20	PBY MC	9735 (RCAF)	—	10.3.42.	20 Sqdn 4.4.42. FTR Coral Sea 6.5.42.
21	PBY MC	9736 (RCAF)	—	10.3.42.	20 Sqdn 7.4.42. Qantas 18.5.42. 11 Sqdn 9.7.42. 20 Sqdn 30.3.43. 107 Sqdn 23.6.43. 3 OTU 10.8.43. Storm damage Rathmines 23.4.46. Sold to J. E. Wood 1.4.48.
22	PBY MC	9710 (RCAF)	—	30.3.42.	11 Sqdn 13.4.42. 20 Sqdn 9.7.42. FTR Lae/Gasmata 8.3.43.
23	PBY MC	9730 (RCAF)	—	30.3.42.	11 Sqdn 20.4.42. Damaged Tulagi by enemy action 5.5.42. Destroyed 14.6.42.
24	PBY MC	9733 (RCAF)	—	30.3.42.	11 Sqdn 29.4.42. Qantas 18.5.42. 20 Sqdn 20.7.42. 107 Sqdn 23.6.43. Crashed 18.8.43 5m off Bowen.
25	PBY MC	9708 (RCAF)	—	14.4.42.	11 Sqdn 18.5.42. FTR ex-A/S patrol Cairns 28.2.43.
26	PBY MC	9711 (RCAF)	—	14.4.42.	11 Sqdn 9.7.42. 3 OTU 15.9.43. Sold to N. R. Carpenter Pty Ltd. 4.10.46.
27	PBY MC	9717 (RCAF)	—	14.4.42.	11 Sqdn 9.7.42. 20 Sqdn 1.10.42. 3 OTU 6.7.43. 107 Sqdn 7.7.43. 3 OTU 2.8.43. Sold to Kingsford-Smith 3.10.46.
28	PBY-5	298	—	5.6.42.	ex-NEI 11 Sqdn 3.12.43. Converted PBY-4 to PBY-5. Sold to Kingsford-Smith 3.10.46.
29	PBY-5	08115 (USN A15)	—	20.6.42.	Qantas 22.6.42. 3 OTU 7.12.42. Sold to Kingsford-Smith 3.10.46.
30	PBY-5	08114 (USN A14)	—	5.7.42.	20 Sqdn 19.10.42. 3 OTU 27.2.43. Sold to Kingsford-Smith 3.10.46.
31	PBY-5	08153	—	15.1.43	3 OTU 23.1.43. Sold to Australair Ltd. 5.11.47.
32	PBY-5	08156	—	15.1.43.	3 OTU 27.1.43. 11 Sqdn 6.2.43. Crashed in open sea rescue attempt 2.5.44.
33	PBY-5	08159	—	15.1.43.	3 OTU 29.1.43. 20 Sqdn 25.10.43. 3 OTU 13.6.44. Damaged 28.6.45. Conversion.
34	PBY-5	08150	—	19.1.43.	3 OTU 7.2.43. 20 Sqdn 11.6.43. 11 Sqdn 6.10.43. FTR Kavieng 7.2.44.
35	PBY-5	08161	—	24.1.43.	20 Sqdn 21.2.43. 11 Sqdn 12.9.43. 43 Sqdn 21.1.44. 11 Sqdn 2.8.44. 20 Sqdn 4.10.45. Sold to Barrier Reef Airways 10.11.47.
36	PBY-5	08190	—	7.2.43.	11 Sqdn 21.2.43. Crash landed Cairns 13.4.43. Conversion.
37	PBY-5	08200	—	7.2.43.	3 OTU 11.3.43. 11 Sqdn 9.11.43. 20 Sqdn 14.12.43. 11 Sqdn 1.8.44. 111 ASRF 24.7.45. Sold to A.N.A. 15.10.46.
38	PBY-5	08203	—	8.2.43.	20 Sqdn 21.2.43. 11 Sqdn 11.3.43. 107 Sqdn 23.6.43. 43 Sqdn 25.8.43. 11 Sqdn 18.2.44. Damaged 20.3.44. Conversion.
39	PBY-5	08206	—	8.2.43.	3 OTU 18.2.43. Crashed during heavy swell, Port Stephen, NSW 24.5.43.
40	PBY-5	08201	—	9.2.43.	11 Sqdn 30.3.43. 43 Sqdn 12.8.43. 3 OTU 11.2.45. Sold to A.N.A. 15.10.46.
41	PBY-5	08203	—	14.2.43.	20 Sqdn 15.3.43. FTR 7.4.43.
42	PBY-5	08208	—	27.2.43.	11 Sqdn 28.3.43. 20 Sqdn 12.12.43. 11 Sqdn 23.3.44. 43 Sqdn 11.6.44. Damaged in heavy seas 15.5.45. Conversion.
43	PBY-5	08202	—	30.3.43.	11 Sqdn 19.4.43. Crashed in Bougainville jungle 26.4.43.
44	PBY-5	08207	—	30.3.43.	20 Sqdn 19.4.43. 43 Sqdn 27.9.43. 111ASRF 8.6.45. Sold 6.1.48. KSAS.
45	PBY-5	08269	—	30.3.43.	11 Sqdn 19.4.43. 43 Sqdn 12.3.44. FTR Namlea 20.7.44.
46	PBY-5	08272	—	30.3.43.	20 Sqdn 15.4.43. 3 OTU 5.7.43. Sold 12.11.47.
47	PBY-5	08284	—	30.3.43.	11 Sqdn 6.5.43. 112 ASRF 18.8.45. Sold to J. E. Wood 13.11.47.
48	PBY-5	08268	—	6.4.43.	20 Sqdn 20.4.43. Wrecked during take-off Bowen lighthouse. Conversion.
49	PBY-5	08285	—	6.4.43.	20 Sqdn 5.5.43. 11 Sqdn 24.6.43. FTR 29.4.44. from Manokwari, Vogelkop.
50	PBY-5	08264	—	6.4.43.	20 Sqdn 2.5.43. 11 Sqdn 23.8.43. FTR 2.9.43 from Sorong, Vogelkop Pen.
51	PBY-5	08333	—	17.4.43.	20 Sqdn 2.6.43. 11 Sqdn 26.7.43. 3 OTU 25.5.44. Sold to Australair 5.11.47.
52	PBY-5	08335	—	17.4.43.	11 Sqdn 14.6.43. Crashed Cleveland Bay, Townsville 7.9.43. Conversion.
53	PBY-5	08334	—	19.4.43.	11 Sqdn 26.5.43. 43 Sqdn 9.9.43. 20 Sqdn 28.11.43. 43 Sqdn 23.12.43. FTR 21.4.44 from Balikpapan.
54	PBY-5	08332	—	6.5.43.	20 Sqdn 15.6.43. 112 ASRF 27.1.45. Destroyed by E/A 6.4.45.
55	PBY-5	08336	—	6.5.43.	20 Sqdn 1.7.43. 11 Sqdn 9.10.43. 43 Sqdn 26.9.44. 111 ASRF 10.6.45. Sold to C. K. Campbell 12.11.47.
56	PBY-5	08286	—	6.5.43.	43 Sqdn 7.8.43. 11 Sqdn 22.12.44. 112 ASRF 16.8.45. 20 Sqdn 15.11.45. Sold to Kingsford-Smith 5.1.48.
58	PBY-5	08341.	—	9.5.43	20 Sqdn 5.7.43. 43 Sqdn 14.11.44. 112 ASRF 4.4.45. 20 Sqdn 6.12.45. Sold to Barrier Reef Airways 10.11.47.
59	PBY-5	08400	—	27.5.43.	20 Sqdn 1.8.43. 43 Sqdn 12.8.44. ASR Sqdn 16.5.46. Sold to *Sydney Morning Herald* 24.3.47.
60	PBY-5	08404	—	27.5.43.	20 Sqdn 11.7.43. 43 Sqdn 6.12.44. 112 ASRF 6.5.45. Sold 12.11.47.
61	PBY-5	08406	—	27.5.43.	20 Sqdn 1.8.43. 11 Sqdn 5.7.45. Sold to C. K. Campbell 12.11.47.
62	PBY-5	c/n1340	JX238	27.5.43.	20 Sqdn 11.8.43. 11 Sqdn 9.12.44. 20 Sqdn 6.8.45. Sold 5.1.48.

205

RAAF No A24-	Type	US No (cn)	RAF No	Rec'd	Abbreviated history
63	PBY-5	c/n1341.	JX239	28.5.43.	20 Sqdn 1.8.43. 43 Sqdn 7.6.44. 11 Sqdn 13.12.45. Sold 5.11.47.
64	PBY-5	08405	—	21.7.43.	43 Sqdn 7.8.43. FTR from Philippines 14.12.44.
65	PBY-5	08489	—	21.7.43.	43 Sqdn 16.9.43. 112 ASRF 6.6.45. Sold to C. K. Campbell 12.11.47.
66	PBY-5	08499	—	21.7.43.	43 Sqdn 2.9.43. 3 OTU 16.7.44. Sold to J. E. Wood 21.11.47.
67	PBY-5	08500	—	21.7.43.	20 Sqdn 25.8.43. FTR from Pomelaa, Celebes 2.10.43.
68	PBY-5	08504	—	26.7.43.	43 Sqdn 8.9.43. 11 Sqdn 31.3.45. 112 ASR F 27.6.45. 43 Sqdn 25.10.45. Sold to Kingsford-Smith 5.1.48.
69	PBY-5A (M)	34056	—	15.12.43.	11 Sqdn 18.2.44. Destroyed by fire Darwin 14.12.45.
70	PBY-5A (M)	34059	—	17.12.43.	43 Sqdn 5.2.44. 20 Sqdn 10.10.44. 3 OTU 20.1.45. Conversion 22.1.46.
71	PBY-5A (M)	34057	—	23.12.43.	11 Sqdn 8.4.44. 20 Sqdn 6.12.44. 43 Sqdn 16.2.45. 11 Sqdn 27.8.45. Sold to Kingsford-Smith 5.1.48.
72	PBY-5A (M)	34058	—	23.12.43.	11 Sqdn 5.2.44. S&R Wg 15.2.49. Sold to Grant Trading Co 14.1.43.
73	PBY-5A (M)	48300	—	8.1.44.	20 Sqdn 8.4.44. FTR from Surabaya 21.5.44.
74	PBY-5A (M)	48298	—	28.12.43.	11 Sqdn 5.2.44. Force landed Clarence River 15.7.44. Conversion 12.2.46.
75	PBY-5A (M)	48297	—	26.1.44.	11 Sqdn 7.4.44. Sold to Mr Kennedy 9.5.47.
76	PBY-5A (M)	48299	—	27.1.44.	20 Sqdn 27.2.44. 43 Sqdn 14.11.44. Crashed at Broome 19.12.44. Conversion.
77	PBY-5A (M)	48301	—	27.1.44.	20 Sqdn 27.2.44. 42 Sqdn 16.4.45. 43 Sqdn 12.7.45. 11 Sqdn 12.11.45. 43 Sqdn 10.1.46. Sold C. K. Campbell 12.11.47.
78	PBY-5A (M)	48302	—	27.1.44.	11 Sqdn 28.2.44. 20 Sqdn 23.9.44. 42 Sqdn 9.10.44. 43 Sqdn 3.9.45. Sold to Barrier Reef Airways 10.11.47.
79	PBY-5A (M)	48344.	—	28.1.44.	43 Sqdn 16.5.44. 11 Sqdn 8.6.44. Sold to Barrier Reef Airways 10.11.47.
80	PBY-5A (M)	48349	—	30.1.44.	3 OTU 1.5.44. 11 Sqdn 6.12.45. Sold to Kingsford-Smith 5.1.48.
81	PBY-5A (M)	48350	—	29.1.44.	20 Sqdn 3.6.44. 42 Sqdn 11.2.45. 11 Sqdn 18.7.45. Sold to Kingsford-Smith 5.1.48.
82	PBY-5A (M)	34056	—	2.2.44.	43 Sqdn 16.5.44. 20 Sqdn 9.9.44. 43 Sqdn 3.2.45. 11 Sqdn 16.8.45. Sold 10.11.47.
83	PBY-5A (M)	48346	—	12.3.44.	20 Sqdn 7.6.44. 42 Sqdn 18.1.45. Sold to Kingsford-Smith 5.1.48.
84	PBY-5A (M)	48345.	—	12.3.44.	20 Sqdn 7.6.44. 3 OTU 19.2.45. 11 Sqdn 12.11.45. 43 Sqdn 10.1.46. Sold 5.1.48.
85	PBY-5A (M)	48351	—	12.3.44.	20 Sqdn 8.6.44. 43 Sqdn 25.9.44. 42 Sqdn 26.1.45. 11 Sqdn 10.8.45. Sold 12.11.47.
86	PBY-5A (M)	48356	—	12.3.44.	20 Sqdn 9.6.44. 42 Sqdn 8.11.44. 11 Sqdn 5.2.46. Sold to J. E. Wood 13.11.47.
87	PBY-5A (M) (M)	48348	—	26.3.44.	20 Sqdn 23.6.44. 3 OTU 17.1.46. Sold to *Sydney Morning Herald* 24.3.47.
88	PBY-5A (M)	48352	—	26.3.44.	3 OTU 25.4.44. 42 Sqdn 8.8.44. 11 Sqdn 8.8.45. Sold to Kingsford-Smith 5.1.48.
89	PBY-5A (M)	48354	—	26.3.44.	43 Sqdn 15.7.44. 42 Sqdn 1.9.44. 11 Sqdn 2.8.45. Sold to Barrier Reef Airways 10.11.47.
90	PBY-5A (M)	48355	—	10.4.44.	3 OTU 26.4.44. 42 Sqdn 9.8.44. FTR from Makassar 15.10.44.
91	PBY-5A (M)	46488	—	12.4.44.	3 OTU 20.6.44. 43 Sqdn 8.9.44. 111 ASRF 18.1.45. 113 ASRF 24.2.45. Caught fire at Morotai 14.6.45.
92	PBY-5A (M)	46491	—	12.4.44.	3 OTU 18.5.44. 113 ASRF 5.5.45. 11 Sqdn 28.10.49. At RAAF Rathmines 1.4.53.
93	PBY-5A (M)	48353	—	12.4.44.	3 OTU 25.4.44. 42 Sqdn 9.8.44. 112 ASRF 1.7.45. 11 Sqdn 13.7.45. Sold 5.1.48.
94	PBY-5A (M)	46489	—	30.4.44.	42 Sqdn 9.7.44. 43 Sqdn 15.7.44. 42 Sqdn 1.9.44. Write off Sermata Is 22.9.44.
95	PBY-5A (M)	46490	—	30.4.44.	20 Sqdn 26.6.44. 42 Sqdn 7.12.44. 20 Sqdn 16.11.45. Sold to *Sydney Morning Herald* 5.11.47.
96	PBY-5A (M)	46532	—	7.5.44.	42 Sqdn 5.8.44. Write off S of Soebra Is. 14.1.45. Destroyed by rescue aircraft.
97	PBY-5A (M)	46533	—	7.5.44.	42 Sqdn 5.8.44. 11 Sqdn 13.7.45. 114 ASRF 15.10.45. Sold to C. K. Campbell 12.11.47.
98	PBY-5A (M)	46434	—	7.5.44.	8 Com Unit 7.7.44. 111 ASRF 1.1.45. 111 ASRF 1.1.45. Sank Balikpapan 1.7.45.
99	PBY-5A (M)	46435	—	14.5.44.	3 OTU 7.6.44. 6 Com Unit 12.7.44. Rathmines ex-11 Sqdn 7.7.50. Rathmines 1.4.53.
100	PBY-5A (M)	46576	—	14.5.44.	42 Sqdn 8.7.44. 43 Sqdn 3.8.44. 42 Sqdn 9.9.44. AA Makassar, ditched 23.10.44.
101	PBY-5A (M)	46577	—	14.5.44.	42 Sqdn 8.8.44. Damaged 3.7.45. Conversion 1.11.45.
102	PBY-5A (M)	46578	—	14.5.44.	42 Sqdn 7.8.44. 114 ASRF 29.9.45. Sold to C. K. Campbell 12.11.47.
103	PBY-5A (M)	46579	—	14.5.44.	3 OTU 6.7.44. 11 Sqdn 6.12.45. 43 Sqdn 10.1.46. Sold to A.N.A. 15.10.46.
104	PBY-5A (M)	46594	—	24.10.44.	8 Com Unit 3.12.44. 111 ASRF 20.2.45. 113 ASRF 18.6.45. 11 Sqdn 15.7.48. Rathmines 7.7.50 and 1.4.53.

RAAF No A24-	Type	US No (cn)	RAF No	Rec'd	Abbreviated history
105	PBY-5A (M)	46580	—	11.11.44.	113 ASRF 28.3.45. 115 ASRF 5.8.45. 112 ASRF 14.2.46. 114 SRF 21.10.46. 11 Sqdn 10.11.49. Crashed 3 ml NNE Georgetown, Qld 7.5.50. Conversion 19.6.50.
106	PBY-5A (M)	46605	—	8.12.44.	113 ASRF 14.12.45. 111 ASRF 11.10.45. 112 ASRF 21.6.46. Hangar collision 26.11.46.
107	PBY-5A (M)	46606	—	8.12.44.	111 ASRF 9.2.45. 113 ASRF 3.5.45. Sank off Balikpapan 22.6.45.
108	PBY-5A (M)	46607	—	18.12.44.	113 ASRF 14.2.45. Crashed on take-off Magee Island 25.3.45.
109	PBY-5A (M)	46608	—	18.12.44.	113 ASRF 19.3.45. 112 ASRF 12.4.46. 11 Sqdn 9.6.49. Rathmines 1.4.53.
110	PBY-5A (M)	46619	—	22.2.45.	113 ASRF 18.2.46. 112 ASRF 13.8.46. 11 Sqdn 18.8.49. Rathmines 1.4.53.
111	PBY-5A (M)	46620	—	22.2.45.	115 ASRF 26.11.45. 114 ASRF 2.9.46. Rathmines 1.4.53.
112	PBY-5A (M)	46621	—	5.3.45.	112 ASRF 2.8.45. 113 ASRF 18.2.46. 111 ASRF 23.4.46. 112 ASRF 20.1.47. 11 Sqdn 18.8.49. Rathmines 22.8.50.
113	PBY-5A (M)	46622	—	5.3.45.	115 ASRF 4.1.46. 113 ASRF 4.4.46. 112 ASRF 7.5.46. Sank Champagny Is 4.6.46.
114	PBY-5A (M)	46623	—	20.3.45.	115 ASRF 10.8.45. 113 ASRF 18.2.46. 112 ASRF 27.2.47. Rathmines 1.4.53.
200	PB2B-1	44227	JX617	11.11.44.	3 OTU 2.12.44. Rathmines 1.4.53.
201	PB2B-1	44215	JX612	27.12.44.	20 Sqdn 8.1.45. Rathmines 1.4.53.
202	PB2B-1	44226	JX616	24.11.44.	20 Sqdn 17.2.44. Sold to Butler Air Trans 21.10.46.
203	PB2B-1	44225	JX615	3.12.44.	20 Sqdn 30.12.44. FTR from Pescadores 7.3.45.
204	PB2B-1	44219	JX613	22.12.44.	20 Sqdn 8.1.45. FTR from Laoet Strait 29.1.45.
205	PB2B-1	44224	JX614	4.1.45.	20 Sqdn 20.1.45. Crashed on take-off, Darwin 9.8.45. Conversion 20.11.45.
206	PB2B-1	44217	JX611	8.2.45.	43 Sqdn 9.3.45. 20 Sqdn 15.6.45. Blown up by DCs Darwin 20.6.45.
300	PB2B-2	44229	JX619	22.11.44.	20 Sqdn 14.12.44. 112 ASRF 3.4.46. Sold to Qantas Empire Airways 28.10.46.
301	PB2B-2	44234	JX624	3.12.44.	20 Sqdn 31.12.44. Struck reef, Jinamoc Is 12.3.45.
302	PB2B-2	44230	JX620	4.1.45.	3 OTU 28.1.45. Sold to Airmotive Supply Corp, NY, 18.5.53.
303	PB2B-2	44231	JX621	4.1.45.	20 Sqdn 23.1.45. 3 OTU 20.9.45. Sold to Asian Airlines Pty, 30.1.48.
304	PB2B-2	44237	JX627	4.1.45.	20 Sqdn 7.2.45. Sold to Poulson & Middlemiss 21.10.46.
305	PB2B-2	44228	JX618	15.1.45.	3 OTU 16.2.45. Sold to Asian Airlines Pty, 30.1.48.
306	PB2B-2	44233	JX623	15.1.45.	20 Sqdn 9.2.45. Sold to Qantas 10.12.46.
307	2B2B-2	44232	JX622	18.1.45.	20 Sqdn 9.2.45. 3 OTU 17.1.46. Sold to Airmotive 18.5.53.
308	2B2B-2	44235	JX625	8.2.45.	43 Sqdn 9.3.45. 20 Sqdn 8.6.45. Damaged by AA off Timor 22.7.45. Conversion 4.9.45.
309	2B2B-2	44236	JX626	22.2.45.	20 Sqdn 24.3.45. Sold to Qantas 12.12.46.
350	2B2B-2	44279	JX661	18.3.45.	3 OTU 12.4.45. Sold to Capt P. G. Taylor 23.10.46.
351	2B2B-2	44286	JZ833	18.3.45.	3 OTU 9.4.45. Sold to Mr A. C. M. Jackaman 13.12.46.
352	2B2B-2	44278	JX660	20.3.45.	3 OTU 12.4.45. 112 ASRF 16.5.46. Qantas 6.12.46. 11 Sqdn 8.9.49. Sold to Airmotove 18.5.53.
353	2B2B-2	44281	JZ828	27.3.45.	43 Sqdn 7.5.45. 112 ASRF 26.11.45. 111 ASRF 2.9.46. Conversion 3.12.48.
354	2B2B-2	44282	JZ829	27.3.45.	43 Sqdn 26.4.45. 42 Sqdn 17.9.45. 112 ASRF 26.11.45. Sold to Qantas 10.12.46.
355	2B2B-2	44289	JZ836	27.3.45.	43 Sqdn 14.4.45. 112 ASRF 26.11.45. Sold to Qantas 10.12.46.
356	2B2B-2	44285	JZ832	14.4.45.	43 Sqdn 18.5.45. 114 ASRF 20.2.46. Sold to Mr Carr 28.10.46.
357	2B2B-2			28.4.45.	43 Sqdn 28.5.45. Sold to Qantas 30.10.46.
358	2B2B-2	44266	JX648	28.4.45.	43 Sqdn 30.5.45. Hailstorm damage, Rathmines 25.4.46. Sold to Capt P. G. Taylor 23.10.46.
359	2B2B-2	44284	JZ831	28.4.45.	43 Sqdn 21.5.45. Sold to Airmotive 18.5.53.
360	2B2B-2	44294	JZ841	28.4.45.	43 Sqdn 30.5.45. 113 ASRF 12.9.45. 115 ASRF 1.12.45. Sold to Airmotive 18.5.53.
361	2B2B-2	44261	JX643	5.5.45.	43 Sqdn 16.6.45. Sold to Mr F. H. Bridgewater 27.9.46.
362	2B2B-2	44288	JZ835	5.5.45.	43 Sqdn 1.6.45. 115 ASRF 19.2.46. Sold to Butler Air Transport 11.10.46.
363	2B2B-2	44247	JX629	29.5.45.	113 ASRF 12.11.45. Sold to Airmotive 18.5.53.
364	2B2B-2	44291	JZ838	29.5.45.	42 Sqdn 23.6.45. 111 ASRF 12.11.45. Sold to Poulson & Middlemiss 27.2.47.
365	2B2B-2	44256	JX638	30.5.45.	42 Sqdn 2.7.45. Crashed SE of Mindanao 10.10.45.
366	2B2B-2	44264	JX646	30.5.45.	43 Sqdn 20.11.45. Sold to Mr Jackaman 13.12.46.
367	2B2B-2	44292	JZ839	30.5.45.	42 Sqdn 23.6.45. 113 ASRF 3.12.45. 111 ASRF 2.5.46. Sold to Qantas 11.10.46.
368	2B2B-2	44254	JX636	31.5.45.	42 Sqdn 3.7.45. 111 ASRF 28.1.46. 11 Sqdn 2.12.48. Sold to Airmotive 18.5.53.
369	2B2B-2	44297	JZ834	31.5.45.	42 Sqdn 5.7.45. 43 Sqdn 20.11.45. Sold to Poulson & Middlemiss 8.10.46.
370	2B2B-2	44246	JX628	6.6.45.	42 Sqdn 20.7.45. Damaged Laban Island reef 18.8.45. Conversion 20.11.45.

RAAF No A24-	Type	US No (cn)	RAF No	Rec'd	Abbreviated history
371	2B2B-2	44259	*JX641*	6.6.45.	42 Sqdn 23.7.45. 20 Sqdn 22.11.45. 43 Sqdn 14.1.46. Sold to Qantas *(VH-EBD)*.
372	2B2B-2	44280	*JX662*	6.6.45.	20 Sqdn 11.7.45. Loaned to Qantas 5.2.48. Exploded 27.8.49 at Rose Bay *(VH-EAW)*.
373	2B2B-2	44249	*JX631*	*16.6.45*	42 Sqdn 30.7.45. 43 Sqdn 30.11.45. Sold to Airmotive 18.5.53.
374	2B2B-2	44258	*JX640*	16.6.45.	43 Sqdn 21.8.45. Sold to Airmotive 18.5.53.
375	2B2B-2	44270	*JX652*	16.6.45.	42 Sqdn 27.8.45. 43 Sqdn 15.10.45. Sold to Airmotive 18.5.53.
376	2B2B-2	44255	*JX637*	4.7.45.	1 APU 6.8.45. Sold to Butler Air Transport 11.10.46.
377	2B2B-2	44290	*JZ837*	5.7.45.	20 Sqdn 18.8.45. 3 OTU 25.1.46. Sold to Airmotive 18.5.53.
378	2B2B-2	44253	*JX635*	7.7.45.	113 ASRF 8.9.45. Loaned to Qantas *(VH-EAX)*. Wrecked Lord Howe Is 24.6.49.
379	2B2B-2	44260	*JX642*	9.7.45.	20 Sqdn 10.9.45. 43 Sqdn 17.1.46. 114 ASRF 19.2.46. Sold to Qantas 11.10.46.
380	2B2B-2	44283	*JZ830*	16.7.45.	115 ASRF 25.8.45. 11 Sqdn 14.7.49. Sold to Airmotive 18.5.53.
381	2B2B-2	44257	*JX639*	16.7.45.	115 ASRF 8.9.45. Crashed off Lord Howe Is 28.9.48.
382	2B2B-2	44250	*JX632*	30.7.45.	3 OTU 17.9.45. Sold to Airmotive 18.5.53.
383	PB2B-2	44263	*JX645*	30.7.45.	113 ASRF 24.8.45. 3 OTU 10.1.46. Sold to Airmotive 18.5.53.
384	PB2B-2	44293	*JZ840*	1.8.45.	3 OTU 17.9.45. Sold to Capt P. G. Taylor 23.10.46.
385	PB2B-2	44252	*JX634*	3.9.45.	43 Sqdn. S&R Wing/11 GR Sqdn 1.10.47. Sold to Airmotive 18.5.53.

*AH534 is given on Pacific Islands Aviation Society list as having c/n 27 but having no RAAF serial No.

FTR = Failed to return (from operational mission).
Conversion = Conversion to components.
STF = Seaplane Training Flight.
ASRF = Air-Sea-Rescue Flight.

Appendix E

Flight data of Catalina *A24-1* which was ferried from San Diego, California, to Sydney, Australia, 12 February 1941 — 28 February 1941.

Aircraft: Model 28/5/MA flying boat with two Pratt & Whitney R-1830, S1C3-G Twin Row Wasp Engines — rated 1,050bhp, 1,200bhp for take-off.

Dimensions:		
	Length overall	65ft 2in.
	Height max on beaching gear	18ft 5in.
	Span	104ft
	Mean chord	165·32in.
	Aspect ratio	7·5 to 1.
	Span of tail	30ft 6in.
	Length of hull	63ft 11in.
	Beam of hull	10ft 2½in.
	Gross displacement of hull	142,295cu in.
	Maximum draft	2ft 7½in.
	Wing area	1,400sq ft.
	Normal fuel tankage	1,460Imp gal.
	Normal oil tankage	100gal.
Performance:	(i) For gross weight of 29,547lb.	
	Useful load	13,140lb.
	Critical altitude	5,700ft.
	Full speed of critical alt.	171kt.
	Stalling speed (sea level power)	62·5kt.
	Service ceiling	19,500ft.
	Climb to 5,000ft (1,050bhp)	7min.
	Climb to 15,000ft (1,050bhp)	25min.
	Max weight for flight on one engine at sea level and 1,050bhp	29,547lb.
	Take off time in calm	43sec.
	Wing loading	21·1lb/sq ft.
	Power loading	12·3lb/hp.

Stage	Distance	Time	Air speed	Ground Speed	Altitude	Fuel used	Average Cons.
San Diego-Honolulu	2,371 naut ml	23hr 40min	100·25kt	114·28kt	5-6,000ft	1,325Imp gal	56gal/hr
Honolulu-Canton Is	1,665 naut ml	14hr 48min	98·61kt	111·5kt	4hr @ 1,000ft 3¹/³ @ 6,000ft 7hr 38 @ 1,000ft or less	960 Imp gal	64gal/hr
Canton Is-Noumea	1,710 naut ml	15hr 12min	101·12kt	112·5kt	1hr @ 1,000ft 14hrs @ 7,500ft	910Imp gal	60gal/hr
Noumea-Sydney	1,069naut ml	10hr	100·54kt	106·9kt	3hr @ 500ft 7hr @ 5,700ft	610Imp gal	61gal/hr

Take off weights and times:

San Diego	33,000lb	46 sec	5-8kt breeze
Honolulu	32,000lb	62 sec	Flat calm
Canton Is	32,600lb	—	Choppy sea, gusts 20-25mph
Noumea	29,700lb	43 sec	Calm; sea smooth.

NB: This data is based on the original twelve pages of data which specifies *A24-1;* the official RAAF list of Catalinas indicates that the aircraft which arrived at Rose Bay, Sydney on 27/28 February, 1941 was *A24-2.*

Performance: (ii) For gross weight of 27,000lb.

Full speed at critical altitude	173kt.
Stalling speed (sea level power)	60kt.
Service ceiling	21,500ft.
Max permissible speed	187kt.
Take-off, calm	37 sec.
Wing loading	19·3lb/sq ft.
Power loading	11·25lb/hp.

Distances in nautical miles:		Time
San Diego-Pearl Harbor	2,371ml.	23hr 40min.
Pearl Harbor-Canton Island	1,665ml	14hr 48min.
Canton Island-Noumea	1,710ml	15hr 12min.
Noumea-Sydney	1,069ml	10hr
Totals	6,815ml	63hr 50min.

Appendix F

Representative aircraft (Catalinas and Canso As) of the RCAF.

Squadron No	Canso A	Catalina
4	9771 9802 11006 11044	JX211 FP291 FP294
5	9737 9738 9739 9740 9741 9742 9743 9744 9745 9753 9756 9764 9773 9807 9858 9875 9879 11004 11052 11055	W8430 W8431 Z2137 Z2139
6	9762 9790 11007 11044 9787 9788	FP202 FP290 FP296 JX572
7	9788 9803 11007 11099	JX209 JX212 JX213
13	9815 11079	
120	9792 9805	JX294 JX571 JX579
9	9790 9800 11005	W8432 FP293 FP297 JX207
116	9701-9707 9741 9742 9745 9746 9748 9749 9750 9781 9757 9758 9772 9777 9778 9798 9806 9808 9819 9823 9825 9828 9829 9830 9831 9832 9836 9839 9844 11034 11057 11061 11064	W8431 W8432 Z2134 Z2137 Z2138 Z2139 DP202 FP294 FP296 FP297
117	9701 9702 9704 9705 9706 9707 9709 9806 9818 JX219 JX572 JX578 JX579 JX580	FP209 FP291 FP292 JX207 JX209 JX212 JX213
160	9752 9785 9786 9789 9768 9780 9793 9794 9797 9798 9799 9812 9814 9813 9817 9818 9822 9840 11023 11047 11048 11078 11080	
161	9750 9840 11004 11040	
162	9764 9766 9768 9769 9812 11023 11033 11039 11056 11067 11075 11077 11089 11091 11093 9754 'P'	
408	11093 11094	W8412 W8421 W8427 W8434 Z2135
413	1103 11018 11047 11075 11079	Z2149 AH549 AH550 AH567 AJ155 AJ161 FP182 FP282 FP306 FP323 JX276 JX280 JX292 JX299 JX311 JX321 JX330 JX333 JX336 JX357
422		FP103 FP105 FP106 FP529 FP533

RCAF code letters

Squadron	Code	Squadron	Code
4	BO	116	ZD, NO
5	QN	117	PQ
6	AF	120	RS
7	FG	162	GK, DZ
9	HJ	413	QL, AX, AP
13	AP	408	AK, MN
		422	DG

Appendix G
Catalinas of the RNZAF

PBY-5s	Serial No	Cons No	Other	PB2B-1s	Serial No	Cons No	Other
	NZ4001	1194	Bu 08280		NZ4023	28086	Bu72997
	NZ4002	1334	JX232		NZ4024	28088	Bu72999
	NZ4003	1336	JX234		NZ4025	28089	Bu73000
	NZ4004	1297	Bu08373		NZ4026	28102	BU73013
	NZ4005	1335	JX233		NZ4027	28087	Bu72998
	NZ4006	1338	JX236		NZ4028	28104	Bu73015
	NZ4007	1339	JX237		NZ4029	28119	Bu73030
	NZ4008	1332	JX230		NZ4030	28105	Bu 73016
	NZ4009	1333	JX231		NZ4031	28120	Bu73031
	NZ4010	1251	JX228		NZ4032	28121	Bu73032
	NZ4011	1337	JX235		NZ4033	28132	Bu73043
	NZ4012	1384	Bu08450		NZ4034	28133	Bu73044
	NZ4013	1402	Bu08468		NZ4035	28134	Bu73045
	NZ4014	1398	Bu08464		NZ4036	28135	Bu73046
	NZ4015	1387	Bu08453		NZ4037	28136	Bu73047
	NZ4016	1400	Bu08466		NZ4038	28137	Bu73048
	NZ4017	1401	Bu08467		NZ4039	28144	Bu73055
	NZ4018	1432	Bu08488		NZ4040	28146	Bu73057
	NZ4019	1372	Bu08438		NZ4041	28147	Bu73058
	NZ4020	1369	Bu08435		NZ4042	28118	Bu73029
	NZ4021	1431	Bu08487		NZ4043	28103	Bu73014
	NZ4022	1470	Bu08516		NZ4044	28148	Bu73059
					NZ4045	28149	Bu73060
					NZ4046	28145	Bu73056
					NZ4047	60956	Bu73095
					NZ4048	60959	Bu73098
					NZ4049	60974	Bu73113
					NZ4050	60957	Bu73096
					NZ4051	60958	Bu73097
					NZ4052	60976	Bu73115
					NZ4053	60977	Bu73116
					NZ4054	60975	Bu73114
					NZ4055	61108	Bu44202
					NZ4056	61109	Bu44203

Appendix H
Catalina aircraft ordered for the United States Navy

First aircraft contract 28.10.33; first flight March 1935; last delivery 9.45.

Total number accepted

2,387	— Consolidated
290	— Boeing
155	— Naval Air Factory
230	— Vickers

Bureau (Serial) numbers:

9459	XP3Y-1	*08124-08549*	PBY-5
0102-0161	PBY-1	*33960-34059*	PBY-5A
0454-0503	PBY-2	*44188-44227*	PB2B-1
0842-0907	PBY-3	*44228-44277*	PB2B-2
1213-1244	PBY-4	*46050-46579*	PBY-5A
1245	XPBY-5A	*46580-46638*	PBY-5A
2289-2455	PBY-5	*46639-46698*	PBY-6A
2456-2488	PBY-5A	*46724*	PBY-6A
7243-7302	PBY-5A	*63992*	PBY-5
02791-02946	PBN-1	*63993-64099*	PBY-6A
02948-02977	PBY-5A	*64101-64107*	PBY-6A
04399-04420	PBY-5A	*67832-68061*	Canso-A
04425-04514	PBY-5	*72992-73116*	PB2B-1
04972-05045	PBY-5A	*99080*	PBY-4
08030-08123	PBY-5A		

Appendix I
USN Seaplane tenders

AVP SMALL SEAPLANE TENDERS

4	*Avocet*	1	*Lapwing*
14	*Childs*	6	*Pelican*
17	*Clemson*	9	*Sandpiper*
8	*Gannet*[1]	7	*Swan*
16	*George E. Badger*	5	*Teal*
18	*Goldsborough*	3	*Thrush*
2	*Heron*	20	*William B. Preston*[2]
19	*Hulbert*[2]	15	*Williamson*[2]

[1]AVP 1-9 converted from minesweepers and AVP 14-20 from destroyers.
[2]Reclassified seaplane tender (destroyer) (AVD) (all of tonnage between 850 and 1,200 tons).

'BARNEGAT' CLASS (1,766 tons)

23	*Absecon*	24	*Chincoteague*
33	*Barataria*	36	*Cook Inlet*
10	*Barnegat*	25	*Coos Bay*
34	*Bering Strait*	37	*Corson*
11	*Biscayne*[1]	38	*Duxbury Bay*
12	*Casco*	40	*Floyds Bay*
35	*Castle Rock*	39	*Gardiners Bay*

[1]Converted to amphibious force flagship (AGC).

41	*Greenwich Bay*	29	*Rockaway*
26	*Half Moon*	51	*San Carlos*
21	*Humboldt*	30	*San Pablo*
13	*Mackinac*	52	*Shelikof*

22	*Matagorda*	53	*Suisun*
48	*Onslow*	31	*Unimak*
49	*Orca*	32	*Yakutat*
50	*Rehoboth*		

AV SEAPLANE TENDERS

5	*Albermarle*
10	*Chandeleur*
17	*Cumberland Sound*
7	*Currituck*
4	*Curtiss*
15	*Hamlin*
14	*Kenneth Whiting*
3	*Langley*¹
11	*Norton Sound*
12	Pine Island
9	Pocomoke
16	*St George*
8	*Tangier*
1	*Wright*'

AVD SEAPLANE TENDERS (destroyers)

1,190 tons converted from destroyers or small submarine tenders

10	*Ballard*
8	*Belknap*'
1	*Childs*
4	*Clemson*'
3	*George E. Badger*'
12	*Gillis*
5	*Goldsborough*'
13	*Greene*'
6	*Hulbert*'
9	*Osmond Ingram*
14	*McFarland*'
7	*William B. Preston*
11	*Thornton*
12	*Williamson*'

'Lost.
'To auxiliary miscellaneous conversion from carrier. AV9&10 C3 cargo type (all about 8-9,000 tons except 3 — 11,000 tons).
'Converted to high-speed trans (APD).
'Converted to destroyer (DD).

Classifications:
PG Gunboat (under 'Patrol Craft').
PG-22 *Tulsa* (between 990-2,000 tons), comm 1923 renamed *Tacloban* 27.11.44.
Classification: cruisers, gunboats & frigates — cities and towns; seaplane tenders — aviation pioneers, bays, sounds & straits.

213

Appendix J
Catalinas operated by the American Army Air Force (AAF) and the US Air Force (USAF)

AAF Catalinas   Observation Amphibians (OA)

Year	Model	Manufacturer	Quantity	Gross wt (lb)	Span	Length	Remarks
1941	OA-10-CO	Consolidated	56	30,300	104ft	63ft 10in	USN type PBY-5A; max speed 185mph
1944-45	OA-10A-VI	Vickers	230	30,700	104ft	63ft 10in	Canadian built; max speed 185mph
1945	OA-10B-CN	Consolidated	75	34,000	104ft	63ft 11in	USN type PBY-6A; max speed 180mph

When the USAF was formed on 18 September 1947 some of the above-mentioned aircraft were subsequently redesignated as follows:

SA-10A-VI	Vickers	230
SA-10B-CO	Consolidated	75

All these aircraft were powered by two P&W R1830-92 1,200 hp engines and in operations specialised in air-sea-rescue.

Serial Nos:	42-109020-42-109025	44-33868-44-34097
	43-3259-43-3270	45-57833-45-57907
	43-43839-43-43863	
	43-47956-43-47961	

Appendix K
Rescue units of the United States Air Force

Unit		Period	Bases
1	ERS	10.43-31.3.46	Boca Raton, Casablanca; Ajaccio, Foggia
	RS	9.46-20.8.50	MacDill (to ARS '49)
	ARS	20.8.50-14.11.52	MacDill
	ARG	14.11.52-8.12.56	Albrook
2	ERS	12.43-	Hamilton, Keesler, Morotai (5 AF, 43-44), (13 AF, 44-)
	RS	c.48-10.8.50	Kadena, Clark (to ARS '49)
	ARS	10.8.50-14.11.52	Clark
	ARG	14.11.52-24.6.58	Clark, Wheeler
3	ERS	15.2.44	Gulfport, Keesler, Biak, Atsugi, Okinawa
	RS	11.4.47-10.8.50	Yokota, Johnson (to ARS '49)
	ARS	10.8.50-14.11.52	Johnson
	ARG	14.11.52-18.6.57	Johnson, Nagoya, Moriyama
	ARRG	8.1.66-31.1.76	Tan Son Nhut, Nakon Phanom, U-Tapao
4	ERS	11.44	Pacific
	RS	c.48-20.8.50	Anderson, Hamilton (to ARS '49)
	ARS	20.8.50-14.11.52	Hamilton
	ARG	14.11.52-8.12.56	Hamilton
5	ERS	26.1.45-	Boxted, Halesworth (65 Fighter Wing)
	RS	21.5.46-10.8.50	Morrison, Keesler
	ARS	10.8.50-14.11.52	Lowry
	ARG	14.11.52-8.12.56	Lowry, Westover
6	ERS	45-3.47	Ie Shima, Okinawa (5th AF)
	RS	c.48-10.8.50	Harmon, Westover
	ARS	10.8.50-14.11.52	Westover, Papperrell
7	ERS	c.45-15.5.46	Hickam, India
	RS	1.9.49-10.8.50	Wiesbaden
	ARS	10.8.50-14.11.52	Wiesbaden
	ARG	14.11.52-8.12.56	Wiesbaden, Wheelus

ERS = Emergency Rescue Sqdn. RS = Rescue Sqdn.
ARS = Air Rescue Sqdn. ARG = Air Rescue Group.

Appendix L
Catalina PBY-5 flying boats of the Royal Netherlands Naval Air Service

Y No	San Diego	Manila	Surabaya	Remarks
38	25.8.41.	3.9.41.	5.9.41.	Sank after collision with tow-boat 9.2.42.
39	25.8.41.	3.9.41.	5.9.41.	Damaged in air attack on Morokrembangan 5.2.42; destroyed with base on 3.3.42.
40	31.8.41.	11.9.41.	—	Shot down near Morokrembangan on 3.2.42.
41	31.8.41.	11.9.41.	—	Damaged in air attack on Morokrembangan 5.2.42; destroyed with base on 3.3.42.
42	2.9.41.	11.9.41.	—	With GVT-3 on 16.1.42; lost in air attack on Morokrembangan 1.3.42.
43	10.9.41.	23.9.41.	—	Lost in air attack on Morokrembangan 5.2.42.
44	13.9.41.	23.9.41.	—	Lost in landing accident at Tandjung Pinang (Banka) 5.12.41.
45	13.9.41.	23.9.41.	—	Served with GVT17, GVT18 & 321 Sqdn; operated until March 1946.
46	18.9.41.	7.10.41.	—	Lost in air attack on Morokrembangan on 1.3.42.
47	18.9.41.	7.10.41.	—	Lost while landing at Tg Priok 23.2.42; had served with GVT17 & GVT18.
48	18.9.41.	7.10.41.	—	Destroyed at Tg Priok during demolition 3.3.42; had served with GVT17 & GVT18.
49	30.9.41.	12.10.41.	—	GVT13 wef 16.1.42. Left Surabaya 19.2.42 for Australia. Later with 321 Sqdn, until 1944.
50	30.9.41.	—	—	Damaged at Wake Is. 9.10.41; repaired at San Diego 13.12.41; Lost 5.2.42.
51	30.9.41.	12.10.41.	—	GVT16 wef 1.2.41; sunk in Barito River, Borneo 21.1.42.
52	—	15.10.41.	10.12.41.	To RAF Singapore — 205 Sqdn.
53	—	15.10.41.	10.12.41.	To RAF Singapore — 205 Sqdn.
54	—	15.10.41.	10.12.41.	To RAF Singapore — 205 Sqdn 7.1.42.
55	18.10.41.	3.11.41.	—	GVT16; Tjilatjap to China Bay, Ceylon 2.3.42. With 321 Sqdn as 'C' until 1944.
56	18.10.41.	3.11.41.		GVT16 wef 1.12.41; Lake Bagendit, Java for Ceylon 2.3.42 with V/Adml Helfrich; 321/'D' until 1945.
57	27.10.41.	3.11.41.		GVT16 wef 1.12.41; Tjilatjap — Ceylon 2.3.42; 321/'E'; scrapped at Morokrembangan in 1946.
58	27.10.41.	3.11.41.		GVT17 wef 5.1.42; lost with crew in air battle Kema, Celebes, on 11.1.42.
59	2.11.41.	9.11.41.		GVT17 wef 5.1.42; Lengkong, Java — Australia 2.3.42. Destroyed at Broome 3.3.42.
60	27.10.41.	3.11.41.		GVT17 wef 5.1.42; Lengkong - Australia 2.3.42. Destroyed at Broome 3.3.42.
61	2.11.41.	9.11.41.		GVT3 wef 14.1.42; lost in air attack on Morokrembangan 3.2.42.
62	8.11.41.	15.11.41.		GVT2 wef 14.1.42; Tjilatjap - Australia 6.3.42; 321/'F' at China Bay; crashed Biak 18.10.45.
63	8.11.41.	15.11.41.		GVT2 wef 14.1.42; lost in air battle Noordbroeder Island, Java Sea, 27.2.42.
64	8.11.41.	15.11.41.		GVT2 wef 14.1.42; Tjilatjap - Ceylon 2.3.42; 321/'G'; scrapped 1945.
65	17.11.41.	2.12.41.		GVT5 wef 12.1.42; severe damage in air battle at Tjilatjap 4.3.42.
66	17.11.41.	2.12.41.		GVT5 wef 12.1.41; destroyed in air attack near Tjilatjap 4.3.42.
67	19.11.41.	2.12.41.		GVT5 wef 12.1.41; GVT17; Java - Australia 2.3.42; destroyed at Broome 3.2.42.
68	27.11.41.	—		Destroyed during attack on Pearl Harbor 8.12.41.
69	27.11.41.	—		At Pearl Harbor 8.12.41; refit at San Diego; Australia - Ceylon; 321/'H'; Morokrembangan 1947.
70	27.11.41.	—		8.12.41. en route to Wake Is; Morokrembangan 27.12.41; destroyed at Broome 3.3.42.
71	—	—		GVT5; Java - Broome 6.3.42; Australia - India; crash-landed 8.11.42 and burnt out.
72	8.12.41.	—		At Morokrembangan 8.1.42; shot down near Waroe south of Surabaya 5.2.42.
73				Surabaya 16.1.42; Morokrembangan 3.3.42 bomb-damaged beyond repair and destroyed by crew.
Y-3				An ex-USN PBY-4 left damaged at Tjilatjap; USN 1219; to Broome 7.3.42; became RAAF A24-28 FJ-L.
Y-74				Ex-San Diego 2.9.42; Ceylon 5.1.43; became 321/'J'; scrapped at Morokrembangan 1946.
Y-75				Ex-San Diego 10.9.42; Ceylon 5.1.43; became 'Skysleeper' transport aircraft 321/'K'; scrapped at Biak 1952.
Y-76				Ex-San Diego 9.9.42; Ceylon 5.1.43; became 321/'L'; renumbered P76 on 15.7.46; scrapped at Biak 25.2.52.
Y-77				Ex-San Diego 13.9.42; Ceylon 5.1.43; became 321/'M'; renumbered P77 on 15.7.46; scrapped at Biak end of 1951.
Y-78				Ex-San Diego 16.9.42; Ceylon 5.1.43; became 321/'N'; lost after emergency landing in Gulf of Bengal 9.12.43.
Y-79				Ex-San Diego 13.9.42; Ceylon 5.1.43; became 321/'O'; renumbered P217 1.12.52; withdrawn 1958, monument at Biak.
Y-80				Ex-San Diego 22.9.42; Ceylon 3.11.42; became 321/'P'; scrapped in Ceylon 1945.
Y-81				Ex-San Diego 23.9.42; crashed with fighter aircraft 26.3.43.
Y-82				Ex-San Diego 26.9.42; Ceylon 3.11.43; became 321/'Q'; crashed near Seroei 28.12.50 while with No 7 Sqdn.
Y-83				Ex-San Diego 27.9.42; Ceylon 1.11.42; became 321/'R'; renumbered P218 1.12.52; scrapped at Biak in 1957.
Y-84				Ex-San Diego 30.9.42; Ceylon 3.11.42; became 321/'S'. Sunk by Y83 after emergency landing off Cape Agulhas, S Africa.

Y-85	Ex-San Diego; Ceylon 20.11.42; became 321/'T'; renumbered *P219* 1.4.53; destroyed by fire at Biak 30.10.54.
Y-86	Ex-USN; Australia 1.4.43 with MLD; 321/'U' on 5.7.43; MLD wef 20.5.45; scrapped at Biak 8.1.49.
Y-87	Ex-USN Australia 1.4.43 with MLD; 321/'V' 12.45 at Priok, Batavia; crashed at Woendi Is 13.10.46.

The following six Catalina Mk IVBs (PB2B-1s) were on loan from the RAF, to serve with 321 Sqdn at China Bay:

Y88	JX315	W/WW received 9.5.44 returned to RAF 4.2.45.
Y89	JX313	X/XX received 14.5.44 returned to RAF 4.2.45.
Y90	JX294	Y/YY received 16.5.44 returned to RAF 4.2.45.
Y91	JX272	Z/ZZ received 7.7.44 returned to RAF 4.2.45.
Y92	JX365	'B' received 1.8.44 returned to RAF 11.44.
Y93	JX205	'N' received 1.8.44 returned to RAF 11.44 (A Mark IV-A)

NB: During 321's 'Liberator' period, Catalina aircraft flight letters were doubled.

The following six aircraft Mark IVBs (PB2B-1s) were received from the RAF-Karachi and 321's Liberators were returned to the RAF as they were too heavy to land at Tandjong Perak, Surabaya. All were renumbered with a 'P' prefix 15.7.46.

Y88	JX276	'C'	Scrapped 11.1.49 and disposed by sinking near Surabaya July 1950.
Y89	JX288	'D'	Scrapped 28.8.49 and disposed by sinking near Surabaya July 1950.
Y90	JX289	'F'	Scrapped 6.49 and disposed by sinking near Surabaya July 1950.
Y91	JX298	'G'	Scrapped 8.49 and disposed by sinking near Surabaya July 1950.
Y92	JX354	'S'	Scrapped 9.49 and disposed by sinking near Surabaya July 1950.
Y93	JX359	'V'	Lost through fire during refuelling at Balikpapan 5.11.47; ex-Bu Aer *73010*.

The following aircraft were received from the RCAF in Canada and delivered direct to the Netherlands East Indies:

P200	DP202(?)	Ex-Toronto 17.9.46; Morokrembangan 28.9.46; scrapped at Biak 14.2.52.
P201	JX206	Ex-Toronto 17.9.46; Morokrembangan 28.9.46; disposed by sinking, Surabaya, 7.50.
P202	JX572	Ex-Toronto 17.9.46; Morokrembangan 28.9.46; disposed by sinking, Surabaya, 7.50.
P203	JX219	Ex-Toronto 2.11.46; scrapped at Biak 5.10.51.
P204	Z2137	Ex-Toronto 26.12.46; crashed near Gili Manoek, Bali, 26.1.47.
P205	JX217	Ex-Toronto 14.12.46; scrapped at Biak 14.11.51.
P206	JX209	Ex-Toronto 24.12.46; scrapped at Morokrembangan in 1950.

The following PB2B-2s with serial Nos *16·207* to *16·210* were received from the RAAF:

P207	44266	JX648	A24-358	In RNNAS 1947; disposed by sinking, Surabaya 25.7.50.
P208	44286	JZ833	A24-351	In RNNAS 1947; disposed by sinking, Surabaya 1950.
P209	44293	JZ840	A24-384	In RNNAS 1947; disposed by sinking, Surabaya 1950.
P210	44264	JX646	A24-366	In RNNAS 1948; disposed by sinking, Surabaya 25.7.50.

The following aircraft were purchased in the USA and flown to Valkenburg for refit and thence to Dutch New Guinea:

P211	46581	PB2B1	Valkenburg 9.2.51; Lost en route from New Guinea 19.12.52.
P212	46521	PB2B-1	Valkenburg 22.2.52; scrapped 8.7.57; restored, and now displayed at the Museum, Soesterberg.
P213	46460	PBY-5A	Valkenburg 16.3.51; crashed at Biak 28.2.52.
P214	33972	PBY-5A	Valkenburg 3.4.51; scrapped at Biak 14.6.56.
P215	46583	PBY-5A	Valkenburg 27.4.51; scrapped at Biak 12.6.56.
P216	48252	PBY-5A	Valkenburg 25.7.51; scrapped at De Kooy 1.5.58; sold as scrap 1962.

The following aircraft ex RAAF were presented by the Australian government on 13.5.53:

P220	46594	A24-104	Scrapped at Biak 1.11.56.
P221	46619	A24-110	Scrapped at Biak 1.8.56.
P222	46620	A24-111	Scrapped at Biak 1.4.58.
P223	46491	A24-92	Used for spare parts.
P224	46535	A24-99	Scrapped at Biak 1.7.57.
P225	46621	A24-112	Scrapped at Biak 28.1.57.

NB: wef = with effect from.

Appendix M

Catalinas in Norwegian service (No 330 Squadron)

Serial No.	Allotted	Code	Remarks
FP525	22.5.42.	GS-Z	Shot down by U-boat 21/22.9.42.
FP526	29.7.42.	GS-Z	To No 4 OTU 21.11.42.
FP527	17.6.42.	GS-O	To No 131 OTU 21.11.42.
FP528	23.7.42.	GS-P	To No 131 OTU; SOC 3.8.44.
FP529	?	?	To No 131 OTU; SOC 1.8.44.
FP531	30.5.42.	GS-W	To RAF Greenock 19.11.42; SOC 3.8.44.
FP533	?	?	To No 4 OTU; SOC 3.8.44.
FP534	?	?	To VP-72 US Navy.
FP535	28.5.42.	GS-X	Missing 5.11.42.
FP536	9.6.42.	GS-Y	To 131 OTU; SOC 3.8.44

Catalinas in Norwegian service (No 333 Squadron) 1942-45

Serial No	Ex-		Letter & Name	Remarks
W8424	210 Sqdn QL-R	18.2.42.	QL-R/B 'Vingtor'	To 131 OTU.
FP121	210 Sqdn QL-Z	24.9.42.	QL-Z/C 'Jössing'	Damaged by U-boat 17.5.44.
FP115	210 Sqdn QL-U	13.2.43.	QL-U	To Pembroke Dock 26.2.43.
FP314	Greenock QL-T	5.3.43.	A 'Viking'	To Scottish Aviation 21.12.44.
FP183	210 Sqdn	28.1.44.	D 'Vingtor II'	SOC 23.12.44.
FP222	302 FTU	4.7.44.	B 'Ulabrand'	To Greenock 1.1.45.
JX582	Felixstowe	23.10.44.	A 'Viking II'	To Kjevik, Norway, 21.11.45.
JX265	Felixstowe	23.10.44.	B 'Vingtor III'	To Scottish Aviation 1.3.45.
JV933	Saunders-Roe	31.5.44.	C 'Jössing II'	To No 57 MU, Wig Bay 12.12.45.
JX224	202 Sqdn	28.3.45.	KK- B 'Vingtor IV'	To Felixstowe 21.6.45; crashed Oakington 14.8.45.
JX583	210 Sqdn	2.6.45.		To 210 Sqdn 8.6.45.
JX573	131 OTU	6.6.45.	B 'Vingtor V'	To 57 MU, Wig Bay, 1.46.
JX382	57 MU, Wig Bay	3.8.45.	A 'Ulabrand II?'	To 57 MU, Wig Bay 31.1.46.

Catalinas in Norwegian Service (No 333 Squadron) 1945-54

Cons No	USN	RAF	Accepted	Codes	Flying hr	Remarks
28160	73071	JX400	6.2.46.	KK-D K-AG KK-G	1099.20	Withdrawn 26.10.51.
28154	73065	JX394	21.12.45.	KK-E K-AD KK-D	1275.50	Damaged 1953; to LTS Kjevik 16.2.54.
28171	73082	JX411	6.2.46.	KK-F K-AI KK-I	1078.20	Withdrawn 26.10.51.
28172	73083	JX412	27.12.45.	KK-G K-AK (KK-K)	770.5	Total damage 6.9.48 Fordesvike.
28116	73027	JX372	27.2.46.	KK-H K-AC KK-C	929.45	Withdrawn 5.6.53.
28170	73081	JX410	4.2.46.	KK-J K-AH KK-H	1023.20	Withdrawn 26.10.51.
27196	73007	JX356	27.12.45.	KK-K (K-AB)		Total damage 6.7.46 Altafjord.
28158	73069	JX398	4.2.46.	KK-L K-AF KK-F	17.50	Withdrawn 16.6.54; write off 10.8.54(?)
28155	73066	JX395	17.2.46.	KK-M K-AE KK-E	1585.10	Withdrawn 20.8.54; sold for Kr25,000 to Vestlandske Luftfartselsap 2.10.54.
28122	73033	JX378	24.4.47.	K-AL KK-L	1499.55	Withdrawn 1.11.54.
28210	44192	JX590	15.5.47.	K-AM (KK-M)	68.20	Withdrawn 1948.
28129	73040	JX385	27.8.48.	K-AN KK-N	1397.50	Ex-LN-OAP Vingtor Luftvaier A/S; total damage 28.3.54 Björnöya.

Appendix N
No 333 Squadron special duty operations to Norway

Date	Aircraft	Captain	Location and passengers
1.5.42.	W8424	Lt Cdr F. Lambrechts	Vikten, Nr Rørvik; Sverre Granlund, Odvar Røstgård, Nordahl Grieg.
22.5.42.	W8424	Lt Cdr F. Lambrechts	Stavenes, Askvold; Ole Snefjellå, Eivind Viken plus man, woman & child.
14.7.42.	W8424	K/Lt Birger Grinde	Langøy, Lofoten; Hugo Munthe-Kaas.
20.7.42.	W8424	Lt H. Offerdal	Lurøy; Ole Snefjellå and Anton Arild.
22.8.42.	W8424	Lt H. Offerdal	Vornes, Sommerøy, Lofoten; Petter Ravik and Ewald Knudsen.
8.12.42.	W8424	K/Lt H. Jørgensen	Melfjord, Helgelandskysten; Tor Jorfald.
1.5.43.	FP121	K/Lt H. Jørgensen	Skjaervaer, Helgelandskysten; Capt E. B. Sjøberg.
14.5.43.	FP183	K/Lt H. Jørgensen	Lines Gård, Melfjord; Ole Snefjellå and Erling Moe.
19.6.43.	FP121	Lt H. B. Anonsen	Alderen 66°26′N 12°48′E; Jon Kristoffersen & Odd Jønland.
11.8.43.	FP314	K/Lt. H. Jørgensen	Svartskaer, Lurøy, Nordlandskysten; Jon Kristoffersen and Odd Jønland.
15.8.43.	FP314	Lt A. Schaaning	Nordlandskysten (to land supplies)
19.11.43.	FP314	Lt A. Schaaning	Lurøy, Nordlandskysten; Jon Kristoffersen and Odd Jønland.
23.4.44.	JX582	S/Lt R. D. Moe	Onøy, Traena; Alfred Henningsen.
5.6.44.	JX582	Lt H. Anonsen	Futøy, Lurøy; Jon Kristoffersen, Erling Moe and Lars or Tredjemann.
6.12.44.	FP222	S/Lt H. Hartmann	Linihamari & Kirkenes; Col Boyd, USAF.
26.3.45.	JV933	S/Lt F. Ferner	Søroya, Graznia; Lts Jansen, P. Danielsen and W/op T. Andersen.
26.4.45.	FP314	Lt K. Garstad	Sandøyfjord, Sørøya; Odd Heløe, Adml Danielsen and evacuate 13 to Kirkenes.

Appendix O
Catalinas of the Royal Danish Air Force

PBY-5A

Danish Nos		RCAF No	Received	Off charge	Name	Remarks
FM51	851	9840	6.6.47.	29.10.53.		Ex-Nos 162 & 160 Sqdns, RCAF.
FM-52	852	11049	6.6.47.	8.12.60.	'Papoose'	
FM-53	L853	11034	29.6.47.	11.12.69.	'Pluto'	Ex-Nos 161, 116 & 162 Sqdns, RCAF.
FM-54	854	11039	22.7.47.	8.12.60.	'Tatterat'	Ex-Nos 161 & 162 Sqdns, RCAF.
FM-55	855	11097	22.6.47.	12.8.58.	'Mallemuk'	Ex-No 162 Sqdn RCAF.
FM-56	856	9831	6.6.47.	9.2.56.	'Nauja'	Ex-Nos 116 & 161 Sqdns, RCAF.
	L857	08109	18.9.51.	14.10.67.	'Munin'	
	858	46603	13.9.51.	3.10.55.	'Hugin'	

PBY-6A

L861		(USN)64035	8.4.57.	13.11.70.		To Danish Air Museum.
L862		64102	24.7.47.	24.10.63.		Lost in hangar fire at Narssarssuaq.
L863		63998	21.8.57.	13.11.70.		Sold as N16KL.
L864		64046	7.10.57.	24.10.63.		Lost in hangar fire at Narssarssuaq.
L865		64032	24.11.57.	10.8.63.		Crashed in mountains, Cape Desolation.
L866		63993	18.12.57.	70		Ex VPB-100 & VPB-71; to RAF Museum, Cosford, 1974.
L867		63997	12.1.58.	3.5.64.		Crashed.
L868		64000	8.2.58.	13.11.70.		Sold as N15KL; crashed with CAF 18.8.75, Harlingen, Texas.

Appendix P
Catalinas in Indonesia

Ex-Military PBY-5As, thirteen passenger aircraft in KLM service from 1947 onwards; Indonesian government property but in use by KLM Interinsular Services, after indepen-dence of Indonesia, aircraft were transferred to Garuda Indonesian Airways.
Maximum take-off weight 13,393kg (29,531lb); max load 1,700kg (3,748lb).

PK-CTA	c/n 9796	'Alor'	8.3.48 crashed at Poso, Celebes.
PK-CTB	c/n 9812	'Buru'	1.1.50 to Garuda.
PK-CTC	c/n 9766	—	1.1.50 to Garuda.
PK-CTD	c/n 9760	'Damar'	1.5.50 to Garuda.

In KLM service from 1949 onwards; new aircraft with big square windows, eighteen passenger aircraft, Model 28-5A max TO 13,393kg (29,531lb); max load 1,500kg (3,307lb).

PK-CPA	c/n 482	'Amboina'	1.1.50 to Garuda.
PK-CPB	c/n 867	'Bali'	1.1.50 to Garuda.
PK-CPC	c/n 886	'Cream'	1.1.50 to Garuda.

The following Model 28-5As were not in service with KLM:

PK-CPD	c/n 394	'Djoranga'
PK-CPE	c/n 385	'Enu'.

The following PBY-5A aircraft were used by the Indonesians during the struggle for independence, using bases at Campur Darat Lake, Tulungagung, Java, and Singkarak Lake in West Sumatra:

RI-005   Sunk following accident in Batanghari River, Jambi Province, 29.12.48.

RI-006   Damaged at Maguwo AFB, Yogyakarta, during Dutch strike 19.12.49.
On 27.6.50 further PBY-5As were received from the Netherlands Militaire Luchvaart.

Appendix Q
Catalinas which were operated in Chile

Type	Call sign	Serial No	Arrived	Out of Service	Remarks
PBY-5	530(401)	*08302*	23.6.43	4.3.60	Accident 20.5.53.
PBY-5	531(402)	*08433*	23.6.43	4.3.60	Accident 5.10.53
PBY-5	400	*08301*	23.6.43	10.9.48	Accident.
OA-10	560(405)	*44-33868*	28.6.48	21.7.61	Accident 15.6.61.
OA-10	561(406)	*44-34093*	28.6.48	11.1.63	
OA-10	652 mod.	*28-5*	28.6.48	28.11.59	Accident 26.1.58.
OA-10	563	*17-87*	22.8.56	22.5.61	
OA-10	564	*16-27*	22.8.56	6.9.63	
OA-10	565	*18-22*	22.8.56	27.12.—	Accident 1.12.60.
OA-10	404	*7295*	23.6.43.	—	

Appendix R
Enemy submarines sunk or damaged by Catalina or Canso aircraft.

Date	Sub Capt	Sqdn	Pilot	Position	Remarks
25.8.41.	U-452 March	209	F/O Jewiss	61°30′N 15°30′W	S; 4 x DCs from AH553; with HMS Vascoma.
25.10.41.	G. Ferraris	202	Sqn Ldr Eagleton	37°07′N 14°19′W	S; convoy HG75; scuttled after attack by AH538 & E/V.
30.10.41.	U-81	209	F/O Ryan		D; 3 x DCs from AH545 and 3x A/S bombs from a Hudson.
6.12.41.	U-332	202	Flt Lt Garnett	36°04′N 07°33′W	D; AH562 attack followed 3hr later by W8424 Flt Lt Stacey.
2.5.42.	U-74 Friederich	202	Flt Lt Powell	37°32′N 00°10′E	S; 7 x 250lb DCs from AJ162.
9.6.42.	Zaffiro Mottura	240	Flt Lt Hawkins	38°21′N 03°21′E	S; Z2143 attempted landing to rescue survivors.
13.7.42.	U-153			09°56′N 81°29′W	S; 'probably damaged' by PBY (SEM 1, p154); sunk by Lansdowne.
20.8.42.	U-464 Harms	VP73	Lt R. Hopgood	61°25′N 14°40′W	S; C/E SN-73.
28.8.42.	U-94 Ites	VP92	Lt G. R. Fiss	17°40′N 74°30′W	S; C/E TAW-15 4 x 650lb DCs & HMCS Oakville.
31.8.42.	RO-61 Tokutomi	VP42	Lt S. Coleman	52°36′N 173°57′W	With Lt Carl Amme, VP43 and USS Reid.
3.9.42.	U-756 Harney	VP73	Lt J. E. Odell	57°30′N 29°00′W	S; C/E SC-97.
23.9.42.	U-253 Friedrichs	210	Flt Sgt J. Semmens	68°19′N 13°50′W	S; C/E QP-14.
1.11.42.	U-664	VP84	Lt P. A. Bodinet	—	D; C/E HX-212; U-664 sunk 9.8.43.
5.11.42.	U-408 v. Hymmen	VP84	Lt R. C. Millard	67°40′N 18°32′W	S; A/S sweep.
10.12.42.	U-611 v. Jacobs	VP84	Lt L. L. Davis	58°09′N 22°44′W	S; C/E HX-217.
6.1.43.	U-164 Fechner	VP83	Lt W. Ford	01°58′S 39°23′W	S; C/E JT-1 80ml NE of Fortaleza.
13.1.43.	U-507 Schacht	VP83	Lt L. Ludwig	01°38′S 39°52′W	S; C/E TR-1; U-507's actions brought Brazil into WW2 (R2/203).
10.2.43.	U-108	202	Sqn Ldr O-Skan	32°24′N 16°08′W	D; C.L.A patrol 2 x DCs; U-108 scuttled May 1945.
14.2.43.	U-620 Stein	202	Flt Lt Sheardown	39°27′N 11°34′W	S; C/E KMS-9; 5DCs + 1DC in two attacks.
8.3.43.	U-156 Hartenstein	VP53	Lt J. E. Dryden	12°38′N 54°39′W	S; 4 x 350lb DCs set at 25ft.
26.3.43.	U-339	190	P/O Fish	?	D; 6 x 250lb DCs.
10.4.43.	U-465	210	Flt Lt Squire	?	D; Leigh-light a/c; 4 x DCs.
15.4.43.	Archimede	VP83	Ens Robertson	03°23′S 30°28′W	S; with 2nd PBY Lt G. Bradford, Jr.
28.4.43.	U-528	VP84	Lt W. A. Shevlin		D; C/E SC-127.
4.5.43.	U-630 Winkler	5Can	Sqn Ldr B. H. Moffit	56°38′N 42°32W	S; C/E ONS-5.
14.5.43.	U-657 Göllnitz	VP84	Lt E. T. Allen	60°10′N 31°52′W	S; C/E ONS-7.
17.5.43.	U-229	190	Flt Lt Gosling	?	D; C/E TA-42; sunk by HMS Keppel 22.9.43.
25.5.43.	U-467 Kummer	VP84	Lt R. C. Millard	62°25′N 14°52′W	S; C/E RU-75.
20.6.43.	U-388 Sues	VP84	Lt E. W. Wood	57°36′N 31°20′W	S; C/E ON-189; 3 x 350lb DCs + 1x Mark 24 'Mine'.
24.6.43.	U-200 Schonder	VP84	Lt J. W. Beach	59°00′N 26°18′W	S; C/E ONS-11; 3 x 350lb DCs + 1x Mark 24 'Mine'.
7.7.43.	U-267	210 ?	?		D; (vide Coastal Command record).
8.7.43.	U-603	202	Flt Lt G. Powell	42°05′N 13°40′W	D.
9.7.43.	U-590 Kruer	VP94	Lt S. Auslander	23°54′S 42°54′W	S; C/E TJ-1; 4 x DCs set at 25ft.
15.7.43.	U-135 Luther	VP92	Lt R. J. Finnie	28°20′N 13°17′W	S; C/E OS-51 with HMS Balsam, Rochester & Mignonette.
21.7.43.	U-662 Müller	VP94	Lt R. H. Howland	03°56′N 48°46′W	S; C/E TF-2; U-662 survivors taken by PC494.
31.7.43.	U-199 Kraus		Cadet A. Torres	23°54′S 42°54′W	S; attacks also by PBM & a Hudson.

Date	Sub Capt	Sqdn	Pilot	Position	Remarks
20.8.43.	U-197 Bartels	259	Flt Lt O. Barnett	28°40'S 42°36'E	S; 6 x DCs followed by 2nd attack (F/O C. E. Robin, 265 Sqdn).
15.9.43.	RO-101 Fujisawa	VP23	Lt W. J. Geritz	10°57'S 163°56'E	S; with USS Saufley (DD-465).
16.12.43.	I-179	VP52	Cdr Flenniken	04°28'S 147°22'E	S; (Ref Jap Shipping Losses, p8; Washington, DC, 1947).
8.1.44.	U-343	202	Flt Lt J. Finch	36°54'N 01°46'W	D; shared with 'R'/179; sunk 10.3.44 by HMS Mull.
24.2.44.	U-761 Geider	VP63	Lt T. Wooley	35°55'N 05°45'W	S; shared with 'G'/202, HMS Anthony & HMS Wishart.
25.2.44.	U-601 Hansen	210	Sqn Ldr F. J. French	70°26'N 12°40'E	S; 2 x DCs; 8-10 survivors seen.
11.3.44.	UIt22 Wunderlich	262	Flt Lt J. Roddick	41°28'S 17°40'E	S; 6 x DCs followed by Flt Lt E. S. Nash with 6 x DCs.
16.3.44.	U-392 Schümann	VP63	Lt R. G. Spear	35°55'N 05°41'W	S; with HMS Affleck.
17.4.44.	U-342 Hossenfelder	162	F/O T. C. Cooke	60°23'N 29°20'W	S.
15.5.44.	U-731 Keller	VP63	Lt M. J. Vopatek	35°54'N 05°45'W	S; with HMS Kilmarock and HMS Blackfly.
17.5.44.	U-668	333	Lt H. Hartmann		D; Sunk in 'Operation Deadlight' post-8.5.45.
18.5.44.	U-241 Werr	210	F/O B. Bastable	63°36'N 01°42'E	S.
24.5.44.	U-476 Niethmann	210	Capt Maxwell	65°08'N 04°53'E	S.
3.6.44.	U-477 Jenssen	162	Flt Lt R. McBride	63°59'N 01°37'E	S.
11.6.44.	U-980 Dahms	162	F/O L. Sherman	63°07'N 00°26'E	S.
13.6.44.	U-715 Röttger	162	Wg Cdr C. Chapman	62°45'N 02°59'W	S.
17.6.44.	U-423 Hackländer	333	Lt C. Krafft	63°06'N 02°05'E	S.
24.6.44.	U1225 Sauerberg	162	Flt Lt D. Hornell	63°00'N 00°50'W	S.
28.6.44.	U-396	210	F/O J. Campbell	62°30'N 01°08'E	D; sunk 23.4.45 by 86 Sqdn, RAF, 59°29'N 05°22'W.
30.6.54.	U-478 Rademacher	162	Flt Lt R. E. McBride	63°27'N 00°50'W	S; with Liberator 'E'/86.
5.7.44.	U-859 Jebson	262	Flt Lt Fletcher	?	D; 5 x DCs; sunk by HMS Trenchant 23.9.44 05°46'N 100°04'E.
17.7.44.	U-347 de Buhr	210	F/O J. Cruickshank	68°35'N 02°30'W	S.
18.7.44.	U-742 Schwassmann	210	F/O R. Vaughan	68°24'N 09°51'E	S.
4.8.44.	U-300	162	F/O W. Marshall	?	D; sunk 22.2.45 36°29'N 08°20'W by HM ships.
30.4.45.	U-1055 Meyer	VPB63	Lt F. G. Lake	48°00'N 06°30'W	S; MAD-equipped.
7.5.45.	U-320 Emmrich	210	Flt Lt K. Murray	61°32'N 01°53'E	S; sono-buoy used after attack.

C/E = Convoy Escort
C.L.A. = creeping line ahead
D = damaged
S = sunk

Appendix S
Japanese ships sunk or damaged by Catalina aircraft of VP-52, USN.

25.11.43.	Lt W. J. Lahodney, USN	Cruiser damaged; 2 x 500lb + 1 x 1,000lb; 75ml west of Rabaul.
1.12.43.	Lt W. J. Pattison, USNR	Tanker 15,000 tons destroyed by fire; 1 x 1,000lb & 1 x 500 lb bomb S of Kavieng.
1.12.43.	Lt C. J. Schauffler, USNR	Two destroyers damaged; 2 x 500lb bombs; S of Kavieng.
10.12.43.	Lt Jg. Rudy Lloyd, USN	8,000-ton MV sunk; 2 x 1,000lb & 1 x 500lb bombs between Dyual Is & New Ireland.
12.12.43.	Lt W. M. Flenniken, USN	4,000-ton MV sunk; 1 x 1,000lb.
13.12.43.	Lt Rudy Lloyd, USN	Cruiser damaged (?); 1 x 1,000lb & 1 x 500lb bomb.
15.12.43.	Lt C. J. Schauffler, USNR	I-type submarine probably damaged by straddle with 4 x 650lb DCs'.
17.12.43.	Lt W. M. Flenniken, USN	Submarine (I-type) damaged; 4 x 650lb DCs.
19.12.43.	Lt A. N. McInnis Jr. USNR	MV set on fire — 7,000 ton MV destroyed; 1 x 1,000lb bomb.
20.12.43.	Lt Cdr H. A. Sommer, USN	MV sunk; 6,000 tons; 1 x 1,000lb bomb.
20.12.43.	Lt W. J. Lahodney, USN	5,000-ton MV; 1 x 500lb bomb.
20.12.43.	Lt Jg. W. B. Squier, USNR	5,000-ton MV set on fire.
24.12.43.	Lt R. D. Dilworth, USNR	12,000-ton MV damaged; 1 x 500lb bomb.
23.12.43.	Lt jg R. John, USNR	Destroyer damaged by 1 x 500 or 1,000 lb bomb.
12.2.44.	Lt R. D. Dilworth, USNR	6,000-ton MV sunk at Wewak; 2 x 250lb bombs (Dilworth awarded Silver Star).
3.6.44.	?	Destroyer.

'I-11 and I-181 were lost in January by unknown cause (ref p176 US Sub Losses WW2).

Appendix T
Japanese ships which have been recorded as sunk by mines laid by Australian Catalinas[1].

24.7.43.	*Mie Maru;* cargo vessel, 2,913 tons, 02°45′S 133°40′E.
16.9.43.	*Seikai Maru;* converted gunboat, 2,663 tons, 02°30′S 150°48′E.
4.11.43.	*Ryusoan Maru;* cargo vessel, 2,455 tons, 02°40′S 150°40′E.
23.7.44.	*Takasan Maru;* cargo vessel, 1,428 tons, 04°35′S 122°17′E.
26.10.44.	*Seito Maru;* cargo vessel, 2,219 tons 03°14′S 116°13′E.
29.10.44.	*Kokko Maru;* cargo vessel, 2,863 tons, 01°17′S 116°48′E.
4.11.44.	*Tsukushi;* survey vessel, 2,000 tons, est 02°40′S 150°40′E.
3.3.45.	*Hario;* misc auxiliary, 4,000 ton, est 18°10′N 109°40′E².

[1]Probable.
²See also *Air War Against Japan 1943-1945* by George Odgers, chap 22.

These ships are all given as having been sunk by Australian laid mines by the Joint Army-Navy Assessment Committee and published in *Japanese Naval and Merchant Shipping Losses During World War II by All Causes* for the Navy Department of USA in February 1947.

Appendix U
The Inscription on the Catalina War Memorial, Cairns, Australia

'During the early critical months of the Pacific war, Catalina flying boats of 11 and 20 Squadrons, Royal Australian Air Force, played a significant part in slowing the initial Japanese advance, operating from northern island bases as emergency bombers and reconnaissance aircraft. Although deficient in speed, arms and armour, they exerted an influence out of all proportion to their limited numbers as these inexorably dwindled and their bases were overrun or became untenable. The survivors withdrew to mainland Australia, and — briefly licking their wounds — renewed the fight from the waters which this memorial overlooks.

'Armed with bombs, depth-charges, mines and torpedoes, they reached out from here in single flight to the Solomons, New Britain, New Guinea and the Netherlands East Indies and by stages and in increasing strength to the Palaus, the Philippines, Formosa and China.

'In January 1942, the two squadrons attacked Truk, the great Japanese naval base in the Caroline Islands; by June the enemy flood had reached the Solomons and the Catalinas were bombing Tulagi the centre of the group: three years later in May 1945 with the reinforcement of 42 and 43 Squadrons, they were mining the south China coast and in July, as the test atom bomb exploded in New Mexico, they were at full stretch mining the Banka Straits off Sumatra.

'In the years between, these four squadrons attacked most of the enemy strongholds within this great rectangle; many of them many times. By night Catalinas bombed them and mined their harbours, swept their sealanes with radar eyes and, parachuting supplies or setting down on unlit reaches, maintained our coast-watchers in their midst, and at all times in the role they were designed for, the flying boats escorted armadas of ships, harried submarines and plucked from the sea, soldiers and sailors and many aircrew — some from within rifle shot of the enemy.

'Not all of these missions were mounted from Cairns, neither the first strikes nor the last took off from here. But from the attacks on Tulagi onwards for two hard years, this city was the Catalinas' operational base and its people the refuge and the strength of those who flew them. It was perhaps unique among the settled communities of Australia in having a fraction of its population in almost daily contact with her enemies and in pulsing night and day to the passage of armed aircraft directly attacking them.

'In those far-off years this placid spot resounded some three thousand times to the labouring take-off of a loaded Catalina and a day later heard its whispered return — but not three thousand times. From all Australian Catalina operations in the South West Pacific theatre three hundred and twenty airmen failed to return.

Nearly all of those who died were temporary citizens of Cairns.

Their resting places are mostly unknown. *This is their memorial.* This memorial was unveiled by his Excellency the Governor of Queensland, Air Marshal Sir Colin Hannah, KCMG, KBE, CB, on 9th October 1976. It was built by the people of this city in 1976, its centenary year, and by the surviving members of the wartime Catalina squadrons.'

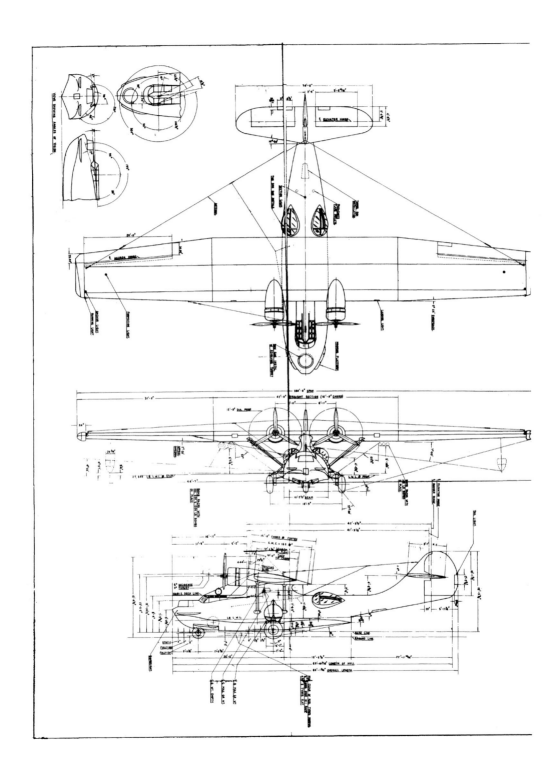

Acknowledgements

Over a period of three years more than 200 people have helped me in this project, largely by correspondence but also by personal contact. May I acknowledge their help and express my thanks to them all.

The Editors of *Air Mail, RAF News, Air Force, Wings, New Zealand Herald, Naval Aviation News, Scuttlebutt, Aerospace Historian* and *Veterans Advocate* were kind enough to include my requests in their publications.

Members of various associations including the Pensacola Veterans, the Aircrew Association, the Air Gunners' Association and the RAF Association, not only assisted me personally, but put me in touch with others.

Authors Capt Richard Knott, Capt W. Scarborough and Roscoe Creed, although actively involved with their own projects, readily responded to my requests, while Chaz Bowyer was one of the first to offer help.

'Hudson' friends, Flt Lt Ray Kelly, Lt Col Bill Amos, Wg Cdr Geoffrey Bartlett and Sqn Ldr John Espie, continued to provide help and advice.

Some 'Cat men' have searched diligently on my behalf over a period of years, namely Cdr Jack Bruce, Lt Col Bob Wardner, John Crawford and Lt Egil Johansen.

Exceptional help was received from official bodies such as the US Naval Historical Center, RAAF Historical Records, and SAAF Museum; the Curator at my last wartime station — Cosford— allowed me to view the PBY-6A in addition to providing data.

From correspondents Rear Adml Paul Foley, Jr, and Capt Carl Krafft came much valuable material covering their respective operations.

Professor Samuel E. Morison is quoted from *The History of United States Naval Operations in World War II* by kind permission of Messrs. Little, Brown & Co.

Sir Winston S. Churchill is quoted from *The Second World War* first published in 1952, by kind permission of Messrs. Cassell, the publishers.

Air Marshal Sir Richard Wakeford who served with Nos 210 and 212 Squadrons, kindly agreed to write a Foreword to this script.

I list now, all those who contributed to this project.

America
Allard, Dr D. C., Head of Naval Archives;
Amme Jr, Carl H., PhD, USN (Ret), VP-43 & VP-45;
Amos, Lt Col William, USAF (Ret), 2nd B Sqdn, 5th AF;
Barker, William A., VP-11;
Berg, Leonard, VP-73;
Brown, Col Walter W., USAF (Ret), 1st ERS & 7th ERS;
Bruce, Cdr Jack D., USN (Ret), VP-92;
Busker, Capt Jules M., USNR (Ret), VPB-34;
Check, Robert T., Editor of *Scuttlebutt*;
Christians, Cdr R. W., USN;
Coley Jr, Capt Jack, USN (Ret), VP-11;
Collyer, Robert, USN;
Crawford, John W., USAF (Ret), 2nd ERS;
Creed, Roscoe;
Dunwoody, Cdr Kirk S., USN (Ret), VP-12;
Favorite, Lt Cdr George U., USNR (Ret), VP-33;
Flenniken, Cdr William M., USN (Ret);
Foley Jr, Rear Adml Paul, USN (Ret), VP-41;
Gregory, Robert L., USCG, VP-6;
Halley, J. J., of Air Britain;
Hendrie, Lt Robert F., USNR (Ret), VP-33;
Higbee, Lt Cdr Joseph, USN (Ret), VPB-33;
Higham, Dr Robin;
Hill, Capt Joe, VP-11;
Hutchings, Rear Adml Curtis, USN (Ret), VP-63;

Johnson, Alfred 'Chief';
Johnson, Don, USN (Ret), VPB-33;
Kelly, William S., USAF (Ret), 3rd ERS;
Knott, Capt Richard C., USN (Ret);
Lahodney, Capt William J., USN (Ret), VPB-52;
Lincoln, Capt John R., USN;
Martin, Capt William H., USNR, VP-101;
McBride, Charles J., USN (Ret), VP-63 & VP-84;
Miller, Lt Cdr B. J., USN (Ret), VP-12;
Politte, Lt Robert, USN (Ret), VP-33;
Quong, Victor W., USN;
Reid, Capt Jack H., USN (Ret), VP-44;
Roberts, Douglas, USN (Ret), VP-54;
Russell, Adml James S., USN (Ret), VP-42;
Ryan, Richard, USN (Ret), VP-52;
San Diego Aero-Space Museum
Scarborough, Capt William E., USN (Ret), VP-72 & VP-91;
Smith, Capt Leonard B., USN (Ret), (209 Sqdn RAF);
Smith, Lt Robert F., USAF (Ret), ER Flt;
Stewart Sr, Cdr Jamie B., USN (Ret), VP-84;
Utgoff, Capt V. V., USN (Ret), VP-34;
Walke, Maj Emil P., USAF (Ret), 6th RS;
Walsh, Lt Cdr James, USNR (Ret), VP-84;
Wardner, Lt Col Robert S., USAF (Ret), ERS & USCG;
Wood, Capt Everett, DFC (British), VP-84;
Zoet, Prof Charles J., USAF (Ret), 12th AAC;
Zubler, Lt Cdr John R., USNR (Ret), VPB-33.

Australia
Borchers, Ray A., RAAF, 205 Sqdn RAF;
Callahan, Geof B., RAAF, 205 Sqdn RAF;
Compagnoni, Harry J., RAAF;
Coote, Elwyn, RAAF, 43 Sqdn;
Defence Air Historical Records;
Denham, Lindsay W., RAAF;
Hodgkinson, Capt Vic. A., DFC, 20 Sqdn;
Kelly, Flt Lt R. A. N., BEM;
Kiddle, Flt Lt George, 45 Group;
Kingsland, Gp Capt Sir Richard, CBE, DFC, RAAF, 11 Sqdn;
Mumford, Radio Officer Glen, Qantas;
Oats, Flt Lt Lindsay J., RAAF, 42 Sqdn;
Parsons, Sqn Ldr Frank K., RAAF, 20 Sqdn & 112 ASR Flt;
Sayer, Flt Lt Chas, RAAF, 42 Sqdn;
Selby, Ron B., RAAF;
Trebilco, Flt Lt Tom, MBE, RAAF, 43 Sqdn;
Webb, W., RAAF, 42 Sqdn.

Brazil
Beraldo, Jose;
Sperry, Col Guilherme Sarmento, BAF.

Canada
Buxton, Flt Lt Harry, RCAF, 45 Group;
Campbell, Flt Lt Jack M., RCAF, 413 Sqdn;
Dickson, Sqn Ldr Don W., RCAF, 6 Sqdn;
Gowans, Sqn Ldr John R., RCAF, 413 Sqdn;
Jamieson, Lloyd D., RCAF, 117 & 413 Sqdns;
Jardine, Gp Capt Alex, AFC, RCAF, 205 Sqdn RAF;
Kirker, P/O Roy, RCAF, 117 & 205 Sqdns;
Knight, Dr McGregor E., RCAF, 7 Sqdn;
Lineham, Sqn Ldr J. L., RCAF, 48 Sqdn RAF;
Moffatt, Charles M., RCAF, 116 Sqdn;
Murphy, F/O Frank, RCAF, 116 Sqdn;
McClymont, Lt Ronald J. H., RCN, 120, 9 & 5 Sqdns RCAF;
Penney, Madeline, Editor of *Veterans Advocate*;
Randall, Gp Capt Lawson H., DFC, RCAF, 413 Sqdn;
Rankin, Flt Lt John P., RCAF, 413 Sqdn;
Robertson, Sqn Ldr J. A., RCAF, 210 Sqdn RAF;
Shortt, A. J., Curator, National Aviation Museum, Rockcliffe;
Veild, Flt Sgt Wes V., RCAF, 5 Sqdn;
Wells, Flt Lt Donald J., RCAF, 413 Sqdn.

Chile
Porras, General L., Air Attaché.

Denmark
Haugbyrd, Ms Lizzie, Secretary, Royal Danish Embassy;
Jensen, Torben, RDAF.

France
Busson, Jean-Pierre, Conservateur en Chef, Historique de la Marine;
Lacau, Le Général de Brigade Aériene Xavier, Attaché de l'Air;
Loite, Jean-Jacques, 6ème Flottille d'Exploration (VFP-1 of the Free French).

Iceland
Ragnarsson, Ragnar J., Esq.

Indonesia
Nataatmaja, Col Jauhari, Defence Attaché;
Suparno, Colonel, Indonesian Air Force, Jakarta.

Italy
Flamigni, Capt A., Italian Navy.

Netherlands
de Bruijn, Capt A. J., RDNAS, 321 Sqdn;
de Liefde, T., RDNAS, 321 Sqdn;
Geldof, Nico, AMIMechE;
Mason, Malcolm, Sec of RAF Assn, Amsterdam;
van Oosten, Cmdr F. C., RNN (Ret), Ministerie van Defensie;
Raven, G. J. A., MA, Ministerie van Defensie;
Zwanenburg, Gerrie J., MBE;

New Zealand
Cowern, Miss Danella;
Darby, Dr. Charles, MSc, PhD
East, Barrie;
Jenks, Cliff;
Mackley, Sqn Ldr W. B., DFC, RNZAF, 6 Sqdn;
Martin, Sqn Ldr Don L. M., RNZAF, 490 Sqdn RNZAF & 422 Sqdn RCAF;
Ministry of Defence
Stokes, John W., RNZAF;
Wakeford, Jack, RNZAF, 6 Sqdn.

Norway
Baldersheim, Erling;
Ferner, Lt Finn Chr., 333 Sqdn;
Krafft, Capt Carl F., DFC, 333 Sqdn;
Hartmann, Capt Harald, 333 Sqdn;
Johansen, Lt Egil D., 333 Sqdn;
Stenersen, Sten, Esq, Historian & Publisher;
Svendsen, Knut, 333 Sqdn;
Vik, Capt Tor, 333 Sqdn.

Russia
Bashkirov, V., Director of the Central House of Aviation & Space M. V. Frunze;
Parshina, Mrs T., Secretary, The Russian Embassy;
Pasychnekov, V., Director of the Central Museum of the USSR Armed Forces.

South Africa
Eden, Maj Des. E., SAAF, No 262 Sqdn RAF & 35 Sqdn SAAF;
Leach, Wg Cmdr A. de V., DFC, 224 & 48 Sqdns RAF;
McGregor, Col P. M. J., SAAF Museum;
Mitchell, Major M. J., SAAF, 262 Sqdn RAF & 25 Sqdn SAAF;

Nash, Wg Cdr E. S. S., DFC, AFC, RAF, 262 Sqdn.

Sweden
Westberg, Gp Capt Jan, Air Attaché;
Törngen, Maj Sven, SAF;
Carleson, Axel, SAF Museum.

Royal Air Force
Armstrong, Sqn Ldr Leon V., 612 Sqdn;
Ayshford, Gp Capt John, DFC, 240 Sqdn;
Banton, Capt David, 212 Sqdn;
Barnes J. W., 240 Sqdn;
Beaumont, Flt Lt Max, 202 & 240 Sqdns;
Bell, Hugh;
Bleach, Wg Cdr D. G., 209 Sqdn;
Boston, Geof A.;
Brazel, Ray, 212 & 628 Sqdns;
Chadwick, Jack;
Chandler, F/Lt Jack, 202 Sqdn;
Cole, W/O Robert J., 191 & 240 Sqdns
Collings, Flt Lt Guy, 191 & 270 Sqdns;
Corbin, Harold;
Creedy, Gordon, 202 Sqdn;
Davis, Harold L.;
Dewdney, Flt Lt N. W. D., 240 Sqdn;
Emmott, Capt Ken, 191 Sqdn;
Farrance, Jim, 205 Sqdn;
Foster, Don, 240 Sqdn;
Fryer, Mark, 205 Sqdn;
Gibbon, Geof, 190 & 210 Sqdns;
Gooding, Flt Lt David, 202 Sqdn;
Green, John;
Griggs, Flt Lt C. A., 270, 212 & 202 Sqdns;
Gwyther, Sqn Ldr H. V., 240 & 210 Sqdns;
Harrison, Wilf, Ferry Command;
Hartshorn, Ray, 201 & 202 Sqdns;
Henry, Peter, 205 Sqdn;
Hossent, Sq Ldr Rev G. W. T., 233 & 209 Sqdns;
Hunt, Eddy, 265 Sqdn;
Jardine, Gp Capt Alex, AFC, CD, RCAF, 205 Sqdn;
Lee, P. D., 490 Sqdn;
Ledbury, W/O J. H. L., 191 Sqdn;
Lowden, Capt Eric, 205 Sqdn & 117 Sqdn RCAF;
McKendrick, Flt Lt G., 265 Sqdn;
Mahoney, W/O Des., 628, 212, 210 & 224 Sqdns;
Martyn, B. A., 202 Sqdn;
Miles, Flt Lt A. E., 45 Group;
Morgan, W/O Wyndham, 265 Sqdn;

Moss, L. J., 240 & 212 Sqdns;
Mudd, Neville, 413 & 205 Sqdns;
Myers, Flt Lt Geof A., DFC, 240 Sqdn;
Owen, D. L., Technical Librarian, British Hovercraft Corp;
Page, Flt Lt Charles, 212 & 202 Sqdns;
Parker, Ralph, 240 Sqdn;
Peace, Maj Guy G., Force 136 (Special Ops, Siam);
Philps, John, 202 Sqdn;
Powell, Sqn Ldr R. Y., DFC, 202 Sqdn;
Risk, Flt Lt Sir Thomas, 205 Sqdn;
Robertson, John, 190, 210 & 262 Sqdns;
Robinson, Flt Lt Frank, DFM, 270 & 210 Sqdns;
Rothery, Gilbert;
Shield, T. L., Ferry Command;
Smith, Sqn Ldr P., 205 Sqdn;
Speer, George, 628 Sqdn;
Spencer, W/O A. F., 205 Sqdn;

Taylor, Chas S., C Eng, MIMechE, Historian, British Hovercraft Corp;
Tebbit, Flt Lt Peter, 270 Sqdn;
Thistlethwaite, Paddy, 240 Sqdn;
Thomas, Flt Lt Andrew, 8 Sqdn;
Thomas, D. J., 259 Sqdn;
Thomas, Mrs Pat;
Usherwood, Capt Ralph, 205 Sqdn;
Wakeford, AM Sir Richard, KCB, MVO, OBE, AFC, RAF Retd, 210 & 212 Sqdns;
Walker, John G., 210, 190 & 265 Sqdns;
Whitley, J., 191 Sqdn;
Williams, Sqn Ldr Eric I., 205 Sqdn;
Woodland, W/O N. N., 413, 210 & 190 Sqdns;
Wright, Flt Lt L. J. B., 209 & 210 Sqdns;
Wyant, John, 205 Sqdn;
Wynn, F/O J. F., 270 Sqdn;
Bromet, Lady Jean, DBE;
Millar, J. H., FRAeS.

Bibliography

Air 27 — 1074, 1154, 1184, 1294, 1300, 1459, 1543, 1556, 1715, 1721, 1731, 1830, 2151.

AP 2036 A, B & D, Pilot's and Flight Engineer's Notes 2nd Edn for Catalinas Marks I, II, III & IV.

Arheim, Tom, *Fra Spitfire Til F-16*, Sem & Stenersen A/S, 1984.

Bertini, Capt. Vasc M., *Sommergibili in Mediterraneo*, Vols 1 & 2, Ufficio Storico M.M., Rome 1972.

Cassagneres, Everett, *The Consolidated PBY Catalina*, Profile Publications.

Churchill, Winston S., *The Second World War*, Vols I-VI Cassell, London.

Craven & Cate, *The Army Air Forces in World War II*, (7 Vols), Washington, 1983.

Darby, Charles, *RNZAF: The First Decade 1937-46*, Kookaburra Tech, 1971.

Eller, R/Adml E. M., *US Submarine Losses in World War II*, 1963.

Evanov P. N., *Wings Across Seas* (Russian Edn), Moscow, 1972.

Fahey, James C., *US Army Aircraft 1908-46*, Ships & Aircraft, 1946; *USAF Aircraft 1947-56*, A.F. Museum Foundation, 1956.

Fetzer, Leland, *The Soviet Air Force in WW2* (English Edn), 1974.

Gilchrist, Andrew, *Bangkok Top Secret*, Hutchinson 1970.

Gillison, Douglas, *Royal Australian Air Force 1939-42*, A.W.M., 1957.

Haga, Arfinn, Vi Fløy Catalina, J. W. Cappelens Forlag, A/S, 1983.

Halley, James J., *The Squadrons of the RAF*, Air-Britain, 1980.

Hashimoto, M., *Sunk*, H. Holt & Co, 1954.

Hendrie, Andrew, *Seek and Strike*, W. Kimber, 1983.

Jenks, C. F. L., *New Zealand Military Aircraft & Serial Nos*, NZ Aviation Historical Soc, 1980.

Joint Army-Navy Assessment Committee, *Japanese Naval & Merchant Shipping Losses During WW2*, Washington, DC, 1947.

Knott, Richard C., *The Black Cats*, Patrick Stephens, 1981.

Kostenuk, Samuel, *RCAF Squadron Histories and Aircraft 1924-1968*, S. Stevens Hakkert & Co, 1977.

Martin, Lt Gen. H. J., *South Africa at War*, Purnell, 1979.

Melnyk, Capt T. W., *Canadian Flying Operations in SE Asia 1941-45*, Dept of National Defence, 1976.

Morison, Samuel, E., *History of United States Naval Operations in WWII*, Vols 115, Little, Brown & Co, Boston.

Odgers, George, *Air War Against Japan 1943-45*, A.W.M., Canberra, 1957.

Pentland, Geoffrey, *Aircraft of the RAAF 1921-78*, Kookaburra Tech, 1971.

Price, Alfred, *Aircraft versus Submarine*, Jane's, 1980.

Pudney, John, *Atlantic Bridge*, HMSO, 1945.

Rechberg, Baron B. von Müllenheim, *Battleship Bismarck*, Triad/Panther, 1982.

Reynolds, Sir Brian, *Coastal Command's War Record 1939-45*.

Richards, Denis, *The Fight Against Odds*, Vol 1, RAF 1939-45, HMSO, 1974; *The Fight Avails*, Vol 2, RAF 1939-45 (with H. St. G. Saunders).

Robertson, John, *Australia at War 1939-45*, W. Heinemann, 1981.

Robinson, Frank, *The British Flight Battalion at Pensacola and Afterwards*, Sunflower University Press, 1984.

Roskill, Capt S. W., *The War at Sea*, Vols I-III, HMSO.

Ross, Sqn Ldr J. M. S., *The Official History of the RNZAF*.

Russell, Adml James S., *US Naval Aviation 1910-70*, Govt Printing Office.

Saunders, H. St. George, *The Fight is Won*, Vol 3, RAF 1939-45, HMSO, 1975.

Scarborough, Capt W. E., *PBY Catalina in Action,* Squadron/Signal Pub, 1983.

Shores, Christopher, *History of the RCAF,* Royce Publications, 1984.

Stenersen, Sten, *Slipp Over Norge,* Norsk Flyhistorisk Forening, 1982.

Swanborough, H. G., *US Naval Aircraft Since 1911,* Funk & Wagnalls.

Thetford, Owen, *Aircraft of the Royal Air Force Since 1918,* Putnam 1979.

Tomlinson, M., *The Most Dangerous Moment,* W. Kimber, 1976.

Ubaldini, U. M., *I Sommergibili Negli Oceani,* 2nd Edn, Ufficio Storico, 1976.

US Army Air Force micro-film records of Rescue Squadrons.

US Navy micro-film records NRS 256, 1977-104, 1978-89, 1978-87.

Vincent, David, *Catalina Chronicle,* LPH, 1978.

Wanderley, L/Brig N. F. L., *The Brazilian Air Force in the 2nd World War,* 1st Edn, 1976; *Correio Aereo Nacional,* 1st Edn, 1976.

Wikene, I., *The Canso and Catalina in the RCAF,* Canadian Aviation Historical Society.

Wrathall, G. A., *No 6 Flying Boat Squadron RNZAF, 1966.*

Glossary and abbreviations

AA	Anti-Aircraft
AAC	Army Air Corps
AAF	Army Air Force
Aldis Lamp	A lamp used to transmit messages in Morse code by operating a mirror and sighting through a fixed telescopic sight
AOC	Air Officer Commanding
ASR	Air-Sea-Rescue
ASV	Aircraft-to-Surface-Vessel. Equipment which transmitted electro-magnetic waves which would be reflected back by vessels to produce a 'blip' on a cathode-ray-tube screen
BAF	Brazilian Air Force
D/F	Direction Finding
DFC	Distinguished Flying Cross
DG	Douglas Gillison (RAAF historian)
DR	Dead reckoning (navigation)
DR	Denis Richards (RAF historian)
E/A	Enemy aircraft **or** Enemy action
ERS	Emergency Rescue Squadron
ETA	Estimated Time of Arrival
Flt Lt	Flight Lieutenant
Flt Sgt	Flight Sergeant
F/O	Flying Officer
GO	George Odgers (RAAF historian)
IFF	Identification, Friend or Foe
JATO	Jet Assisted Take-Off
JR	John Robertson (Australian historian)
Lt	Lieutenant
MAD	Magnetic Anomaly Detection
Mae West	A life-jacket which could be inflated by mouth or by a CO_2 bottle. The term is derived from a buxom American lady!
OTU	Operational Training Unit
PLE	Prudent Limit of Endurance
P/O	Pilot Officer
PPC	Patrol Plane Commander (USN term)
RAAF	Royal Australian Air Force
Radar	The American term applied to equipment such as the British ASV
RCAF	Royal Canadian Air Force
RNZAF	Royal New Zealand Air Force
RNethNAS	Royal Netherlands Naval Air Service
R/T	Radio Telephony
SAAF	South African Air Force
SE	Special Equipment
SEM	Samuel Eliot Morison (USN historian)
Sqn Ldr	Squadron Leader
Square Search	A search of a square area in which it is calculated a vessel of known maximum speed should be after a given period of time
SWR	Capt S. W. Roskill, DSC, RN, (British Naval historian)
USAAF	United States Army Air Force
USAF	United States Air Force
USCG	United State Coast Guard
USN	United States Navy
W/AG	Wireless operator/Air Gunner
Wg Cdr	Wing Commander
W/O	Warrant Officer
WSC	Winston Spencer Churchill
W/T	Wireless Telegraphy

Index

234

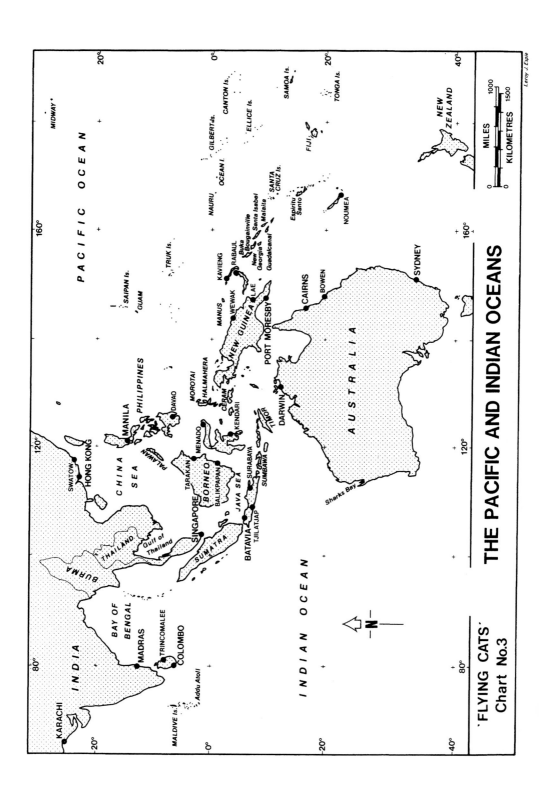

THE PACIFIC AND INDIAN OCEANS

'FLYING CATS'
Chart No.3

Leroy J. Espie

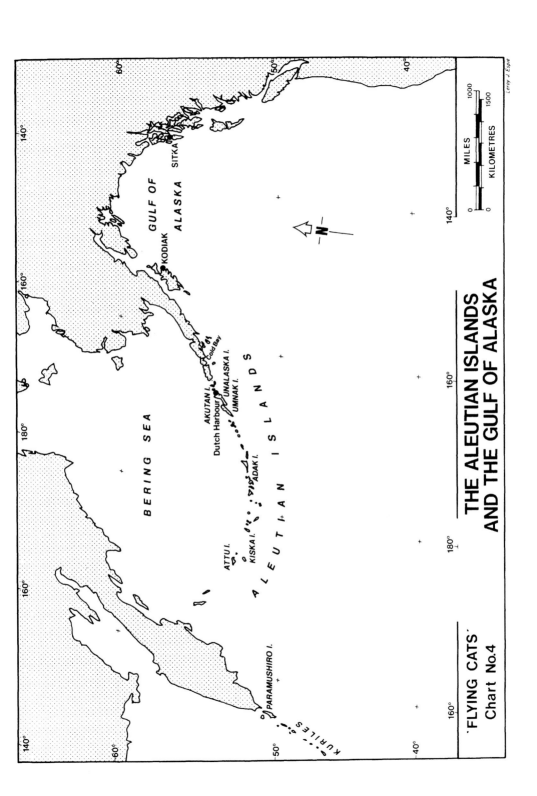

THE ALEUTIAN ISLANDS
AND THE GULF OF ALASKA

'FLYING CATS'
Chart No.4

Leroy J. Espie